The College of Law
of England and Wales

LIBRARY SERVICES

The College of Law, Christleton Hall, Christleton, Chester CH3 7AB
Telephone: 01483 216849 Library.Chester@lawcol.co.uk

**This book MUST be returned on or before the last date stamped below.
Failure to do so will result in a fine.**

Birmingham • Bristol • Chester • Guildford • London • Manchester • York

FAMILY LAW AND THE INDISSOLUBILITY OF PARENTHOOD

There are few areas of public policy in the western world where there is as much turbulence as in family law. Often the disputes are seen in terms of an endless war between the genders. Reviewing developments over the last forty years in North America, Europe, and Australasia, Patrick Parkinson argues that, rather than just being about gender, the conflicts in family law derive from the breakdown of the model on which divorce reform was predicated in the late 1960s and early 1970s. Experience has shown that although marriage may be freely dissoluble, parenthood is not. Dealing with the most difficult issues in family law, this book charts a path for law reform that recognizes that the family endures despite the separation of parents, while allowing room for people to make a fresh start and prioritizing the safety of all concerned when making decisions about parenting after separation.

Patrick Parkinson is a Professor of Law at the University of Sydney and an internationally renowned expert on family law. He has played a major role in shaping family law in Australia. His proposal for the establishment of a national network of family relationship centers, made to the prime minister in 2004, became the centerpiece of the Australian government's family law reforms. He was also instrumental in reforming the child support system and has had extensive involvement in law reform issues concerning child protection. He was made a Member of the Order of Australia for his services to law, legal education, policy reform, and the community. Parkinson has published widely on family law and child protection, as well as other areas of law. His most recent books include *Tradition and Change in Australian Law* (4th edition, 2010) and *Australian Family Law in Context* (4th edition, 2009), among many others.

Family Law and the Indissolubility of Parenthood

Patrick Parkinson

The University of Sydney

CAMBRIDGE
UNIVERSITY PRESS

CAMBRIDGE UNIVERSITY PRESS
Cambridge, New York, Melbourne, Madrid, Cape Town,
Singapore, São Paulo, Delhi, Tokyo, Mexico City

Cambridge University Press
32 Avenue of the Americas, New York, NY 10013-2473, USA

www.cambridge.org
Information on this title: www.cambridge.org/9780521116107

First published 2011

Printed in the United States of America

A catalog record for this publication is available from the British Library.

Library of Congress Cataloging in Publication data
Parkinson, Patrick.
  Family law and the indissolubility of parenthood / Patrick Parkinson.
    p. cm.
  Includes index.
  ISBN 978-0-521-11610-7 (hardback)
  1. Domestic relations. 2. Divorce – Law and legislation.
  3. Custody of children. I. Title.
  K670.P375 2011
  346.01′5–dc22   2010043976

ISBN 978-0-521-11610-7 Hardback

In memory of Kari Theobald

Contents

Preface

Families in modern, developed societies take many different forms. There are heterosexual couples with and without children, married couples, those who live together outside marriage, couples who live "together apart," single parents, separated parents who share care, same-sex couples with and without children, blended families, stepfamilies, and grandparents who are primary carers of young children. Even such a long list is not at all exhaustive.

In recent years, perhaps disproportionate attention has been focused in the academic literature on less traditional and emerging family forms. Issues such as same-sex marriage engage the attention of many, as do other matters that give people a sense that they are exploring the frontiers of progress in terms of recognition and regulation. There is a natural human inclination to gravitate to the excitement of the new and to place most importance on those issues that fit with one's values and beliefs. However, many of these family law issues, interesting and important as they are, only affect a very small proportion of the population in modern societies.

The vast majority of those who are personally affected by family law, who seek the advice of lawyers on these matters, and who have cases before the courts, are heterosexual men and women who have had children. It is with the vast majority of people who are affected by family law rules and processes that this book is concerned.

There was a time when an analysis of issues and conflicts arising from the breakdown of heterosexual relationships would be primarily an analysis of marriage breakdown. The historical reflections in the first part of the book are, for that reason, focused on the assumptions and expectations that surrounded divorce some forty years ago. Marriage no longer has the central place it once did, at least in western countries – that is, those countries in Europe, North America, and beyond with a shared heritage derived from

Greek, Roman, and Judeo-Christian thought. These days, many parents who have family law disputes after separation have lived together without marrying or have never lived together at all. The thesis of this book is that whatever the status of the relationship between the partners prior to their separation, they are tied together by the bonds of parenthood and these bonds are more enduring than the ties that marriage once involved.

For these reasons, although the focus of this book is on issues arising for the biological parents of children born from heterosexual relationships, it is not only about marriage and divorce. In many countries, the majority of those who have children together in heterosexual relationships do at some stage marry. Yet even those who have never lived together may find themselves tied to one another by the bonds of parenthood. There may well be aspects of this analysis that apply to separated same-sex couples who have had the care of children as well, and to family law disputes between biological parents and stepparents. The extent to which such disputes are similar to, or different from, those between heterosexual, biological parents might be the subject of other research.

The idea for this book was first conceived ten years ago, as I contemplated the raging gender war in Australia surrounding parenting after separation, and the way in which complex issues about parents and children seemed to be reduced to forms of analysis that allowed people to raise flags, dig trenches, and find common cause against somewhat imaginary enemies. Analyzing issues in terms of the interests and perspectives of just one gender did not seem to hold out much promise for resolving the conflicts between the genders. Further reflection on the issues, coupled with analysis of developments in other countries, suggested to me another explanation for the seemingly intractable problems of gender conflict within family law: that the issue was not necessarily about gender, but about two irreconcilable conceptualizations of the meaning of separation and divorce.

That is the theme of this book. A first version of the thesis, as it was applied to parenting after separation, was published by the *Family Law Quarterly* in 2006, and further aspects were included in a chapter in Robin Wilson's edited book, *Reconceiving the Family: Critical Reflections on the American Law Institute's Principles of the Law of Family Dissolution*, published by Cambridge University Press in the same year. The thesis was further developed in the ensuing years and was the subject of the second International Family Law Lecture, given in London in 2009.

People will no doubt react in many different ways to this thesis. There will be some who will welcome the analysis contained in the book because it fits with what they perceive the law ought to be. There will be others who will wish that the trends I identify are not so, just as we may wish a diagnosis of a serious illness is not so.

Discerning international trends is different from endorsing them as positive developments. Yet whether one welcomes them or not, the argument of this book is that we need to come to terms with the profound implications of the shifts in law and society that have occurred over the last forty years and that have so fundamentally changed the meaning of separation and divorce. There are no doubt some who would like to turn back the clock to another age when divorce meant the end of the family unit, with only vestigial ties remaining between parents, and when the family formed by unmarried parenthood was a mother-child dyad; but the argument of this book is that the old order has irretrievably disappeared.

Although the pace of change has been much faster in some jurisdictions than in others, I would argue that legal systems across the western world will sooner or later follow the same patterns. In the book, I seek to show how issues such as family violence and relocation can be addressed in a context of accepting those trends. Too many, however, are still stuck in a polarized rhetoric based on a refusal to accept that the world has changed. Canutian zeal might be admirable in some respects, but trying to hold back the waves is futile. It is better to learn to surf them.

In the years since the idea for this book was conceived, I have had the privilege of being able to help shape the family law system in Australia in very practical ways. Although this has delayed the writing and publication of the book, it has also meant that its ideas do not remain purely theoretical. The concept of Family Relationship Centers, which formed the centerpiece of the Australian government's reforms to the family law system in 2006, emerged from this thinking; so too did some aspects of the reforms to the Child Support Scheme, which came into effect in 2008, implementing recommendations from a committee I chaired. Other ideas that made their way into legislation, and which had their origins in submissions to parliamentary inquiries or advice to the Australian government from the Family Law Council, also stem from the same reflections on both the causes and possible solutions to the complex problems of our day.

Along the way, I accumulated a great debt of gratitude to many. Numerous research assistants have worked on this project at various stages, finding materials not only in English but in a variety of other languages, which they were able to translate for me. My thanks in particular to Heidrun Blackwood, Sophie Crosbie, Alex Daniel, Edwina Dunn, Antoine Kazzi, Severine Kupfer, Tharini Mudaliar, Annett Schmiedel, and Kari Theobald for their excellent research assistance and translation work. Antoine Kazzi did a large amount of work in the final stages of the project and also prepared the index.

Particular mention should be made of Kari Theobald. Kari was a Canadian student who came on exchange to Sydney for a semester and worked with me on this project during that time, translating materials from French. Tragically, she passed away in 2006 at the age of 29, from ovarian cancer. Kari was an exceptionally bright, vivacious, and optimistic young woman who took a great interest in issues concerning family life. She graduated with a master's degree from Yale and a law degree from the University of Toronto. Her life was full of promise and was tragically cut short before she could experience the joys and travails of parenthood. This book is dedicated to her memory.

I am grateful also to many friends and colleagues in the International Society of Family Law who have assisted me along the way. Judge Svend Danielsen helped me understand the system of County Governors' Offices in Denmark and arranged meetings with government officials in Copenhagen. Associate Professor Eva Ryrstedt of the University of Lund provided great assistance on issues concerning the law in Scandinavia generally. Professor Bea Verschraegen of the University of Vienna was kind enough to read the whole manuscript in draft and made many helpful comments. I am most grateful also to many colleagues in North America with whom I have discussed issues over the years. Any inaccuracies in the recording or analysis of these legal and social developments remain my responsibility alone.

My thanks also go to my colleague at the University of Sydney, Dr Judy Cashmore, with whom I have done much of my empirical research in family law, as well as much other work in the field of child protection. Her support and encouragement over many years have been invaluable. Judi Single and other members of the research team at the University of Sydney have also played an important part in shaping the ideas in this book as issues have emerged from interviews with parents, children, and professionals who experience the practice of family law in their different ways.

This research was supported by a Discovery Project Grant from the Australian Research Council, DP0450827. The research on relocation, referred to in Chapter 7, was supported by two Discovery Project Grants from the Australian Research Council, project numbers DP0665676 and DP0988712. I am most grateful to the Council for this financial support.

Sydney, Australia
October 2010

PART ONE

Family Law and the Meaning of Divorce

I

Family Law and the Issue of Gender Conflict

Family law is largely about distributing loss. Of course, it is rarely described as such. When judges make decisions about where children will live and how much contact the other parent will have, their decisions are cloaked in the optimistic language of the "best interests" of children. Similarly, when making decisions about property, courts may use the language of equitable distribution of assets, as if what is being divided are the gains of the marriage. In one sense it may be so. Yet in divorce, as is often said, there are no winners. When it is not possible for the children to live in the same household with both parents, neither parent will usually have as much time with the children as he or she had during the intact marriage. When one household is divided into two, neither party to the marriage can keep as much of the property as they enjoyed during the marriage. The courts must endeavor to split the loss equitably between them.

Because marriage breakdown involves so much loss, it is also a period of grieving. Anger is a natural stage in grieving, and whereas in the death of a loved one, the grieving person may be able to rail only against the heavens, in the death of a marriage, there are far more tangible targets. There is the ex-spouse, his or her solicitor, men's groups, the feminist movement, the courts, or perhaps the family law legislation itself.

It is not surprising, then, that family law is continually being "reformed." Family law is in a state of flux in many countries. Pressure builds up in the system as one group feels more keenly a sense of grievance than another; dissatisfaction finds its expression in the political sphere, and a Committee is established or another report is commissioned.

Family law is thereby politicized in a way that is not true of most other areas of private law. Indeed, there can be few areas of law or public policy where there is as much conflict and turbulence as in family law. This conflict arises in most aspects of family law, including issues about the nature of marriage, what legal consequences should flow from cohabitation, legal responses to domestic violence, the rules concerning property division and spousal support, and of course, the issue of what level of child support should be paid by nonresident parents.

The greatest conflict – at least in English-speaking countries – concerns parenting arrangements after separation. These debates are often presented in terms of a gender war.[1] Lobby groups abound – some representing single mothers, others representing nonresident fathers – campaigning for changes to the law on issues that matter most to each gender.

As with other social issues, the war is waged on many levels, not least the semantic level. Some groups promote shared parenting, but these largely reflect the agendas of the men's groups.[2] Around the English-speaking world, groups representing men are often characterized by those opposing them as "father's rights groups";[3] but this reflects the semantic

---

[1] MARY ANN MASON, THE CUSTODY WARS: WHY CHILDREN ARE LOSING THE LEGAL BATTLES AND WHAT WE CAN DO ABOUT IT (1999); Nicholas Bala, *A Report from Canada's 'Gender War Zone': Reforming the Child Related Provisions of the Divorce Act*, 16 CAN. J. FAM. L. 163 (1999); Richard Collier, *From Women's Emancipation to Sex War? Men, Heterosexuality and the Politics of Divorce, in* UNDERCURRENTS OF DIVORCE 123 (Shelley Day Sclater & Christine Piper eds., 1999); Barbara Bennett Woodhouse, *Child Custody in the Age of Children's Rights: The Search for a Just and Workable Standard*, 33 FAM. L. Q. 815 (1999); Herma Hill Kay, *No-Fault Divorce and Child Custody: Chilling Out the Gender Wars*, 36 FAM. L.Q. 27 (2002); Helen Rhoades, *Children's Needs and 'Gender Wars': The Paradox of Parenting Law Reform*, 24 AUSTRALIAN J. FAM. L. 160 (2010).

[2] In the United States, groups include the American Coalition for Fathers and Children, (http://www.acfc.org), Fathers for Equal Rights (http://www.fathers4kids.com), the Alliance for Non-Custodial Parents Rights (http://ancpr.com), and a range of other, more local organizations. For a list, *see* http://themenscenter.com/National/national06.htm. In Great Britain, the lead organization is known as the Equal Parenting Council http://www.equalparenting.org. In Canada, there is also an Equal Parenting Council (http://www.canadianepc.com). *See also* the Canadian Equal Parenting Groups Directory (http://www.canadianequalparentinggroups.ca). In Australia, there is the Shared Parenting Council (http://www.spca.org.au).

[3] In the United States, *see* Leora Rosen, Molly Dragiewicz, & Jennifer Gibbs, *Fathers' Rights Groups: Demographic Correlates and Impact on Custody Policy* 15 VIOLENCE AGAINST WOMEN 513 (2009). In Australia, *see* Miranda Kaye & Julia Tolmie, *Fathers' Rights Groups in Australia and Their Engagement with Issues in Family Law*, 12 AUSTRALIAN J. FAM. L. 19 (1998); Miranda Kaye & Julia Tolmie, *Discoursing Dads: The Rhetorical Devices of Fathers' Rights Groups*, 22 MELB. U. L. REV. 162 (1998); Michael Flood, *"Fathers' Rights" and the Defense of Paternal Authority in Australia*, 16 VIOLENCE AGAINST WOMEN 328 (2010). In Britain, *see* Richard Collier, *Fathers' Rights, Gender and Welfare: Some Questions for Family Law*, 31 J. SOCIAL WELFARE & FAM. L. 357 (2009); FATHERS' RIGHTS ACTIVISM AND LAW REFORM IN COMPARATIVE PERSPECTIVE (Richard Collier and Sally Sheldon eds., 2006).

war. Such groups would not generally characterize themselves as being motivated by a concern for their own rights, although in practice, those rights often feature prominently. Rather, they present their concerns as being about the best interests of children. They are supported in this by organizations that promote shared parenting in the context of a wider concern for children's rights.[4]

June Carbone has provided a good summary of the competing claims of these interest groups:[5]

> [T]he battle lines in the custody wars at divorce are so well drawn that they can better be described as opposing trenches. On one side are those who would identify children's wellbeing with continuing contact with both parents. They favor joint custody, liberal visitation, and limitations on custodial parent's autonomy that secure the involvement of the other parent. In the other camp are those who argue that genuinely shared custody approaching an equal division of responsibility for the child is rare, and that children's interests lie with the well-being of the parent who assumes the major responsibility for their care. This group favors primary caretaker provisions to govern custody, greater respect for the custodial parent's autonomy (including greater freedom to move), and greater concern for both the physical and psychological aspects of domestic violence.

With politicization often comes an oversimplification of the issues. Complex problems are reduced to propositions that may readily be articulated within an adversarial political framework. When that adversarial contest has been expressed in terms of gender, the vastly different experiences of women from different backgrounds and circumstances are homogenized into a common experience of separation and divorce, which is often fitted into a victim framework. Men's groups also compete for the status of being aggrieved, and the courts exercising family law jurisdiction are attacked on all sides for "bias" without any common or agreed-upon view of what "neutrality" might look like. When debates are conducted in these terms, it is no wonder that the result is either insufficient consensus to achieve reform or unsatisfactory compromises that lead to laws filled with contradiction.

---

[4] One such organization in the United States is called the Children's Rights Council: http:// www.crckids.org. It proclaims its mission as being to assure a child "the frequent, meaningful and continuing contact with two parents and extended family the child would normally have during a marriage." It has an equivalent in Canada: www.canadiancrc.com.

[5] June Carbone, From Partners to Parents: The Second Revolution in Family Law, 180 (2000).

The Changing "Problem" of Fatherhood

The turbulence in relation to policy about postseparation parenting in particular is largely the result of nonresident fathers wanting a greater level of involvement with their children.[6] This may be contrasted with the position a couple of decades ago, where the dominant concern of public policy was with the disappearance of fathers from children's lives.

This can be seen, for example, in American research on parenting after separation. Judith Seltzer, using data from a national survey in the United States conducted in 1987–1988, found that almost 60 percent of nonresident fathers saw their children less than once per month, according to mothers' reports.[7] She concluded that "for most children who are born outside of marriage or whose parents divorce, the father role is defined as much by omission as commission."[8] Her findings were consistent with other general population studies in the United States conducted in the 1980s and early 1990s, which revealed a pattern of disengagement by a majority of nonresident fathers over a period of years.[9] Furstenberg and Cherlin, writing in 1991, concluded, based on the available evidence, that "over time, the vast majority of children will have little or no contact with their fathers."[10] Stewart, reporting on data collected from young people between 1994 and 1996 in the U.S. National Longitudinal Study of Adolescent Health, found a similar level of disengagement. Sixty-one percent of these young people saw their fathers less than once a month.[11]

The nonengagement and disengagement of nonresident fathers was particularly evident in representative national population studies in the United States, which accessed not only divorced parents but also those

---

[6] Stephanie Goldberg, *Make Room for Daddy*, 83 A.B.A.J. 48 (1997); William Smith, *Dads Want Their Day: Fathers Charge Legal Bias Towards Moms Hamstrings Them as Full-Time Parents*, 89 A.B.A.J. 38 (2003). On the growth of the fatherhood movement, *see* Wade Horn, *You've Come a Long Way, Daddy*, POLICY REVIEW, 24, (July–Aug. 1997).

[7] Judith Seltzer, *Relationships between Fathers and Children Who Live Apart: The Father's Role after Separation*, 53 J. MARRIAGE & FAM. 79 (1991).

[8] *Id* at 97.

[9] Frank Furstenberg, Christine Winquist Nord, James Peterson, & Nicholas Zill, *The Life Course of Children of Divorce: Marital Disruption and Parental Contact*, 48 AM. SOC. REV. 656 (1983); Judith Seltzer & Suzanne Bianchi, *Children's Contact with Absent Parents*, 50 J. MARRIAGE & FAM. 663 (1988); Joyce Munsch, John Woodward, & Nancy Darling, *Children's Perceptions of Their Relationships with Coresiding and Non-Coresiding Fathers*, 23 J. DIV. & REMARRIAGE 39 (1995).

[10] FRANK FURSTENBERG & ANDREW CHERLIN, DIVIDED FAMILIES: WHAT HAPPENS TO CHILDREN WHEN PARENTS PART, 26 (1991).

[11] Susan Stewart, *Nonresident Parenting and Adolescent Adjustment: The Quality of Nonresident Father-Child Interaction*, 24 J. FAM. ISSUES 217 (2003).

who have not lived together or who have cohabited outside marriage. Research with formerly married parents presented a different picture from the general population, with most fathers remaining involved in their children's lives in the first few years after divorce;[12] even with divorced parents, however, involvement declined over time.

All that has changed now. U.S. research indicates that there has been a steady increase in the levels of contact between nonresident fathers and their children. Comparing national datasets in four different time periods between 1976 and 2002, Amato, Meyers, and Emery found that levels of contact between nonresident fathers and their six- to twelve-year-old children increased significantly. The number of fathers who had weekly contact, for example, rose from 18 percent in 1976 to 31 percent in 2002. The greatest rate of increase was between the mid-1970s and the mid-1990s.[13] The increase was particularly marked in families where the parents had previously been married. The rapid rise in the proportion of ex-nuptial births[14] suppressed the rate at which father-child contact increased, because levels of contact are typically much lower between nonresident fathers who had not been married, and their children.[15] Recent research has also demonstrated that many nonresident fathers retain a consistent level of involvement in their children's lives over many years, contradicting the assumption that contact with most nonresident fathers declines as the years go by.[16]

A significant cultural change in attitudes of fathers toward contact with their children following separation has led to a redefinition of the

[12] Eleanor Maccoby, Christy Buchanan, Robert Mnookin, & Sanford Dornbusch, *Postdivorce Roles of Mothers and Fathers in the Lives of Their Children*, 7 J. FAM. PSYCH. 33 (1993). *See also*, in relation to young adults' contact with divorced fathers, Teresa Cooney, *Young Adults' Relations with Parents: The Influence of Recent Parental Divorce*, 56 J. MARRIAGE & FAM. 45 (1994).

[13] Paul Amato, Catherine Meyers, & Robert Emery, *Changes in Nonresident Father-Child Contact From 1976 to 2002*, 58 FAM. REL. 41 (2009).

[14] In 1980, the birth rate for unmarried women aged 15–44 was 29 per 1,000. By 2007, it was 53 per 1,000. The percentage of all births to unmarried women rose from 18% of total births in 1980 to 40% in 2007. Federal Interagency Forum on Child and Family Statistics, *America's Children: Key National Indicators of Well-Being*, 4, (2009). There is similar evidence of growth in ex-nuptial births from a longitudinal study in Canada. The proportion of children born within marriage dropped from 85% of the children born in 1983–1984 to 69% of the children born in 1997–1998. The proportion of children born within a cohabiting relationship more than doubled, from 9% to 22% between the two surveys, whereas the proportion of births to single mothers increased from less than 6% to 10%: HEATHER JUBY, NICOLE MARCIL-GRATTON, & CÉLINE LE BOURDAIS, WHEN PARENTS SEPARATE: FURTHER FINDINGS FROM THE NATIONAL LONGITUDINAL SURVEY OF CHILDREN AND YOUTH 6–7 (2005).

[15] Amato et al., *supra* note 13, at 49.

[16] Jacob Cheadle, Paul Amato, & Valarie King, *Patterns of Nonresident Father Contact*, 47 DEMOGRAPHY 205 (2010).

"problem" of fatherhood. No longer, in modern family law, is it a problem of absence. Rather, it has become a problem of insistent presence. Because fathers demand a greater involvement in their children's lives after separation, there has been increasing conflict both at a policy level and at the individual level of litigated cases.

THE TURMOIL IN POLICY ABOUT PARENTING
AFTER SEPARATION

Western countries – and in particular Europe, North America, Australia and New Zealand – seem to be caught in an endless pattern of reform or pressure for reform, with periods of fierce debate followed by periods when there is a temporary cessation of hostilities. Canada provides one example. In that country, a gender war raged over the future of custody law after initial proposals for reform were made by a Parliamentary committee in 1998.[17] The Canadian government, in its response, endorsed the need for legislative reform.[18] An acrimonious debate, largely along gender lines, culminated in a final report[19] that provided the basis for a bill introduced into Parliament at the end of 2002 (Bill C-22). The bill sought to remove the terms "custody" and "access" in favor of the term "parenting time," with neither parent seen to be reduced to the role of a visitor in their children's lives.[20] The bill was not enacted before the government of the day went to an election in 2003.[21] Following a change of government, and in the wake of continuing fierce debate about the bill, it was shelved,[22] but agitation for reform continues.[23]

---

[17] Parliament of Canada, *For the Sake of the Children: Report of the Special Joint Committee on Child Custody and Access* (1998).

[18] *Government of Canada's Response to the Report of the Special Committee on Child Custody and Access: Strategy for Reform* (1999). For discussion, *see* SUSAN BOYD, CHILD CUSTODY, LAW, AND WOMEN'S WORK (2003).

[19] Department of Justice, *Putting Children First: Final Federal-Provincial-Territorial Report on Custody and Access and Child Support* (2002).

[20] Bill C-22, An Act to Amend the Divorce Act, the Family Orders and Agreements Enforcement Assistance Act, the Garnishment, Attachment and Pension Diversion Act and the Judges Act and to amend other Acts in consequence, 2nd Session, 37th Parliament, 2002. For a summary, *see* Helen Rhoades, *Custody Reforms in Canada*, 17 AUSTRALIAN J. FAM. L. 81 (2003).

[21] For discussion, *see* Susan Boyd, *Walking the Line: Canada's Response to Child Custody Law Reform Discourses*, 21 CAN. FAM. L. Q. 397 (2004).

[22] *See* Helen Rhoades & Susan Boyd, *Reforming Custody Laws: A Comparative Study*, 18 INT. J. L. POL'Y & FAM. 119, 121, 123 (2004).

[23] *See,* e.g., EDWARD KRUK, CHILD CUSTODY, ACCESS AND PARENTAL RESPONSIBILITY: THE SEARCH FOR A JUST AND EQUITABLE STANDARD (2008), *available at* http://www.fira.ca/cms/documents/181/April7_Kruk.pdf.

THE PROBLEM OF TRENCH WARFARE

Around the western world, the conflict between the different lobby groups has eventuated in huge territorial battles that are, rightly or wrongly, perceived as having some strategic value. Every gain by men's groups in altering the language of legislation – however symbolic or trivial – is seen as a loss by women's groups. Conversely, gains by women's groups are mourned as a loss to fathers. With each reform, evidence is gathered by researchers that appears to demonstrate the successes or failures of the legislative change. Too often, however, such research is marred by the all-too-obvious alignment of the researchers with particular interest groups and the selective presentation of research findings. In the partisan desire to influence evidence-based policy, there is far too much policy-based evidence.

In these conflicts, there is little meeting in the middle, little search for common ground, common values, shared interests. The best interests of children might, theoretically, provide that common ground, but of course, what is in the best interests of children is, beyond various generalities, highly contested terrain.

THE GROWTH IN LITIGATION ABOUT PARENTING

The escalation of gender conflict over postseparation parenting is taking place not only at the policy level. It is also reflected at the level of individual families, with a dramatic growth in litigation about parenting. Statistics on such issues are surprisingly hard to obtain. Many countries either do not publish statistics about family law disputes at all or do so only in a form that makes it impossible to disaggregate different kinds of disputes. However, some data is available on parenting disputes.

In the United States, an indication of the increase in custody disputes can be seen in the data of the National Center for State Courts. Evidence from seven states indicates a 44 percent increase in custody filings between 1997 and 2006.[24] In the same period, divorces had decreased nationally by 3 percent. There had previously been a 43 percent increase in custody filings in twenty-nine states between 1988 and 1995.[25] In Australia,

---

[24] EXAMINING THE WORK OF STATE COURTS 29 (Robert LaFountain, Richard Schauffler, Sandra Strickland, William Raftery, Chantal Bromage, Cynthia Lee, & Sarah Gibson, eds., 2008).

[25] BRIAN OSTROM & NEAL KAUDER, EXAMINING THE WORK OF STATE COURTS, 1995: A NATIONAL PERSPECTIVE FROM THE COURT STATISTICS PROJECT (1996); Jessica Pearson, *A Forum for Every Fuss: The Growth of Court Services and ADR Treatments for Family*

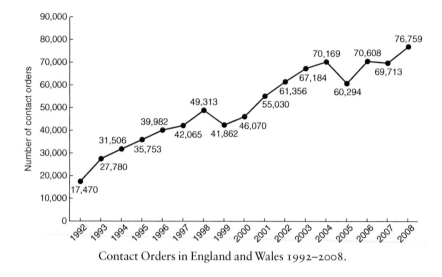

Contact Orders in England and Wales 1992–2008.

the number of contact applications nearly doubled between 1994 and 2000,[26] although this upward trend was evident long before 1995.[27] In Britain, contact (visitation) orders increased more than fourfold between 1992 and 2008.[28]

Law Cases in the United States, in CROSS CURRENTS: FAMILY LAW AND POLICY IN THE US AND ENGLAND 513 (Sanford Katz, John Eekelaar, & Mavis Maclean, eds., 2000). *See also* ANDREW SCHEPARD, CHILDREN, COURTS AND CUSTODY: INTERDISCIPLINARY MODELS FOR DIVORCING FAMILIES, 38–40 (2004).

[26]   In 1994–1995, there were 14,144 applications in the Family Court of Australia. In 1999–2000, there were 27,307. Family Court of Australia *Statistics 1999/00* table 4.10. No figures are available after 2000 because of changes to the court system.

[27]   As a result of a transfer of powers from state governments to the federal government in 1987, the Family Court gained jurisdiction over custody and access disputes involving ex-nuptial children. In 1988–1989, the first full year in which this expanded jurisdiction existed, there were 10,619 contact applications in the Family Court of Australia. In 1993–1994, there were 16,256. Family Court of Australia *Statistics 1989/90* table 5, *1999/00* table 4.10. Indeed, the rise in the level of contact applications can be seen since 1981. In that year, there were 4,214 applications, and by 1986 it had risen to 7,208. Family Court of Australia *Statistics 1989/90* table 5.

[28]   In 1992, there were 17,470 contact orders. In 2008, there were 76,759. This table is derived from the statistics published annually by the Ministry of Justice and its predecessor departments. *See, e.g.,* Ministry of Justice, *Judicial and Court Statistics* 2008, ch 5; Lord Chancellor's Department, *Judicial Statistics 1986–2000. See also* Gwynn Davis & Julia Pearce, *Privatising the Family?* 28 FAM. L. 614 (1998). For discussion of the explanations for this rise in litigation, *see* Gwynn Davis, *Love in a Cold Climate – Disputes About Children in the Aftermath of Parental Separation, in* FAMILY LAW: ESSAYS FOR THE NEW MILLENIUM 127, 128–29 (Stephen Cretney, ed., 2000).

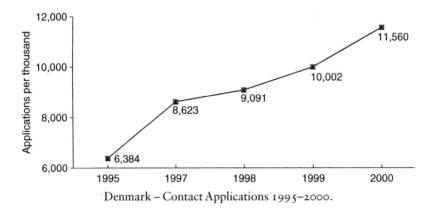

Denmark – Contact Applications 1995–2000.

Nor are these increases confined to English-speaking countries. In France, new applications in relation to parenting and visitation arrangements following separation and divorce increased by 25 percent between 1996 and 2001.[29] In Germany, there was a 27 percent increase in litigation over contact between 1999 and 2003.[30] In Denmark, the total number of visitation applications nearly doubled between 1995 and 2000, rising from 6,384 in 1995 to 11,560 in 2000.[31] After that time, the numbers remained relatively stable, even falling in 2006 to 10,184 cases. However, in 2008, the numbers rose sharply again, to 13,412.[32]

---

[29] Department of Justice, France, *Annuaire Statistique de la Justice, 1996–2000* and *1997–2001*. The increase in applications in relation to children born to unmarried parents was even greater. They rose from 42,005 in 1996 to 62,201 in 2001. By 2006, the figure was 78,986, almost a 100% increase within ten years: Department of Justice, France, *Annuaire Statistique de la Justice, Édition 2008*, 49. The rate of disputes between unmarried couples is likely to reflect increases in the ex-nuptial birth rate as a percentage of all births, which has been rising in western countries: Kathleen Kiernan, *Childbearing Outside Marriage in Western Europe*, 98 POPULATION TRENDS 11 (1999).

[30] Kerima Kostka, *Die gemeinsame elterliche Sorge bei Trennung und Scheidung – ein Blick auf die Begleitforschung zur Kindschaftsrechtsreform*, 1 AKTUELLE INFORMATIONEN 22, 23 (2006).

[31] CivilRetsDirektoratet, *Samvær Børnesagkyndig Rådgivning Konfliktmægling, Statistik 2001* (2002). In Denmark, any parent may apply for contact. It used to be the case that contact rights would only arise if the parents had lived together for most of the first year of the child's life, usually at least eight months in practice. This restriction was removed in 1995.

[32] Personal communication from Mariam Khalil, Danish Department of Family Affairs, by email, December 15, 2009. This followed the enactment of the Danish Act on Parental Responsibility, which took effect beginning October 1, 2007.

These massive increases in litigation about parenting after separation have passed largely unnoticed even in the few jurisdictions that publish statistics. Their effects are certainly noticed in the courts. Family lawyers and judges around the western world bemoan the fact that courts are overwhelmed with cases, leading to long delays in bringing to trial the disputes that cannot be settled.

However, there has been little discussion in the academic or professional literature about why this has been occurring and what its implications are for the family law system. What happened to all those disappearing fathers who did not want to see their children? They still exist, of course, but at a systemic level, the "problem" of fatherhood has changed. It is not clear whether their absence is a greater or lesser problem than the numbers of fathers who are now fighting through the court system to maintain their involvement with their children.

REFRAMING THE ISSUES

It is unfortunate that these conflicts – at both an individual level and a policy level – should so often be seen as just another front in the gender war. Undoubtedly this is one legitimate (and perhaps inevitable) characterization of the way in which the conflict is perceived and played out. However, seeing the problem in these terms masks a much more fundamental issue that has profound implications for every aspect of modern family law.

The thesis of this book is that many of the conflicts about family law around the western world today derive from the breakdown of the model on which divorce reform was predicated in the late 1960s and early 1970s. That model, which assumed a sharp differentiation in the respective roles of custodial and noncustodial parents, presupposed that divorce could end the relationship between parents in such a way that people could get on with their lives with only residual ties to their former partners. The assumption was that once the property and the children had been allocated to one household or the other, each parent was autonomous. The divorce freed him or her from being entangled with the life of the other parent, except to a limited extent. Those ties were through child support obligations, which were poorly enforced, spousal maintenance where ordered, and ongoing visitation with the children.

The experience of the last forty years has shown that whereas marriage may be freely dissoluble, parenthood is not.[33] In the modern

---

[33] It follows that parents can be divorced in one respect but not in others. Maccoby and Mnookin have distinguished between four aspects of divorce. Firstly, there is the spousal

law, the biblical idea that in marriage, the two become one flesh[34] finds its expression not in the law of marriage itself but rather in the consequences of procreation whether or not the parents were married. This is reflected in the multitude of ways in which parents are treated as an enduring family unit, whatever their relationship may become and whatever new relationships they may form. Parenthood creates enduring connections, ties that outlast the severance of the adult relationship.

One aspect of this is financial. Parenthood has economic consequences that often justify and necessitate ongoing financial transfers between separated and divorced parents for a long time after a marriage or nonmarital relationship has ended. Spousal maintenance, once strictly limited by reference to need or rehabilitative purposes, is experiencing a revival. In countries such as Canada, there is a now a focus on its utility in compensating for lost earning capacity as a result of marital roles and circumstances.[35]

Whereas the requirement to pay spousal maintenance is more common in some jurisdictions than others, the obligation to pay child support is more universal, and it is now vigorously enforced in many countries.[36] In both contexts, the fortunes of one parent affect the other. Career success or career reversals for the primary earner may affect his or her liability for child support or spousal maintenance. The primary caregiver is thus often affected financially by the success or otherwise of the primary breadwinner. The parent liable to pay child support may also be affected by the life choices and circumstances of the primary caregiver in jurisdictions that take account of the income of both parents in the assessment of child support.

The entwinement of parents' lives is also to be seen in terms of parenting arrangements after separation. The ties that bind parents together are, of course, only as strong as the bond between each parent and the children. Where one parent is prepared to let go of a close connection with his or her child, or is resigned to that outcome, or alternatively, the connection is severed by court order, then autonomy is possible for the other parent, and the involvement of the nonresident parent is mainly through child support;

---

divorce, which is the process by which the couple separate as husband and wife. Secondly, there is the legal divorce, which makes spousal divorce effective and gives an entitlement to remarry. Thirdly, there is the economic divorce, by which the financial resources of one household economy are divided. Fourthly, there is the parental divorce: ELEANOR MACCOBY & ROBERT MNOOKIN, DIVIDING THE CHILD: SOCIAL AND LEGAL DILEMMAS OF CUSTODY (1992).

[34] Genesis 2:24; Matthew 19:4–6.
[35] *See* Chapter 11.   [36] *See* Chapter 10.

but where each parent wants to retain a close connection and involvement with the child, the parents' lives continue to be entwined with each other through the children in ways beyond the financial. This manifests itself in terms of joint parental responsibility and the continuing need to negotiate with one another about the time children spend with each parent, as well as in sorting out the logistics of such arrangements. A desire of a primary caregiver to relocate to another area or country has profound implications for the other parent.

The continuing interconnectedness of the lives of parents following separation also has implications for governments. Child support enforcement is one aspect of this, but efforts are increasingly being made to improve the enforceability of orders for contact between nonresident parents and children as well.[37] The state is no less involved in seeking to preserve family relationships through law than a century ago, but the focus of its involvement has shifted. Whereas once the state played a role in maintaining the principle of the indissolubility of marriage by forbidding or severely restricting divorce, now it has largely abandoned that role. Instead, the state's emerging role in the regulation of family life is to maintain the indissolubility of biological parenthood, with limited recognition being given also to other quasi-parental relationships.

THE INDISSOLUBILITY OF PARENTHOOD AND LIMITATIONS ON AUTONOMY

The history of family law reform over the last few years is not only, or even mainly, a history of a gender war. It reflects the piecemeal recognition of the difficulties inherent in the idea that divorce can bring an end to a parental relationship, as opposed to a transformation in its character.

This book explores how family law has changed to recognize the indissolubility of parenthood, why it has changed so significantly over the last forty years or so, and why this trend is probably irreversible despite strong opposition to these developments. This is explored through a comparative study of jurisdictions around the western world, in

---

[37] In Britain, *see, e.g.*, Advisory Board on Family Law, Children Act Sub-Committee, *Making Contact Work: A Report to the Lord Chancellor on the Facilitation of Arrangements for Contact Between Children and Their Non-Residential Parents and the Enforcement of Court Orders for Contact* (2002). In Australia, *see, e.g.*, Family Law Council, *Child Contact Orders: Enforcement and Penalties* (1998); Helen Rhoades, *Contact Enforcement and Parenting Programmes – Policy Aims in Confusion?* 16 CHILD & FAM. L.Q. 1 (2004).

particular Australia, Britain, Canada, France, Germany, New Zealand, the Scandinavian countries, and the United States. It will be argued that many of the problems and conflicts concerning family law with which courts and legislatures are now grappling reflect a tension between two irreconcilable conceptualizations of what the divorce of parents is all about. One conceptualization emphasizes the importance of postseparation autonomy for each parent. The other rests on the notion that even though separation may lead to or bring about the dissolution of a marital or quasi-marital relationship, the lives of the parents remain inextricably entwined with one another as a consequence of the continuing obligations of parenthood.

Resolving the tensions caused by these two irreconcilable conceptualizations requires a clear choice to be made at the political level. The challenge for the future of family law is coming to terms with the implications of this in a more systematic and principled way than has occurred so far.

2

The Divorce Revolution and the
Process of Allocation

THE INDISSOLUBILITY OF MARRIAGE

For many centuries, marriage was regarded as indissoluble. In countries founded on the western legal tradition, the indissolubility of marriage can be traced back to Christian teaching on the nature of marriage itself. Jesus Christ quoted the very earliest chapters of the book of Genesis as evidence of the Creation ordinance that on marriage, a man leaves his father and mother and is joined to his wife, and "they will become one flesh."[1] The sexual union, consummated, according to traditional Christian sexual ethics, on the wedding night, was an expression of a more fundamental union – not the erotic yet transitory joining together of vaginal intercourse, but a union of lives until death parted them. "So they are no longer two, but one," Jesus explained. "Therefore what God has joined together, let no-one separate."[2]

Christian teaching on divorce was thus a strict code, replacing the Jewish teaching based on the law of Moses, which allowed divorce. Jesus said that Moses permitted divorce because people's hearts were hard.[3] By his time, a rabbinic teaching had emerged that effectively allowed a man to divorce his wife for any reason.[4] Questioned about this teaching by the Pharisees, Jesus was unequivocal in calling his followers to a higher standard. He permitted divorce on the grounds of adultery, thus indicating the great importance of sexual fidelity to preserve the uniqueness of the union between a man and a woman. However, he rejected firmly the teaching

---

[1] Genesis 2:24 (New International Version).
[2] Matthew 19:6 (New International Version).
[3] Matthew 19:8.
[4] ANDREW CORNES, DIVORCE AND REMARRIAGE: BIBLICAL PRINCIPLES & PASTORAL PRACTICE, 183–84 (1993).

of those who said that a man could divorce his wife merely because of dissatisfaction with her. Marriage, in Jesus' teaching, irrevocably changed the nature of a man's familial relationships. He left one familial unit and, with his wife, formed another that was intended to be as enduring as the relationship he had with his own parents.

In modern western societies, we have largely lost the sense that marriage is a union that is transformative. In many western countries, men and women may experience multiple unions serially – sexual relationships without living together, cohabiting relationships, and marriages. Even though marriage may still have a special place culturally, for many people, the first divorce may not be the last.

The transformative nature of marriage is, however, not unique to the historic western legal tradition. Societies throughout history and around the world have certainly varied in the ease of divorce and in its frequency in practice. Yet the fundamental significance of marriage – and its transformative nature in terms of a person's relationships – is not at all unique to cultures based on a Christian heritage. In China and Japan, for example, the cultural meaning of marriage also involves leaving one family and joining another. Mostly, it is the woman who does the leaving, transferring from the family line of her father and mother and joining the dynastic line of her husband's family. This is known as viri-patrilocal marriage. It is possible also for a man to join the wife's dynastic line – an occurrence most likely to take place if the woman's family has no male heir and her family line would die out (uxorilocal marriage). Marriage, in these cultures also, is much more than a contract.[5]

The Prohibition on Divorce

In societies that adopted Christian teaching as normative, it was centuries before the standard of indissolubility of marriage really became established. Christian devotion competed with preexisting customs and understandings of marriage. The Church could not really develop an effective prohibition on divorce without first establishing dominion over marriage. To the extent that marriage was a matter of custom and practice, it may not be properly evidenced. It followed that the first step in establishing the indissolubility of marriage was to ensure it was held in public.

---

[5] *See generally*, WILLIAM PARISH & MARTIN KING WHYTE, VILLAGE AND FAMILY IN CONTEMPORARY CHINA (1978).

First, this occurred through insisting that a marriage should be concluded at the door of the Church (*ad ostium ecclesiae*) where it could be seen by villagers. It had to be in the presence of a priest, as a witness to the union. It was only much later, with the Council of Trent in 1563, that the notion became established that the priest was essential to the solemnization of the marriage, and not merely a witness.[6]

As Mary Ann Glendon has documented, the history of marriage has been first one of juridification and then later one of dejuridification, as over time divorce first became permitted and then gradually liberalized.[7] That liberalization is a twentieth-century story.[8]

THE EMERGENCE OF NO-FAULT DIVORCE

The story of the no-fault divorce revolution is often told as if it was a western invention, with California being in the vanguard of social change.[9]

In fact, there had been a few flirtations with a liberal law of divorce in western countries in previous centuries, for example, Napoleonic France; but none lasted longer than a brief period.[10] Divorce on the basis of a legal separation for one year was permitted in Sweden by a law enacted in 1915.[11] The concept of no-fault divorce was also introduced early on in the communist world. Lenin's government in Russia declared freedom of divorce soon after coming to power in 1917. It was seen as the counterpart to freedom of marriage. Both kinds of freedom were regarded as aspects of the freedom of individuals.[12] The Russian Family Code of 1918 introduced "mutual consent of both spouses as well as the wish of one of them" as grounds for divorce. Article 18 of the Russian Family Code of 1926 carried this freedom of divorce even further by allowing that application to the Civil Registry for a letter of divorce could be made *ex parte*, without knowledge or consent of the other spouse. In 1929, the requirement of

---

[6] LAWRENCE STONE, ROAD TO DIVORCE: ENGLAND 1530–1987, 51–66 (1990).

[7] MARY ANN GLENDON, STATE, LAW, AND FAMILY: FAMILY LAW IN TRANSITION IN THE UNITED STATES AND WESTERN EUROPE (1977).

[8] RODERICK PHILLIPS, PUTTING ASUNDER: A HISTORY OF DIVORCE IN WESTERN SOCIETY, 568–70 (1988); MARY ANN GLENDON, ABORTION AND DIVORCE IN WESTERN LAW (1987).

[9] For accounts of the American history of no-fault divorce, *see* HERBERT JACOB, SILENT REVOLUTION: THE TRANSFORMATION OF DIVORCE LAW IN THE UNITED STATES (1988); Lynn Wardle, *No-Fault Divorce and the Divorce Conundrum*, 1991 B.Y. U. L. REV. 79.

[10] *See* JOHN EEKELAAR, REGULATING DIVORCE, 11–12 (1991).

[11] GLENDON, *supra*, note 7, 224–26 (1977).

[12] Yuri Luryi, *Soviet Family Law*, 10 MAN. L. J. 117, 170 (1980). *See also* KENT GEIGER, THE FAMILY IN SOVIET RUSSIA (1968).

any legal action for divorce of registered marriages was abolished by the courts, allowing termination by informal mutual agreement, unilateral declaration, or desertion.[13] The experiment did not last long. In July 1944, following an exponential rise in divorce, bigamy, abortion, and juvenile delinquency, freedom of divorce was severely restricted.[14]

Stalin's Russia was not the only country to experiment with family law reform. In Nazi Germany, divorce on the basis of a three-year separation was added to fault-based grounds through a law passed by Hitler's National Socialist regime in 1938.[15]

After World War II, the new communist countries of Eastern Europe also reformed their family laws. For example, in Czechoslovakia, reforms in 1955 permitted no-fault divorce based on the fact of lengthy separation. In 1963, a new Family Code was introduced that allowed divorce when the relations between the spouses were so seriously disturbed that the marriage could no longer fulfill its social purpose.[16] Fresh reforms in the Soviet Union in 1968 made divorce by consent available by registration after a three-month "cooling off" period if there were no minor children.[17]

The divorce revolution only came to western countries at the end of the 1960s. In England and Wales, divorce law was reformed in 1969. Even though the English Parliament persisted with fault-based grounds for divorce, divorce by mutual consent was made available following two years' separation. Unilateral divorce without fault was only possible five years after separation.[18]

---

[13] Jan Gorecki, *Communist Family Pattern: Law as an Implement of Change*, 1 U. ILL. L. F. 121, 124 (1972); Jacob Sundberg, *Recent Changes in Swedish Family Law: Experiment Repeated*, 23 AM. J. COMP. LAW 34, 44 (1975).

[14] GEIGER, *supra*, note 12, at 95–98, 255–58.

[15] *See* GLENDON, *supra*, note 7.

[16] Olga Plankova, *Relations Between Husband and Wife Under Czechoslovak Family Law*, 9 BULLETIN OF CZECHOSLOVAK LAW 1, 2–3, 11 (1968); Act no 94/1963, The Family Code s.24.

[17] Principles of Legislation of the USSR and the Union Republics on Marriage and the Family, July 3rd 1968, [1968] 27 Ved. Verkh. Sov. S.S.S.R. Item 241. For a summary of the law as it developed in the former Soviet bloc after the demise of the communist government, *see* Marko Mladenovic, Marina Janjic-Komar, & Christa Jessel-Holst, *The Family in Post-Socialist Countries*, *in* INTERNATIONAL ENCYCLOPEDIA OF COMPARATIVE LAW VOL IV Chapter 10, 3, 80–85 (1998).

[18] Divorce Reform Act, 1969 (Eng.). A new law of divorce was enacted in 1996 (Family Law Act, 1996) but the government decided not to proceed with these divorce reforms following the perceived failure of its pilot program to steer people into mediation as part of the divorce reform package. On the practical experience of the fault-based grounds for divorce in England and Wales, *see* GWYNN DAVIS & MERVYN MURCH, GROUNDS FOR DIVORCE (1988).

France also retained a mixture of fault-based and no-fault grounds in its reforms. The legislature's intent in enacting the 1975 Reform Law was that divorce by mutual consent be considered the preferred form of dissolution. However, the law offered a list of other possible avenues for divorce; these included divorce on the ground of acts constituting a "serious or repeated violation of the duties and obligations of marriage." [19]

Elsewhere in Europe, the trend emerged to enact a simple form of no-fault divorce, based on a separation period. The Divorce Law Reform of 1973 in Sweden introduced divorce by consent immediately when the couple did not have children, and imposed a six-month period of consideration if the divorce was not sought by agreement or there is a child under the age of sixteen. [20] In West Germany, the various grounds for divorce were replaced in 1976 with a single ground that the marriage has failed. [21] This can be demonstrated irrebuttably if the spouses have lived apart for one year and both spouses petition for divorce, or the respondent consents to divorce. A divorce could also be granted if the spouses have lived apart for three years. [22]

These trends were reflected also in the various laws of the United States. Whereas in the majority of U.S. states, the no-fault ground for divorce was added to fault-based grounds, some states adopted pure no-fault divorce. [23] In this movement, the Uniform Marriage and Divorce Act, developed by the Commissioners for Uniform State Laws in 1970, was an influential model for divorce reform. [24] The Act proposed that fault-based grounds for divorce be swept away and replaced with divorce based on a period of separation. Marriage, once treated as indissoluble unless an innocent spouse was given "relief" on the basis of fault, was now freely dissoluble, and in most western countries by the unilateral decision of one person against the wishes of the other.

---

[19] *See* GLENDON, *supra*, note 7, 202–12 (1977). The law of divorce has been amended by legislation passed on May 26, 2004. The new legislation preserves the multiple bases for divorce but sets up an initial common procedure as well as pathways between the various routes to divorce: Christian Dadomo, *The Current Reform of French Law of Divorce*, 2004 INT. FAM. L. 218.

[20] Glendon, *supra*, note 7, 224–26. *See also* Sundberg, *supra* note 13.

[21] "Wenn sie gescheitert ist."

[22] The Marriage and Family Law Reform of 1976: BGB §§ 1564–1568.

[23] Herma Hill Kay, *Beyond No-Fault: New Directions in Divorce Reform*, in DIVORCE REFORM AT THE CROSSROADS, 6, 7–8 (Stephen Sugarman & Herma Hill Kay eds., 1990); thirty-three states still retained fault-based divorce as of 2002: SANFORD KATZ, FAMILY LAW IN AMERICA 79 (2003).

[24] Uniform Marriage and Divorce Act 9A U.L.A. 169 (1998).

GIVING MARRIAGES A DECENT BURIAL

The central idea of no-fault divorce was that dead marriages should be given a decent burial and that it should be possible for the parties to get on with their lives and start fresh once decisions had been made about financial matters and custody.

The concept was well expressed in the statement of principles put forward by the Law Commission of England and Wales as early as 1966. A good divorce law, said the Law Commission, should aim to buttress marriage, but if the marriage was at an end, the role of the law should be "to enable the empty legal shell to be destroyed with the maximum fairness, and minimum bitterness, distress and humiliation."[25]

A similar view was taken by the Governor's Commission on the Family in California, which also reported in 1966. It urged reform of the law of divorce to eliminate fault both in the grounds for divorce and as a determinant in the division of community property and alimony. It further recommended the creation of a statewide Family Court that would have a therapeutic rather than a forensic purpose:[26]

> The direction of the law must be ... toward family stability – toward preventing divorce where it is not warranted, and toward reducing its harmful effects where it is necessary ... if a marriage is viable, it is the job of the Court, through any available personnel, to afford the parties what help they need and the Court can give. If the marriage has irretrievably foundered, then it must be the goal of the Court to aid the litigants to respond as maturely as possible to the difficult experience of the divorce. If the procedure, by "relieving tensions, or offering comfort or interpretation," can enable the litigants to respond less hysterically or vindictively and more reasonably to the experience of divorce, the legal issues can be more intelligently and constructively analyzed by the Court and counsel, and the Court may more easily develop final orders which will operate to the best interests of the parties – and children – involved.

The courts were to be both intensive-care doctors and undertakers, both saving and burying marriages; but where the marriage was clearly at an end, it should make final orders, not to adjudicate on rights or to make

---

[25] Law Commission, Reform of the Grounds of Divorce: The Field of Choice 10, Cmnd 3123 (1966). The second objective was said to have two facets. "First the law should make it possible to dissolve the legal tie once that has become irretrievably broken in fact ... Secondly, it should achieve this in a way that is just to all concerned, including the children as well as the spouses." *Id.* at 10–11.

[26] Report of the Governor's Commission on the Family 33–34 (1966).

hard choices between competing interests, but to help the parties move on without attribution of blame. Altruism about the role of law was combined in both England and California with a surreal optimism that the courts could take on the role of helping both parties to a failed marriage to adjust to the future without bitterness, distress, vindictiveness, or hysteria. Therapy was not a role to which courts hitherto had been accustomed.

As the no-fault divorce revolution began to sweep the western world in the late 1960s and early 1970s, a number of features were quite typical. One defining feature of such regimes was that issues of custody and property were dealt with by a once-for-all process of allocation.

THE ALLOCATION OF THE CHILDREN

As a consequence of divorce, the court allocated the children.[27] Typically, the courts would award "custody" to one parent, usually the mother, and grant "access" or "visitation" to the other. There was little difference in this respect between common law countries and civil law countries of Western Europe. "Custody" included virtually all the rights and powers that an adult needed to bring up a child, including the right to make decisions about a child's education and religion.[28] Both parents were legal guardians at common law, but this meant little, because the powers classified as those of "guardianship" were few and far between. They included such matters as consent to marriage, among others.

---

[27] ANDREW SCHEPARD, CHILDREN, COURTS AND CUSTODY: INTERDISCIPLINARY MODELS FOR DIVORCING FAMILIES 3–4 (2004) ("The court's function was to resolve the parents' dispute by choosing one or the other as the custodial parent and awarding the other parent visitation."). For histories of the development of custody law, *see* MARY ANN MASON, FROM FATHER'S PROPERTY TO CHILDREN'S RIGHTS: THE HISTORY OF CHILD CUSTODY IN THE UNITED STATES (1994); SUSAN MAIDMENT, CHILD CUSTODY AND DIVORCE: THE LAW IN SOCIAL CONTEXT (1984) (England); CAROL SMART, THE TIES THAT BIND: LAW, MARRIAGE, AND THE REPRODUCTION OF PATRIARCHAL RELATIONS, (1984) (England); SUSAN B. BOYD, CHILD CUSTODY, LAW, AND WOMEN'S WORK (2003) (Canada).

[28] Lerner v. Superior Court In and For San Mateo County, 242 P.2d 321 (Cal) (1952) ("The essence of custody is the companionship of the child and the right to make decisions regarding his care and control, education, health, and religion," Traynor J. at 323); Griffin v. Griffin, 699 P.2d 407 (Colo. 1985) (power to decide the child's education, health care, and religious training is vested in the custodial parent); Frizzell v. Frizzell, 323 P.2d 188 (Cal. Ct. App.) (1958) (custodial parent has the power to determine what school the child will attend); Jenks v. Jenks, 385 S.W.2d 370 (Mo. App.) (1964) (award of custody carries with it the right to determine the child's education, including the place of education); Majnaric v. Majnaric, 347 N.E.2d 552 (Ohio. App.9.Dist., 1975) (noncustodial parent generally has no right to determine the child's education); Boerger v. Boerger 97 A.2d 419 (N.J. Super. Ch 1953); Bentley v. Bentley 86 A.D.2d 926, 448 NYS 2d 559 (3d Dep't 1982) (custodial parent has the right to determine the child's

Custody law was binary in character.[29] The assumption universally held at that time was that custody decisions involved a definitive choice between one home and another. This understanding of the meaning of custody was not, of course, a product of the divorce revolution in the same way that the clean-break principle was in regard to financial matters.[30] Rather, the law as it then stood provided a context in which it was possible to hold out to parents a promise of postdivorce autonomy once the custody issue had been settled. The law of custody was not shrouded in much uncertainty in terms of its practical application. There was, after all, no such thing as joint custody in the late 1960s and early 1970s, and the maternal preference remained sufficiently strong that women could be all but guaranteed of keeping custody of younger children,[31] unless there were serious deficiencies in their capacity to care for the child.[32] Indeed, the motives of fathers who sought primary care of their children were questioned.[33] In the aftermath of parental separation, there were fairly clearly assigned roles for

religious upbringing). In Canada, *see*, e.g., Krueger v. Krueger, [1979] 25 O.R. 2d 673 (Ont. C.A.) ("In my view, to award one parent the exclusive custody of a child is to clothe that parent, for whatever period he or she is awarded the custody, with full parental control over, and ultimate parental responsibility for, the care, upbringing and education of the child, generally to the exclusion of the right of the other parent to interfere in the decisions that are made in exercising that control or in carrying out that responsibility" (Thorson J.A, ¶54). In relation to English and Australian common law, *see* ANTHONY DICKEY, FAMILY LAW 265–66 (1985).

[29] For discussion of this in the context of autopoietic theory, *see* GUNTHER TEUBNER, LAW AS AN AUTOPOIETIC SYSTEM (Anne Bankowska And Ruth Adler Trans., 1993); MICHAEL KING & CHRISTINE PIPER, HOW THE LAW THINKS ABOUT CHILDREN (2d ed. 1995); MICHAEL KING & JUDITH TROWELL, CHILDREN'S WELFARE AND THE LAW: THE LIMITS OF LEGAL INTERVENTION (1992).

[30] The clean-break philosophy in financial matters was explicit in the 1975 reforms in Australia. Section 81 of the Family Law Act, 1975 provides: "In proceedings under this Part ... the court shall, as far as practicable, make such orders as will finally determine the financial relationships between the parties to the marriage and avoid further proceedings between them."

[31] For example, the commentary to the Uniform Marriage and Divorce Act's best-interests test stated: "The preference for the mother as custodian of young children when all things are equal, for example, is simply a shorthand method of expressing the best interest of children ..." Uniform Marriage and Divorce Act 9A U.L.A. 169 at 282 (1998), Comment on s. 402.

[32] *See*, in the United States, Linda Elrod & Milfred Dale, *Paradigm Shifts and Pendulum Swings in Child Custody: The Interests of Children in the Balance* 42 FAM. L. Q. 381 (2008).

[33] Thus leading American family law scholar Herma Hill Kay could write: "Gender wars over custody preceded no-fault divorce and were initially waged by fathers, not to obtain physical custody of their children, but to reduce their support obligations." Herma Hill Kay, *No-Fault Divorce and Child Custody: Chilling Out the Gender Wars*, 36 FAM. L.Q. 27, 34 (2002).

each gender: for one, the demands of single parenthood; for the other, a substantial loss in terms of parental status and involvement.

Irène Théry, the French sociologist, characterized the original divorce reform model as the substitution model of postdivorce parenting.[34] The marriage breakdown marked the dissolution of the nuclear family. The future upbringing of the child depended on a choice between two alternatives: the home of the mother or the home of the father. Parental authority was awarded to the sole custodial parent, and there was a strong differentiation between the roles of the custodial and noncustodial parents. This way of seeing divorce was expressed pithily by the New York Court of Appeals in 1978: "Divorce dissolves the family as well as the marriage."[35] Divorce thus reversed the transformative nature of marriage.

In this traditional conceptualization of what was involved in custody decision making, visitation (or "access") was simply a "legal concession to the loser."[36] Once this allocation had occurred, people could get on with their lives with the past behind them. The old marriage was dead and they could begin anew, repartner, and build a new family life with only vestiges of continuity with the old.

To the extent that this view of custody allocation after divorce was underpinned by any theory, it was that children needed continuity of relationships with at least one parent, and if that continuity was assured, children would survive the divorce experience well. This view was most famously expressed by Goldstein, Freud, and Solnit in their influential book, *Beyond the Best Interests of the Child*.[37] Writing

---

[34] Irène Théry, *The Interest of the Child and the Regulation of the Post-Divorce Family*, 14 INT'L. J. SOC. L. 341 (1986).

[35] Braiman v. Braiman, 44 N.Y.2d 584, 407 N.Y.S. 2d 449, 378 NE 2d 1019 at 1022 (1978). For a summary of the facts of this case, *see* SCHEPARD, *supra* note 27, at 33–34.

[36] LYNNE HALEM, DIVORCE REFORM: CHANGING LEGAL AND SOCIAL PERSPECTIVES, 213–14 (1980). Although judges everywhere maintained the stance that visitation was a right of the noncustodial parent, concerns were expressed by some experts that visitation may threaten the security of the children and make things more difficult where the custodial parent has remarried: *Id.* at 214–15, citing LOUISE DESPERT, CHILDREN OF DIVORCE 59 (1953) (the father's presence "may be a threat to the new security [the children] have worked hard to build without him"). One writer even suggested that a clean-cut break with one parent should be part of the divorce agreement: Wayne Oates, *A Minister's Views on Children of Divorce, in* EXPLAINING DIVORCE TO CHILDREN 157 (Earl Grollman ed., 1969).

[37] JOSEPH GOLDSTEIN, ANNA FREUD, & ALBERT SOLNIT, BEYOND THE BEST INTERESTS OF THE CHILD (1973). The book, while highly influential, also attracted a lot of criticism. For a review of reviews, *see* R. Crouch, *An Essay on the Critical and Judicial Reception of Beyond the Best Interests of the Child*, 13 FAM. L.Q. 49 (1979). *See also* Martin Richards,

within the psychoanalytic tradition of psychology, they argued that the interests of a child were best served if courts ensured the continuity of a relationship with one "psychological parent" to which the child was already attached. To minimize disruption in a child's life resulting from the marriage breakdown, child custody decisions should be made speedily and, once made, should be final. They took the substitution model of postseparation parenting to its extreme when they argued – controversially – that noncustodial parents should have no legally enforceable right of access:[38]

> Children have difficulty in relating positively to, profiting from and maintaining the contact with two psychological parents who are not in positive contact with each other. Loyalty conflicts are common and normal under such conditions and may have devastating consequences by destroying the child's positive relationships to both parents.... Once it is determined who will be the custodial parent, it is that parent, not the court, who must decide under what conditions he or she wishes to raise the child. Thus the non-custodial parent should have no legally enforceable right to visit the child, and the custodial parent should have the right to decide whether it is desirable for the child to have such visits.

Even though the courts did not embrace the most radical aspects of Goldstein, Freud, and Solnit's views, the consequence of the prevailing view of custody decision making was that divorce involved a clean break in terms of parental responsibility once the issue of custody allocation was decided.

THE CLEAN-BREAK PRINCIPLE AND THE GOAL OF SELF-SUFFICIENCY

Another aspect of the divorce revolution was the emphasis, in many jurisdictions, on achieving a clean financial break between the parties, limiting spousal support, spousal maintenance, or alimony (as it was variously called) to cases of need. This is, however, the one aspect of the divorce revolution where the most diversity was observable around the western world, at least in the first wave of the divorce revolution.

Behind the Best Interests of the Child: An Examination of the Arguments of Goldstein, Freud and Solnit Concerning Custody and Access at Divorce, 1986 J. Soc. Welfare L. 77; Michael Freeman, *The best interests of the child? Is 'The Best Interests of the Child in the best interests of children?*, 11 Int'l. J.L. Pol'y & Fam. 360 (1997).

[38] Goldstein, Freud, & Solnit, *id* at 38.

Canada

Nowhere perhaps was the clean-break approach better articulated than by the Law Reform Commission of Canada in a 1976 report that recommended the adoption of a rehabilitative philosophy of spousal support:[39]

> The main purpose of financial provision on dissolution of marriage should be to meet the reasonable needs of the spouse who performed, on behalf of both spouses, family functions that carry economic disadvantages. Just as the law should characterize financial provision during marriage as a mutual responsibility, it should also treat the economic advantages accruing to the spouse who performs the wage-earning role on behalf of both spouses as a mutual asset. The right to continue to share in this asset after the partnership ends should last as long as the economic needs following from dependency during marriage continue to exist in the face of reasonable efforts by the dependent person to become self sufficient. The duration of the post-dissolution dependency period should be governed by the principle that everyone is ultimately responsible to meet his or her own needs. The financial guarantee provided by law should be one of rehabilitation to overcome economic disadvantages caused by marriage and not a guarantee of security for life for former dependent spouses. The obligation of the former spouse who is required to pay should be balanced by the obligation of the other eventually to become self-sufficient, as all other unmarried persons must be, within a reasonable period of time. The law should still provide for the possibility of a permanent obligation where the economic disability of a spouse flowing from the marriage is permanent.

Self-sufficiency for each spouse was the goal in most cases, and although spousal support had an important part to play in addressing the economic disadvantages for mothers on marriage breakdown, it was to last only so long as needed in order for the mother to be able to provide for herself. The Divorce Act 1985 in Canada removed any linkage between the parties' conduct that may have led to the breakdown of the marriage and either spouse's entitlement to spousal support. Similar changes occurred in provincial matrimonial legislation throughout Canada.[40] The Divorce Act provided that spousal support awards should "in so far as practicable, promote the economic self-sufficiency of each spouse within a reasonable

---

[39]   Law Reform Commission of Canada, Report on Family Law, 40–41 (1976).
[40]   Kristen Douglas, Spousal Support under the Divorce Act: A New Direction (1991), available at: http://dsp-psd.pwgsc.gc.ca/Collection-R/LoPBdP/BP/bp259-e.htm

period of time."[41] Although the legislation offered a range of bases for child support, judicial interpretation by the Supreme Court of Canada in the latter half of the 1980s emphasized the importance of promoting a clean break, and spousal support was viewed as transitional and rehabilitative in nature.[42]

In jurisdictions that adopted an approach of equitable distribution of property, a clean break could be achieved by awarding the majority of the assets to the children's primary caregiver, almost invariably the mother, while leaving the father with a minority of the assets but with what in many cases was the most valuable asset of the marital partnership – his earning capacity. Equitable distribution statutes give courts in many cases the possibility to secure the matrimonial home for the mother and children, with or without the need for a mortgage to pay out the other parent.

United States

The Uniform Marriage and Divorce Act (UMDA) in the United States, which influenced the development of state laws on the subject,[43] reflected this clean-break approach. The focus was on achieving equity between divorced spouses through the division of property.[44] Indeed, Robert Levy, the reporter for the UMDA, had initially made a strong plea that property division rather than spousal support should be the primary vehicle for financial settlement between the parties to the marriage. He also saw an element of spousal support as being contained within child support

---

[41] Divorce Act 1985 s.15(7)(d) (as originally enacted). *See* now Divorce Act 1985 s.15.2(6)(d).

[42] Pelech v. Pelech [1987] 1 S.C.R. 801, Richardson v. Richardson, [1987] 1 S.C.R. 857, and Caron v. Caron, [1987] 1 S.C.R. 892. These cases were known collectively as the "Pelech trilogy." They all concerned the issue of whether the applicants could claim spousal support that was inconsistent with the parties' prior agreements limiting such support. However, the judgments were interpreted as promoting clean-break approaches even where there was no prior agreement. *See* James McLeod, *Case Comment on Pelech v. Pelech* 7 R.F.L. (3d) 225 (1987). For a retrospective on the decisions, *see* Robert Leckey, *What Is Left of Pelech?* 41 SUP. CT. L. REV. (2d) 103 (2008). For developments since then, particularly following the decision of the Supreme Court of Canada in Moge v. Moge, [1992] 3 S.C.R. 813, *see* Chapter 11.

[43] The UMDA was only adopted (in part) in eight states, but its ideas influenced the content of other state laws. For a review of developments in U.S. state law following the UMDA, *see* Grace Blumberg, *The Financial Incidents of Family Dissolution, in* CROSS CURRENTS: FAMILY LAW AND POLICY IN THE US AND ENGLAND 387 (Sanford Katz, John Eekelaar, and Mavis Maclean, eds., 2000).

[44] *See*, for example, Gray's comparative study of jurisdictions, KEVIN GRAY, REAL LOCATION OF PROPERTY ON DIVORCE (1977).

payments,[45] and proposed to the drafting committee that spousal support be abolished except for those cases where children were no longer living at home, the wife was unlikely to remarry or be able to support herself, and the division of property was inadequate to do justice given her contributions to the marriage.[46] Although the drafting committee eventually adopted a more liberal approach to the award of spousal support, the UMDA still reflected Levy's clean-break orientation to a significant extent.[47]

Making provision for future needs out of the property settlement required a new way of thinking about the division of property, which took account of disparities in the economic circumstances of the parties as well as their past contributions. Property division thus was to take over some of the functions hitherto assigned to spousal support. The 1973 version of § 307 of the UMDA, Alternative A (for separate property states), made all the property, whenever and howsoever acquired, available for distribution between the parties. It also combined both retrospective and prospective elements in the list of considerations for the court:[48]

> In a proceeding for dissolution of a marriage, legal separation, or disposition of property following a decree of dissolution of marriage ... the court, without regard to marital misconduct, shall, and in a proceeding for legal separation may, finally equitably apportion between the parties the property and assets belonging to either or both however or whenever acquired, and whether the title thereto is in the name of the husband or wife or both. In making apportionment the court shall consider the duration of the marriage, any prior marriage of either party, antenuptial agreement of the parties, the age, health, station, occupation, amount and sources of income, vocational skills, employability, estate, liabilities, and needs of each of the parties, custodial provisions, whether the apportionment is in lieu of or in addition to maintenance, and the opportunity of each for future acquisition of capital assets and income. The court shall also consider the contribution or dissipation of each party in the acquisition, preservation, depreciation, or appreciation in value of the respective estates, and as the contribution of a spouse as a homemaker or to the family unit.

---

[45] Robert Levy, Uniform Marriage and Divorce Legislation: A Preliminary Analysis 140ff (1969), cited in Herma Hill Kay, *Equality and Difference: A Perspective on No-Fault Divorce and Its Aftermath*, 56 U. Cincinnati L. Rev. 1, 47 (1987).

[46] Kay, *id* at 47.

[47] Levy later noted that the UMDA did offer grounds for judges to provide substantial protection to displaced homemaker spouses through the award of spousal support. Robert Levy, *A Reminiscence about the Uniform Marriage and Divorce Act – and Some Reflections about Its Critics and Its Policies*, 1991 B.Y.U.L. Rev. 43, at 72ff.

[48] UMDA § 307 (1973).

In this long list of considerations, factors going to future needs and earning capacity were listed ahead of retrospective issues about contributions to the asset pool or to the family.

The UMDA § 308 provided that spousal support could be ordered only if the applicant "lacks sufficient property to provide for his reasonable needs" and is "unable to support himself through appropriate employment or is the custodian of a child whose condition or circumstances make it appropriate that the custodian not be required to seek employment outside the home."[49] From a modern standpoint, the generic use of the male pronoun seems particularly inapposite in this context, for the situations where men were recipients of spousal support were almost as rare as tropical heat in the Arctic.

The comment to § 308 stated clearly that the intention of the section, taken together with § 307 concerning property division, was:

> ... to encourage the court to provide for the financial needs of the spouses by property disposition rather than by an award of maintenance. Only if the available property is insufficient for the purpose and if the spouse who seeks maintenance is unable to secure employment appropriate to his skills and interests or is occupied with child care may an award of maintenance be ordered.[50]

Mary Ann Glendon commented on the huge implications of the shift brought about by the UMDA:[51]

> The language of the newer statutes is significant. Traditionally, alimony was payable *unless* there were circumstances indicating that there was no need. The Uniform Act and other recent statutes provide alimony will *not* be payable *except* in special cases of need. This means that in principle, legal marriage no longer carries with it the effect of economic responsibility for the other spouse.

Australia

Like the UMDA, Australia also adopted a clean-break approach. Indeed, the desirability of a clean break was emphasized in legislation.[52] Australian law gives judges an enormous discretion to allocate all the property of the

---

[49] Uniform Marriage and Divorce Act § 308, 9A U.L.A. 169, 446 (1998).
[50] Uniform Marriage and Divorce Act § 308, 9A U.L.A. 169, 447 (1998).
[51] Mary Ann Glendon *Marriage and the State: The Withering Away of Marriage*, 62 VIRGINIA L. REV. 663, 706 (1976).
[52] *See* s.81 of the Family Law Act 1975.

parties as the court sees fit, not just the fruits of the marriage partnership.[53] Family law practitioners and the courts seek to deal with the equity of the case entirely through property division, even if, as is quite commonly the case, women with the primary care of the children receive 70 percent of the property.

Spousal support was confined to cases where a spouse does not have the means for self-support. The threshold criterion for spousal support in s.72 of the Family Law Act 1975 is that the other party is unable to support herself or himself adequately whether:

(a) by reason of having the care and control of a child of the marriage who has not attained the age of 18 years;
(b) by reason of age or physical or mental incapacity for appropriate gainful employment; or
(c) for any other adequate reason.

A study conducted in the late 1990s concluded that apart from interim payments prior to the property settlement, spousal maintenance had all but disappeared from the landscape.[54] Researchers described it as "rare, minimal, and brief."[55] Seven percent of respondents had paid or received periodic spousal support since separation. Respondents who had not yet finalized their property were more than twice as likely as those who had settled their property to receive or pay periodic support (5 percent versus 13 percent). This indicated that periodic maintenance was being used as a form of "bridging finance" to tide women over until there was a final property division.

The notion of equitable distribution of the marital assets (or, in some jurisdictions, all the assets) is foreign to certain European jurisdictions in which property ownership is based on the idea of community property. In such community property jurisdictions, the normal approach is to divide the acquests of the marriage equally (or all of the property, depending on the matrimonial regime in each jurisdiction or which was applicable as between the spouses). An equal division of the property alone is much less likely to result in a fair division of the assets given the disadvantages flowing from caring for children. In jurisdictions such as France, other forms of adjustment have been developed to address the inequities flowing from the breakdown of the relationship.

---

[53] Patrick Parkinson, *The Yardstick of Equality: Assessing Contributions in Australia and England* 19 INT J. L. POL'Y & FAM. 163 (2005).
[54] JULIET BEHRENS AND BRUCE SMYTH, SPOUSAL SUPPORT IN AUSTRALIA: A STUDY OF INCIDENCE AND ATTITUDES (1999).
[55] *Id.* at 7.

France

One such approach can be seen in the way that French law dealt with alimony in the aftermath of its divorce revolution in 1976. The French Divorce Reform Law of that year created multiple different forms of divorce, which varied in the economic consequences attaching to them. These were divorce by mutual consent, divorce for prolonged disruption of the life in common, and divorce for fault. Divorce on the basis of the prolonged disruption of the life in common could be sought unilaterally. It required either that the parties had been separated for six years or that, for the same period, one spouse had been suffering from an apparently incurable mental illness. Divorce for fault included shared fault; that is, an applicant could petition on one of the fault-based grounds even though it would be possible for a petition to be brought against him or her on fault-based grounds.

Divorce ended the duty of spousal support,[56] subject to provisions concerning certain kinds of divorce. The economic effects of marriage breakdown were to be dealt with in a manner other than through spousal support.[57] Central to this was the notion of the compensatory payment (*prestation compensatoire*), meant to compensate one spouse "for the disparity which the disruption of the marriage creates in the conditions of their respective lives."[58] Considerations included such factors as the age and the state of health of the spouses, the time already devoted or which they will have to devote to the upbringing of the children; their professional qualifications; and loss of pension rights. The legislation envisaged that this would be a lump-sum payment where possible, but also made provision for it to be paid in instalments, thus resembling spousal support but for the fact that the obligation was final and, barring quite exceptional circumstances, unmodifiable. Where divorce was granted on the basis of fault, the compensatory payment was available to the plaintiff but not the defendant. Although not expressed as such, the compensatory payment was akin to a severance payment on the termination of employment.[59]

---

[56] CIVIL CODE, Article 270.

[57] Glendon, writing soon after the introduction of the new laws, explained the approach French law took to the notion of ongoing support. It was not very different from the clean-break concept in Anglophone countries. She wrote: "The major goal of the new law, so far as effects of divorce are concerned, is to minimize 'after-divorce' contact and conflict between the ex-spouses." Mary Ann Glendon, *The French Divorce Reform Law of 1976*, 24 AM. J. COMP. L. 199, 213–14 (1976).

[58] English translation of Article 270 given in Glendon, *id*, 215 at note 71.

[59] GLENDON, *supra* note 7, 252.

The position was entirely different for unilateral divorce based on six years of separation or on mental illness under the original reforms to divorce law in 1976. Here the petitioner was obliged to pay spousal support indefinitely. Indeed the obligation even bound his estate and only ended with the death of the creditor-spouse. This form of divorce represented "a limited continuation of marriage."[60] In this way, French law reconciled unilateral no-fault divorce with traditional notions of the indissolubility of marital obligations. A wife could agree to a divorce – in which case a compensatory payment would need to be worked out; or she could petition for divorce on the basis of the husband's fault, in which case she was entitled to a compensatory payment and could also seek an award of damages to compensate for the material or moral prejudice caused by the dissolution of the marriage.[61] Otherwise, under the original 1976 reforms, she could be divorced against her will only to the extent that her former husband was entitled to remarry. The economic marriage continued, in sickness and in health, for richer or for poorer, until her death or remarriage.[62]

Sweden

The clean-break concept was also introduced in Sweden. By the time the divorce reform process began in Sweden in the late 1960s, spousal support was already a moribund concept.[63] The reform of divorce law, commenced by directives from the Minister of Justice in 1969, proceeded on the basis that in principle there should be no spousal support after divorce and that each party should be self-sufficient.[64] Writing in 1989, Mary Ann Glendon concluded that Sweden had implemented the clean-break principle more thoroughly than any other country under examination in her comparative law study, and that postdivorce spousal support was rare in practice.[65]

West Germany

Other jurisdictions did not take such an absolute approach but still emphasized the objective that both parties should become self-sufficient, with spousal support directed toward that goal. So for example, West Germany's

---

[60] Glendon, *supra* note 57, 218. [61] *Id*, 219.
[62] French law has evolved since then. In particular, changes to the law made on May 26, 2004 made an award of *prestation compensatoire* available irrespective of the nature of the divorce.
[63] Zona Sage, *Dissolution of the Family under Swedish Law* 9 FAM. L. Q. 375, 388 (1975).
[64] Note, *Current Legal Developments – Sweden*, 19 INT. & COMP. L. Q. 164 (1970).
[65] GLENDON, *supra* note 7, 224.

Marriage and Family Law Reform of 1976 provided that spousal support was to be available after divorce only for a transitional period to allow the economically weaker partner to become economically self-sufficient.[66] That at least, was the theory.

England and Wales

Other countries took a different approach, at least in the early years after the divorce revolution. In England and Wales, for example, the view that the laws of divorce should be liberalized was accompanied by a great deal of concern about the position of women who would thereby be economically disadvantaged. The Law Commission, in its landmark report setting out the field of choice in terms of divorce reform in 1966, clearly identified the need for the "economically weaker party" to be protected.[67] The legislative response to this need was to engage in wishful thinking. In the early years after the changes to the divorce law, the courts were instructed to exercise their powers in relation to property division and maintenance so "as to place the parties, so far as practicable and, having regard to their conduct, just to do so, in the financial position in which they would have been if the marriage had not broken down and each had properly discharged his or her financial obligations and responsibilities towards the other."[68]

Ten years on, it was recognized that this approach was utterly impracticable as a goal for financial provision on divorce, and it was abandoned by 1984. The legislation passed in that year gave priority to the needs of the children and otherwise contained a number of provisions that required consideration of how spouses could move toward self-sufficiency.[69] This included a statutory duty on courts, when exercising powers for financial provision, "to consider whether it would be appropriate so to exercise those powers that the financial obligations of each party towards the other will be terminated as soon after the grant of the decree as the court considers just and reasonable."[70] Over the ensuing years, there was a significant decline in spousal maintenance orders made on divorce. In 1985, 29,617

---

[66] BGB §§ 1569–76. GLENDON, *supra*, note 7, 258–59.

[67] Law Commission, *supra* note 27 at 50.

[68] *Matrimonial Causes Act* 1973 s.25 as originally enacted. The financial provisions were first enacted in the *Matrimonial Proceedings and Property Act* 1970. This followed recommendations from the Law Commission: THE LAW COMMISSION, FAMILY LAW: REPORT ON FINANCIAL PROVISION IN MATRIMONIAL PROCEEDINGS (Law Com. No. 25, 1969).

[69] STEPHEN CRETNEY, PRINCIPLES OF FAMILY LAW 761–66 (4th ed, 1984); JOHN EEKELAAR & MAVIS MACLEAN, MAINTENANCE AFTER DIVORCE 50–51 (1986).

[70] Matrimonial Causes Act 1973 s.25A. *See also Harman v Glencross* [1986] 1 All ER 545, CA at 557 per Balcombe LJ; *B v B (Financial Provision)* [1990] 1 FLR 20 at 26 (Ward J).

orders were made out of 157,491 divorces. By 1994, 17,193 orders were made out of 154,873 divorces.[71]

CHILD SUPPORT AND PARENTAL SEPARATION

In theory, at least, the one obligation that routinely ought to have tied mothers and fathers together, even in clean-break jurisdictions, was child support. Yet even that obligation was far from universal in practice.

In the United States, for example, data from the Panel Study of Income Dynamics, which oversamples low-income households, showed that only 39 percent of female-headed single-parent households had any spousal or child support award in 1968.[72] Official government statistics indicated that only 30 percent of single mothers actually received child support in 1976.[73] One reason was the gap between having an award and actually receiving payment. In 1978, 3,424,000 women had child support due to them but only 64 percent of the money due was paid.[74] Thus although in theory, the obligation to pay child support – at least by those who had sufficient earned income – was universal, the practical reality was very different.

Behind the practice, there seems to have been a cultural assumption that the support of one's former family was not an expected and enduring obligation years after that family had been dissolved. Harry Krause, writing in 1989, summarized the position twenty-five years earlier:[75]

> Twenty-five years ago, child support was not a public issue. Absent parents were not pursued. Even for a legally established child support obligation, the absent father could all but choose not to pay. The obligation was rarely enforced effectively – especially not across state lines. Paternity – where in doubt – was rarely ascertained.

[71] John Eeekelaar, *Post-divorce Financial Obligations in* Cross Currents: Family Law and Policy in the United States and England, 405, 417 (Sanford Katz, John Eekelaar, & Mavis Maclean eds., 2000).

[72] Anne Case, I-Fen Lin, & Sara McLanahan, *Explaining Trends in Child Support: Economic, Demographic and Policy Effects*, 40 Demography 171, 177 (2003).

[73] Elaine Sorensen & Ariel Halpern, Child Support Enforcement: How Well Is It Doing? Urban Institute, Discussion Paper, p.1 (1999). This data was from the March Current Population Surveys (CPS). This is a nationally representative survey of approximately 50,000 households, conducted by the U.S. Census Bureau.

[74] U.S. Census Bureau, *Child Support and Alimony: 1989*, data available at http://www.census.gov/hhes/www/childsupport/cstabf.html

[75] Harry Krause, *Child Support Reassessed: Limits of Private Responsibility and the Public Interest* 1989 U. Ill. L. Rev. 367, 370.

He noted further that the dominant social work view of the time was that enforcement should not be pursued because this would inconvenience the mother, and that children in need should be supported from the public purse.

Only a minority of fathers, it appears, felt a moral obligation to support their children once they were no longer one family, and no doubt many of those who did pay did so under compulsion. In the United States, motivation to pay child support was particularly weak when the mother was in receipt of welfare support because this money simply meant reduced welfare payments.[76] In Britain, at least, this attenuated level of commitment to child support was reinforced by the courts, which were willing enough to allow nonresident parents to prioritize the needs of second families over first families.[77] As men formed new families, their primary commitments were seen to be to that new family unit.

Writing in 1982, David Chambers anticipated the possibility that the moral obligation to pay child support might become further attenuated; that "family," with its attendant responsibilities, might come to mean nothing more than the people who live together in an intimate relationship at a given point in time.[78] As fathers felt squeezed out of their children's lives, the more time passed after the separation, the less sense of commitment they would feel to support the children financially.[79] He expected that with the rapid rise in divorce rates and children being raised outside marriage, the father's sense of diminished obligation to children with whom he had little contact would come to be seen as reasonable. The no-fault divorce revolution was changing the landscape of what family meant, with possibly dramatic impacts on the old notions of obligation between parents and children.

---

[76] Irwin Garfinkel, Daniel R. Meyer, & Sara S. McLanahan, *A Brief History of Child Support Policies in the United States, in* FATHERS UNDER FIRE: THE REVOLUTION IN CHILD SUPPORT ENFORCEMENT, 14, 15–16 (Irwin Garfinkel, Sara McLanahan, Daniel Meyer, & Judith Seltzer, eds., 1998).

[77] Mavis Maclean, *The Making of the Child Support Act of 1991: Policy Making at the Intersection of Law and Social Policy,* 21 J. L. & SOC. 505 (1994). *See also* Carol Smart, *Wishful Thinking and Harmful Tinkering? Sociological Reflections on Family Policy,* 26 J. SOC. POL'Y. 301, 311–15 (1997).

[78] David Chambers, *The Coming Curtailment of Compulsory Child Support,* 80 MICH. L. REV. 1614, 1622 (1982).

[79] Chambers wrote: "Especially if the custodial parent remarries, but even if she does not, most noncustodial parents participate less and less in the tiny events important to the sense of family, the events that make one feel the child's protector, teacher and companion. Over time, many fathers come to regard child support as a form of taxation without representation." *Id.* at 1624.

THE BREAKDOWN OF THE ALLOCATION MODEL AND THE
EMERGENCE OF THE ENDURING FAMILY

It was not long after the first flush of the divorce revolution that the idea
that divorce ended the family as well as the marriage began to change. This
change was most marked in thinking about the arrangements for postseparation parenting. In a perceptive article written in 1986, Théry argued that
the substitution model of the postseparation family was gradually being
displaced. Under this model, the parents' legal divorce necessarily required
a divorce between them not only as partners but also as parents. Only one
of the two parents could continue in that role after the divorce, and the
other's role would be no more than a visiting one in most cases.

Théry argued that a new concept of postseparation parenting was
emerging. This she called the idea of the enduring family. In this conceptualization, divorce was a "transition between the original family unit
and the re-organisation of the family which remains a unit, but a bipolar
one."[80] She noted that this conceptualization of postseparation parenting
implied the refusal of a choice between parents in favor of joint parental
authority.

A similar view was expressed in the early 1980s by social work
professor Constance Ahrons, who argued that the child's postdivorce
family should be regarded as being "binuclear," with membership in two
households rather than one.[81] Writing in 1983, she saw a trend emerging
toward shared custody and coparenting, and observed that this would
have "profound implications for the postdivorce family."[82] In her later
writing, Ahrons characterized the binuclear family as a form of limited
partnership established for a single purpose – to be coparents to the
children. She argued that the partnership agreement, which might have
to be renegotiated from time to time as circumstances change, needs to
establish rules for how parenting is to be managed across two households
and make practical provision for how to deal with holiday time, illnesses,
and other such issues.[83]

---

[80] Théry, *supra* note 33 at 356.
[81] Constance Ahrons, *Redefining the Divorced Family: A Conceptual Framework*, 25 SOC.
      WORK 437 (1981).
[82] Constance Ahrons, *Divorce: Before, During and After, in* STRESS AND THE FAMILY, VOL
      1, COPING WITH NORMATIVE TRANSITIONS 102, 112 (Hamilton McCubbin & Charles
      Figley, eds., 1983).
[83] CONSTANCE AHRONS, THE GOOD DIVORCE: KEEPING YOUR FAMILY TOGETHER WHEN
      YOUR MARRIAGE COMES APART 128–29 (1994).

The family mediation movement that began to emerge in the late 1970s in the United States was also influenced by the concept that divorce is not the end of the family, but rather a reorganization of the family. New ways of describing this idea emerged.[84]

This emerging view about postseparation parenting had its outworking in major changes in the law of custody. In various jurisdictions, the law has moved from a binary, winner-takes-all model of parenting after separation, based on the idea of allocating custody to one parent or the other, presumptively for the duration of childhood, toward a much more fluid and contingent approach to postseparation parenting arrangements. In this new conceptualization, the assumption was that both parents should be given the opportunity to remain involved in children's lives and to spend time with them. The details of that would depend more on logistics than the law.[85]

THE DIVORCE REVOLUTION AND THE FEMINIZATION OF POVERTY

Changes also occurred from the 1980s onward in thinking about financial issues. It did not take long for the issue to emerge that the divorce revolution, by increasing substantially the numbers of women experiencing divorce, would have serious adverse repercussions for women,[86] for it was almost always women, rather than men, who sacrificed their earning capacity in order to give primary focus to child rearing.

One of the most oft-cited pieces of research on this issue was that of Lenore Weitzman, who reported dramatic differences between the financial positions of men and women one year after divorce in California. Weitzman claimed that, on average, women were 73 percent worse off after divorce and men were 42 percent better off.[87] Her figures were later shown to be in error. Reexamination of her data demonstrated that the decline in women's financial circumstances was 27 percent and the

---

[84] One suggestion was to describe parents after marriage breakdown as being "divorced to" rather than "divorced from" one another. Hugh McIsaac, *Preface to* HOWARD H. IRVING & MICHAEL BENJAMIN, FAMILY MEDIATION, at ix-x (1995).

[85] *See* Chapter 3.

[86] Margaret Brinig & June Carbone, *The Reliance Interest in Marriage and Divorce*, 62 TUL. L. REV. 855 (1988); Stephen Sugarman, *Dividing Financial Interests on Divorce*, in DIVORCE REFORM AT THE CROSSROADS 130 (Stephen Sugarman & Herma Hill Kay, eds., 1990).

[87] LENORE WEITZMAN, THE DIVORCE REVOLUTION (1985).

increase in men's was 10 percent.[88] Even if Weitzman's dramatic headline figures were erroneous, a multitude of studies around the western world published in the 1980s and early 1990s reached broadly similar conclusions.[89]

Whatever the detail on the economic consequences of divorce, it should not have been surprising that women who had cared for children would be particularly vulnerable on separation. The generation of women who went through divorce in the 1970s and 1980s were quite likely to have withdrawn from workforce participation entirely either after marriage or at least with the arrival of the first child, and they also frequently did a great variety of unpaid work outside the home, such as involvement in schools, charitable organizations, and community groups.

While the economic effects of separation and divorce were often expressed in terms of the positions of women and men as a whole, the research even in the 1980s and early 1990s revealed a significant degree of heterogeneity in terms of the adverse economic effects of relationship breakdown for women. The evidence was that those women who are able to form a stable and enduring new partnership with another man typically recover their former financial position, owing to the fact that people tend to form relationships with others of similar educational background and social status, and that is likely to mean that their new partner has an earning capacity not dissimilar to that of the former husband.

---

[88] Richard Peterson, *A Re-evaluation of the Economic Consequences of Divorce*, 61 Am. Soc. Rev. 528 (1996). Weitzman admitted that the figures she reported were in error: Lenore Weitzman, *The Economic Consequences of Divorce Are Still Unequal*, 61 Am. Soc. Rev. 537 (1996). Sanford Braver has suggested that the error in relation to the decline of women's standard of living arose from the simple error of reading that women's standard of living was 73% of the previous standard of living (i.e., a 27% decline) as being a drop of 73%. Sanford Braver & Diane O'Connell, Divorced Dads: Shattering the Myths 59–61 (1998). For other criticisms of Weitzman's work, *see* Levy, *supra* note 43 at 52–54 and 60ff; Jana Singer, *Divorce Reform and Gender Justice*, 67 N.C. L. Rev. 1103 (1989).

[89] In the United States, *see* e.g., James McLindon, *Separate but Unequal: The Economic Disaster of Divorce for Women and Children*, 21 Fam. L.Q. 351 (1987); Saul Hoffman & Greg Duncan, *What Are the Economic Consequences of Divorce?*, 25 Demography 641 (1988); Marsha Garrison, *Good Intentions Gone Awry: The Impact of New York's Equitable Distribution Law on Divorce Outcomes*, 57 Brook. L.R. 621 (1991). In Britain, *see* John Eekelaar & Mavis Maclean, Maintenance after Divorce (1986). On the international evidence generally, *see* The Economic Consequences of Divorce: The International Perspective (Lenore Weitzman & Mavis Maclean, eds., 1992). On methodological issues in the studies conducted in the 1980s, including Weitzman's, *see* Annemette Sørensen, *Estimating the Economic Consequences of Separation and Divorce: A Cautionary Tale from the United States*, at 263 in that volume.

This pattern was seen very clearly, for example, in longitudinal Australian research carried out in the 1980s. The overall picture of women's loss of household income, comparing pre- and postseparation standards of living some three-to-five years after separation, was similar to the patterns in other countries. The greater the standard of living prior to separation, the greater was the fall. However, women who repartnered typically regained the economic position they had before their divorce.[90] A follow-up study three years later confirmed the pattern. As more women repartnered, more were able to recover something like their preseparation standard of living; but for those who remained single parents, their financial position had not improved markedly since separation.[91]

Concern about the feminization of poverty, together with the related concern for governments about the cost of supporting single-parent families through welfare budgets, drove numerous reforms from the 1980s onward. Changes in patterns of familial relationships came at an enormous cost to governments acting as social insurers for children and their primary caregivers. They in turn sought to reduce or recoup that expenditure through increased financial transfers between former spouses and parents. The major focus around the world was on the proper assessment and collection of child support obligations, but spousal support also began to experience a revival, at least in certain jurisdictions.[92] Men, whether or not they had been married to the mother of their children, increasingly found themselves constrained financially by the enduring obligations associated with parenthood.

THE GENDER WAR AND THE ENDURING FAMILY

This shift toward the recognition of the enduring family could also be interpreted in less benign terms. The same developments can be seen in both positive and negative ways. For example, Dawn Borque, a Canadian author, saw the trends in terms of the reconstruction of the patriarchal, nuclear family after separation, with individual male authority being

---

[90] *See* SETTLING UP (Peter MacDonald ed., 1986). Australian research indicates that statistically, the opportunities to repartner diminish with age for women. Jody Hughes, *Repartnering after Divorce: Marginal Mates and Unwedded Women*, FAMILY MATTERS 55, 16 (2000).

[91] KATE FUNDER, MARGARET HARRISON, & RUTH WESTON, SETTLING DOWN (1993).

[92] In Canada for example,, the Supreme Court gave a major stimulus to the revival of spousal support in Moge v. Moge, [1992] S.C.R. 813. *See* Chapter 11.

reestablished. As a consequence, women were forced to remain bound to their former partners and, to a large extent, subject to their control.[93]

However, feminist opposition to the idea of the enduring family was only partial. The notion that there should be a clean break between mothers and fathers when it came to the allocation of responsibility for children was one thing, but financial responsibility was another. Feminist writers were in the vanguard of emphasizing the indissolubility of parenthood when it came to economic issues. Another Canadian scholar, Anne Marie Delorey, like Borque, saw the move toward joint legal custody as being about the reassertion of patriarchal power and control, but still wanted men to contribute financially:[94]

> I would suggest that fathers who favour joint legal custody are actually seeking more rights and control without a corresponding increase in responsibility for their children. It is also significant that fathers' rights groups are demanding that the courts pay more attention to 'parents' rights' (otherwise known as men's rights) rather than focusing on such things as support obligations and enforcement. Emphasis on men's custody rights increases men's power, while emphasis on support enforcement, of course, requires men to be responsive to the economic needs of women and children. Men's rights groups want to uphold patriarchal law, under which ... [m]others have obligations without reciprocal rights. Fathers have rights without reciprocal obligations.[95]

Such views certainly played to the gallery of those who saw the law on parenting after separation mainly in terms of a struggle between the genders. However, those who saw the motivations of fathers seeking more involvement after separation purely in terms of the assertion of power and the avoidance of financial responsibility took altogether too little account of the possibility that fathers might want to be more involved in postseparation parenting because they loved their children and grieved the loss of their companionship.

Far from a one-sided shift in the balance of power between the warring genders, the shift to a recognition of the indissolubility of parenthood required both former partners to recognize the continuing rights that each of them had, and for nonresident parents to fulfill their financial obligations to their children through payments to their former partners. In their different

---

[93] Dawn Borque, *Reconstructing the Patriarchal Nuclear Family: Recent Developments in Child Custody and Access in Canada* 10 CANADIAN J. L. & SOC. 1 (1995).

[94] Anne Marie Delorey, *Joint Legal Custody: A Reversion to Patriarchal Power*, 3 CANADIAN J WOMEN & L. 33, 39 (1989).

[95] Citing PHYLLIS CHESLER, MOTHERS ON TRIAL, 365 (1986).

ways, both men's and women's advocacy groups expressed concerns about the shift toward the recognition of the enduring family. Every step of the way, whether it has been in relation to parenting after separation or financial transfers between parents, legislative reform has been controversial and contested; change, nonetheless, has been inexorable.

RESTRUCTURING THE FAMILY AFTER SEPARATION

The history of family law reform in the last twenty years could be said to be the history of abandonment of the assumption, fundamental to the divorce reform movement of the early 1970s, that divorce could dissolve the family as well as the marriage when there are children.[96] Margo Melli, surveying the changes over her career as an American family law professor, has commented on the magnitude of the changes since the emergence of no-fault divorce:[97]

> [A]s we have begun to develop a legal structure more responsive to the consequences of divorce and the needs of children and their parents, we have changed the nature of divorce. The modern institution of divorce has become quite different from its predecessors; in particular, it differs from the 'clean break' vision of divorce of the early no-fault period. Today, divorce is not the end of a relationship but a restructuring of a continuing relationship.

Similarly, British sociologists Bren Neale and Carol Smart observe that divorce in the 1970s "was a personal step that separated the old life from the new; the original family was effectively disbanded as parents opted for a clean break and entered into a tacit agreement not to interfere in each other's lives."[98] In contrast, modern divorce has "been recast as a 'stage' (albeit a painful one) in the newly extended life course of the indelible nuclear family."[99]

---

[96] Of course, no change has been made to the fundamental premise of the no-fault divorce revolution, that marriages should be freely dissoluble on the application of one party. If there has been a counterrevolution of any sort, then it has been to allow for the possibility of choice about the law to govern one's marriage, reflected in the development of the Covenant Marriage movement in the United States: *see e.g.*, Katherine Shaw Spaht, *Louisiana's Covenant Marriage Law: Recapturing the Meaning of Marriage for the Sake of the Children, in* THE LAW AND ECONOMICS OF MARRIAGE AND DIVORCE 92 (Anthony Dnes & Robert Rowthorn eds., 2002).

[97] Marygold Melli, *Whatever Happened to Divorce?*, WIS. L. REV. 637, 638 (2000).

[98] Bren Neale & Carol Smart, *In Whose Best Interests? Theorising Family Life Following Parental Separation or Divorce, in* UNDERCURRENTS OF DIVORCE 33, 35 (Shelley Day Sclater & Christine Piper, eds., 1999).

[99] *Id.* at 37.

However, with the abandonment of the assumption that divorce could mean the end of the family, there has been no conceptual reevaluation that would offer a new theoretical framework for policy formulation on family law issues. To a great extent, legal change has been driven not by any philosophical shift in the meaning of divorce, but in a piecemeal way as a reaction to the mounting body of evidence that the allocation model of divorce was inadequate to deal with the consequences of relationship breakdown.

That conceptual reevaluation can only emerge from an exploration of the tension that exists between the two irreconcilable ideas of what divorce is all about – one that emphasizes enduring familial relationships after separation and another that recognizes the reality of the breakdown of those relationships. This tension is the story of modern family law, and the resolution of the tension requires clear political choices to be made. Family law cannot continue to muddle through, caught between two irreconcilable conceptualizations of what divorce is all about.

PART TWO

Parenthood in the Enduring Family

3

Redefining Parenthood after Separation

Over the last few years, different jurisdictions have retreated from the winner-takes-all notion of custody in different ways. That process has moved further in some European jurisdictions than it has in most of the United States, but the direction of the movement is the same.

THE MOVEMENT TOWARD JOINT CUSTODY
IN THE UNITED STATES

That process began in the early 1980s with the movement toward joint legal custody in many States. Courts and legislatures began to respond to a shift in emphasis from the need of the child to have an attachment to one "psychological parent" to a need for children to maintain relationships with both parents.[1] Pressure for a legal presumption that the court should award joint legal custody was particularly strong in North America,[2] but it was also experienced in other western countries.

The term "joint custody" is a term with multiple usages in different parts of the United States. The position is well summed up by Ann Estin:[3]

> [I]n practice "joint custody" is not a single, unitary category.... Joint custody sometimes refers to sole legal custody in one parent combined with some form of shared residence. This arrangement allows parents to "share access to children and child-rearing responsibilities," and, depending on the time-sharing provisions, may permit frequent and prolonged contact.

---

[1] The work of Wallerstein and Kelly was perhaps most influential in bringing about a shift in emphasis: JUDITH WALLERSTEIN & JOAN KELLY, SURVIVING THE BREAKUP (1980).

[2] Andrew Schepard, *Taking Children Seriously: Promoting Co-operative Custody after Divorce*, 64 TEX. L. REV. 687 (1985).

[3] Ann Estin, *Bonding after Divorce: Comments on Joint Custody: Bonding and Monitoring Theories*, 73 IND. L.J. 441, 442 (1998).

While some monitoring can occur with this pattern, it does not give the nonprimary parent a right to control or even to participate in decisions concerning the children. Alternatively, divorced parents might have joint decisionmaking authority, while the children reside primarily (or almost exclusively) with one of them. This allows the nonprimary parent a greater measure of authority, but not much opportunity for a relationship with the children. At the other extreme, joint custody is sometimes understood to imply an equal division of both decisionmaking and residence ...

As originally developed, joint custody meant joint *legal* custody. In a joint legal custody arrangement, parents share responsibility for the children and there is a duty to consult on at least some issues. In an arrangement for joint legal custody, one parent is still awarded either "physical custody" – designated the primary domiciliary parent – or able to decide the child's "primary residence." Although it usually implies that there should be liberal visitation rights for the nonresident parent, an award of joint custody in itself says nothing about how much time a child will spend with each parent.

Increasingly, however, joint custody is used to describe joint physical custody, in which the children spend such significant amounts of time living with each parent that the arrangement cannot accurately be characterized as one in which there is a primary caregiver and a secondary, visiting parent. Joint physical custody does not necessarily mean equal time. For example, in California, the Family Code defines joint physical custody as meaning that "each of the parents shall have significant periods of physical custody. Joint physical custody shall be shared by the parents in such a way so as to assure a child of frequent and continuing contact with both parents."[4] By way of contrast, in Arizona and Georgia, joint physical custody is defined as "substantially equal time with each parent."[5] Some jurisdictions differentiate very clearly between these different meanings of joint custody whereas others do not.

---

[4]   Cal. Fam. Code § 3004. The definition of joint physical custody in Missouri is similar. "Joint physical custody" means "an order awarding each of the parents significant, but not necessarily equal, periods of time during which a child resides with or is under the care and supervision of each of the parents. Joint physical custody shall be shared by the parents in such a way as to assure the child of frequent, continuing and meaningful contact with both parents": Mo. Rev. Stat. § 452.375(3).

[5]   *See* Ariz. Rev. Stat. § 25-402(3): "'Joint physical custody' means the condition under which the physical residence of the child is shared by the parents in a manner that assures that the child has substantially equal time and contact with both parents." Ga. Code Ann. § 19-9-6(3): "'Joint physical custody' means that physical custody is shared by the parents in such a way as to assure the child of substantially equal time and contact with both parents."

All states in America authorize joint custody or its equivalent as an option, but only a few states now have a presumption in favor of joint custody or its equivalent. Other states have a presumption in favor if the parties agree to it. In the remaining states, the focus is on the best interests of the child, and the issue of joint custody, apart from being an option available, is not specifically addressed.[6]

The movement toward joint custody reached its zenith as a legislative reform movement in the United States in the late 1980s. Since then, there has been a move toward different language, which reflects an entirely different understanding of postseparation parenting.

PARENTING PLANS

Washington State led the way to a new conceptualization of parenting after separation. Its radical approach was adopted as long ago as 1987. Washington State law requires each of the parents on divorce to propose a parenting plan, and if an agreement cannot be reached, a plan can be determined by the court.[7] Parenting plans are framed in linguistic terms that avoid the assumptions inherent in the language of custody that one parent has the primary responsibility while the other is assigned a marginal, visiting role. Washington's Code provides that the plan shall include a residential schedule that designates in which parent's home each minor child shall reside on given days of the year, including provision for holidays, birthdays of family members, vacations, and other special occasions."[8] It also requires that there be a dispute resolution process stipulated in the plan to try to resolve future disagreements without court action.[9]

---

[6] *See* Linda Elrod and Robert Spector, *A Review of the Year in Family Law 2007–2008: Federalization and Nationalization Continue*, 42 FAM L.Q. 713 (2009) Chart 2. *See also* Susannah May, *Child Custody and Visitation*, 11 GEORGETOWN J. GENDER & L. 381 (2001).

[7] WASH. REV. CODE § 26.09.181.

[8] WASH. REV. CODE § 26.09.184(6). For commentary on these reforms, *see* Jane Ellis, *Plans, Protection and Professional Intervention: Innovations in Divorce Custody Reform and the Role of Legal Professionals*, 24 U. MICH. J. L. REFORM 1 (1990). Ellis reported in this article on an empirical study of the operation of the legislation based on a study of files and interviews with lawyers. The file study indicated greatly increased shared parenting provisions following the effective date of the Act (*Id.* at 125). *But see* John Dunne, Wren Hudgins, & Julia Babcock, *Can Changing the Divorce Law Affect Post-Divorce Adjustment?*, 33 J. DIV. & REMARRIAGE 3 (2000).

[9] WASH. REV. CODE § 26.09.184(2) and (4).

Katherine Bartlett notes the connection between the emergence of the concept of the mandatory parenting plan and the changes both in attitudes toward postseparation parenting and parents' working circumstances: [10]

> The trend in favor of mandatory parenting plans recognizes not only the advantages of advance planning for children, but also the changing demographics of the family. Once upon a time, when one parent was to receive primary custody and the other visitation every other weekend, an order so providing may have seemed adequate enough. Such simple, straightforward arrangements have outworn their usefulness in this era, when, increasingly, both parents seek active involvement in the child's life. The need for greater specificity comes also from the increasing complexity of family life, with both parents likely to be working, children involved in a greater number of after-school activities, and higher expectations for family, social and intellectual life.

The idea of encouraging parents to draw up parenting plans in sorting out arrangements after separation has now become a widespread practice used by mediators around the western world, and the language of parenting plans has now been incorporated into the legislation of a number of U.S. states.[11] Often it is grafted onto the traditional language of custody. West Virginia's statute is an example of this old wine in new bottles. The Court may order a parenting plan that makes "provision for the child's living arrangements and each parent's custodial responsibility." The plan should include a "custodial schedule that designates in which parent's home each minor child will reside on given days of the year," or a formula by which such a schedule is to be determined. The Court must also make an "allocation of decision-making responsibility as to significant matters reasonably likely to arise with respect to the child."[12] Gone is the notion of "custody" as a bundle of rights, including the right of residence, to be allocated to one or other parent, or perhaps to both. The notion of custodial responsibility is largely to be equated with actual care.

OTHER LINGUISTIC FORMULATIONS

Other U.S. jurisdictions combine new terminology somewhat interchangeably with the old language of custody. Illinois, for example,

---

[10] Katherine Bartlett, *US Custody Law and Trends in the Context of the ALI Principles of the Law of Family Dissolution*, 10 VA. J. SOC. POL'Y & L. 5, 7–8 (2002).

[11] *See* e.g. MONT. CODE § 40-4-234; N.M. STAT. § 40-4-9.1; TN CODE § 36-6-404.

[12] WV CODE § 48-11-205(c)(1).

encourages parents to try to reach a Joint Parenting Agreement, failing which the Court will make a Joint Parenting Order or a Sole Custody Order. The language of joint parenting is used in the same section of the statute as joint custody.[13] In Utah, all the possible bases are covered. The legislation provides that "any party requesting joint custody, joint legal or physical custody, or any other type of shared parenting arrangement, shall file and serve a proposed parenting plan."[14] It is a linguistic smorgasbord. In Wisconsin, the statute uses the term "custody" only to refer to legal custody, while referring to the issue of how much time the child will spend with each parent as being an order about physical placement, without distinguishing between the resident and nonresident parent.[15] In Minnesota, the parties may agree that their parenting plan will utilize language other than "custody" and "parenting time," but if a parenting plan is included in a final judgment, the court must specify whether the parties have joint or sole legal and physical custody for enforcement purposes.[16]

The acceptance that the notion of custody is now outdated is also seen in the American Law Institute's proposals for the reform of the law concerning family dissolution.[17] The term "custodial responsibility" used in the Principles is something different from the traditional notion of custody, for it does not imply the necessity for a binary choice between the mother and the father as caregiver. The parties are required to devise a parenting plan that should include a "custodial schedule that designates in which parent's home each minor child will reside on given days of the year," or a formula or method for determining such a schedule.[18] In this way, the either/or choice between the parents of traditional custody adjudication is abandoned in favor of an approach that recognizes that in the absence of reasons to restrict or prohibit one parent's contact with the child, both will have caring responsibility for the child, and the parent who is not in a primary caregiving role is nonetheless something more than a visitor in the children's lives.

---

[13] 750 ILL. COMP. STAT. 5/602.1(b).   [14] UTAH CODE § 30–3-10.8(1).

[15] WIS. STAT. § 767.41(4)(a)1: "Except as provided under par. (b), if the court orders sole or joint legal custody … the court shall allocate periods of physical placement between the parties in accordance with this subsection. The exception, provided for in par. (b) is where "after a hearing, the court finds that physical placement with a parent would endanger the child's physical, mental or emotional health."

[16] MINN. STAT. § 518.1705 (subds 2–4).

[17] AMERICAN LAW INSTITUTE, PRINCIPLES OF THE LAW OF FAMILY DISSOLUTION: ANALYSIS AND RECOMMENDATIONS (2002).

[18] PRINCIPLES § 2.05(5)(a). This is similar to the approach adopted in Washington's Code.

EUROPE: THE CONTINUATION OF PARENTAL
RESPONSIBILITY AFTER SEPARATION

At about the same time as U.S. jurisdictions were debating the merits of joint legal custody, other countries began to adopt very different approaches. Rather than making joint custody (in the sense of joint legal responsibility) an option, or even establishing a presumption in favor of this, other countries made joint parental responsibility the default position in the absence of a court order to the contrary. That is, parental rights, powers, and responsibilities were seen as continuing after separation and divorce, unaffected by the change in the legal status or living arrangements of the parents.

Britain: Parental Responsibility, Residence, and Contact

In England and Wales, a radical reconceptualization of postseparation parenting occurred in 1989. On the recommendation of the Law Commission of England and Wales, the language of custody, guardianship, and access was abolished. In its place, the Children Act 1989 provided that each parent has "parental responsibility" and retains that responsibility after the marriage breakdown. Instead of making a custody order giving to one parent, to the exclusion of the other, a bundle of rights and powers to make decisions about the welfare of the child, the new law provided that court orders should focus on the practical issues, in a way similar to the approach taken in the "parenting plan" jurisdictions of the United States. The Children Act introduced the new terminology of "residence" and "contact" orders. Such orders say nothing about parental responsibility – that is, they do not carry with them a bundle of parental powers and responsibilities to the exclusion of the other parent, except to the practical extent required in the terms of the order. When a child is living primarily with one parent, this diminishes the nonresident parent's rights, powers, and responsibilities in a practical sense, to the extent that those rights, powers, and responsibilities depend on the child living physically with that parent, but they are in all other respects unaffected by the parental separation.

The philosophy of the Children Act 1989 is that parental responsibility continues after separation as it existed before the relationship breakdown, subject to any orders to the contrary by the court. Where there is a dispute about a particular aspect of parental responsibility, such as schooling or medical treatment, it can be dealt with by making a specific order in relation to that issue. In 1995, Scotland passed legislation using similar terminology and concepts.[19]

British sociologist Carol Smart has described well the significance of this legislation for the movement toward the indissolubility of parenthood:[20]

> The Children Act ... is ... part of a trend towards changing the fundamental nature of divorce. Contained within the Act are three newly articulated principles. The first is the principle of "non-intervention." This means that the courts are reluctant to become involved in matters over children and actively encourage parents to negotiate outcomes without the need for a court order. The second is the principle of joint parenting. This means that the old idea of one parent having "custody" and the other having "access" is abandoned in favour of a system where parents simply go on being parents with the same legal duties and obligations as existed during the marriage. The terms custody and access are replaced by residence and contact. The third principle is the welfare of the child. This is not a new principle, but in this Act it has come to be synonymous with the idea of the right of a child to have two parents. This means that joint parenting is meant to be an active sharing of the upbringing of the child in which both parents are as much involved as they were before the divorce. I want to suggest that these new principles have in fact introduced a new marriage contract by another name. This new marriage contract ends the possibility of confluent love[21] for mothers (although not necessarily for fathers) – by which I mean that it ends the possibility of divorce finishing a relationship with a person one no longer loves or cares for.

As Smart notes, whether or not parenthood is in practice indissoluble for primary caregivers (predominantly women) depends to a great extent on the attitude of the nonresident parent. If a nonresident father desires to remain closely involved with his children, the new ideas on postseparation parenting give him much leverage. However, little can be done in practice to compel nonresident parents to remain involved with their children.

---

[19] *Children (Scotland) Act* 1995, s. 11.
[20] Carol Smart, *Wishful Thinking and Harmful Tinkering? Sociological Reflections on Family Policy*, 26 J. Soc. Pol'y. 301, 315 (1997).
[21] The idea of confluent love is taken from the sociological writing of Anthony Giddens. Giddens defines confluent love in terms of a contrast with romantic love. "Confluent love is active, contingent love, and therefore jars with the 'for-ever', 'one-and-only' qualities of the romantic love complex." ANTHONY GIDDENS, THE TRANSFORMATION OF INTIMACY 61 (1992).

France: The Emergence of Coparentalité

Similar developments have occurred in France, where the law is now based on a principle of *coparentalité*.[22] In France, reforms were introduced in 1993 that were similar to those enacted by the Children Act 1989 in England. By legislation passed on January 8, 1993,[23] the Civil Code was amended to remove the language of custody.[24] It was replaced with the language of "parental authority." The legislation provided that parental authority is to be exercised in common[25] and that parental separation does not change this.[26] Where parents are unmarried, joint parental authority applies as long as both parents acknowledge the child within a year of the birth. Otherwise the parent who is first to acknowledge the child – almost invariably the mother – has sole parental authority. The position can of course be changed by a joint declaration of the parents or by judicial decision.[27] Prof. Hugues Fulchiron summarizes the approach of the French Parliament: "legislators have sought to assert the enduring nature of the ties between the child and both of its parents. It takes two to be parents, and parents remain parents forever." [28]

The legislation also created a new specialist judge for family disputes – the *juge aux affaires familiales*. In the event of a dispute between the parents about parental authority following separation, the judge decides the issues

---

[22] Frédéric Vauvillé, *Du Principe de Coparentalité*, 209 Les Petites Affiches 4 (2002). The *coparentalité* principle is also examined by Hugues Fulchiron in *L' Autorité Parentale Renovée*, Répertoire Du Notariat Defrénois 959 (2002). *See also* Philippe Malaurie and Hugues Fulchiron, La Famille (3rd ed, 2009).

[23] Loi 93–22, 1993–01–08, modifiant le code civil, relative à l'état civil à la famille et aux droits de l' enfant et instituant le juge aux affaires familiales. *Available at* http://www. legifrance.gouv.fr. For an examination of the 1993 reform, *see* François Boulanger, *Faut-il Revoir les Règles D'attribution de L'autorité Parentale?*, 1999 Recueil Dalloz Chroniques 233; *see also* Françoise Dekeuwer-Défossez, Rénover Le Droit De La Famille: Propositions Pour Un Droit Adapté Aux Réalités Et Aux Aspirations De Notre Temps (1999), in particular at 64.

[24] In French, "la garde."

[25] French C. Civ. Art. 372. *See* Hugues Fulchiron, La Mise en Oeuvre du Droit de L'enfant à être Elevé par ses Deux Parents et la Généralisation de L'exercice en Commun de L'autorité Parentale, (1997).

[26] French C. Civ. Art. 373–2. *See also* Jean Carbonnier, Droit Civil Tome 2 – La Famille, l'enfant, le couple, 633 (21st ed. 2002). The author states that "the overall spirit of the 1987–1993 legislation was to ensure that parental authority continues to be exercised after divorce in the same conditions as during marriage." (Severine Kupfer trans.)

[27] French C. Civ. Art. 372. This provision has been maintained in article 372 of the French Civil Code modified by the 2002 reform. *See* Hugues Fulchiron, *Custody and Separated Families: The Example of French Law*, 39 Fam. L. Q. 301, 306 (2005).

[28] Fulchiron, *ibid.*

of primary residence and contact.[29] The judge is also given the power to make an order vesting parental authority in one parent only if it is in the best interests of the child to do so.[30] In a study of 300 judicial decisions in 1994–95, 91.6 percent of the orders were found to be for joint parental authority, and this was the position in every case where the parties had petitioned jointly for divorce.[31]

Germany

The idea of continuing parental authority despite separation and divorce was also the basis of law reform in Germany. The *Gesetz zur Reform des Kindschaftrechtes*, 1997,[32] provides for joint parental responsibility to continue after separation as the default position whether or not the parents were married. Before this, joint parental responsibility for divorced parents was an exception rather than a rule, and a father who had never been married to the mother could not be awarded joint parental responsibility.[33] The 1997 law amended the Civil Code[34] to provide that the parents have joint parental responsibility during the marriage, and unmarried parents can agree to joint parental responsibility by formal declaration. Effectively, however, it is up to the mother whether to agree that the father be recognized, and the lack of judicial review has been held to breach the European Convention on Human Rights and to violate the German constitution.[35] Where there

---

[29] This is referred to in French as a right of access and "housing" (*hébergement*) of the child.

[30] French C. CIV. Article 373–2-1 created by the 2002 law reform (further amended in 2010). However, the other parent would keep his "monitoring right" on the child's maintenance and education (Article 373–2-1 para 5) and he would still be informed of the important choices concerning the child and could be refused his right of access only for "serious reasons" (article 373–2-1, para 2), see François Boulanger, *Modernisation ou Utopie?: La Reforme de L'autorité Parentale par la Loi du 4 Mars 2004*, 2002 RECUEIL DALLOZ CHRONIQUES 1571.

[31] Hugues Fulchiron & Adeline Gouttenoire-Cornut, *Réformes Législatives et Permanence des Pratiques: à Propos de la Généralisation de L'exercice en Commun de L'autorité Parentale par la Loi du 8 Janvier 1993*, 1997 RECUEIL DALLOZ CHRONIQUES 363.

[32] This legislation came into force on July 1, 1998.

[33] Eva Ryrstedt, *Joint Decisions – A Prerequisite or a Drawback in Joint Parental Responsibility?*, 17 AUSTRALIAN J. FAM. L. 155, 196 (2003).

[34] See generally, Nina Dethloff, *Parental Rights and Responsibilities in Germany*, 39 FAM. L. Q. 315 (2005).

[35] § 1626a para 2, BGB (*Bürgerliches Gesetzbuch*). The provision was held by the European Court of Human Rights to be in breach of the European Convention on Human Rights because it violated Article 8 (right to respect for private and family life) and Article 14 (protection against discrimination: Zaunegger v Germany [2009] ECHR 22028/04 (3 December 2009). See further, Bea Verschraegen, *Elterliche (Ob-)Sorge – Regel und*

is joint responsibility, it continues after separation unless the court orders otherwise on the application of one of the parties.[36]

Scandinavia

Likewise in the Scandinavian countries, the default position is that joint parental responsibility continues after divorce.[37] The legislative approach is one of nonintervention. Instead of allocating custody as one of the matters to be dealt with in granting a divorce, joint custody is deemed to continue after separation unless one parent seeks a court order to the contrary. This was how joint custody became the norm in Norway,[38] Sweden,[39] and Finland[40] from the early 1980s onward. In Sweden,[41] the possibility of having a joint custody arrangement by consent after divorce was introduced by legislative amendment in 1977. In 1983, the Children and Parents Code was further amended to provide that joint legal custody existed between the parents on divorce unless the court was asked to make an order for sole custody, and from 1998, the court could make an order for joint custody in the absence of agreement.[42]

In Denmark, prior to 2007, the position was that both parents retained parental responsibility after separation unless the Court ordered otherwise. Parents could agree on joint custody, but the court could not order joint custody if the parents did not agree.[43] They had to make a binary choice between the parents, and the decision about residence was a corollary of the award of custody to one parent or the other. In 2006,

---

Ausnahme: Wer bestimmt, wer entscheidet? 1/2010 INTERDISZIPLINÄRE ZEITSCHRIFT FÜR FAMILIENRECHT 4 (2010). The Federal Constitutional Court in 1 BvR 420/09, 21st July 2010 held that the provision violated Article 6 of the Basic Law (concerning care for children).

[36] BGB § 1671, para 1. The applicant may seek that parental responsibility, or part of it, be conferred on him or her alone. The change from joint parental responsibility to sole parental responsibility may be made if the other parent agrees (and a child of 14 years old or more does not object), or it is in the best interest of the child. (BGB § 1671, para 2).

[37] *See* Ryrstedt, *supra* note 33. *See also* Kirsti Kurki-Suonio, *Joint Custody as an Interpretation of the Best Interest of the Child in a Critical and Comparative Perspective*, 14 INT'L J. L. POL'Y & FAM. 183, 188 (2000).

[38] Children and Parents Act 1981, Lov 1981–04–08 nr. 7 om barn og foreldre.

[39] Children and Parents Code 1949 (*Föräldrabalken*). *See generally* Eva Ryrstedt, *Custody of Children in Sweden*, 39 FAM. L. Q. 393 (2005).

[40] Custody of Children and Rights of Access Act 1983 (Lag angående vårdnad av barn och umgängesrätt 8.4 1983/361).

[41] Ryrstedt, *supra* note 33, at 172–73.   [42] *Id.* at 174.

[43] Lov nr 387 af 14 juni 1995 om forældremyndighed og samvær (Custody and Access Act 1995).

a Commission proposed modest reforms to this position, but its caution was cast aside by the Minister of the day who announced major reforms to the law. The law on Parental Responsibility, passed in 2007,[44] removed the old language of custody. Joint parental responsibility became the normal position in all cases unless there were serious grounds for an order of sole parental authority, and the courts could determine who would be the primary caregiver.[45]

THE MEANINGFUL INVOLVEMENT OF BOTH PARENTS

The transition from the old language of custody to the new language of parenting time and its equivalents, in which there is no linguistic distinction between the roles of the separated parents, may, on one view, represent nothing more than a semantic shift. However, it has been accompanied by other legislative provisions that emphasize the importance of maintaining the involvement of the nonresident parent in the children's lives.

One way this has been done is to give content to the notion of the "best interests of the child" by legislative findings or directions, or the statement of principles. Whereas some legislatures have been content with semantic change, others have combined this with legislative provisions that strongly encourage some level of shared parenting. An example is the legislation in Colorado. The legislature's declaration provides:

> The general assembly finds and declares that it is in the best interest of all parties to encourage frequent and continuing contact between each parent and the minor children of the marriage after the parents have separated or dissolved their marriage. In order to effectuate this goal, the general assembly urges parents to share the rights and responsibilities of child-rearing and to encourage the love, affection, and contact between the children and the parents.

Consistent with this goal, Colorado is one of the few American jurisdictions that avoids entirely the language of custody. The legislation refers instead to "proceedings concerning the allocation of parental responsibilities"[46] and utilizes the generic language of "parenting time" to refer to the time the child spends living with each parent, and not just

---

[44] *Lov om Foroeldreansvar* (Law on Parental Responsibility), 20.08.2007.
[45] Annette Kronborg and Christina Jeppesen de Boer, *The CEFL Principles of European Family Law Regarding Parental Responsibilities and Danish Law, in* JUXTAPOSING LEGAL SYSTEMS AND THE PRINCIPLES OF EUROPEAN FAMILY LAW ON PARENTAL RESPONSIBILITIES, 195 (Jane Mair and Esin Örücü, eds., 2010).
[46] COLO. REV. STAT. § 14-10-123.

the nonresident parent. Colorado courts are required to "determine the allocation of parental responsibilities, including parenting time and decision-making responsibilities."[47]

In Florida, the law states the public policy of the State as being "to encourage parents to share the rights and responsibilities, and joys, of childrearing" despite parental separation.[48] Amendments to the law in 2008 provide that the court must approve a parenting plan that includes provisions about "how the parents will share and be responsible for the daily tasks associated with the upbringing of the child" and "the time-sharing schedule arrangements that specify the time that the minor child will spend with each parent."[49] The language of time-sharing goes beyond that in other jurisdictions, for it assumes that time with the child will be shared between the parents. Of course, this presumption may be rebutted if there are grounds for making an order of sole parental responsibility.[50] While the statute uses the language of time-sharing, it also provides that there "is no presumption for or against ... any specific time-sharing schedule when creating or modifying the parenting plan of the child."[51]

BEYOND CUSTODY

Although the language of "custody" remains in common use in the United States and Canada, and the concept is also integral to postseparation parenting in jurisdictions using other languages, the clear trend is for both the language and the concept to be phased out. The Commission on European Family Law – a body set up in 2001 with representation from twenty-two countries – has sought to develop common principles for family law across jurisdictions, with the idea that these principles will inspire law reform

---

[47] Colo. Rev. Stat. § 14–10–124. The approach in Colorado is consistent with the recommendation of the U.S. Commission on Child and Family Welfare. It recommended that courts and legislatures should replace the terms "custody" and "visitation" with terms that more accurately describe parenting responsibilities and are less likely to foster conflict. They gave the examples of "parental decision-making," "parenting time," and "residential arrangements" for children. U.S. Commission on Child and Family Welfare, Parenting Our Children: In the Best Interest of the Nation, A Report to the President and Congress, Recommendation One, 34 (1996).

[48] Fla. Stat. Title VI, 61.13(2)(c)(1).

[49] Fla. Stat. Title VI, 61.13(2)(b). While the statute uses the language of "sharing," subsection (c)(1) provides that: "There is no presumption for or against the father or mother of the child or for or against any specific time-sharing schedule when creating or modifying the parenting plan of the child."

[50] Fla. Stat. Title VI, 61.13(2)(c)(2).

[51] Fla. Stat. Title VI, 61.13(2)(c)(1).

in the jurisdictions that do not already adhere to them. In setting out the principles for parenting, it used the generic language of parental responsibilities.[52] Principle 3.10 provides:

> Parental responsibilities should neither be affected by the dissolution or annulment of the marriage or other formal relationship nor by the legal or factual separation between the parents.

This is the new mantra of family law. Marriage may be dissoluble, parents may split up, but parenthood continues unaffected.

RESOLVING DISPUTES ABOUT PARENTING DECISIONS IN THE ENDURING FAMILY

Joint custody, shared parental responsibility, *coparentalité*, and its equivalents raise issues in relation to decision making in the postdivorce family. How is a committee of two, whose personal relationship is in tatters, able to resolve conflicts about schooling, religious upbringing, disciplinary issues, medical treatment, and other such matters? This problem did not arise with the traditional view of custody. The position was straightforward. The custodial parent had the power to make all the major decisions in relation to the child, subject perhaps to challenge by the other parent if a decision was seen to be severely detrimental to the child's well-being.

However, with the emergence of joint legal custody and its equivalent as a default position in legislation in many jurisdictions, new issues have had to be resolved. What duty is there on parents to consult one another in relation to major decisions concerning a child? How, if at all, is this to be enforced? In the event of a dispute that is taken to court, should the wishes of the primary caregiver be treated as presumptively valid, with the onus on the other parent to justify interference, or should the court be asked to evaluate the competing positions without recourse to presumptions?

One view is that the courts should not decide these disputes at all. Just as child-rearing disputes between married couples would be regarded as nonjusticiable, at least in the United States, so the same rationale should be applied to such disputes between separated, divorced, or never-married parents on the basis that they are simply not appropriate for judicial resolution. Parents should instead be assisted to negotiate changes

---

[52] KATHARINA BOELE-WOELKI, FRÉDÉRIQUE FERRAND, CRISTINA GONZÁLEZ-BEILFUSS, MAARIT JÄNTERÄ-JAREBORG, NIGEL LOWE, DIETER MARTINY & WALTER PINTENS, PRINCIPLES OF EUROPEAN FAMILY LAW REGARDING PARENTAL RESPONSIBILITIES, European Family Law Series No 16 (2007).

to parenting plans by agreement, just as married couples have to, rather than using litigation to resolve their postseparation conflicts about child-rearing matters.[53]

This is consistent with the approach that has been adopted in Sweden, where there is no presumption either in favor of joint custody or sole custody, although in most cases, parents agree to joint custody. This means they retain equal decision-making power, but in the event of dispute about any parental decision – for example, where there are disputes about education or about religious practice – the only orders a court can make are in regard to a different allocation of custody. They have no authority to resolve other disputes about a child's upbringing. Thus in Sweden, neither parent in a joint custody arrangement has any greater authority than the other, and there is no umpire.[54] The consequence is that in the event of disagreement, the status quo is likely to prevail. The child will remain in the same school, or will not have the medical operation to which one parent is resistant. The only other alternative is for a parent to petition the court for sole custody.[55]

Norway resolves the tension between the two conceptualizations of divorce in a different way. Although parental responsibility is joint, primary caregivers can make major decisions concerning the care of children without involving the nonresident parent.[56] However, in the event of disputes between parents on major issues of upbringing that are not within the sole

---

[53] Robert Emery and Kimberly Emery, *Should Courts or Parents Make Childrearing Decisions?: Married Parents as a Paradigm for Parents Who Live Apart*, 43 WAKE FOREST LR 365 (2008). An Australian judge has refused to make orders in relation to the religious upbringing of a young child born to a Jewish mother and a Catholic father. Altobelli FM wrote: "There are some matters of parental responsibility that are simply best left to parents to decide" (C & B [2007] FMCAfam 539 at para 113).

[54] Ryrstedt, *supra* note 33, at 177, and personal communication to the author (June 14, 2010).

[55] *Id.* at 172–180. Proposals for change were made in a report to the Government on July 26, 2007. This report raised the possibility that one of two legal custodians could be given the right to make certain decisions, e.g., regarding the health of the child: STATENS OFFENTLIGA UTREDNINGAR, BESLUTANDERÄTT VID GEMENSAM VÅRDNAD M.M. (SOU 2007:52) (State Government Investigations, *Discretion in cases of Joint Custody*) available at: http://www.sweden.gov.se/content/1/c6/08/58/19/aac497a6.pdf. However, a government response in February 2010 indicated an unwillingness to contemplate change to the law. See Umgängesstöd och Socialtjänstens Förutsättningar att Tala med Barn (Social Support and Social Services' Ability to Talk to Children) available at: http://www.sweden. gov.se/content/1/c6/13/98/20/763f076e.pdf

[56] Section 37, *Children and Parents Act* 1981 in Norway provides: "If the parents have joint parental responsibility, but the child lives permanently with only one of them, the other parent may not object to the parent with whom the child lives making decisions concerning important aspects of the child's care, such as the question of whether the child shall

province of the primary caregiver, Norway, like Sweden, has no umpire, and the only option is to seek a court order dissolving joint custody.

In contrast to Norway and Sweden, the courts in England and Wales are empowered to make specific issue orders.[57] Such orders can be made at the time of resolving a dispute about residence and contact, or at some subsequent time if a parent challenges the decision of the other parent by taking the matter to court. The difficulty with this approach is that it places the court in the position of a decision maker about such issues as a child's schooling or religious upbringing. The role of the court in making specific decisions on parenting issues raises particular challenges for the application of the best-interests test. Faced, for example, with a conflict between parents about the best private school for a child, and in a context where the court can no longer fall back on the primacy of the custodial parent's wishes in an age of shared parental responsibility, what does it mean to search for the best interests of the child? There are unlikely to be any issues of law or fact finding involved in such decisions, except to the extent that previous agreements between the parents during happier periods in their relationship need to be taken into account.

For practical reasons, there have to be presumptions to deal with such disputes, for example, that the decision of the primary caregiver is to be presumed to be in the best interests of the child, or that the court will not disturb the status quo unless satisfied on the balance of probabilities that changing the situation, authorizing the disputed medical treatment, or whatever, will be better for the child.

The position in France is similar to that in Britain. If parents cannot agree on an issue concerning the exercise of parental authority, the matter has to be resolved by the *juge aux affaires familiales*. A study of the cases taken to the court in 1994–95 in Lyon and Nanterre puts into perspective the extent to which disagreements need to be resolved by litigation. Fulchiron studied 1,493 decisions. He found that disputes relating to the exercise of joint parental authority only appear in twenty cases. As he noted, "the litigation is not very significant compared to the number of joint parental authority cases that 'work'."[58]

A fourth approach is in evidence in Finland and Germany, where through different mechanisms, it is possible for the court to divide aspects of parental responsibility between the parents, giving one parent the

---

attend a day-care centre, where in Norway the child shall live and other major decisions concerning everyday life." *See also* Ryrstedt, *supra* note 33, at 185–91.

[57] *Children Act* 1989 § 8(1) (Eng. and Wales).

[58] Fulchiron, *supra*, note 25 at 5.

power to make the decisions in a given area while specifying that other decision-making responsibilities should be exercised by the other parent or exercised jointly. Thus although the court cannot make a decision for the parents where there is a dispute, it can decide who should be empowered to make the decision. In Finland, it has become common practice for first-instance courts to order that some aspects of parental responsibility, such as religious upbringing, should be excluded from the operation of joint custody to avoid conflict between the parents. In high-conflict families, the court may give only one issue to decide jointly, such as the right to decide about the child's name.[59] In Germany, *Burgerliches Gesetzbuch* (BGB) §1687 provides that in situations where parents with joint parental responsibility are living apart, agreement is required for decisions of particular importance to the child. However, the parent with whom the child usually lives as a result of either the agreement of the other parent or a judicial decision has the authority to make decisions alone in matters of day-to-day care, which are defined as matters in everyday life that arise often and have no irreversible impact on the development of the child. While the child is with the other parent, that parent has the authority to decide on day-to-day matters.[60]

If parents with joint parental responsibility cannot reach an agreement on a certain matter, the court may, on the application of one parent, order that the parent in question shall have the power to make decisions on the specific issue or in the area of parental responsibility that is in dispute, for example, decision making on educational matters: BGB §1628. Alternatively, under §1671, a parent may seek an order for sole parental responsibility, either wholly or in part, allowing an aspect of parental decision making to be exercised by that parent alone.

A similar approach is adopted in certain jurisdictions in the United States. In Oregon, for example, the legislation provides that an order for joint custody "may specify one home as the primary residence of the child and designate one parent to have sole power to make decisions about specific matters while both parents retain equal rights and responsibilities for other decisions."[61]

<hr>

[59] *See* Kurki-Suonio, supra note 37 at 195. *See also* Ryrstedt, *supra* note 33, at 180–85.
[60] *See further* REINER SCHULZE ET AL., BÜRGERLICHES GESETZBUCH HANDKOMMENTAR (6th ed, 2009) § 1687 Nr.
[61] O.R.S. § 107.169(1). *See also* Florida, FLA. STAT § 61.13(2)(c)2a: "In ordering shared parental responsibility, the court may consider the expressed desires of the parents and may grant to one party the ultimate responsibility over specific aspects of the child's welfare or may divide those responsibilities between the parties based on the best interests of the child. Areas of responsibility may include primary residence, education,

THE IDEALIZATION OF THE POSTSEPARATION FAMILY

The move away from a norm of sole custody after separation, and the shift in language to emphasize the importance of both parents in children's lives, has been accompanied by another trend, namely toward the idealization of agreement about postseparation parenting. Laws that encourage the meaningful involvement of both parents are aspirational. They seek to deal not only with the consequences of people's actual behavior for parenting after separation, but to prescribe how they should behave. They express the hope that even if parents cannot or should not stay together for the sake of the children, at least they should live apart harmoniously, cooperating in the postseparation parenting. It has been suggested in France that this represents a new moralizing about the family.[62]

In some instances, such laws have an exhortatory tone to them. This is not a new phenomenon in the countries of continental Europe. In civil law systems, legislative statements about what spouses and parents ought to do have long had a place in the drafting of civil law codes. Such codes self-consciously seek an educational role. This may be illustrated by provisions in the law of some European countries concerning decision making in the intact family. In France, for example, Article 371 of the Civil Code provides that "A child, at any age, owes honour and respect to his father and mother," while Article 371-1 para 3 provides that "parents shall make a child a party to decisions relating to him, according to his age and degree of maturity."[63] In civil law countries, it is therefore not surprising to find statements about what parents should do and how they should behave, and which do not necessarily give rise to enforceable obligations.[64]

Such provisions, teaching parents how to exercise their responsibilities and about the importance of children's participation, are alien to common law systems. Aspirational or normative statements are not an established

---

medical and dental care, and any other responsibilities that the court finds unique to a particular family."

[62] Benoiît Bastard and Laura Cardia-Vonèche, *Children Contacts in France: An Overview of the Law, Professional Practice and Current Debates*, 7 (Paper given at the European Conference of the Working Group for Comparative Study of Legal Professions, Berder, June 30–July 3, 2004), ("Un nouveau moralisme familial").

[63] S Kupfer trans.

[64] In Norway, for example, the *Children and Parents Act* 1981 § 31 provides: "As and when the child becomes able to form its own point of view on matters that concern it, the parents shall listen to the child's opinion before making a decision on the child's personal situation. Attention shall be paid to the opinion of the child, depending on the age and maturity of the child. The same applies to other persons with whom the child lives or who are involved with the child."

part of the tradition of legislative drafting in common law countries. However, laws concerning parenting after separation provide an exception. In the United States, it is common to find aspirational ideas expressed through statements of legislative policy. In Australia, the Family Law Act 1975 contains the principle that "except when it is or would be contrary to a child's best interests ... parents share duties and responsibilities concerning the care, welfare and development of their children; and ... should agree about the future parenting of their children."[65] The idea that parents should agree is otiose when they are litigants before a judge and seeking an adjudication in the absence of agreement.

A later section provides:[66]

The parents of a child are encouraged:

(a) to agree about matters concerning the child; and
(b) to take responsibility for their parenting arrangements and for resolving parental conflict; and
(c) to use the legal system as a last resort rather than a first resort; and
(d) to minimize the possibility of present and future conflict by using or reaching an agreement; and
(e) in reaching their agreement, to regard the best interests of the child as the paramount consideration.

This is quite a different style of drafting to the norm in common law countries, where legislation concerning the resolution of disputes is written for judges, setting out rules or principles to apply, or factors to consider in the exercise of a discretionary judgment.

Yet the idealization of postseparation harmony may even be seen in the factors that the court must use to determine the best interests of the child. In New Zealand, for example, these emphasize harmony not only in the nuclear family but beyond it, including the extended family and tribe of Maori culture, the whānau, hapu, or iwi. In the Care of Children Act 2004, the principles relevant to children's welfare and best interests are:

(a) the child's parents and guardians should have the primary responsibility, and should be encouraged to agree to their own arrangements, for the child's care, development, and upbringing:
(b) there should be continuity in arrangements for the child's care, development, and upbringing, and the child's relationships with his or her family, family group, whānau, hapu, or iwi, should be

---

[65] Family Law Act 1975 s.60B.   [66] Family Law Act 1975 s.63B.

stable and ongoing (in particular, the child should have continuing relationships with both of his or her parents):

(c) the child's care, development, and upbringing should be facilitated by ongoing consultation and cooperation among and between the child's parents and guardians and all persons exercising the role of providing day to day care for, or entitled to have contact with, the child:

(d) relationships between the child and members of his or her family, family group, whānau, hapu, or iwi should be preserved and strengthened, and those members should be encouraged to participate in the child's care, development, and upbringing:

(e) the child's safety must be protected and, in particular, he or she must be protected from all forms of violence (whether by members of his or her family, family group, whānau, hapu, or iwi, or by other persons):

(f) the child's identity (including, without limitation, his or her culture, language, and religious denomination and practice) should be preserved and strengthened.

Most of these factors emphasize the enduring family, characterized by agreement, continuity of relationships, consultation, cooperation, and strengthening of cultural identity. This contrasts with lists of factors concerning best interests in other jurisdictions, which are written to assist the court in choosing between parents' competing claims in the event of a dispute.[67]

THE GOOD DIVORCE

For whom are such legislative provisions written? The most obvious users of law are those who are unable to resolve their disputes without recourse to law. A primary purpose of such laws appears to be persuasion.[68] For those parents who separate and are able to resolve the parenting arrangements either by default or by agreement without the need for mediation or legal advice, such laws may have little role to play, except to the extent

---

[67] The New Zealand legislation can, for example, be compared with s.60CC(2) and (3) of the Australian Family Law Act 1975 that, like other jurisdictions, provides adjudicatory considerations in determining what is in the best interests of children, rather than aspirational goals.

[68] Concerning the Australian legislation, Justice Richard Chisholm concluded that the purpose of reforms passed in 1995 to encourage the greater involvement of both parents was to change hearts and minds: Richard Chisholm, *Assessing the Impact of the Family Law Reform Act 1995*, 10 AUSTRALIAN J. FAM. L. 177 (1996).

that they influence cultural norms about parenting after separation. Such parents may well have no idea of what the legislation says and have no particular need to find out. For other parents who have a great need to find out what the legislation says because they are involved in litigation, the role of the law seems to be to assist them to resolve their conflicts for themselves.

Yet statements of policy or principle to the effect that both parents should remain actively involved in the care of children and should cooperate in the work of parenting may be unrealistic for many families. They express a hope about what might be, or a statement about what should be, rather than necessarily what is possible or desirable in the actual circumstances of many individual families. The legislation may put forward the ideal of the good divorce, but working this out in the harsh reality of bitter postseparation conflict between many parents is another matter. French sociologist Benoit Bastard, a leading critic of the idea of coparentalité, observes:[69]

> What we expect of couples in this regard is difficult to comprehend: they must be able to consider themselves separated yet must also maintain a connection with their children and, in this respect, with each other. Are we not trying to fit a square peg in a round hole? Moreover, this model necessitates a capacity for negotiation the majority of couples lack…. Such individuals don't know how to accommodate, post separation, a partner, usually the father, who is "no longer part of the family."

Even where familial relationships are not marred by serious ongoing hostility, the shift from a sole-custody approach, to parenting after separation, to one that involves both parents is not straightforward. Parenting in the enduring family is usually not a continuation of the parenting patterns in the unitary family, but requires entirely new patterns to be developed. Divorce therefore means a reinvention of the parenting of the children rather than a continuation of a previously established pattern. This is because in the aftermath of separation, it is frequently the case that fathers who have played a secondary role as parents are placed in a position where for significant periods of time, especially during the school holidays, they are the primary caregiver – a role that may well be foreign to them in the course of an intact marriage.

---

[69] Benoit Bastard, *Une Nouvelle Police de la Parentalité?* 5 ENFANCES, FAMILLES, GÉNÉRATIONS 11, 16-17 (2006) (Sophie Crosby trans.). *See also* Benoit Bastard, *Controverses Autour de la Coparentalité: Coparentalité, Homoparentalité, Monoparentalité … Où va la Famille?* (2005) 156 SCIENCES HUMAINES 40; Sylvie Cadolle, *La Transformation des Enjeux du Divorce: La Coparentalité à L'épreuve des Faits* 122 INFORMATIONS SOCIALES 136 (2005).

To describe the role of a father as a secondary role in an intact marriage or other relationship is not to diminish either its extent or its importance. It is merely to describe the way in which parents work together in an intact, role-divided relationship. The typical pattern of parenting is not that each of them acts as a parent, but that at times one of them is active in a parental role while at other times both are. At least this is the most common pattern in which one parent – almost invariably the mother – alters his or her patterns of workforce participation to become the primary caregiver of the child, whereas the other parent makes no major changes in this regard. In such a role-divided marriage, the primary caregiver typically spends significant periods of time during the weekdays as the sole caregiver to the child, while at evenings and weekends, both parents are involved in the parenting enterprise. The father might be the sole caregiver for certain periods – for example, to give the mother a break or to allow her to do other things – but he is rarely the sole caregiver for extended periods of time.

For this reason, the changes for fathers after separation in the enduring family are particularly great. While for mothers, divorce brings an expansion of an already established pattern of sole caregiving, it propels fathers into a role that they may never have had for more than a few hours at a time when the marriage was intact – the role of a sole caregiver without having the other parent for support. The changes required of fathers in maintaining an active engagement with the children in turn require a great deal of mothers. They must trust the father with a much greater level of sole parental responsibility than he has previously exercised, and must seek to negotiate this parenting at a time when her relationship with him is likely to be very strained.

By no means can all parents manage this transition from parenting together to parenting apart. There are numerous barriers to the creation of good-enough coparenting relationships and multiple reasons why, despite significant involvement as a parent while the relationship was continuing, this does not translate into successful postseparation involvement.[70] The changes in the law do not ensure that nonresident parents maintain meaningful relationships with their children, but they do help create the conditions that give this a greater likelihood of success.

---

[70] For insights from a French study, *see* Laura Cardia-Vonèche & Benoit Bastard, *Why Some Children see their Father and Others do not; Questions Arising from a Pilot Study*, in PARENTING AFTER PARTNERING: CONTAINING CONFLICT AFTER SEPARATION 29 (Mavis Maclean ed, 2007).

4

Reasons for the Demise of Sole Custody

How are we to understand the profound change in the language and content of custody laws over the last forty years, and the equally profound changes in patterns of parenting after separation? The legislative changes have been all the more remarkable because they have not gone unchallenged. Yet in the main, the tide of change has flowed inexorably away from traditional conceptualizations of custody and toward an understanding of divorce as a restructuring of the arrangements in a family that continues after separation.

One way of understanding this tide of change is in terms of winners and losers, with every gain for men being a defeat for women in a zero-sum game.[1] This was, for example, how the movement toward joint legal custody was characterized by some in the 1980s.[2] Although there can be little doubt that debates about custody law reform have been strongly influenced by the advocacy of gender-based pressure groups,[3] this advocacy has

[1]   See e.g. CHILD CUSTODY AND THE POLITICS OF GENDER (Carol Smart & Selma Sevenhuijsen, eds., 1989); Susan Boyd, *Backlash against Feminism: Canadian Custody and Access Reform Debates of the Late Twentieth Century*, 16 CANADIAN J. WOMEN & L. 255 (2004); Michael Flood, *"Fathers' Rights" and the Defense of Paternal Authority in Australia*, 16 VIOLENCE AGAINST WOMEN 328 (2010).

[2]   See e.g. Anne Marie Delorey, *Joint Legal Custody: A Reversion to Patriarchal Power*, 3 CANADIAN J. WOMEN & L. 33 (1989). For the different feminist positions on joint custody in the 1980s, *see* Katharine Bartlett & Carol Stack, *Joint Custody, Feminism and the Dependency Dilemma*, 2 BERKELEY WOMEN'S L.J. 9 (1986).

[3]   For an analysis of the competing arguments and rhetorical devices used by fathers' groups and mothers' groups respectively in the United States, *see* Scott Coltrane & Neal Hickman, *The Rhetoric of Rights and Needs: Moral Discourse in the Reform of Child Custody and Child Support Laws*, 39 SOC. PROB. 400 (1992). For an analysis of the views and influence of different pressure groups in Canada from the late 1960s to the mid-1980s, *see* Susan Boyd & Claire Young, *Who Influences Law Reform? Discourses on Motherhood and Fatherhood in Legislative Reform Debates in Canada*, 26 STUDIES IN LAW, POLITICS & SOCIETY 43 (2002).

reflected larger social trends and attitudinal changes. Away from the dust of battle in legislatures and the rhetoric of law reviews and Internet sites, it is evident that there has been a quiet sea change occurring in the hearts and minds of the general population around the western world concerning parenting after separation, including those who are separated or divorced.

CHANGES IN COMMUNITY ATTITUDES
TOWARD PARENTAL RESPONSIBILITY

The extent of change in community attitudes about parenting after separation can be illustrated by reference to studies in Australia that indicate that the concept of shared parenting has very widespread support, including in the divorced population. This can be seen from community surveys conducted in the mid-1990s. Significant legislative change occurred in Australia at that time with the enactment of the Family Law Reform Act 1995,[4] which was intended to bring about a greater emphasis on the involvement of both parents.[5] The Act emphasized the equal responsibility of both parents after divorce and the child's right of contact with both parents unless it was contrary to the child's best interests.[6] It has since been overtaken by further reforms in 2006.[7]

Around the time that the legislation was being passed through Parliament, the Australian Institute of Family Studies was commissioned to conduct research on attitudes to parental responsibility in Australia.[8] What it found was that the 1995 legislation reflected views already held by the great majority of the population. Funder and Smyth, the researchers at the Institute, reported that 78 percent of Australians thought that children should always be cared for by both parents, sharing the duties and responsibilities for their care, welfare, and development when the parents are married. Another 20 percent thought this should mostly be the case.[9] When asked more specifically about whether both parents should remain involved when they are separated or divorced, assent was still strong for

4 *See* Chapter 3.
5 *See generally*, John Dewar, *The Family Law Reform Act 1995 (Cth) and the Children Act 1989 (UK) Compared – Twins or Distant Cousins?*, 10 AUSTRALIAN J. FAM. L. 18 (1996).
6 Family Law Act 1975 s.60B.   7 *See* Chapter 5.
8 KATHLEEN FUNDER & BRUCE SMYTH, EVALUATION OF THE IMPACT OF PART VII (1996). *See also* Kathleen Funder, *The Australian Family Law Reform Act 1995 and Public Attitudes to Parental Responsibility*, 12 INT'L J.L. POL'Y & FAM. 47 (1998). The research was conducted mostly in November 1995, with some further interviewing done in January 1996: Funder & Smyth, *id* at 14. The legislation commenced in July 1996.
9 FUNDER & SMYTH, *supra* note 8, at Table 3.1.7.

this proposition, although somewhat more conditional; 50 percent of Australians thought that this should always be the case and another 33 percent thought this should mostly be the way parents care for their children after separation.[10] These were the views of respondents in the survey taken as a whole. But even among the subset of those who had experienced separation and divorce, the results were very similar.[11]

Further community surveys in 2006 and 2009 showed continuing strong support for the involvement of both parents. Seventy-five percent of fathers and 79 percent of mothers in 2006 agreed or strongly agreed with the statement that "children generally do best after separation when both parents stay involved in their lives." In 2009, even more agreed with this proposition (79 percent of fathers and 83 percent of mothers).[12] More mothers than fathers strongly agreed.[13] When comparing nonseparated parents with separated parents, a more differentiated pattern emerged. Eighty-four percent of separated fathers agreed that the continuing involvement of both parents was beneficial for children, compared to 72 percent of nonseparated fathers in 2006. In 2009, the proportions were 86 percent compared to 77 percent. Conversely, 76 percent of separated mothers agreed with the statement in 2006, compared with 80 percent of the nonseparated mothers in 2006, whereas in 2009, the proportions were 77 percent compared to 86 percent.[14] Although fathers' belief in the importance of involving both parents increases with the actual experience of separation, and mothers' belief in its importance decreases, there remains assent for the proposition among more than three-quarters of separated mothers and around 85 percent of separated fathers.

The available research in Australia also shows quite strong support for the idea of a presumption of equal time. During a period when there was a parliamentary inquiry into the idea of equal time in 2003, the Australian Institute of Family Studies conducted phone interviews with more than 1,000 parents who had been either separated, divorced, or had never lived with the other parent. They were asked their reactions to the "idea that if parents separate, children should spend equal time with each parent.

---

[10]   *Id*, at Table 3.1.10.
[11]   *Id*, at Tables 3.7.8, 3.7.9, 3.7.12, 3.7.15, 3.7.17, & 3.7.18.
[12]   RAE KASPIEW, MATTHEW GRAY, RUTH WESTON, LAWRIE MOLONEY, KELLY HAND, & LIXIA QU, EVALUATION OF THE 2006 FAMILY LAW REFORMS 113 (2009).
[13]   In 2006, 36% of mothers compared to 31% of fathers. In 2009, 47% of mothers compared to 40% of fathers): *Ibid*.
[14]   *Ibid*, at pp.114–15.

That is, children would have two homes and would move between each." Sixty-nine percent of fathers and 31 percent of mothers agreed with this proposition.[15] Mothers with children under six years of age were more likely than other mothers to reject the notion of equal time, as were mothers who had a lot of conflict with the other parent.

Evidence from the United States points to a similar level of support for the involvement of both parents after separation. For example, a ballot in Massachusetts in 2004 asked voters whether their state representative should support legislation that would effectively provide a strong presumption in favor of joint legal and physical custody of children. The provision was passed overwhelmingly, securing a ratio of about five people who supported it to every one who was against it.[16]

PRESSURE FROM FATHERS

Although the legislative shift toward greater involvement by nonresident parents appears to have the support of both genders, it is clear that the major reason for the shift in favor of joint custody and shared parenting arrangements around the western world is pressure from fathers for more time with their children.[17] Governments have been very receptive to lobbying by fathers' groups.[18] Shared parenting offers an answer to the difficult politics of divorce. It speaks in the language of compromise in contrast to the winner-takes-all concept of custody. It draws on the cultural persuasiveness of the idea of equality between men and women.

However, it is not just that one lobby group has been more effective than another in the continuing gender wars over parenting after separation. The pressure from fathers for changes in law and practice reflects very substantial cultural shifts in attitudes of fathers across the population in

---

[15] Bruce Smyth & Ruth Weston, *The Attitudes of Separated Mothers and Fathers to 50/50 Shared Care*, FAMILY MATTERS no.67, 8 (2004).

[16] Cited in Judith Greenberg, *Domestic Violence and the Danger of Joint Custody Presumptions*, 25 NTH ILLINOIS L. REV. 403, 403 (2005).

[17] For an empirical study of the complaints of fathers about the divorce process in the United States, *see* Joyce Arditti & Katherine Allen, *Understanding Distressed Fathers' Perceptions of Legal and Relational Inequities Post-Divorce*, 31 FAM. & CONCIL. CTS. REV. 461 (1993).

[18] For the view that the Family Law Reform Act 1995 in Australia was the result of campaigning by men's groups *see*, e.g., HELEN RHOADES, REGINA GRAYCAR, & MARGARET HARRISON, THE FAMILY LAW REFORM ACT 1995: THE FIRST THREE YEARS 23 (2000); Regina Graycar, *Law Reform by Frozen Chook: Family Law Reform for the New Millenium?*, 24 MELB. U. L. REV. 737 (2000).

many western countries. Over time, there have been significant changes in the ideal of fatherhood, with a greater emphasis on emotional closeness and active involvement with the children. This has led to greater involvement in parenting in intact relationships, with a consequential impact upon fathers' attitudes toward postseparation parenting.[19] Despite the rhetoric of equality, more fathers want to assist in the parenting role after separation than to take over as primary caregiver.[20]

Fathers' desire for greater involvement after separation can be seen in research in a number of countries. For example, Fabricius and Hall found in their interviews with college students who had experienced parental divorce that both men and women reported that their fathers had wanted more time with them than they had or their mothers wanted them to have. Forty-four percent reported that their fathers had wanted them to spend equal time with them or more.[21]

There is similar evidence from studies in Australia. In one study, 41 percent of fathers contacted in a random telephone survey of divorced parents in 1997 indicated that they were dissatisfied with the residence arrangements for the children. Two-thirds of this group said that they wanted to be the primary residence parent, and the remaining one-third wanted to have equal time with their children. On average, this was about five years after the divorce. The study also indicated a very high level of dissatisfaction with levels of contact.[22]

In another Australian study of a nationally representative sample of separated parents, interviewed in 2001, three-quarters of the nonresident fathers indicated dissatisfaction with the amount of contact they had. Fifty-seven percent of fathers indicated that they had nowhere near enough time with their children and a further 18 percent said they did not have quite enough time with their children.[23]

---

[19] Carol Smart, *Towards an Understanding of Family Change: Gender Conflict and Children's Citizenship*, 17 AUSTRALIAN J. FAM. L. 20 (2003).

[20] Carl Bertoia & Janice Drakich, *The Fathers' Rights Movement: Contradictions in Rhetoric and Practice*, 14 J. FAM. ISSUES 592 (1993) (presenting interviews with members of fathers' groups in Canada).

[21] William Fabricius & Jeff Hall, *Young Adults' Perspectives on Divorce: Living Arrangements*, 38 FAM. & CONCIL. CTS. REV. 446 (2000).

[22] Bruce Smyth, Grania Sheehan, & Belinda Fehlberg, *Patterns of Parenting after Divorce: A Pre-Reform Act Benchmark Study*, 15 AUSTRALIAN J. FAM. L. 114 (2001).

[23] Patrick Parkinson & Bruce Smyth, *Satisfaction and Dissatisfaction with Father-Child Contact Arrangements in Australia*, 16 CHILD & FAM. L. Q. 289 (2004). The greatest levels of satisfaction for both mothers and fathers were with shared parenting arrangements. The data came from the Household Income and Labour Dynamics in Australia survey (HILDA). Interviews were conducted with 13,969 members of 7,682 households.

This does not mean, of course, that there has been a complete change in fathers' attitudes toward postseparation parenting. Many fathers drop out of their children's lives after separation or, in the case of fathers who never lived with the mother, do not pursue active engagement with the child. This is clear from a significant body of American research,[24] although levels of contact have increased in recent years.[25] Australian research also shows a significant level of paternal disengagement. In 1997, Australian Bureau of Statistics data based on reports of resident parents indicated that 30 percent of children saw their nonresident parent less than once per year, or not at all.[26] Thirty-six percent of nonresident fathers who were interviewed in 2001 had not seen their youngest child in the previous twelve months.[27]

Yet as the Australian research shows, disengagement does not necessarily mean disinterest. Only 20 percent of those fathers with no contact interviewed in 2001 considered that the level of contact was about right. Most wanted time with their children.[28] There have been similar findings in Britain. In one study, 76 percent of fathers who never saw their children were dissatisfied with this.[29] There are numerous reasons why fathers lose contact with, or disengage from, their children.[30] The main factors are

It is not only fathers who want more time with their children. Mothers also want to see more contact between the children and their fathers. In this study, although the majority of resident mothers expressed satisfaction with the contact arrangements, 25% reported that they thought there was nowhere near enough father-child contact taking place, and a further 15% said there was not quite enough contact. Only 5% thought that there was too much contact: *Id*, at 297.

24 Judith Seltzer, *Relationships between Fathers and Children Who Live Apart: The Father's Role after Separation*, 53 J. MARRIAGE & FAM. 79 (1991); Frank Furstenberg, Christine Nord, James Peterson, & Nicholas Zill, *The Life Course of Children of Divorce: Marital Disruption and Parental Contact*, 48 AM. SOC. REV. 656 (1983); Judith Seltzer & Suzanne Bianchi, *Children's Contact with Absent Parents*, 50 J. MARRIAGE & FAM. 663 (1988); Joyce Munsch, John Woodward, & Nancy Darling, *Children's Perceptions of Their Relationships with Coresiding and Non-Coresiding Fathers*, 23 J. DIV. & REMARRIAGE 39 (1995); Susan Stewart, *Nonresident Parenting and Adolescent Adjustment: The Quality of Nonresident Father-Child Interaction*, 24 J. FAM. ISSUES 217 (2003). *See further,* Chapter 1.

25 Paul Amato, Catherine Meyers, & Robert Emery, *Changes in Nonresident Father-Child Contact From 1976 to 2002*, 58 FAM. REL. 41 (2009).

26 AUSTRALIAN BUREAU OF STATISTICS. FAMILY CHARACTERISTICS SURVEY, 1997, Catalogue No. 4442.0 (1998).

27 Parkinson & Smyth, *supra* note 23.

28 Parkinson & Smyth, *ibid*, at p.299.

29 BOB SIMPSON, PETER MCCARTHY, & JANET WALKER, BEING THERE: FATHERS AFTER DIVORCE 32 (1995).

30 For a review of the literature in the American context, *see* Solangel Maldonado, *Beyond Economic Fatherhood: Encouraging Divorced Fathers to Parent* 153 U. PA. L. REV. 921, 962–82 (2004–2005).

serious conflict in the relationship with the mother,[31] leading to maternal gateclosing;[32] repartnering and responsibilities to children in the new family;[33] physical distance;[34] feelings of disenfranchisement by the legal system;[35] and limited financial resources.[36] Most of these men would want a much greater involvement in the children's lives if their circumstances were different.

One explanation for the growth in fathers' desire to be actively involved in their children's lives after separation is that it represents a reaction to the disappointment about failed adult relationships. German sociologists Beck and Beck-Gernsheim make the point that following marriage breakdown:[37]

> The child becomes the last remaining, irrevocable, unique primary love object. Partners come and go, but the child stays. Everything one vainly hoped to find in the relationship with one's partner is sought in or directed at the child. If men and women have increasing difficulty in getting on with one another, the child acquires a monopoly on companionship, sharing feelings, enjoying spontaneous physical contact in a way which has otherwise

[31] James Dudley, *Increasing Our Understanding of Divorced Fathers Who Have Infrequent Contact with Their Children* 40 Fam. Rel. 279 (1991); Geoffrey Greif, *When Divorced Fathers Want No Contact with Their Children: A Preliminary Analysis*, 23 J. Divorce & Remarriage 75 (1995).

[32] Liz Trinder, *Maternal Gate Closing and Gate Opening in Postdivorce Families*, 29 J. Fam. Issues 1298 (2008).

[33] Wendy Manning, Susan Stewart, & Pamela Smock, *The Complexity of Fathers' Parenting Responsibilities and Involvement with Nonresident Children*, 24 J. Fam. Issues 645 (2003).

[34] Dudley, *supra* note 31; Greif, *supra* note 31.

[35] Edward Kruk, *Divorce and Disengagement: Patterns of Fatherhood Within and Beyond Marriage* (1993); Sanford Braver & Diane O'Connell, Divorced Dads: Shattering the Myths (1998).

[36] Bruce Smyth, *Postseparation Fathering: What Does Australian Research Tell Us?* 10 J. Fam. Stud. 20, 30–33 (2004); Anne Skevik, *'Absent Fathers' or 'Reorganized Families'? Variations in Father-child Contact after Parental Break-up in Norway*, 54 Sociological Rev. 114 (2006).

[37] Ulrich Beck & Elisabeth Beck-Gernsheim, The Normal Chaos of Love 37 (Mark Ritter & Jane Wiebel trans., 1995). A similar view is expressed by French scholar, Benoit Bastard, who writes: "… it is quite clear that the instability of the couple explains the growth of interest in the child-parent relationship. Break-ups are commonplace and have become a part of the normal life experience of the individual and of the contemporary marriage model. As such, being hardly able to count on parents remaining in an enduring couple relationship, we cannot but hope to reinforce child-parent relationships instead. We arrive thus at an exclusive focus point: it is the existence of a child which confirms a parent's identity both as an adult and as a person." Benoit Bastard, *Une Nouvelle Police de la Parentalité?* 5 Enfances, Familles, Générations 11, 15 (2006) (Sophie Crosby trans.).

become uncommon and seems risky. Here an atavistic social experience can be celebrated and cultivated which in a society of individuals is increasingly rare, although everyone craves it. Doting on children, pushing them on to the centre of the stage … and fighting for custody during and after divorce are all symptoms of this. The child becomes the final alternative to loneliness, a bastion against the vanishing chances of loving and being loved. It is a private way of "putting the magic back" into life to make up for general disenchantment. The birth-rate may be declining but children have never been more important.

To some extent, then, the new focus on parenting after separation reflects nonresident parents' desire for meaning and connection, and also represents a response to the fear of loneliness and social isolation. Separation motivates some fathers to rethink their priorities and to try to maintain their connections to children even if this means struggle and conflict.

THE BENEFITS OF PATERNAL INVOLVEMENT IN THE POSTSEPARATION FAMILY

Encouraging the greater involvement of fathers in children's lives after separation, at least in the absence of violence, abuse, or high conflict, is also supported now by a large body of research on outcomes of divorce for children. This research indicates that although more frequent contact with the nonresident parent does not in itself lead to improved well-being for the children of divorce,[38] children do benefit from a close relationship with the nonresident parent. In a 1999 meta-analysis of sixty-three prior studies on parent-child visitation, Amato and Gilbreth confirmed that frequency of contact in itself does not appear to be associated with better outcomes for children.[39] However, emotional closeness, and particularly "authoritative parenting," is highly beneficial to children.[40] Authoritative parenting includes helping with homework, talking about problems, providing

---

[38] This has been a basis for feminist objections to legislative reforms promoting more shared parenting after separation. *See*, e.g. SUSAN BOYD, CHILD CUSTODY, LAW, AND WOMEN'S WORK (2003).

[39] Paul Amato & Joan Gilbreth, *Nonresident Fathers and Children's Well-Being: a Meta-analysis*, 61 J. MARRIAGE & FAM. 557 (1999).

[40] Authoritative parenting refers to a style of parenting that is neither authoritarian nor permissive. *See* Diana Baumrind, *Authoritarian v. Authoritative Control*, 3 ADOLESCENCE 255 (1968). *See also* MAVIS HETHERINGTON & JOHN KELLY, FOR BETTER OR FOR WORSE: DIVORCE RECONSIDERED 127–130 (2002); ELIZABETH SEDDON, CREATIVE PARENTING AFTER SEPARATION 26–28 (2003). Further research is needed to determine what aspects of authoritative parenting by a nonresident parent after separation are

emotional support to children, praising children's accomplishments, and disciplining children for misbehavior. The researchers concluded that "how often fathers see children is less important than what fathers do when they are with their children."[41]

Parental separation and divorce are a significant risk factor for children both in terms of long-term emotional well-being and educational performance.[42] Greater involvement of fathers in postseparation parenting has at least the potential to ameliorate these risks, particularly the risk of depression and other indications of emotional distress. Adolescents who have no contact with their nonresident parent, and those who have infrequent contact, have been shown to be more depressed than those in frequent-visit and married families.[43] Although the research evidence is not unequivocal, closeness to nonresident fathers has also been found to be related to less depression in adolescents, better school performance, and a perception that their worst problem was less severe, independently of the effect of closeness to the mother.[44] Measures to encourage a continuing relationship between nonresident parents and their children should therefore be seen as highly desirable in the absence of high levels of ongoing

---

particularly beneficial to children and young people: Susan Stewart, *Nonresident Parenting and Adolescent Adjustment: The Quality of Nonresident Father-child Interaction*, 24 J. FAM. ISSUES 217 (2003).

[41] Amato & Gilbreth, *supra* note 39, at 569.

[42] Joan Kelly & Robert Emery, *Children's Adjustment Following Divorce: Risk and Resilience Perspectives*, 52 FAM. REL. 352 (2003); PAUL AMATO & ALAN BOOTH, A GENERATION AT RISK (1997); Paul Amato, *The Consequences of Divorce for Adults and Children*, 62 J. MARRIAGE & FAM. 1269 (2000); Jane Elliott & Martin Richards, *Children and Divorce: Educational Performance and Behaviour Before and After Parental Separation*, 5 INT'L J.L. & FAM. 258 (1991).

[43] Bonnie Barber, *Support and Advice from Married and Divorced Fathers: Linkages to Adolescent Adjustment*, 43 FAM. REL. 433 (1994).

[44] CHRISTY BUCHANAN, ELEANOR MACCOBY, & SANFORD DORNBUSCH, ADOLESCENTS AFTER DIVORCE 193, 204 (Fig. 10.6) (1996). Buchanan et al. could not say whether a better relationship with the nonresidential parent leads to better adjustment in the adolescent, or whether adolescents who are better adjusted maintain better relationships with their nonresident parent. They theorized that both processes are at work (*id*, at p.198). They also found that the better adjustment of adolescents in dual-residence families compared to single-residence families was a reflection of the level of closeness they felt to both parents (*id*, at pp. 204–05). *See also* Susan Stewart, *Nonresident Parenting and Adolescent Adjustment: The Quality of Nonresident Father-Child Interaction*, 24 J. FAM. ISSUES 217 (2003) (closeness to nonresident fathers after separation associated with significantly less emotional distress in young people independently of the effect of closeness to the resident mother). *But see* Frank Furstenberg, Philip Morgan, & Paul Allison, *Paternal Participation and Children's Well-Being after Marital Dissolution*, 52 AM. SOC. REV. 695 (1987) (closeness to fathers was not associated with lower levels of delinquency or distress, although the association between emotional closeness and children's reports of

conflict between the parents, irrespective of the division of roles between the parents when the marriage was intact.[45]

These generalizations about what is likely to benefit children and young people after parental separation and divorce must, however, be qualified by the extensive evidence that serious ongoing conflict between the parents after separation is likely to be harmful to children.[46] There is evidence, for example, that contact with nonresident fathers decreases boys' behavior problems when parental conflict is low but increases their behavior problems when levels of conflict are high.[47] In particular, when children are caught up as messengers or spies in these conflicts, contact may impact negatively on children's well-being.[48] The risk of ongoing emotional harm to children is particularly great where the relationship between the parents after separation is characterized by ongoing physical violence.[49]

---

dissatisfaction approached significance); ELAINE WELSH, ANN BUCHANAN, EIRINI FLOURI, & JANE LEWIS, 'INVOLVED' FATHERING AND CHILD WELL-BEING: FATHERS' INVOLVEMENT WITH SECONDARY SCHOOL AGE CHILDREN (2004) (no relationship found between non-resident parent involvement and young people's well-being).

[45] For reviews of the literature, *see* JAN PRYOR & BRYAN ROGERS, CHILDREN IN CHANGING FAMILIES: LIFE AFTER PARENTAL SEPARATION (2001); Joan Kelly, *Legal and Educational Interventions for Families in Residence and Contact Disputes*, 15 AUSTRALIAN J. FAM. L. 92 (2001); Robert Emery, *Post-Divorce Family Life for Children: An Overview of Research and Some Implications for Policy, in* THE POST-DIVORCE FAMILY: CHILDREN, PARENTING AND SOCIETY 3 (Ross Thompson & Paul Amato eds., 1999); Michael Lamb, *Noncustodial Fathers and Their Impact on the Children of Divorce, in* THE POST-DIVORCE FAMILY, *id*, at 105.

[46] Michael Lamb, Kathleen Stemberg, & Ross Thompson, *The Effects of Divorce and Custody Arrangements on Children's Behavior, Development, and Adjustment*, 35 FAM. & CONCIL. CTS. REV. 393 (1997); Jennifer McIntosh, *Enduring Conflict in Parental Separation: Pathways of Impact on Child Development*, 9 J. FAM. STUD. 63 (2003); Liz Trinder, Joanne Kellet, & Louise Swift, *The Relationship Between Contact and Child Adjustment in High Conflict Cases after Divorce or Separation*, 13 CHILD & ADOLESCENT MENTAL HEALTH 181 (2008); Laura Minze, Renee McDonald, Erica Rosentraub, & Ernest Jouriles, *Making Sense of Family Conflict: Intimate Partner Violence and Preschoolers' Externalizing Problems*, 24 J. FAM. PSYCH 5 (2010).

[47] Paul Amato & Sandra Rezac, *Contact with Non-Resident Parents, Interparental Conflict, and Children's Behavior*, 15 J. FAM. ISSUES 191 (1994). The findings in relation to girls were in the same direction, but did not reach significance (*id*, at p.200).

[48] Christy Buchanan, Eleanor Maccoby, & Sanford Dornbusch, *Caught between Parents: Adolescents' Experiences in Divorced Homes*, 62 CHILD DEV. 1008 (1991).

[49] Catherine Ayoub, Robin Deutch, & Andronicki Maraganore, *Emotional Distress in Children of High-Conflict Divorce. The Impact of Marital Conflict and Violence*, 37 FAM. & CONCIL. CTS. REV. 297 (1999); Claire Sturge & Danya Glasser, *Contact and Domestic Violence – The Experts Court Report*, 30 FAM. L. 615 (2000); PETER JAFFE, NANCY LEMON, & SAMANTHA POISSON, CHILD CUSTODY AND DOMESTIC VIOLENCE: A CALL FOR SAFETY AND ACCOUNTABILITY (2003).

Whereas frequency of contact is not in itself beneficial to children, some degree of frequency of contact is a precondition for the kind of parenting that is beneficial to children.[50] When fathers have only brief or relatively infrequent contact with their children, they are less likely to feel comfortable about disciplining their children and engaging in other aspects of involved, authoritative parenting. Instead, they tend to make the visits "fun" and entertaining so that the children want to continue the visits.[51] As Thompson and Wyatt have written:

> Divorced from the routines, settings and everyday activities of the child's usual life, a visiting relationship with the nonresidential parent quickly becomes constrained and artificial, making it easier for fathers and their children to drift apart as their lives become increasingly independent.

A minimum amount of time is necessary to foster and maintain a "real parenting" relationship instead of merely a visiting relationship, whether it is through frequent and regular contact arrangements[52] or sustained periods of visiting during school holidays.[53] Regular overnight stays play an important role in fostering emotional closeness between children and nonresident parents.[54] Indeed, new thinking is emerging about the value of at least some overnight stays with the nonresident parent even for infants, with proponents arguing that this will promote stronger attachments.[55] Adolescents who stay overnight with their nonresident parent also report greater closeness and

---

[50] Judy Dunn, *Contact and Children's Perspectives on Parental Relationships, in* CHILDREN AND THEIR FAMILIES: CONTACT, RIGHTS AND WELFARE 15 (Andrew Bainham, Bridget Lindley, Martin Richards, & Liz Trinder eds., 2003) (more contact associated with closer relationships with nonresident fathers).

[51] Ross Thompson & Jennifer Wyatt, *Values, Policy, and Research on Divorce: Seeking Fairness for Children, in* THE POST-DIVORCE FAMILY, *supra* note 45, 222. The artificiality of the contact relationship may help to explain why some fathers disengage from their children after separation and divorce: Bob Simpson, Julie Jessop, & Peter McCarthy, *Fathers after Divorce, in* CHILDREN AND THEIR FAMILIES, *supra* note 50 at 201.

[52] William Fabricius, *Listening to Children of Divorce: New Findings that Diverge from Wallerstein, Lewis and Blakeslee*, 52 FAM. REL. 385, 389 (Fig. 3) (2003).

[53] Eleanor Maccoby, Christy Buchanan, Robert Mnookin, & Sanford Dornbusch, *Postdivorce Roles of Mothers and Fathers in the Lives of Their Children*, 7 J. FAM. PSYCH. 33 (1993). *See also* BUCHANAN ET AL., *supra* note 44.

[54] Bruce Smyth & Anna Ferro, *When the Difference Is Night and Day: Parent-Child Contact after Separation*, 63 FAM. MATTERS 54 (2002).

[55] Joan Kelly & Michael Lamb, *Using Child Development Research to Make Appropriate Custody and Access Decisions for Young Children*, 38 FAM. & CONCIL. CTS. REV. 297 (2000); Richard Warshak, *Blanket Restrictions: Overnight Contact between Parents and Young Children*, 38 FAM. & CONCIL. CTS. REV. 422 (2000). Marsha Kline Pruett, Rachel Ebling & Glendessa Insabella, *Parenting Plans and Visitation: Critical aspects of Parenting Plans for Young Children: Interjecting Data into the Debate about Overnights*. 42 FAM. CT

better quality of relationships with their nonresident parent than those who have daytime-only contact – an association that remains significant after taking account of the overall frequency of contact and the level of conflict between the parents. Greater closeness in the father-child relationship does not seem to affect the closeness of the mother-child relationship.[56]

FAIRNESS BETWEEN PARENTS

There are good reasons, in terms of children's well-being, for promoting greater involvement from fathers after separation in the absence of violence, abuse, or high conflict, but the greater value now placed on connection with children after separation does not necessarily mean that children are more at the center of attention and focus. One other theme in the pressure for law reform has been fairness between the parents. Increasingly, the focus is on parents' interests and concerns, which reflects a move away from highly discretionary and welfare-oriented decision making in favor of greater attention to demands for justice. This shift is reflected, for example, in the American Law Institute's Principles of the Law of Family Dissolution.[57] In this model law, children's best interests remain the paramount objective, but fairness between the parents is a secondary objective.[58] The commentary explains:

> Paragraph (1) states the Chapter's primary objective as serving the child's best interests. The priority of the child's interests over those of the competing adults is premised on the assumption that when a family breaks up, children are usually the most vulnerable parties and thus most in need of the law's protection.

REV. 39 (2004). There are nonetheless significant issues concerning the effect of overnight stays on a child's attachment to the primary caregiver, from whom the child is temporarily separated. For the debates on this issue, see the articles and rejoinders in response to these articles published in the Family Court Review in 2001–02. *See also* Judith Younger, *Post-Divorce Visitation for Infants and Young Children – the Myths and the Psychological Unknowns*, 36 FAM. L. Q. 195 (2002); Jennifer McIntosh, Bruce Smyth, Margaret Kelaher, Yvonne Wells, & Caroline Long, *Post-separation Parenting Arrangements and Developmental Outcomes for Infants and Children*, (2010), http://www.ag.gov.au/www/agd/agd.nsf/Page/Families_FamilyRelationshipServicesOverviewofPrograms_ResearchProjectsonSharedCareParentingandFamilyViolence

[56] Judith Cashmore, Patrick Parkinson, & Alan Taylor, *Overnight Stays and Children's Relationship with Resident and Nonresident Parents after Divorce*, 29 J. FAM ISSUES 707 (2008).

[57] AMERICAN LAW INSTITUTE, PRINCIPLES OF THE LAW OF FAMILY DISSOLUTION: ANALYSIS AND RECOMMENDATIONS (2002).

[58] *See ibid*, at § 2.02.

Fairness to the parents when it can also be achieved, however, is another objective of Chapter 2. Fairness to parents is not only a valid objective in itself, but it is intertwined with the child's interests. The Chapter assumes that without confidence in the basic fairness of the rules, parents are more likely to engage in strategic, resentful or uncooperative behavior, from which children may suffer; conversely, when parents believe that the rules are fair, they are more likely to invest themselves in their children and to act fairly toward others. Accordingly, when more than one rule could be expected to serve the interests of children equally well, or when the impact of the alternative rules upon children is uncertain, Chapter 2 adopts the rule most likely to produce results that achieve the greatest fairness between parents.

The significance of parents' rights and interests has also made its way onto the statute book. For example, the law of Massachusetts provides that, "In making an order or judgment relative to the custody of children, the rights of the parents shall, in the absence of misconduct, be held to be equal ..."[59]

Arguments about fairness to parents are also being heard in Europe, with claims for parental rights being founded upon the European Convention on Human Rights. British law had hitherto moved to a situation in which contact was expressed to be the right of the child, whereas parents had responsibilities rather than rights. When Britain in 1998 adopted the European Convention on Human Rights into its domestic law,[60] it opened up avenues for argument by nonresident parents that contact with their children was an aspect of the human right to the protection of family life.[61] Such a claim has been reinforced by the European Convention on Contact Concerning Children (2003), which refers to contact as a right of both parent and child.[62]

One challenge is to maintain the focus on the best interests of children when much louder voices are demanding to be heard with legitimate claims in relation to postseparation parenting arrangements. This is particularly an issue in relation to equal-time arrangements, where a desire for such an arrangement may be motivated more by concerns for equal treatment of

[59] Massachusetts General Laws, Ch 208, s.31.
[60] Human Rights Act, 1998 (Eng.).
[61] Andrew Bainham, *Contact as a Right and Obligation, in* Children and Their Families, *supra* note 50, at 61.
[62] European Convention on Contact Concerning Children, Council of Europe, Strasbourg, 15 May 2003, Article 4, available at http://conventions.coe.int/Treaty/en/Treaties/ Html/192.htm. This article states that such contact may be restricted or excluded only where necessary in the best interests of the child. *See also* Brussels IIa Regulation No 2201/2003.

parents than any belief that this is what would work best for the children. Indeed, children may say they want an equal-time arrangement out of a desire to be fair to each parent rather than to be fair to themselves.[63]

The desire for equality has a powerful gravitational force in people's thinking about gender relationships. Sir Bob Geldof, the veteran singer, poverty relief campaigner, and advocate for father's rights, put the case simply when he said: "The principle of 50 per cent of everything, the same for mother and father, must pertain."[64] In Geldof's view, this justified a presumption of equal time between mothers and fathers; however, children are not commodities and their time is not an asset to be allocated between parents.

CHILDREN'S VIEWS ON TIME WITH NONRESIDENT PARENTS

One way of maintaining the focus on the best interests of children is to hear the voices of children concerning their experiences of family life after separation.[65] Generally, research on what children and young people say from their own experience has fortified the case for rethinking conventional notions of custody and visitation.[66] Recent studies in Australia and New Zealand have shown that substantial numbers of children and young people would like to see their nonresident parents more than they do. In Australia, a study of the views of sixty young

---

[63] Smart et al. found in their study of children who were in arrangements involving substantially equal time for each parent, that children took on a sense of responsibility about being fair to each parent: Carol Smart, Amanda Wade, & Bren Neale, *Objects of Concern? – Children and Divorce*, 11 CHILD & FAM. L. Q. 365 (1999).

[64] Bob Geldof, *The Real Love That Dare Not Speak Its Name*, in CHILDREN AND THEIR FAMILIES, *supra* note 50, at 186.

[65] Barbara Bennett Woodhouse, *Talking about Children's Rights in Judicial Custody and Visitation Decision-Making*, 36 FAM. L. Q. 105 (2002); Richard Warshak, *Payoffs and Pitfalls of Listening to Children*, 52 FAM. REL. 373 (2003).

[66] There is now a substantial literature on children's voices in working out postseparation parenting arrangements. *See*, e.g., PATRICK PARKINSON & JUDITH CASHMORE, THE VOICE OF A CHILD IN FAMILY LAW DISPUTES (2008); Megan Gollop, Anne Smith, & Nicola Taylor, *Children's Involvement in Custody and Access Arrangements after Parental Separation*, 12 CHILD & FAM. L.Q. 383 (2000); Jennifer McIntosh, *Child Inclusive Divorce Mediation: Report on a Qualitative Research Study*, 18 MED. Q. 55 (2000); Ian Butler, Lesley Scanlan, Margaret Robinson, Gillian Douglas, & Mervyn Murch, *Children's Involvement in Their Parents' Divorce: Implications for Practice*, 16 CHILDREN & SOCIETY 89 (2002); Christine Szaj, *The Fine Art of Listening: Children's Voices in Custody Proceedings*, 4 J. L. & FAM. STUD. 131 (2002); Carol Smart, *From Children's Shoes to Children's Voices*, 40 FAM. CT REV. 307 (2002); Anne Smith, Nicola Taylor, & Pauline Tapp, *Rethinking Children's Involvement in Decision-Making after Parental Separation*, 10 CHILDHOOD 201 (2003).

people ages twelve to nineteen, who had experienced their parents' separation a few years earlier, found that 50 percent said they did not have enough time alone with the nonresident parent.[67] In contrast, most young people (72 percent) said they had enough time alone with their resident parent.[68] A New Zealand study that interviewed 107 children and young people from 73 families who had experienced divorce found that 52 percent of the children felt that the levels of contact were about right, 34.7 percent wanted to see the other parent more often, and 11 percent wanted to see the other parent much more often. Only 2 percent wanted less time on access.[69]

This is consistent with the findings of earlier research in Australia,[70] Britain,[71] Canada,[72] and the United States.[73] It is also consistent with the available evidence of young adults' views in the United States. Laumann-Billings and Emery found that young adults who lived in sole-custody arrangements expressed more feelings of loss and more often viewed their lives through the lens of divorce, compared to those young adults who grew up in more shared physical custody arrangements.[74] In another study, Fabricius and Hall interviewed students in psychology classes at Arizona State University over a four-year period about their experiences of parental divorce and their views on what would have been the best custody and visitation arrangements.[75] Three hundred forty-four men and 485 women participated in the study. They found that both men and women wanted significantly more time with their fathers than they actually had, although more men reported wanting more time with their fathers than women.[76]

---

[67] Patrick Parkinson, Judith Cashmore, & Judi Single, *Adolescents' Views on the Fairness of Parenting and Financial Arrangements after Separation*, 43 FAM. CT REV. 430 (2005).

[68] *Ibid.* This did not differ according to whether they lived mostly with their mother or father, or by their age or gender.

[69] Anne Smith & Megan Gollop, *Children's Perspectives on Access Visits*, 2001 BUTTERWORTHS FAM. L. J. 259; *see also* Gollop, Smith, & Taylor, *supra* note 66.

[70] MARGARET McDONALD, CHILDREN'S PERCEPTIONS OF ACCESS AND THEIR ADJUSTMENT IN THE POST-SEPARATION PERIOD (Family Court Research Report No.9, 1990).

[71] YVETTE WALCZAK & SHEILA BURNS, DIVORCE: THE CHILD'S POINT OF VIEW (1984). *See also* ANN MITCHELL, CHILDREN IN THE MIDDLE: LIVING THROUGH DIVORCE (1985).

[72] Richard Neugebauer, *Divorce, Custody and Visitation: The Child's Point of View*, 12 J. DIVORCE 153 (1989).

[73] JUDITH WALLERSTEIN & JOAN KELLY, SURVIVING THE BREAKUP (1980); Buchanan et al., *supra* note 44.

[74] Lisa Laumann-Billings & Robert Emery, *Distress among Young Adults from Divorced Families*, 14 J. FAM. PSYCH. 671 (2000).

[75] Fabricius & Hall, *supra* note 21.   [76] *Id*, at p. 451.

Children's voices may also speak against extensive contact in their situation. There are some children who do not want more time with their nonresident parent. Children may blame one parent for the marriage breakdown, or find that the nonresident parent does not do enough interesting things with them. Some fathers do not make enough time for their children because of the demands of work or new relationships. Others cannot be more involved with their children's lives because of the tyranny of distance. Listening to children involves listening to their individual needs and views, without romanticizing the parent-child relationship in such a way that it is assumed that children want to have a close relationship with the nonresident parent. Listening to children also involves being sensitive to their needs as circumstances change.

While children's voices, from the available research, do not speak in favor of any single custody rule or standard, they do indicate that traditional patterns of custody and visitation, as a general rule, are utterly inconsistent with the needs of many children. Although usually, the most practical and sensible arrangement will be to have a primary caregiver with whom the children live the majority of the time, children's interests are best served by encouraging active parenting by both parents following separation,[77] at least where the nonresident parent wants this and there are no concerns about women's or children's safety arising from such involvement.

THE COUNTERTHRUST – CONTINUING THE PRESEPARATION PATTERNS OF CARE

Whereas the trend has been mainly toward laws that encourage the involvement of both parents, supported by principles that promote significant parenting time for nonresident parents, there has been criticism of this, centered on the argument that laws encouraging greater involvement by fathers in postseparation parenting are inconsistent with the realities of parenting before the separation. Van Krieken summarizes well the way in which this focus on preseparation parenting arrangements conflicts with the pressures for nonresident parent involvement in child-rearing after separation:[78]

> The dispute seems to be between a position that there either ought to be or simply is consistency and continuity between [the preseparation division of

---

[77] Marsha Freeman, *Reconnecting the Family: A Need for Sensible Visitation Schedules for Children of Divorce*, 22 WHITTIER L. REV. 779 (2001).

[78] Robert van Krieken, *The 'Best Interests of the Child' and Parental Separation: On the 'Civilizing of Parents'* 68 MODERN L. REV. 25, 36 (2005).

domestic labour and the post-separation arrangements] – so that the parent who has done most of the child care before separation has most say in their upbringing after separation – and one in which separation allows for a renegotiation of the child-rearing contract, such that fathers play a new and different role in their children's lives. From the perspective of the first position, the second constitutes "a tendency to disparage mothers' roles as primary carers during marriages."[79] Within the zero-sum model of power often characterizing this approach, any discussion of fathers' needs, interests and rights necessarily requires a denial of mothers' needs, interests and rights.

As feminist scholars have pointed out, there is a difference between caring about and caring for, and the majority of the "caring for" in parenting after divorce remains a female responsibility.[80] Even though fathers are playing a more active role in their children's lives, mothers even in dual-earner households continue to carry most of the family's domestic responsibilities.[81]

The "Past Caretaking Standard"

A number of proposals concerning custody law make the patterns of "caring for" during the intact relationship the primary consideration in determining the allocation of time between parents after separation. Primary caregivers have long been favored in terms of allocating custody, that is, in choosing whether the mother or the father will have the child living with them most of the time. Courts have tended to preserve the status quo unless it is not working well, and in most cases, this means that children continue to be cared for by the parent who was the primary caregiver

---

[79] Citing CAROL SMART & BREN NEALE, FAMILY FRAGMENTS? 147 (1999).

[80] *See*, e.g., Carol Smart, *Losing the Struggle for Another Voice: The Case of Family Law*, 18 DALHOUSIE L.J. 173 (1995).

[81] The difference in role does not necessarily indicate a difference in total hours spent in paid and unpaid work. For U.S. research, *see* BETH SHELTON, MEN, WOMEN, AND TIME: GENDER DIFFERENCES IN PAID WORK, HOUSEWORK AND LEISURE (1992), Ch 5 (men and women have approximately the same amount of leisure time, although patterns of availability and use are different). *See also* Herbert Smith, Constance Gager, & Philip Morgan, *Identifying Underlying Dimensions in Spouses' Evaluations of Fairness in the Division of Household Labor*, 27 SOCIAL SCIENCE RESEARCH 305 (1998); NANCY DOWD, REDEFINING FATHERHOOD 48–57 (2000). For Australian research, *see* MICHAEL BITTMAN, JUGGLING TIME: HOW AUSTRALIAN FAMILIES USE THEIR TIME (1991); Australian Bureau of Statistics, No. 4150.0, *Time Use Survey* (1997); Kenneth Dempsey, *Men and Women's Power Relationships and the Persisting Inequitable Division of Housework*, 6 J. FAM. STUDIES 7 (2000); Human Rights and Equal Opportunity Commission, *It's About Time: Women, Men, Work and Family*, (2007), Ch 5; Janeen Baxter, Belinda Hewitt, & Michele Haynes, *Life Course Transitions and Housework: Marriage, Parenthood, and Time on Housework*, 70 J. MARRIAGE & FAMILY 259 (2008).

while the parents were living together, and who has continued in that role since separation.

However, no longer is the law of parenting after separation merely about how courts should make binary choices. In terms of how much time the children should spend with each parent, there is now a smorgasbord of options, depending on the circumstances of the parents, their proximity to one another, and their work schedules.

The counterthrust to the greater emphasis on the involvement of nonresident parents has been to emphasize the importance of the preseparation pattern of caregiving not only in choosing a primary caregiver but also in determining levels of contact for the other parent. The most prominent recent version of the presumption that postseparation parenting should be based on preseparation patterns has been the approximation standard, proposed by Elizabeth Scott[82] and adopted (as the past caretaking standard) by the American Law Institute.[83]

The past caretaking standard has its origins in a rule that existed for a while in West Virginia and Minnesota, known as the primary caretaker presumption. This was a rule about how to make binary choices between two parents' homes. It said little or nothing about appropriate levels of contact for the nonresident parent. The rule was first developed in West Virginia. In *Garska v McCoy*,[84] the West Virginia Supreme Court held that there should be a presumption in favor of the primary caretaker parent if he or she meets the minimum, objective standard for being a fit parent.[85] Chief Justice Neely enumerated a list of practical tasks that

---

[82] Elizabeth Scott, *Pluralism, Parental Preferences, and Child Custody*, 80 CAL. L. REV. 615 (1992).

[83] PRINCIPLES OF THE LAW OF FAMILY DISSOLUTION § 2.08, *supra* note 57. For an explanation and defense, *see* Katherine Bartlett, *Preference, Presumption, Predisposition, and Common Sense: From Traditional Custody Doctrines to the American Law Institute's Family Dissolution Project*, 36 FAM. L. Q. 11 (2002).

[84] Garska v McCoy 278 SE 2d 357 (1981). Chief Justice Neely, who wrote the court's opinion in Garska, has written extrajudicially in support of the presumption: Richard Neely, *The Primary Caretaker Parent Rule: Child Custody and the Dynamics of Greed*, 3 YALE L. & POL. REV. 168 (1984).

[85] One source of difficulties with the primary caretaker presumption, both in Minnesota and West Virginia, is identified by Laura Sack who in a study of the reported decisions in West Virginia and Minnesota (*Women and Children First: A Feminist Analysis of the Primary Caretaker Standard in Child Custody Cases* (1992) 4 YALE J. L. & FEM 292) found numerous examples of trial judges using the unfit-parent exception to disqualify women from custody on the basis of their sexual conduct. Even though generally these decisions were overturned on appeal, Sack noted that the need for appellate intervention undermines one of the proposed benefits of the presumption, and the cost of an appeal might well deter many women from seeking to do so.

could be examined in determining who was the primary caretaker.[86] He wrote:

> In establishing which natural or adoptive parent is the primary caretaker, the trial court shall determine which parent has taken primary responsibility for, inter alia, the performance of the following caring and nurturing duties of a parent: (1) preparing and planning of meals; (2) bathing, grooming and dressing; (3) purchasing, cleaning, and care of clothes; (4) medical care, including nursing and trips to physicians; (5) arranging for social interaction among peers after school, i.e., transporting to friends' houses or, for example, to girl or boy scout meetings; (6) arranging alternative care, i.e., babysitting, day-care, etc.; (7) putting child to bed at night, attending to child in the middle of the night, waking child in the morning; (8) disciplining, i.e. teaching general manners and toilet training; (9) educating, i.e. religious, cultural, social, etc.; and, (10) teaching elementary skills, i.e., reading, writing and arithmetic.

The presumption was an absolute one for children of tender years. The trial judge was required to give such weight to the opinions of older children as he or she considered justified. The primary caretaker standard in West Virginia replaced the maternal preference rule.[87] It is an approach that has been strongly advocated by some feminist scholars.[88]

Garska v McCoy was adopted by the Minnesota Supreme Court in *Pikula v Pikula* in 1985.[89] However, it only survived there for four years before it was overturned by legislation. Further amendment to the

---

[86] Garska v McCoy 278 SE 2d at 363.

[87] For strong critiques of the primary caretaker presumption, *see* Bruce Ziff, *The Primary Caretaker Presumption: Canadian Perspectives on an American Development*, 4 INT. J. L. POL'Y & FAM. 186 (1990); Carl Schneider, *Discretion, Rules and Law: Child Custody and the UMDA's Best Interest Standard*, 89 MICH. L. REV. 2215, 2283–87 (1991).

[88] Martha Fineman, *Dominant Discourse, Professional Language, and Legal Change in Child Custody Decisionmaking*, 101 HARV. L. REV. 727 (1988); Pamela Laufer-Ukeles, *Selective Recognition of Gender Difference in the Law: Revaluing the Caretaker Role*, 31 HARV. J L. & GENDER 1 (2008). The advantages of the primary caretaker presumption, as advanced in the academic literature, are summarized by Katherine Munro in *The Inapplicability of Rights Analysis in Post-Divorce Child Custody Decision-Making* 30 ALBERTA L. REV. 852, at 893–95 (1992). For a discussion from an Australian perspective, *see* Juliet Behrens, *Australian Legislation on Parenting Orders: A Case for the Principles of Care and Diversity and Presumptions Based on Them*, 24 J. SOC. WELFARE & FAM. L. 401 (2002). The primary caretaker presumption has not gained universal approval from feminist writers.

The debates among feminists are reviewed in Susan Boyd, *Potentialities and Perils of the Primary Caregiver Presumption*, 7 CAN. FAM. L. Q. 1, at 24–28 (1990). *See also* Susan Boyd, Helen Rhoades, & Kate Burns, *The Politics of the Primary Caregiver Presumption* 13 AUSTRALIAN J. FAM. L. 233 (1999).

[89] (1985) 374 N.W. 2d 705.

legislation in 1990, designed to overcome continuing judicial support for the presumption, was emphatic in abolishing it. It stated that: "The primary caretaker factor may not be used as a presumption in determining the best interests of the child."

The past caretaking standard is in some respects similar, but in other respects different, to the primary caregiver presumption. Both utilize past caregiving practices as the presumptive basis for determining postseparation parenting arrangements. However, the primary caretaker presumption was only concerned with the allocation of physical custody. By way of contrast, the past caretaking standard deals with the allocation of time between the parents, as well as the issue of the child's primary residence.

The central operating idea is found in § 2.08 of the ALI Principles. It is that the court should allocate custodial responsibility so that the proportion of custodial time the child spends with each parent approximates the proportion of time each parent spent performing caretaking functions for the child prior to the parents' separation. It is based on the concept of continuity between the intact and separated family.

The presumptive allocation of custodial responsibility that results from this assessment can be modified, but only to the extent necessary to achieve a list of other objectives contained in § 2.08(1).[90]

---

[90] PRINCIPLES § 2.08(1). The objectives are as follows:

(a) to permit the child to have a relationship with each parent which, in the case of a legal parent or a parent by estoppel who has performed a reasonable share of parenting functions, should be not less than a presumptive amount of custodial time set by a uniform rule of statewide application;

(b) to accommodate the firm and reasonable preferences of a child who has reached a specific age, set by uniform rule of statewide application;

(c) to keep siblings together when the court finds doing so is necessary to their welfare;

(d) to protect the child's welfare when the presumptive allocation under this section would harm the child because of a gross disparity in the quality of the emotional attachment between each parent and the child or in each parent's demonstrated ability or availability to meet the child's needs;

(e) to take into account any prior agreement, other than under § 2.06, that would be appropriate to consider in light of the circumstances as a whole, including the reasonable expectations of the parties, the extent to which they could have reasonably anticipated the events that occurred and their significance, and the interests of the child;

(f) to avoid an allocation of custodial responsibility that would be extremely impractical or that would interfere substantially with the child's need for stability in light of economic, physical, or other circumstances, including the distance between the parents' residences, the cost and difficulty of transporting the child, each parent's and the child's daily schedules, and the ability of the parents to co-operate in the arrangement;

There are also exceptions provided by § 2.11. This section sets out a number of justifications for limiting the parental responsibility of a parent in order to protect the child, the child's parent, or other member of the child's household from harm. This includes abuse, neglect, or abandonment of a child, domestic violence, abuse of drugs, alcohol, or another substance in a way that interferes with the parent's ability to perform caretaking functions, and interfering persistently with the other parent's access to the child.

The past caretaking approach is also relevant to the allocation of responsibility for making significant parental decisions. The Principles § 2.09 provides that in the absence of parental agreement, the court should allocate responsibility for making significant life decisions on behalf of the child, including decisions regarding the child's education and health care, to one parent or to two parents jointly, in accordance with the child's best interests. Factors to consider in making this allocation include the allocation of custodial responsibility under § 2.08 and the level of each parent's participation in past decision making on behalf of the child.

When it comes to explaining how the past caretaking standard applied to the allocation of time with the children to the nonresident parent, the ALI principles are somewhat opaque. Although it might be thought that if the parents shared the care of the children equally while they were living together, then there should be an equal time arrangement after separation, the ALI's Principles appear to indicate that in such circumstances, the best-interests test would be applied instead. The Principles are also somewhat opaque when it comes to the allocation of time with the nonresidential parent.[91] Elizabeth Scott, in her original formulation of the approximation standard, was somewhat clearer. Broadly speaking, in her view, the more involved the parent was in caregiving during the marriage, the more time he or she should be allocated after separation. She wrote that for the standard to have practical application, the courts would need to "characterize predivorce family arrangements by using simplifying categories or rules of

---

(g) to apply the Principles set forth in § 2.17(4) if one parent relocates or proposes to relocate at a distance that will impair the ability of a parent to exercise the presumptive amount of custodial responsibility under this section;

(h) to avoid substantial and almost certain harm to the child.

[91] For a detailed analysis, *see* Patrick Parkinson, *The Past Caretaking Standard in Comparative Perspective, in* ROBIN WILSON (ED), RECONCEIVING THE FAMILY: CRITICAL REFLECTIONS ON THE AMERICAN LAW INSTITUTE'S PRINCIPLES OF THE LAW OF FAMILY DISSOLUTION 446 (2006).

thumb to ease the judicial task of applying the rule."[92] She thought that three categories could be constructed that would roughly reflect various patterns of parental involvement, spanning a continuum from a family in which both parents equally share caretaking responsibility to one in which one parent is uninvolved while the other shoulders most of the burden. In the first category, an arrangement for joint physical and legal custody would be appropriate. Where one parent is uninvolved in caretaking, the appropriate order would be for sole custody and visitation. Scott then described the third category as follows. It would:

> include families with two involved parents, one of whom bears the greater burden of child care responsibility. A family in this third category might have a custody arrangement that is similar to joint legal custody, with the child's principal residence being with the primary caretaker and secondary residence with the other parent. The actual time allocation between residences would be based on each parent's participation in the child's life before divorce. Thus, a court ordering custody for a family in this group might use a variety of formulas to allocate the child's time between households, designating time with each parent as a proportion of the month or week. For example, the order might direct that the child live with an actively participating secondary caretaker twelve days a month (or three days a week), while a less involved secondary parent might be awarded physical custody eight days a month (or two days a week).

The past caretaking standard clearly represents an alternative to the approach in many American jurisdictions that encourages the substantial involvement of both parents in the absence of violence or abuse, without a particular reference to past caregiving practices. By requiring that disputed custody cases should be resolved by allocating to each parent the same proportion of time as each spent in caretaking functions before the parents' separation, the past caretaking standard has been hailed as a way of promoting a compromise in the gender war over custody.[93]

---

[92] Scott, *supra* note 82, at 640.

[93] Herma Hill Kay, for example, welcomes the approximation standard, as articulated in the ALI principles, as offering "both mothers and fathers a way to retreat from this particular battlefield [of custody law] with their honor intact": Herma Hill Kay, *No-Fault Divorce and Child Custody: Chilling Out the Gender Wars*, 36 FAM. L. Q. 27, 40 (2002). The standard has also been praised for being gender-neutral: Kathy Graham, *How the ALI Child Custody Principles Help Eliminate Gender and Sexual Orientation Bias from Child Custody Determinations*, 8 DUKE J. GENDER L. & POL'Y 301 (2001).

Issues with the Past Caretaking Standard

There can be no question that the division of roles in the intact marriage is a very significant factor in decision making about parenting after separation. However, the question is the extent to which it should be used to guide postseparation parenting arrangements. Its main relevance is in terms of qualification to be the primary caregiver. The primary caregiver's better qualifications to continue in that role justify the allocation of primary caregiving to them after separation in the majority of cases. Children are likely to have developed a closer attachment to their primary caregivers. Primary caregivers also play an anchor role emotionally in the lives of children. This can be seen in the aftermath of separation. The great majority of children and young people in families where the parents are not living together report that they feel close to their mothers.[94] Primary caregivers are more likely to be attuned to the needs of the children.

However, should the patterns of parenting before separation be determinative of the amount of time the nonresident parent has with the children after separation? The argument that fathers should not have a greater role in parenting after separation than they had before separation ignores the significance of the change that separation can make to fathers' attitudes to the parenting role. Smart and Neale found in their research in Britain that some fathers adjust to divorce by making a new commitment to parenting.[95] They leave the workforce or adjust the extent of their workforce participation in order to invest in a relationship that they feel could not be sustained without a substantial new investment of time and energy. The process of divorce then has an effect of causing them to reorder their priorities.

This is far from a belated conversion on the road to Damascus. Role division within the marriage partnership makes sense for a great many couples as long as the relationship remains intact. Economists have sought to demonstrate how role specialization maximizes benefit.[96] Laws that allocate custody on the basis of the patterns of parenting before separation may be appropriate to the extent that the primary caregiver is better attuned to

---

[94] Buchanan et al., *supra* note 44, at 188, Table 5.1. The picture in relation to fathers is rather more mixed. For example, recent British research with children of divorce found that half of the children interviewed reported that their fathers knew nothing, or very little, of their feelings about the divorce, whereas this was true of only 20% of mothers: Ian Butler, Lesley Scanlan, Margaret Robinson, Gillian Douglas, & Mervyn Murch, Divorcing Children: Children's experience of Their Parents' Divorce 39 (2003).

[95] Carol Smart & Bren Neale, Family Fragments? (1999) Ch 3.

[96] Gary Becker, A Treatise on the Family (1991).

the needs of the children. However, it may act unfairly if the strength of a presumption in favor of the primary caregiver operates to the prejudice of men who fulfilled their role as primary breadwinners within a role-divided partnership, but who want to restructure their working arrangements significantly after separation to ensure that they can remain actively involved with their children's lives. The point is well made by Guidubaldi in his minority report for the U.S. Commission on Child and Family Welfare in 1996: [97]

> A frequently heard rationale for sole mother custody concerns the issue of pre-divorce parenting role performance serving as a precedent for post-divorce parenting roles. In response, it should be noted that during the marriage, traditional role complementarity provides for efficient childrearing, wherein one of the parents usually serves as the primary bread-winner, providing for the child's food shelter, clothing, etc. while the other parent's main focus is on utilizing these resources in providing direct services for the child. Neither contribution should be denigrated in determining post-divorce childrearing privileges or responsibilities. Since both roles were essential for child welfare, since both parties may be presumed to have had at least a tacit agreement to these role divisions, and since in many families the roles are not mutually exclusive and may involve a considerable amount of overlap, the pre-divorce parenting roles should not be the basis for post-divorce parenting time and should not place either parent at a disadvantage in custody conflicts.

Another flaw in the past caretaking standard is that it assumes that the coparenting arrangement after separation can mirror the patterns of caregiving within an intact relationship. This takes too little account of the emotional, geographical, and financial earthquake that separation can involve for parents. Coparenting after divorce, whatever form it takes, requires new patterns of parenting to be developed in the very different circumstances that exist for the enduring family. As Smart and Neale observe, "Pre-divorce parenting may be a poor preparation for post-divorce parenting, and the skills, qualities and infrastructural supports required for the former may be rather different to those required for the latter."[98]

---

[97] U.S. COMMISSION ON CHILD AND FAMILY WELFARE, PARENTING OUR CHILDREN: IN THE BEST INTEREST OF THE NATION, A REPORT TO THE PRESIDENT AND CONGRESS, 87 (1996).

[98] SMART & NEALE, *supra* note 95, at 46. Similarly, Warshak writes: "Parents change after divorce. Being a single parent is a very different challenge from being one of two parents in the same home": Richard Warshak, *Punching the Parental Time Clock: The Approximation Rule, Social Science and the Baseball Bat Kids*, 45 FAM. CT REV. 600, 606 (2007).

While preseparation roles certainly can play a part in decision making, numerous other factors need to be taken into account in terms of what will work following separation, not least the practical issues. What arrangements are feasible following separation may depend on how far the parents live from one another, what their work schedules are like, and how long it takes them to get to and from work. These logistical factors are likely to change over time. Postseparation parenting relationships cannot remain stuck in a preseparation time warp.

Whatever view one takes of the past caretaking standard, what is most noteworthy is the absence of adoption of this idea even when recommended by as influential a body as the ALI. It has been adopted in West Virginia[99] but, like most other aspects of the Principles,[100] has not gained further traction. This suggests that despite significant academic support, the past caretaking standard is not in harmony with the zeitgeist. There may be widespread support still, both in theory and practice, for the idea of the role-divided marriage; however, there appears to be little political support for the idea of the role-divided divorce in cases other than those where there are safety concerns. For these reasons, it is unlikely that the past caretaking standard will provide a viable solution to the problem of finding an organizing principle for postseparation parenting.

THE RISE OF SHARED PARENTING LAWS

The factors that have led parliaments and legislatures to support joint custody and shared parenting are in combination so significant that it is unsurprising that legislatures around the western world have been responsive to such calls for law reform. Although there is a consensus that shared parenting is contraindicated in cases where there are safety concerns, in other cases, the new frontier is working out ways of achieving substantially shared parenting time to the extent that the logistics of the parents' circumstances allow. Those logistics, which include being able, financially and otherwise, to remain within a reasonable proximity of one another, may make shared care unrealistic for the majority of families. It is possible for many, though, and the numbers of parents who are trying shared-care arrangements is on the increase in many jurisdictions.

---

[99] W. Va. Code §48–9–206.
[100] Robin Wilson, *American Law Institute's Principles of the Law of Family Dissolution, Eight Years after Adoption: Guiding Principle or Obligatory Footnote?*, 42 Fam. L.Q. 573 (2008).

5

Shared Parenting: The New Frontier

There are indications in many western countries of a very significant growth in shared parenting arrangements over the last ten-to-fifteen years, particularly where parents had previously been married. A substantial number of children, even quite young children, alternate between their parents' homes. At the policy level, a number of jurisdictions now have legislation that gives some encouragement to consider shared parenting arrangements, and the trend in terms of law reform is strongly in that direction in situations where there are no issues of violence or abuse.

THE GROWTH OF SHARED PARENTING

There is no set definition of what shared parenting means, but there is widespread agreement that it need not mean equal time. In some jurisdictions, the definition is set by legislation. In Utah, for example, joint physical custody is defined to mean that the child stays with each parent overnight for more than 30 percent of the year.[1] In Australia, shared care is defined as 35 percent of nights or more per year for each parent as a result of changes made in 2008 to the child support legislation.[2]

Perhaps the most dramatic example of the growth of shared parenting is Sweden, where equal time, or alternating residence arrangements, have become quite common. In 1984–85, 1 percent of Swedish parents who were living apart had equal time arrangements. By 2006–07 it had increased to

---

[1] UTAH CODE § 30-3-10.1.
[2] Child Support (Assessment) Act, 1989 (Austl.). *See* Patrick Parkinson, *The Future of Child Support*, 33 U. W. AUST. L. REV. 179 (2007).

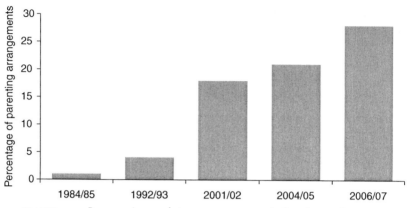

FIGURE 5.1. Increase in equal time arrangements in Sweden, 1984–2007.

28 percent.[3] Almost half of the children aged six to nine whose parents do not live together live in approximately equal time arrangements.[4]

This growth in the incidence of equal time arrangements has risen substantially over the last twenty years without a legislative environment that specifically encourages it. Prior to 1998, a joint custody arrangement could only operate after divorce if both parties consented to it. In 1998, the law was amended to empower the court to make an order for joint custody in the absence of agreement if this was in the best interests of the child. This was certainly seen as controversial by some, although it mirrored the developments elsewhere.[5] However, joint custody might mean no more than joint legal custody and said nothing about the time the child should spend with each parent.

Notwithstanding a relatively neutral legal environment, the growth in equal time arrangements has been very rapid indeed. Court decisions have in all probability contributed very little to this growth, given that most people manage to resolve parenting disputes without the need for a judicial decision. A study of 125 District Court cases in 2002, in which the parents were in conflict about the child's residence, found that a claim for alternating residence was made by one parent in 66 cases. The court decided on

---

[3]   Karin Lundström, *Växelvis Boende ökar Bland Skilsmässobarn*, VäLFäRD No 4, 3–5 (2009), http://www.scb.se/statistik/_publikationer/LE0001_2009K04_TI_02_A05TI0904.pdf; *See also* Statistics Sweden, http://www.scb.se/Pages/TableAndChart____279897.aspx

[4]   Lundström, *supra* note 3, at 5.

[5]   For a critical view, *see* Anna Singer, *Active Parenting or Solomon's Justice? Alternating Residence in Sweden for Children with Separated Parents*, 4 UTRECHT L.R. 35, 40 (2008).

alternating residence against the wishes of one parent in only fifteen of these cases.[6]

This growth in shared parenting has not occurred without generating some level of concern. Amendments introduced in 2006 now require the court to consider particular factors before ordering joint custody. These include the risk of harm to a child or any other member of the family as a consequence of abuse, or the child being unlawfully abducted. The court must also examine the parties' ability to cooperate.[7]

It may well be that one motivation for the popularity of alternating residence for fathers is that they have no need to pay child support if there is an alternating residence arrangement.[8] However, this ought to make it *less* likely that mothers would agree. The growth in shared care in this jurisdiction is much more likely to be the outcome of favorable economic and social welfare conditions that support parents in the workforce, as well as cultural factors. A study of domestic labor among couples with one-year-old children found that when women were working full time, men shared the child care responsibilities equally (although they were less likely to do the laundry and cleaning).[9] This relatively equal division of the child-caring workload translates into quite high levels of shared care after separation.

In Britain, the proportion of parents reporting equal time arrangements is rather lower, but still significant. In a survey of 559 parents, mostly resident parents, British researchers found that 12 percent reported that they shared the care of the child more or less equally.[10] The Children Act 1989 in England and Wales gives no guidance on how children's time with each parent should be allocated.

In Canada, a national longitudinal survey in 1998–99 found that 8 percent of children aged four to fifteen were in equal time arrangements.[11] There was a significant increase in the incidence of shared parenting during the 1990s, comparing those who separated in the first half of the decade

---

[6]   *Id.* at 41.   [7]   *Id.* at 38–39.

[8]   Anna Singer, *Time Is Money? – Child Support for Children with Alternating Residence in Sweden, in* FAMILY FINANCES 591 (Bea Verschraegen ed., 2009).

[9]   Jan Thomas & Ingegerd Hildingsson, *Who's Bathing the Baby? The Division of Domestic Labour in Sweden*, 15 J. FAM STUD. 139 (2009).

[10] VICTORIA PEACEY & JOAN HUNT, PROBLEMATIC CONTACT AFTER SEPARATION AND DIVORCE? A NATIONAL SURVEY OF PARENTS 19 (2008). This was an unweighted figure. Seventy-eight percent of the parents who said that there was an even split were women. The researchers estimated equal time arrangements to exist for between 9% and 17% of separated parents across the population.

[11] HEATHER JUBY, NICOLE MARCIL-GRATTON, & CÉLINE LE BOURDAIS, WHEN PARENTS SEPARATE: FURTHER FINDINGS FROM THE NATIONAL LONGITUDINAL SURVEY OF CHILDREN AND YOUTH 27 (2005). Thirteen percent of children were in shared custody,

with those who separated in the second half.[12] A later survey, in 2001, found that according to mothers' reports, 9.1 percent of children were in approximately equal time arrangements. Fathers reported 15.5 percent, but the researchers noted that studies based on fathers' reports are likely to comprise a larger fraction of those who are closely involved with their children, and thus such studies overestimate the frequency of father-child contact for all children of separated parents.[13]

The Canadian statistics represent a snapshot of all parents who live apart and have children. A study of this kind will yield lower levels of shared care than a study of recent or new divorces. By way of contrast, the available U.S. data is taken from studies of divorce cases. Wisconsin provides a particularly good example of the growth of shared care, as indicated in such files, because researchers have been following these trends over time. In that jurisdiction, where a shared parenting arrangement is defined as involving at least 30 percent of the time with each parent, the incidence of shared care among divorced couples increased from 2.2 percent to 14.2 percent between 1980 and 1992.[14] By 2001, it had reached 32 percent.[15] In a study of 590 divorced mothers and fathers who shared the care of their children, the researchers found that over two-thirds had equal time arrangements at the time of the court orders.[16]

Since 1999 at least, the growth of shared care may have been encouraged by the legislation, although the trend was evident well before that time. The Wisconsin statute was amended in that year to provide that the "court shall set a placement schedule that allows the child to have regularly occurring, meaningful periods of physical placement with each parent and that maximizes the amount of time the child may spend with

---

as defined by the respondents. However, shared custody appeared to have a range of meanings for those who responded to the survey, and included every other weekend contact.

[12] *Id.*, at 28.

[13] Liam Swiss & Céline Le Bourdais, *Father–Child Contact after Separation: The Influence of Living Arrangements*, 30 J. FAM. ISSUES 623, 632–33 (2009).

[14] Marygold Melli, Patricia Brown, & Maria Cancian, *Child Custody in a Changing World: A Study of Post-Divorce Arrangements in Wisconsin*, 3 U. ILL. L. REV. 773 (1997).

[15] Steven Cook & Patricia Brown, *Recent Trends in Children's Placement Arrangements in Divorce and Paternity Cases in Wisconsin*, (2006), http://www.irp.wisc.edu/home.htm. In 59% of cases, the mother had sole custody, and in 7% the father had sole custody. These figures from the Institute for Research on Poverty, University of Wisconsin-Madison, are taken from cases with final judgments dated 2000–02.

[16] Marygold Melli & Patricia Brown, *Exploring a New Family Form – The Shared Time Family*, 22 INT. J. L. POLICY & FAM. 231, 241 (2008).

each parent, taking into account geographic separation and accommodations for different households."[17] The Supreme Court of Wisconsin has nonetheless made it clear that the legislature did not intend the term "maximizing" to mean equal placement or equal time.[18]

The popularity of shared care as an option in the twenty-first century is also evident in Washington State, a jurisdiction in which there is no particular statutory language that encourages shared parenting. According to government statistics in that jurisdiction, 46 percent of parenting plans filed in dissolution cases gave at least 35 percent of the time with the child to the father in 2007–08, in cases where there were no risk factors present. This data was based on forms that were required to be filed with the Parenting Plan on divorce. Sixteen percent of the arrangements gave equal time to mothers and fathers.[19]

A study of a sample of child support files in Arizona in 2007 yielded similar statistics for equal time arrangements to those in Washington State. Fifteen percent of these orders involved essentially equal parenting time.[20]

The statistics from Wisconsin and Washington State only reflect the levels of shared care among couples who have divorced. These figures are not readily comparable with the statistics from Britain, Canada, and Sweden, which are based on general population snapshots. This is for three reasons.

First, levels of shared care are likely to be lower if account is taken of all parents who are living apart, including those who cohabited outside of marriage and those who have never lived together. Levels of non-resident parental involvement with children is typically lower in these groups, and in particular where the parents did not live together prior to separation.[21]

---

[17] WIS. STAT. § 767.41(4)(a)2.

[18] Landwehr v. Landwehr, 2006 WI 64, 291 Wis.2d 49, 715 N.W.2d 180, 185 (2006); Melli & Brown, *supra* note 16, at 235.

[19] Thomas George, *Residential Time Summary Reports Filed in Washington from July 2007 – March 2008*, (2008), http://www.courts.wa.gov/wsccr/docs/ResidentialTimeSummaryReport.pdf (citing statistics by county and statewide). In 86% of the cases, there were no risk factors. Risk factors included "committed DV, abused or neglected child, chemical dependency, mental health issues, or other" (at 3, 5).

[20] Jane Venohr & Rasa Kaunelis, *Arizona Child Support Guidelines Review: Analysis of Case File Data*, 5 (2008), http://supreme.state.az.us/csgrc/Documents/2009-CaseFileRev.pdf

[21] Paul Amato, Catherine Meyers, & Robert Emery, *Changes in Nonresident Father–Child Contact From 1976 to 2002*, 58 FAM. REL. 41 (2009).

Second, the statistics from these states also reflect recent divorces, as contrasted with a snapshot of all children whose parents live apart. As the Wisconsin figures demonstrate, there has been a substantial increase in the incidence of shared care arrangements as found in divorce files over time. It follows that if only recent separations and divorces are examined (for example, those who separated in the last three years), it is likely that the proportions who have shared care arrangements would be higher than taking account of the entire population of separated parents with minor children, which includes those who separated, or whose children were born outside of a cohabiting partnership, up to seventeen years ago.

Thirdly, shared care arrangements do not necessarily last. They may well be a transitional phase in the first few years after separation. The evidence from a variety of studies of shared care in the 1980s and 1990s is that shared care arrangements have a tendency to revert back to primary mother care (most frequently) or primary father care (infrequently).[22]

That there should be change in shared care arrangements over time is not surprising. It is common for parenting arrangements, and in particular contact arrangements, to change as circumstances change. Shared care is dependent on the parents living in relatively close proximity to one another and, for school-age children, to the child's school. New partnerships or job opportunities for one or other parent, or the need for one or both parents to move to an area of cheaper housing following the property settlement, may necessitate some adjustment to the shared care arrangement. In cases where the move amounts to a relocation, that move may be hotly contested.

Notwithstanding these factors, some research on shared care indicates much higher levels of stability than in previous studies. In Wisconsin, researchers found that three years after the divorce, there had been some diminution in the actual practice of shared care, but 80 percent of fathers with shared care time were still engaged in shared care and 11 percent were looking after the child more than 54 percent of the time.[23] The researchers found also that children in shared care experience living arrangements that are as stable, or more stable, than children in the primary care of their mothers.[24]

---

[22] For a review of the international literature, including the United States, *see* Bruce Smyth & Lawrie Moloney, *Changes in Patterns of Post-Separation Parenting Over Time: A Brief Review*, 14 J. FAM. STUDIES 7 (2008).

[23] Melli & Brown, *supra* note 16, at 260.

[24] Lawrence Berger, Patricia Brown, Eunhee Joung, Marygold Melli, & Lynn Wimer, *The Stability of Child Physical Placements Following Divorce: Descriptive Evidence from Wisconsin*, 70 J. MARRIAGE & FAM. 273, 282 (2008).

In Australia, the evidence indicates a more complex picture. Researchers comparing the care arrangements in large-scale longitudinal studies at a three-year interval found that where the parents had a shared care arrangement involving 30 percent or more nights in the first survey, many of the children had reverted to the primary care of the mother three years later. Shared care, defined in this way, proved more unstable than primary care with either the mother or the father.[25] These studies included not only formerly married parents but also those parents who had cohabited outside of marriage or never lived together. However, equal time arrangements have been found to be quite durable. In another large-scale study involving 2,000 separated parents, 60 percent of the children who were in equal care arrangements at separation had the same arrangement four-to-five years later.[26] They were much more durable than unequal shared care arrangements in which the child spent the majority of the time with one parent.[27]

LEGISLATIVE SUPPORT FOR SHARED PARENTING

Although the growth in shared care in some jurisdictions has occurred without significant support from legislatures, there is a growing trend toward legislative encouragement for courts to give serious consideration to shared parenting in adjudicating disputes, in cases other than where there are issues of domestic violence or child abuse. [28]

In most jurisdictions, to be sure, legislatures have resisted the temptation to be too prescriptive. Courts have retained the flexibility to try to discern what will be in the best interests of the child in each case. Over the years,

---

[25] Bruce Smyth, Ruth Weston, Lawrie Moloney, Nick Richardson, & Jeromey Temple, *Changes in Patterns of Post-Separation Parenting Over Time: Recent Australian Data*, 14 J. FAM. STUDIES 23 (2008). *See also* JUDITH CASHMORE, PATRICK PARKINSON, RUTH WESTON, ROGER PATULNY, GERRY REDMOND, LIXIA QU, JENNIFER BAXTER, MARIANNE RAJKOVIC, TOMASZ SITEK, & ILAN KATZ, SHARED CARE PARENTING ARRANGEMENTS SINCE THE 2006 FAMILY LAW REFORMS: REPORT TO THE AUSTRALIAN GOVERNMENT, ATTORNEY-GENERAL'S DEPARTMENT 37–39 (2010), *available at* http://www.ag.gov.au/www/agd/agd.nsf/Page/Families_FamilyRelationshipServicesOverviewofPrograms_ResearchProjectsonSharedCareParentingandFamilyViolence

[26] RAE KASPIEW, MATTHEW GRAY, RUTH WESTON, LAWRIE MOLONEY, KELLY HAND, & LIXIA QU, EVALUATION OF THE 2006 FAMILY LAW REFORMS 127 (2009), *available at* http://www.aifs.gov.au/institute/pubs/fle/index.html

[27] *Id.*

[28] Helen Rhoades, *The Rise and Rise of Shared Parenting Laws*, 19 CAN. J. FAM. L. 75, 75 (2002); Margaret Brinig, *Does Parental Autonomy Require Equal Custody at Divorce?*, 65 LOUISIANA L. REV. 1345 (2005).

various jurisdictions in the United States have responded to the arguments about whether there should be a presumption in favor of joint custody by stating that there should be neither a presumption for nor against. In California, for example, the law provides:[29]

> This section establishes neither a preference nor a presumption for or against joint legal custody, joint physical custody, or sole custody, but allows the court and the family the widest discretion to choose a parenting plan that is in the best interest of the child.

However, even these kinds of legislative statements, designed to quell arguments in a previous era, may well be covered over by accretions to the legislation emphasizing shared parenting. Illinois offers an example of the somewhat mixed messages the legislature can give on such matters. Illinois law provides that there is no presumption in favor of or against joint custody, but this provision is preceded by the statement that:[30]

> Unless the court finds the occurrence of ongoing abuse ... the court shall presume that the maximum involvement and cooperation of both parents regarding the physical, mental, moral, and emotional well-being of their child is in the best interest of the child.

This sounds very much like a presumption in favor of shared parenting in the absence of violence or abuse.

One example of the trend toward shared parenting is the law in Iowa, where the legislative formulation of policy is that:[31]

> The court, insofar as is reasonable and in the best interest of the child, shall order the custody award, including liberal visitation rights where appropriate, which will assure the child the opportunity for the maximum continuing physical and emotional contact with both parents after the parents have separated or dissolved the marriage, and which will encourage parents to share the rights and responsibilities of raising the child unless direct physical

---

[29] CAL. FAM. CODE § 3040(b). It is sometimes thought that California had a joint custody presumption in the 1980s. In fact, it is not at all clear that California ever had a joint custody presumption – intentionally at least. People presumed there was such a presumption until amendments were made in 1988, because the legislature named joint custody first in the list of options. The 1988 amendment made it clear that there was no presumption for or against any particular kind of custodial arrangement. Herma Hill Kay, *Beyond No-Fault: New Directions in Divorce Reform, in* DIVORCE REFORM AT THE CROSSROADS 6, 26–27 (Stephen Sugarman & Herma Hill Kay eds., 1990).

[30] 750 ILL. COMP. STAT. 5/602(c).

[31] IOWA CODE § 598.41(1)(a).

harm or significant emotional harm to the child, other children, or a parent is likely to result from such contact with one parent.

The law provides for a presumption in favor of joint custody,[32] and if joint custody is awarded, then:[33]

> [T]he court may award joint physical care to both joint custodial parents upon the request of either parent ... If the court denies the request for joint physical care, the determination shall be accompanied by specific findings of fact and conclusions of law that the awarding of joint physical care is not in the best interest of the child.

There is a similar provision in Maine.[34]

THE MOVE TOWARD EQUAL TIME: DEVELOPMENTS IN THE UNITED STATES

What about equal time? In a number of jurisdictions, there has been pressure for change from fathers' groups based on the idea that for parents to be treated equally, there ought to be a presumption that children should spend an equal amount of time with each parent after separation.[35] Some legislatures have responded to this issue by explaining that joint custody does not mean necessarily that there is entitlement to an equal time arrangement. In Idaho, for example, the legislation provides that:

> 'Joint physical custody' means an order awarding each of the parents significant periods of time in which a child resides with or is under the care and supervision of each of the parents ... but does not necessarily mean the

---

[32] IOWA CODE § 598.41(2)(a) and (b): "On the application of either parent, the court shall consider granting joint custody in cases where the parents do not agree to joint custody.
   If the court does not grant joint custody under this subsection, the court shall cite clear and convincing evidence ... that joint custody is unreasonable and not in the best interest of the child to the extent that the legal custodial relationship between the child and a parent should be severed."

[33] IOWA CODE § 598.41(5)(a).

[34] 19A ME. REV. STAT. § 1653(2)(D)(1): "If either or both parents request an award of shared primary residential care and the court does not award shared primary residential care of the child, the court shall state in its decision the reasons why shared primary residential care is not in the best interest of the child."

[35] The U.S. Commission on Child and Family Welfare considered this option but did not adopt it, to the disappointment of the minority. U.S. COMMISSION ON CHILD AND FAMILY WELFARE, PARENTING OUR CHILDREN: IN THE BEST INTEREST OF THE NATION, A REPORT TO THE PRESIDENT AND CONGRESS (1996), John Guidubaldi, minority report, 87, 93–97.

child's time with each parent should be exactly the same in length nor does it necessarily mean the child should be alternating back and forth over certain periods of time between each parent.[36]

In Texas, the same concept is expressed in the unique foreign language of that jurisdiction: "Joint managing conservatorship does not require the award of equal or nearly equal periods of physical possession of and access to the child to each of the joint conservators."[37]

By way of contrast, Louisiana is one jurisdiction that has responded affirmatively, if somewhat ambiguously, to the idea of promoting equal time. In that jurisdiction, there is a presumption in favor of joint custody.[38] In determining what the arrangements for joint parenting should be, the courts are instructed that "to the extent it is feasible and in the best interest of the child, physical custody of the children should be shared equally."[39] This may be little more than a rhetorical flourish, however, as the court is also required to identify a "domiciliary parent" who is the parent with whom the child "shall primarily reside."[40] The domiciliary parent also has the authority to make all decisions affecting the child unless an implementation order provides otherwise, and there is a statutory presumption that all major decisions made by the domiciliary parent are in the best interest of the child.[41] Thus while including a presumption in favor of equal time arrangements on the one hand, Louisiana law also assumes that there will always be a primary caregiver with the major decision-making powers. Such legislative schizophrenia illustrates the tensions with which lawmakers must grapple in determining custody policy, and the impact of inconsistent amendments being made to the law in different time periods.

In Oklahoma, legislative policy is in favor of shared parenting, and the court is required to order "substantially equal access" at the time

---

[36] IDAHO CODE § 32–717B(2).

[37] TEX. FAMILY CODE § 153.135. *See also* UTAH CODE § 30-3-10(1)(d); N. M. STAT. § 40-4-9.1 (L)(4).

[38] Art. 132 of the Civil Code provides: "If the parents agree who is to have custody, the court shall award custody in accordance with their agreement unless the best interest of the child requires a different award.

In the absence of agreement, or if the agreement is not in the best interest of the child, the court shall award custody to the parents jointly; however, if custody in one parent is shown by clear and convincing evidence to serve the best interest of the child, the court shall award custody to that parent."

[39] CIVIL CODE ANCILLARIES 9–335 A(2). In Arizona and Georgia also, joint physical custody is defined as substantially equal time, but, unlike in Louisiana, there is no presumption in those states in favor of joint physical custody. *See* ARIZ. REV. STAT. § 25-402(3); GA. CODE ANN. § 19-9-6(3).

[40] CIVIL CODE ANCILLARIES 9–335 B.   [41] *Id.*

of making temporary orders, if requested by one parent to do so.[42] The legislation states:

> It is the policy of this state to assure that minor children have frequent and continuing contact with parents who have shown the ability to act in the best interests of their children and to encourage parents to share in the rights and responsibilities of rearing their children after the parents have separated or dissolved their marriage, provided that the parents agree to cooperate and that domestic violence, stalking, or harassing behaviors ... are not present in the parental relationship. To effectuate this policy, if requested by a parent, the court may provide substantially equal access to the minor children to both parents at a temporary order hearing, unless the court finds that shared parenting would be detrimental to the child.

The presumption in favor of substantially equal access does not carry through to the legislative requirements governing final orders.

THE MOVE TOWARD EQUAL TIME: DEVELOPMENTS IN EUROPE

Agitation for an equal time presumption is also occurring in parts of Europe, notably France and Belgium.[43] Specifying alternating parenting in the legislation as an option is obviously much less controversial than establishing it as a presumption, although it has still proved too controversial for some countries.[44] In France, an intermediate position has been adopted. Even though amendments made in 1993 established the principle of joint parental authority after separation, the legislature, at that time, rejected the idea of alternating residence.[45] However, some judges were persuaded to

---

[42] OKLA. STAT. § 43–110.1. This provision is confined to temporary orders. *See* Redmond v Cauthen, (2009) OK CIV. APP. 46; 211 P.3d 233 (Ct. Civ. App.).

[43] In Britain *see, e.g.,* Ann Buchanan & Joan Hunt, *Disputed Contact Cases in the Courts, in* CHILDREN AND THEIR FAMILIES: CONTACT, RIGHTS AND WELFARE 371, 380 (Andrew Bainham, Bridget Lindley, Martin Richards, & Liz Trinder eds., 2003); Bob Geldof, *The Real Love That Dare Not Speak Its Name, in* CHILDREN AND THEIR FAMILIES, 171. For an examination of the earlier case law on shared residence in England, compared with New Zealand, *see* Caroline Bridge, *Shared Residence in England and New Zealand – a Comparative Analysis,* 8 CHILD & FAM. L. Q. 12 (1996).

[44] For example, in Portugal, proposals for legislation to introduce joint custody as an option included specific reference to the possibility of alternating parenting, but it was omitted from the final version of the legislation in 1995. Maria Clara Sottomayor, *The Introduction and Impact of Joint Custody in Portugal,* 13 INT. J. L. POL'Y & FAM. 247, 252 (1999).

[45] This was implicit in the text, because the principle of a primary or usual residence was maintained, but explicit in the legislative debates. Hugues Fulchiron in *L' autorité Parentale Renovée,* RÉPERTOIRE DU NOTARIAT DEFRÉNOIS 959 (2002).

fix a primary residence while allowing contact with the nonresident parent to such an extent that the arrangements were equivalent, in practice, to an alternating residence system.[46] Two commissions were established in the 1990s to advise the government concerning possible reforms to the law of parental authority. One took a sociological view, under the presidency of Irène Théry.[47] The other focused more on legal issues under the presidency of Françoise Dekeuwer-Défossez.[48] Dekeuwer-Défossez recommended that the notion of principal residence should be removed from the Code because it led judges to refuse shared residence arrangements when such arrangements would not have been contrary to the child's best interests.[49]

The consequence of these proposals for reform, and subsequent governmental consideration, was legislation on parental authority passed in 2002. This legislation was intended to promote alternating residence arrangements. Mme Ségolène Royal, the Minister for Family Affairs, indicated in the legislative debates that the reform's purpose was to encourage the parents to reach agreement on the principle of alternating residence, arguing that it had the advantage of maintaining parity between them.[50] However, in the Senate, concerns were expressed about the imposition of an alternating residence arrangement on parents without their agreement.[51]

---

[46] *See* Hugues Fulchiron & Adeline Gouttenoire-Cornut, *Réformes Législatives et Permanence des Pratiques: à Propos de la Généralisation de L'exercice en Commun de L'autorité Parentale par la Loi du 8 Janvier 1993*, Recueil Dalloz Chroniques 363 (1997) and the cases cited therein. *See also* Paris, 10 Fevrier 1999, Juris Classeur Périodique 99, 2, 10170, Garé (appeal court affirmed trial judge's decision in favor of alternating residence. The court commented that the traditional division into "usual" residence and visiting and housing rights for the other parent, contributed to a weakening of the bond between the child and the nonresident parent. Consequently, shared residence was to be encouraged). A decision of the Cour d'Appel de Toulouse on May 2, 2000 took a different view. It considered that the Civil Code did not allow for an order for alternating residence because it required the child's primary residence to be fixed, with the other parent having visiting and housing rights. *See* Agnes Bigot, *Autorité Parentale: L'article 374 Alinea 3 du Code Civil Interdit de Fait la Résidence Alternée*, 26 Les Petites Affiches 131 (2001).

[47] Iréne Théry, Couple, Filiation et Parenté Aujourd'hui: Le Droit Face aux Mutations de la Famille et de la Vie Privée (1998).

[48] Françoise Dekeuwer-Défossez, Rénover Le Droit De La Famille: Propositions Pour Un Droit Adapté Aux Réalités Et Aux Aspirations De Notre Temps (1999).

[49] *Id.* at 82.

[50] Assemblée Nationale, session of Jun. 14, 2001, J.O. 15 Juin 2001, Debat Ass. Nat. at 4251. For an examination of parental agreements since the March 4, 2002 reform, *see* Olivier Laouenan, *Les Conventions sur L'autorité Parentale Depuis la Loi du 4 Mars 2002*, 28 Juris Classeur Périodique (2003). *See also* Fulchiron, *supra* note 45.

[51] This position was expressed particularly by the Senate's reporter on the Bill, Mssr Béteille. He emphasized in the debate that it was important to be careful about the adoption of

In the result, a compromise position was adopted. Article 373-2-9 para 1 of the Civil Code now provides, as a result of the 2002 amendments, that the residence of a child may be fixed alternately at the domicile of each of the parents or at the domicile of one of them. The listing of alternating residence first, before sole residence, was intended to indicate encouragement of this option. At the insistence of the Senate, the same Article, in para 2, also provides that when alternating residence is not agreed on by the parties, the judge may order a temporary alternating residence arrangement to determine its workability. However, alternating residence may also be ordered without a trial period.[52]

Despite the emphasis on alternating residence in the debates leading up to the 2002 legislation, such arrangements remain uncommon in France. Figures published by the French Department of Justice in 2003 indicated that this kind of arrangement was not commonly sought.[53] Only 10 percent of the cases involving minor children included such a request, whether it originated from both parents or only one of them. In the context of consensual divorces, these requests were much more frequent (15.8 percent) than in the contested divorces, where they represented only 6.1 percent of the cases. In 80.7 percent of the cases, the alternating residence requests were jointly made by the parents. Where the parents disagreed on the issue, alternating residence was only ordered in 25 percent of the cases.[54]

In Belgium, the law was amended in 2006 to provide encouragement for alternating residence – indeed that emphasis was expressed in the title of the legislation.[55] A decade earlier, in a law of 13 April 1995,

---

an alternating residence schedule without the agreement of the parents because of the practical constraints in terms of housing, the constant collaboration needed, and the uncertainties of the experts about the consequences of alternating residence for the child's development. Rapport Sénat, 71, Session Ordinaire 2001–02, 18.

[52] Frédérique Granet, *Alternating Residence and Relocation: A View from France*, 4 UTRECHT L.R. 48, 51 (2008), citing a decision of the French Supreme Court, 14th February 2006. *See* also Hugues Fulchiron, *Custody and Separated Families: The Example of French Law*, 39 FAM. L. Q. 301, 307-08 (2005).

[53] DEPARTMENT OF JUSTICE, ETUDES ET STATISTIQUES JUSTICE, 23, LA RÉSIDENCE EN ALTERNANCE DES ENFANTS DE PARENTS SÉPARÉS (2003). For discussion, *see* Sylvie Cadolle, *La Transformation des Enjeux du Divorce: La Coparentalité à L'épreuve des Faits* 122 INFORMATIONS SOCIALES 136 (2005). Chaussebourg provides a higher figure for alternating residence in 2003: 12%: Laure Chaussebourg, *La Contribution à L'entretien et L'éducation des Enfants Mineurs dans les Jugements de Divorce* 93 INFOSTAT JUSTICE 1 (2007).

[54] *See also* Granet, *supra* note 52, at 51.

[55] The Law of 18 July 2006 is entitled "*Loi tendant à privilégier l'hébergement égalitaire de l'enfant dont les parents sont séparés et réglementant l'exécution forcée en matière d'hébergement d'enfant*" ("Law tending to favor equal residency for children of separated

Belgium had enacted reforms similar to France adopting the principle of *coparentalité* and endorsing as a norm the notion of continuing coparental authority (*autorité coparentale*) that is unaffected by parental separation. The language of "custody" was removed from the law. The law of 18 July 2006 provides that when parents are in dispute about residency, the court is required to examine "as a matter of priority" the possibility of ordering equal residency if one of the parents requests it to do so. The proviso is that if the court considers that equal residency is not the most appropriate arrangement, it may decide to order unequal residency.

This is not the same as saying that there is a presumption in favor of equal time. An equal time arrangement is not presumed to be in the best interests of the child; nonetheless, according to Belgian law, it is the first option that ought to be considered when parents cannot agree on the arrangements.

SHARED CARE IN AUSTRALIAN LAW

In Australia, there have also been significant legislative reforms to encourage shared parenting, through the Family Law Amendment (Shared Parental Responsibility) Act 2006. One of the objectives of the Family Law Act, as amended by that legislation, is to ensure that "children have the benefit of both of their parents having a meaningful involvement in their lives, to the maximum extent consistent with the best interests of the child."[56] This is importantly balanced by another object of the legislation, the need to protect children from physical or psychological harm from being subjected to, or exposed to, abuse, neglect, or family violence, which may necessitate restraints on contact by one parent. When determining the best interests of the child, the "benefit to the child of having a meaningful relationship with both of the child's parents" and protection from harm are the two primary considerations, consistent with the objects of the legislation. There are a large number of other factors that are described as "additional" considerations. It is the additional considerations that help

---

parents and regulating enforcement in child residency matters"): MONITEUR BELGE, 4 Septembre 2006. The legislation amended Article 374 of the Civil Code by adding a new para 2. For commentary, *see* YVES-HENRI LELEU, RIGHTS OF INDIVIDUALS AND FAMILIES, UPDATE: FILIATION AND PARENTAL AUTHORITY. THE LAWS OF 1 JULY 2006 AND 18 JULY 2006 (2007).

[56] Compare the laws in Illinois and Iowa. *See supra* notes 30–33.

determine how it is that the objectives of the legislation, and the primary considerations, are to be achieved.[57]

The emphasis on the meaningful involvement of both parents in the absence of violence or abuse does not translate into a presumption of shared parenting and still less of equal time. The most that the legislation imposes by way of presumed outcome is a presumption in favor of equal shared parental responsibility. This can be rebutted in cases where there is a history of violence or abuse. If there is equal shared parental responsibility, parents have a duty to consult, and to try to reach agreement, on major decisions such as education, health, religion, and changes in children's living arrangements, at least when that has a significant impact on the ability of the other parent to spend time with the child.

Even though equal shared parental responsibility says nothing, per se, about how time is to be allocated between parents – because the circumstances of separated families are so varied – there is at least strong encouragement in the legislation to consider shared parenting, and to do so positively. First of all, the court has a duty to consider whether an equal time arrangement is in the best interests of the child and reasonably practicable. If equal time is not appropriate, then the court must consider what is termed "substantial and significant time." This is defined in the following way:[58]

> a child will be taken to spend *substantial and significant time* with a parent only if:
>
> (a) the time the child spends with the parent includes both:
>   (i) days that fall on weekends and holidays; and
>   (ii) days that do not fall on weekends or holidays; and
> (b) the time the child spends with the parent allows the parent to be involved in:
>   (i) the child's daily routine; and
>   (ii) occasions and events that are of particular significance to the child; and
> (c) the time the child spends with the parent allows the child to be involved in occasions and events that are of special significance to the parent.

The best interests of the child remain the court's paramount concern. Furthermore, the arrangement must be "reasonably practicable." Australia's

---

[57] Patrick Parkinson, *Decision-Making about the Best Interests of the Child: The Impact of the Two Tiers*, 20 AUSTRALIAN J. FAM. L. 179 (2006).
[58] Family Law Act, 1975 s.65DAA(3).

final court of appeal, the High Court of Australia, has indicated that unless the court makes a finding of fact that the arrangement for equal time or substantial and significant time is reasonably practicable, the court has no power to make such an order.[59] Reasonable practicability is given meaning by a further subsection of the Act:[60]

> In determining ... whether it is reasonably practicable for a child to spend equal time, or substantial and significant time, with each of the child's parents, the court must have regard to:
> (a) how far apart the parents live from each other; and
> (b) the parents' current and future capacity to implement an arrangement for the child spending equal time, or substantial and significant time, with each of the parents; and
> (c) the parents' current and future capacity to communicate with each other and resolve difficulties that might arise in implementing an arrangement of that kind; and
> (d) the impact that an arrangement of that kind would have on the child; and
> (e) such other matters as the court considers relevant.

The Full Court of the Family Court of Australia has summarized the legislative intent as follows: [61]

> In our view, it can be fairly said there is a legislative intent evinced in favour of substantial involvement of both parents in their children's lives, both as to parental responsibility and as to time spent with the children, subject to the need to protect children from harm, from abuse and family violence and provided it is in their best interests and reasonably practicable.

This represents a very clear statement of the emphasis to be found in the legislation on shared parenting, and a rejection of the focus on the mother-child dyad as representing the norm for the postseparation family.

Origins

The origins of these reforms lie in the report of a Parliamentary Committee that was established by the then-Prime Minister, John Howard,[62] in June

---

[59] MRR v. GR (2010) 42 Fam. L.R. 531.
[60] Family Law Act, 1975 s.65DAA(5).
[61] Goode & Goode (2006) F.L.C. 93–286 para, 72.
[62] The Prime Minister indicated that he wanted to explore the option of a rebuttable presumption of "joint custody." He expressed concern that many boys growing up in single-parent families lack male role models both at home and in school until their teenage

2003 to explore the option of a rebuttable presumption that children will spend equal time with each parent. [63]

The Committee reported at the end of 2003, after a major public inquiry.[64] It received more than 1,700 submissions and collected evidence all over the country. The issue of a presumption of equal time also generated a great deal of discussion in the media.

One of the major concerns of the Committee was to get away from what they saw as the standard pattern of contact for nonresident parents of every other weekend and half the school holidays. This they dubbed the 80–20 rule, on the basis that it gave nonresident parents approximately 20 percent of the time with their children. The Committee wrote:[65]

> Out of court negotiated outcomes have favoured sole residence because they have been influenced by community perceptions, by experience of women as primary carers and by perceptions and outcomes in court decisions. This has been illustrated by suggestions in evidence to the committee that there is an 80–20 rule in the courts. This is the perception of a common outcome of, usually, the mother with sole residence and the father with alternate weekends and half the school holiday contact.

In the end, the Committee concluded against a presumption of equal time in its Report. The Committee's reasons for this were as follows: [66]

> Two aspects of an equal time template have been highlighted. First, there are dangers in a one size fits all approach to the diversity of family situations and the changing needs of children. Secondly, there are many practical hurdles for the majority of families to have to overcome if they are to equally share residence of children. Many have pointed to the increased risk of exposure of children to ongoing conflicted parental relationships and the instability that constant changing would create for children. Family friendly

---

years: Misha Schubert, *New law to share children in divorce*, THE AUSTRALIAN, Jun. 18, 2003, at 3.

The Government utilized the traditional language of custody despite the removal of the language of custody by the Family Law Reform Act, 1995. This Act adopted reforms on similar lines to the Children Act, 1989 (Eng.), with the terms "custody" and "access" being replaced by "residence" and "contact," and the rhetoric of "parental responsibility" driving out notions of parental rights.

[63] The Committee was also asked to consider whether changes should be made to the formula for calculating child support liabilities and issues concerning grandparents' rights to contact. For a commentary on the issues raised by the terms of reference, *see* Patrick Parkinson, *Custody Battle*, 18 ABOUT THE HOUSE 16 (2003).

[64] HOUSE OF REPRESENTATIVES STANDING COMMITTEE ON FAMILY & COMMUNITY AFFAIRS, PARLIAMENT OF AUSTRALIA, EVERY PICTURE TELLS A STORY: REPORT OF THE INQUIRY INTO CHILD CUSTODY ARRANGEMENTS IN THE EVENT OF FAMILY SEPARATION (2003).

[65] *Id.* at 21.   [66] *Id.* at 31.

workplaces are rare, as are the financial resources necessary to support two comparable households. Some parents lack the necessary child caring capabilities. Distance between households creates problems for transport and for schooling. Second families can also bring complications. Indigenous families' approach to parenting does not fit with the expectations of equal time.

Instead, it recommended in favor of equal parental responsibility. It made clear, however, that it felt the system should move away from any assumption that the normal pattern of contact should be every other weekend and half the school holidays. It considered that "the goal for the majority of families should be one of equality of care and responsibility along with substantially shared parenting time."[67]

Encouraging outcomes for "the majority" of families through legislation is not straightforward. Legislation is typically written in terms of guiding judges on how to exercise their discretion if matters have to be decided by the Court following a trial. The cases that result in a judicial determination are atypical; only about 6 percent of all parenting cases that are commenced in the courts end up in a judgment following a trial.[68]

Richard Chisholm has posited that the population of parents who separate can be divided into three groups when it comes to thinking about how legislation concerning postseparation parenting should be written.[69] There are those who litigate, those who sort out their parenting issues without reference to the law at all, and a group in the middle, who, at some level or another, engage with the family law system in resolving their disputes and "bargain in the shadow of the law."

The Committee saw legislation as a means of reaching this third group by imposing obligations not only on courts but on other professionals involved in helping resolve parenting disputes. The Committee wrote:[70]

> Legislation can have an educative effect on the separating population outside the context of court decisions, if its messages are clear, it is accessible to the general public and well understood by those who offer assistance under it.

---

[67] *Id.* at 30.   [68] *Id.* at 6–7.

[69] The Hon Justice Richard Chisholm, *Softening the Blow – Changing Custody to Residence*, Paper given at The Third World Congress on Family Law and Children's Rights, Bath, England, 2001, http://www.childjustice.org/docs/chisholm2001.pdf

[70] House of Rep. Standing Committee on Family & Community Affairs, *supra* note 66, para 2.74.

It recommended that the legislation should require mediators, counselors, and legal advisers to assist parents who will share parental responsibility to first consider a starting point of equal time, where practicable.[71] This eventually made its way into the legislation.

After much further deliberation and consideration by the government, the 2006 legislation emerged to give expression to the Committee's intent. It came into force on July 1, 2006.

Evaluating the 2006 Reforms

Aware that the 2006 reforms represented a significant change in social policy, the government commissioned a comprehensive research program to examine the outcomes of the reforms. The evaluation was conducted by the Australian Institute of Family Studies (AIFS) and reported at the end of 2009.[72]

The research indicates that there has been an acceleration of the preexisting trend toward shared care. In the late 1990s, shared care was a comparatively rare phenomenon in Australia. In 1997, for example, the Australian Bureau of Statistics (ABS) recorded that only 3 percent of children under eighteen years of age whose parents lived apart were in a shared care arrangement in which each parent cared for the child at least 30 percent of the time.[73] The proportion of children in shared care has nonetheless been rising significantly since that time. By 2003, the ABS was reporting that 6 percent of children were in shared care.[74] A study of the first wave of the Household, Income and Labour Dynamics in Australia (HILDA) Survey found even higher figures of shared care when including daytime contact. Sixteen percent of children who saw their fathers did so on at least 30 percent of the days of the year, but only 7 percent stayed overnight at least 30 percent of the time.[75]

After the 2006 reforms, there was certainly a significant increase in substantially shared care. The Australian Institute of Family Studies' evaluation found that among people who had separated since 2006,

---

[71] *Id.* Recommendation 5.   [72] KASPIEW ET AL., *supra* note 26.

[73] AUSTRALIAN BUREAU OF STATISTICS, Cat No. 4442.0, FAMILY CHARACTERISTICS SURVEY 1997, (1998).

[74] AUSTRALIAN BUREAU OF STATISTICS, Cat No. 4442.0, FAMILY CHARACTERISTICS SURVEY 2003, (2004).

[75] Patrick Parkinson & Bruce Smyth, *When the Difference Is Night & Day: Some Empirical Insights into Patterns of Parent–child Contact after Separation,* Paper presented at the 8th Australian Institute of Family Studies Conference, Melbourne, 2003, http://www.aifs. gov.au/institute/afrc8/papers.html#p

16 percent had a shared care arrangement of 35 percent of nights or more. Seven percent had an equal time arrangement.[76] These were people who have recently separated. Across the population of separated parents, including those who separated many years ago, the levels of shared care are lower. In 2006–07, nearly 8 percent of children who had a parent living elsewhere had a shared care arrangement of 35 percent of nights or more with each parent. Four percent were in an equal time arrangement.[77]

There has also been a substantial increase in shared care in judicially determined cases.[78] Shared care (35–65 percent with each parent) rose from 4 percent to 33.9 percent of cases where contact arrangements were specified. Prior to the 2006 reforms, 65.2 percent of the mothers had primary care. After the reforms, it was 47.8 percent – a 26.7 percent decrease as a proportion of the previous levels of maternal primary care. Fathers in 30.8 percent of cases had primary care prior to the reforms, and this dropped to 18.3 percent afterward – a 40.6 percent decrease as a proportion of the previous levels of paternal primary care. It is clear then that the reforms have had a major impact on the outcomes of judicially determined cases, with many more shared care arrangements being made, at the expense of both maternal and paternal primary care, but, to a greater extent, at the expense of paternal primary care. It appears then that fathers may have more to lose, proportionately, than mothers by legislation that encourages judges to consider shared parenting arrangements.

These court statistics also suggest that shared care may be emerging as a court-imposed compromise when both parents seek primary care awards in their favor. This raises issues of how well the parents are likely to be able to manage a shared care arrangement when they have been unable to work out such a compromise for themselves.

Generally, the evaluation of shared care arrangements was quite positive. The results from the evaluation by the AIFS indicated that children in shared care arrangements (defined as 35 percent of nights with each parent or more) were doing as well as, or better than, children who were in primary mother care. Fathers reported that children in shared care arrangements had higher levels of well-being based on a range of standardized measures, than children who were primarily in maternal care. Mothers reported that the well-being of children in these two groups did not differ significantly.[79] In another study, based on a survey of more than 1,000

---

[76] KASPIEW ET AL., *supra* note 26, at 119.
[77] CASHMORE ET AL., *supra* note 25, at 18.
[78] KASPIEW ET AL., *supra* note 26, at 132–33.   [79] *Id.* at 267.

separated parents, over one-third of whom had a shared care arrangement, fathers with shared care arrangements reported that children were faring better than in other forms of care, after controlling for a range of other factors, whereas mothers' reports did not differ significantly between shared care and moderate levels of care by the nonresident parent.[80]

One of the major objections to the encouragement of shared care in Australia is that it exposes mothers and children to a greater risk of violence and abuse than if there was no such encouragement toward shared care.[81] This does not necessarily arise from the legislation itself, which makes clear that the presumption of equal shared parental responsibility does not apply if there are reasonable grounds to believe that a parent of the child (or a person who lives with a parent of the child) has engaged in abuse of the child or family violence (s.61DA(2)). However, the issue is that women in particular will feel pressured into accepting a shared care arrangement when they have significant safety concerns for themselves or their children because they feel the system is weighted in favor of shared care.

The AIFS evaluation certainly indicates grounds for concern. It found that families in which there was a reported history of physical violence or emotional abuse were as likely to have shared care time arrangements as those where there were no such reports.[82] However, it is not only mothers in shared care arrangements who have safety concerns. Indeed, while 16 percent of mothers who reported equal time arrangements had concerns about their own safety or the safety of the child in the other parent's care, the percentage of fathers expressing such concerns was higher (17.9 percent).

Not all of these concerns relate to family violence or child abuse perpetrated by the other parent. As the researchers pointed out, the safety concerns could also be about harm inflicted by someone other than the other parent, such as a new partner or a relative. Nonetheless, the vast majority of parents with safety concerns indicated that they had experienced physical violence or emotional abuse.[83]

---

[80] CASHMORE ET AL., *supra* note 25.

[81] Zoe Rathus, *Shifting the Gaze: Will Past Violence Be Silenced by a Further Shift of the Gaze to the Future under the New Family Law System?*, 21 AUSTRALIAN J. FAM. L. 87 (2007); Tracey de Simone, *The Friendly Parent Provisions in Australian Family Law – How Friendly Will You Need to Be?*, 22 AUSTRALIAN J. FAM. L. 56 (2008).

[82] KASPIEW ET AL., *supra* note 26, at 164–65.

[83] *Id.* at 166.

The researchers found that mothers who reported safety concerns also reported lower child well-being than for children whose mothers did not indicate any safety concerns. This was true irrespective of the care time arrangement, but when children were in shared care time arrangements and the mother had safety concerns, the children fared worse than those who were living primarily with their mother.[84]

SHARED PARENTING AND HIGH-CONFLICT FAMILIES

It may be that where shared care is imposed as a compromise in cases that are litigated through to trial, children are exposed to higher levels of conflict than would have been the case if a clearer choice between maternal and paternal care had been made. Writing in the Australian context, Jennifer McIntosh, a clinical psychologist, observes:[85]

> The attributes that increase the likelihood of shared arrangements working smoothly ... are not typically characteristic of parents who litigate or who otherwise require significant support to determine and administer their post-separation parenting plans.

Although it is unlikely that many imposed parenting arrangements work better than arrangements that the parties have agreed to themselves, there may be particular issues about imposed shared care because of the level of cooperation required to make it work, and the level of interaction between parents.

McIntosh and former Family Court judge Richard Chisholm expressed particular caution about shared care arrangements in high-conflict families, based on findings concerning children's well-being in McIntosh's clinical sample.[86] McIntosh found that shared care was a risk factor for poor mental health where there was high, ongoing conflict between parents. Conversely, children seemed most likely to benefit from shared care arrangements where there were low levels of hostility. Similar findings have been reached in another study. Mothers with shared care arrangements who also reported high conflict (as compared with just some conflict) perceived their children to be doing much

---

[84] *Id.* at 270.
[85] Jennifer McIntosh, *Legislating for Shared Parenting: Exploring Some Underlying Assumptions*, 47 FAM. CT REV. 389, 393 (2009).
[86] Jennifer McIntosh & Richard Chisholm, *Cautionary Notes on the Shared Care of Children in Conflicted Parental Separation*, 14 J. FAM. STUD. 37 (2008).

less well than mothers who had primary maternal care but also reported high conflict.[87]

While high levels of conflict are problematic for children whatever the amount of time the nonresident parent spends with the children, it is particularly problematic in shared care arrangements, given the greater degree of interaction between parents that is typically involved. For that reason, it is to be expected that a shared care arrangement may add to the burdens these children suffer.

Evidence from the United States also suggests that shared care arrangements in the context of high conflict may not be very durable. Margo Melli and her colleagues in Wisconsin, in their research on shared parenting arrangements, examined differences between equal time arrangements and unequal time arrangements.[88] The average figures for 1980–92 were 6.3 percent equal time arrangements and 5 percent for unequal time (in over 80 percent of which, the mother was the primary residential parent). The unequal time arrangements were usually between 30 percent and 39 percent of the time to the parent who was not the primary caregiver. They found significant differences between these two groups. The equal time arrangement families appeared to have sorted out this arrangement fairly amicably. The unequal time families were much more likely to have reached such a compromise after protracted legal conflict. This group had the highest incidence of returns to court of any of the custody arrangements in the study.

Not all conflict between parents is problematic for children; it is how conflict is resolved that matters.[89] Where there are destructive patterns of conflict, there are often dynamics that ought to indicate that children are not the focus of the arrangement. The desire of one parent for an equal time arrangement may be driven by concerns about fairness to that parent, or equality, rather than the needs or interests of the children. It may also be motivated by a desire to control or punish the other parent. These motivations do not assist in creating the conditions that are necessary to make an equal time arrangement work, which include a child-focused orientation and flexibility rather than rigidity in the arrangements.

[87] CASHMORE ET AL, *supra* note 25, at 88–89.

[88] Melli et al., *supra* note 14.

[89] Kathleen McCoy, Mark Cummings, & Patrick Davies, *Constructive and Destructive Marital Conflict, Emotional Security and Children's Prosocial Behavior*, 50 J. CHILD PSYCHOLOGY & PSYCHIATRY 270 (2009).

CHILDREN'S VIEWS ON EQUAL TIME ARRANGEMENTS

Interviews with children and young people concerning shared care indicate both pros and cons in such arrangements. It does seem that an equal time arrangement is something that many children and young people might choose for themselves. An Australian study of the views of sixty young people ages twelve to nineteen found that when the young people were asked about how parents should divide looking after children when they divorce, the most common responses were that it should be "equal," or "half and half," or fair.[90] An American study of college students also found a very high level of support for shared care.[91] When asked what they thought would be the best living arrangement for children after divorce, 70 percent said an equal time arrangement was optimal. There were no significant differences between men and women in their responses.[92] However, only slightly more than 20 percent of the respondents wanted equal time given their particular family circumstances.[93]

Whereas in that study, 93 percent of the eighty young adults who had actually lived in an equal time arrangement believed it was best,[94] research studies in Britain, Sweden, and Australia have found that children in equal time parenting arrangements have a more diverse range of reactions to it.

In interviews with thirty children and young people in shared care arrangements in Britain, Smart and colleagues found that for some children, where the arrangement was inflexible and the idea of "equal time" was invested with heavy ideological or emotional significance by a parent, it could be very oppressive and constricting. This was particularly so if the parents were rigid in maintaining the schedule and not focused

---

[90] Patrick Parkinson, Judith Cashmore, & Judi Single, *Adolescents' Views on the Fairness of Parenting and Financial Arrangements After Separation*, 43 FAM. CT REV. 430 (2005).

[91] William Fabricius & Jeff Hall, *Young Adults' Perspectives on Divorce: Living Arrangements*, 38 FAM. & CONCIL. CTS. REV. 446 (2000).

[92] *Id.* at 453–54.

[93] *Id.* at 457. It was more common for respondents to indicate that they would have liked to have lived with their mother while seeing their father a lot of the time (*id.* at 452).

[94] *Id.* at 454. The number of students who had lived in equal time arrangements is reported in a later review of the research. William Fabricius, *Listening to Children of Divorce: New Findings That Diverge from Wallerstein, Lewis and Blakeslee*, 52 FAM. REL. 385, 387 (2003).

on the needs of the children. For others, the arrangement worked very well and provided benefits not only in having the regular involvement of both parents, but also in giving chances for a brief "sabbatical" in the relationship with each of them as the child moved from one household to the other.[95]

In a follow-up of these children three-to-four years later, Smart identified three factors that made the difference between successful and unsuccessful shared care arrangements.[96] These were: a) whether the arrangement was based on the needs and wishes of the parents or those of the children; b) whether the arrangements were flexible enough to accommodate changing needs and circumstances; and c) whether the children felt equally "at home" in both of their parents' homes.

A Swedish study involving responses from twenty-two young people in shared care arrangements also found a range of reactions to shared care.[97] The interviewees were generally satisfied with the living arrangements, with interviewees valuing the opportunity to spend a great deal of time with both parents. However, they also indicated a downside, in particular the feeling of rootlessness deriving from the need to pack up and move between homes. Some would have preferred to have one primary abode but feared to say so for fear of upsetting whichever parent they did not want to live with. Like the children and young people in the study by Smart et al., some young people also expressed frustration at the lack of flexibility, feeling ruled by fixed schedules. The young people who were most satisfied with an equal time arrangement were those who had parents who were flexible, could cooperate, and lived near each other.[98]

An Australian study utilized responses by 136 children and young people to an online survey carried on various Web sites for children seeking help. About 20 percent were in shared care arrangements. There

---

[95] CAROL SMART, BREN NEALE, & AMANDA WADE, THE CHANGING EXPERIENCE OF CHILDHOOD: FAMILIES AND DIVORCE (2001); Carol Smart, *From Children's Shoes to Children's Voices*, 40 FAM. CT REV. 307 (2002); Bren Neale, Jennifer Flowerdew & Carol Smart, *Drifting Towards Shared Residence?*, 33 FAM. L. 904 (2003).

[96] Carol Smart, *Equal Shares: Rights for Fathers or Recognition for Children?*, 24 CRITICAL SOCIAL POLICY 484 (2004).

[97] MARGARETA CARLBERG, ANNA HARDY, EVA ELFVER-LINDSTRÖM, & SUZANNE JULIN, VÄXELVIS BOENDE: ATT BO HOS BÅDE PAPPA OCH MAMMA FAST DE INTE BOR TILLSAMMANS (2004). (Alternating residency: living with both mother and father even though they do not live together) (trans. Hugh Storlien).

[98] *Id.* at 28–31.

was no significant difference in children's reported happiness with their arrangements between those in shared care and those living mostly with one parent. What mattered most to children in shared care and other parenting arrangements was having enough good time with both parents – where those relationships were satisfactory – and having some choice and flexibility in the parenting arrangements.[99]

SHARED CARE AND TRADITIONAL PARENTING ARRANGEMENTS AFTER SEPARATION

Shared care will always be a minority parenting arrangement. Shared care is contra-indicated with infants and toddlers, if it involves significant periods of separation from the child's primary caregiver, thereby disrupting a secure attachment. Shared care probably begins to be compatible with a child's developmental needs when he or she reaches school age.[100] With young children, therefore, shared care is not an appropriate option.

There are many other nonresident parents for whom the sole custody/visitation model and its equivalents is the only realistic option. Fathers whose orientation toward the world of work makes it difficult to take on the primary care of children for significant periods of time, especially during school holidays, are likely to recognize the sense in a traditional custody/visitation arrangement. So too may those fathers whose parenting skills are insufficiently developed to make them satisfactory custodians of children for long periods of time following separation. Geographical distance between homes when one or other parent has relocated after separation may make extensive contact impractical. Lack of suitable accommodation for the children may also limit the capacity of the nonresident parent to have the children stay overnight. Shared parenting might be an optimal arrangement for some families if it could

---

[99] CASHMORE ET AL., *supra* note 25, at 111–37.

[100] Jennifer McIntosh, Bruce Smyth, Margaret Kelaher, Yvonne Wells, Caroline Long, *Post-separation Parenting Arrangements and Developmental Outcomes for Infants and Children,* (2010), http://www.ag.gov.au/www/agd/agd. nsf/Page/Families_FamilyRelationshipServicesOverviewofPrograms_ ResearchProjectsonSharedCareParentingandFamilyViolence. *See also* Joan Kelly & Michael Lamb, *Using Child Development Research to Make Appropriate Custody and Access Decisions for Young Children,* 38 FAM. & CONCIL. CTS. REV. 297 (2000); Marsha Kline Pruett, Rachel Ebling & Glendessa Insabella, *Parenting Plans and Visitation: Critical aspects of Parenting plans for Young Children: Interjecting Data into the Debate about Overnights.* 42 FAM. CT REV. 39 (2004).

be managed, but the logistics and expense of doing so may mean it is out of the reach of many separated parents. For these reasons, there can be no one-size-fits-all policy for postseparation parenting.[101] Nonetheless, shared parenting continues to grow in popularity, and laws that at least encourage this option seem to be gaining ground.

---

[101] French scholars Benoit Bastard and Laura Cardia-Vonèche argue that French law fails to acknowledge pluralism in relation to the circumstances of divorced parents. Benoit Bastard & Laura Cardia-Vonèche, *Children Contacts in France: An Overview of the Law, Professional Practice and Current Debates*, 7, Paper given at the European Conference of the Working Group for Comparative Study of Legal Professions, Berder, June 30–July 3, 2004, at 4.

PART THREE

Parents Forever?

Issues about Postseparation Parenting

6

Violence, Abuse, and Postseparation Parenting

Happy families do not break up, and while every unhappy family may be unhappy in its own way,[1] violence and various forms of abuse are common features of separated families. Indeed, research evidence from large-scale community or national surveys has established that domestic violence is a pervasive and common problem in all intimate relationships. A general population survey in Canada found that 8.6 percent of women and 7 percent of men reported some kind of physical abuse from a current or ex-partner within the last five years. Women reported much more severe abuse.[2] Levels of abuse and violence are particularly high in intimate relationships between younger people. In one major study in New Zealand, domestic conflict was present in 70 percent of the intimate relationships of twenty-five-year-olds, with this conflict ranging from minor psychological abuse to severe assault.[3]

It is therefore unsurprising that a history of violence and abuse should be common among families who have separated. The pervasiveness of violence and abuse among parents who have separated is evident in Australian research. Sheehan and Smyth, reporting on interviews with a general population of separated parents, found that 65 percent of women and 55 percent of men indicated that they had experienced violence against them within the criminal law definition of assault. Fifty-three percent of

---

[1] "Happy families are all alike; every unhappy family is unhappy in its own way". LEO TOLSTOY, ANNA KARENINA, Chapter 1.

[2] For Canadian research, see Sarah Romans, Tonia Forte, Marsha Cohen, Janice Du Mont, & Ilene Hyman, *Who Is Most at Risk for Intimate Partner Violence? A Canadian Population-Based Study*, 22 J. INTERPERSONAL VIOLENCE 1495 (2007).

[3] These were findings from the longitudinal Christchurch Health and Development Study. David Fergusson, John Horwood, & Elizabeth Ridder, *Partner Violence and Mental Health Outcomes in a New Zealand Birth Cohort*, 67 J. MARRIAGE & FAM. 1103 (2005).

women and 24 percent of men reported violence or threats of violence that induced fear.[4] Fourteen percent of women, and 3 percent of men reported injuries resulting from violence that required medical treatment.

Parents who need the assistance of the courts and related services to resolve their disputes are likely to report particularly high levels of violence and abuse. This is evident, for example, in a study of 864 former couples using free, court-mandated mediation in Arizona.[5] Asked about that relationship in the last twelve months, 58 percent of women and 54 percent of men reported some physical abuse, such as pushing, shoving, punching, biting, or scratching. Sixty-two percent of women and 50 percent of men reported escalated abuse. Escalated abuse included such violence as broken bones, choking, and threats of, or actual use of weapons, strangling, or suffocating. Fifty-six percent of women and 29 percent of men reported sexual abuse. Ninety-eight percent of women and 97 percent of men reported at least one incident of psychological abuse in the last twelve months, defined by such items as putting the person down or insulting them or shaming them in front of others. Although respondents did not indicate that this abuse was a frequent or regular occurrence,[6] the high incidence of complaints of abuse in a court-mandated cohort indicates how commonly litigants in family law disputes may be able to point to behavior that falls within the definition of violence or abuse in family law statutes – and particularly in those that have a broad definition that includes emotional abuse, verbal abuse, economic abuse, and social isolation within the definition of violence.[7]

---

[4]   Grania Sheehan & Bruce Smyth, *Spousal Violence and Post-Separation Financial Outcomes*, 14 AUSTRALIAN J. FAM. L. 102 (2000).

[5]   Connie Beck, Michele Walsh, & Rose Weston, *Analysis of Mediation Agreements of Families Reporting Specific Types of Intimate Partner Abuse*, 47 FAM. CT REV. 401 (2009).

[6]   The frequency was measured on a scale from 0–6, 0 meaning it had not occurred, 1 meaning it occurred very rarely, and 2 meaning it occurred a little of the time. The scale rose to 6, meaning all of the time. Apart from psychological abuse, the mean scores for both men and women were all below 0.65 on that 6 point scale, that is, well below "very rarely." As this study shows, findings about the quantity of people reporting abuse in any given cohort should not be taken to imply that such incidents were frequent occurrences.

[7]   This is, for example, a feature of some Australian statutes concerning restraining orders. For example, Victoria's Family Violence Protection Act, 2008, s.5 offers a broad definition of family violence that includes emotional, psychological, and economic abuse. Economic abuse includes behavior that unreasonably controls another person without that person's consent, in a way that denies that person the economic or financial autonomy the person would have had but for that behavior (s.6). Emotional or psychological abuse includes behavior that is "offensive to the other person" or that prevents a person from making or keeping connections with the person's family, friends, or culture (s.7). In the Australian Capital Territory, where Canberra is located, conduct offensive to a relevant person is

Family violence, in its many different facets, is a dark reality of family life. How should it be dealt with in the age of the enduring family? Do the levels of violence and abuse among the population who have separated indicate that the idea of the enduring family is just too altruistic and unrealistic?

Devising appropriate laws and policies in this area is complicated. There is now an extensive literature on the relevance of domestic violence to decision making on postseparation parenting.[8] Although there has been a tendency in the past to treat all domestic violence as if it were male-perpetrated violence involving subjugation and control, a pervasive theme that is now emerging is the need to differentiate between different patterns of violence in terms of the risk to parents and children, and the likelihood that parent-child contact can be made safe for the future.[9] This takes account of the heterogeneity, and differences in the severity, of violent episodes in intimate partner relationships, only some of which are characterized by male dominance and the use of power and control to subjugate women.

PATTERNS OF VIOLENCE WITHIN FAMILIES

Thirty years of research on domestic violence has now established that there is a variety of different patterns of violent conflict between intimate

also deemed to be "domestic violence." Domestic Violence and Protection Orders Act, 2008, s. 13(1). *See also* Family Violence Act, 2004, s. 7 (Tasmania).

[8]   *See e.g.* Naomi Cahn, *Civil Images of Battered Women: The Impact of Domestic Violence on Child Custody Decisions*, 44 VANDERBILT L.R. 1041 (1991); Mildred Pagelow, *Effects of Domestic Violence on Children and Their Consequences for Custody and Visitation Agreements*, 7 MEDIATION Q. 347 (1990); MARIANNE HESTER & LORRAINE RADFORD, DOMESTIC VIOLENCE AND CHILD CONTACT ARRANGEMENTS IN ENGLAND AND DENMARK (1996); Carol Smart & Bren Neale, *Arguments against Virtue – Must Contact Be Enforced?*, 27 FAM. L. 332 (1997); Martha Fineman, *Domestic Violence, Custody and Visitation*, 36 FAM. L.Q. 211 (2002); PETER JAFFE, NANCY LEMON, & SAMANTHA POISSON, CHILD CUSTODY AND DOMESTIC VIOLENCE: A CALL FOR SAFETY AND ACCOUNTABILITY (2003); Miranda Kaye, Julie Stubbs, & Julia Tolmie, *Domestic Violence, Separation and Parenting: Negotiating Safety Using Legal Processes*, 15 CURRENT ISSUES IN CRIMINAL JUSTICE 73 (2003); Prentice White, *You May Never See Your Child Again: Adjusting the Batterer's Visitation Rights to Protect Children from Future Abuse*, 13 AM. U. J. GENDER, SOCIAL POLICY & L. 327 (2005).

[9]   Peter Jaffe, Janet Johnston, Claire Crooks & Nicholas Bala, *Custody Disputes Involving Allegations of Domestic Violence: The Need for Differentiated Approaches to Parenting Plans*, 46 FAM. CT REV. 500 (2008); Bruce Smyth, Lawrie Moloney, Ruth Weston, Nick Richardson, Lixia Qu, & Matthew Gray, *Allegations of Family Violence and Child Abuse in Children's Proceedings: A Pre-Reform Empirical Snapshot*, 21 AUSTRALIAN J. FAM. L. 252 (2007); Janet Johnston, *Domestic Violence and Parent-Child Relationships in Families Disputing Custody*, 9 AUSTRALIAN J. FAM. L. 12 (1995).

partners.[10] The terminology used by researchers varies, but broadly they describe similar categorizations of violent conflict within intimate relationships. The research also includes both heterosexual and same-sex relationships.[11] There are differences of view as to whether intimate partner violence is best explained by typologies or should rather be seen as a continuum from mild conflict to severe controlling violence and homicide.[12] These differences of conceptualization do not diminish the level of consensus among social science researchers concerning the heterogeneity of what is termed "family violence."

Four types of violence are commonly described in the literature, sometimes under different names. These are coercive controlling violence, violence driven by conflict, violent resistance, and separation-instigated violence. These categorizations are useful for understanding the dynamics of individual family relationships and identifying the degree of risk involved in proposed arrangements for parenting after separation, but it should not be thought that they are entirely discrete categories. Each intimate partner relationship has its own unique features, and there is some continuity between types.[13]

Coercive Controlling Violence

When domestic violence first emerged into public and professional consciousness through the efforts of the women's movement, domestic

[10] Janet Johnston & Linda Campbell, *A Clinical Typology of Interparental Violence in Disputed-Custody Divorces*, 63 AM. J. ORTHOPSYCHIATRY 190 (1993); Joan Kelly & Michael Johnson, *Differentiation among Types of Intimate Partner Violence: Research Update and Implication for Interventions*, 46 FAM. CT REV. 476 (2008); Nancy Ver Steegh, *Differentiating Types of Domestic Violence: Implications for Child Custody*, 65 LOUISIANA L. R. 1379 (2005); Stacey Williams & Irene Frieze, *Patterns of Violent Relationships, Psychological Distress, and Marital Satisfaction in a National Sample of Men and Women*, 52 SEX ROLES 771 (2005).

[11] On violence in gay and lesbian relationships, *see e.g.* Mary Eaton, *Abuse by Any Other Name: Feminism, Difference, and Intra-Lesbian Violence, in* MARTHA FINEMAN & ROXANNE MYKITIUK, THE PUBLIC NATURE OF PRIVATE VIOLENCE 195 (1994); CLAIRE RENZETTI & CHARLES MILEY, VIOLENCE IN GAY AND LESBIAN DOMESTIC PARTNERSHIPS (1996); Gail Mason, *Boundaries of Sexuality: Lesbian Experience and Feminist Discourse on Violence Against Women*, 7 AUSTRALASIAN GAY & LESBIAN L. J. 41 (1997); Dena Hassouneh & Nancy Glass, *The Influence of Gender Role Stereotyping on Women's Experiences of Female Same-Sex Intimate Partner Violence*, 14 VIOLENCE AGAINST WOMEN 310 (2008).

[12] Michael Johnson, *Domestic Violence: It's Not About Gender—Or Is It?*, 67 J. MARRIAGE & FAM. 1126 (2005); David Fergusson, John Horwood, & Elizabeth Ridder, *Response to Johnson*, 67 J. MARRIAGE & FAM. 1131 (2005).

[13] Janet Johnson, *Response to Clare Dalton's "When Paradigms Collide: Protecting Battered Parents and Their Children in the Family Court System,"* 37 FAM. & CONCIL. CTS REV. 422, 426 (1999).

violence was primarily understood in terms of wife battering and was associated with a variety of forms of intimidation and control that extended beyond physical violence or the threat of it. Women who report coercive controlling violence report a pattern of intimidation, social isolation, and control, as well as assault. Behaviors include economic control, verbal abuse, and emotional abuse. This form of coercive controlling violence,[14] or "intimate terrorism," as Johnson has called it,[15] involves male perpetrators and female victims almost without exception. The period around separation can be a particularly dangerous time for women who are victims of coercive controlling violence.[16]

This type of violence certainly justifies a presumption against joint custody and, in the most serious cases, a presumption against any contact with the nonresident parent at all.[17] One indication of coercive controlling violence is litigation abuse. Repeated use of the court system may be a means by which a violent partner seeks to maintain control or to reassert it or as a means of harassment or oppression of primary caregivers.[18] For this reason, continuing recourse to the courts to resolve parenting disputes ought to be a reason to regard joint parental responsibility as unworkable, leading to an order for sole custody or its equivalent.

Intimate Partner Conflict and Violence

Whereas the patterns of violence most often seen by police, women's refuge workers, and hospital emergency wards is coercive controlling violence, in

---

[14] Mary Ann Dutton & Lisa Goodman, *Coercion in Intimate Partner Violence: Toward a New Conceptualization*, 52 SEX ROLES 743 (2005).

[15] Michael Johnson, *Conflict and Control: Gender Symmetry and Asymmetry in Domestic Violence*, 12 VIOLENCE AGAINST WOMEN 1003 (2006). He used to call it "patriarchal" terrorism. *See* Michael Johnson, *Patriarchal Terrorism and Common Couple Violence: Two Forms of Violence Against Women*, 57 J. MARRIAGE & FAM. 283 (1995). The use of the language of "terrorism" in relation to domestic violence may be traced to LEWIS OKUN, WOMAN ABUSE: FACTS REPLACING MYTHS (l986), who used the term "conjugal terrorism."

[16] Margo Wilson & Martin Daly, *Spousal Homicide Risk and Estrangement*, 8 VIOLENCE & VICTIMS 3 (1993); PATRICIA EASTEAL, KILLING THE BELOVED: HOMICIDE BETWEEN ADULT SEXUAL INTIMATES 85–87 (1993); Holly Johnson & Tina Hotton, *Losing Control: Homicide Risk in Estranged and Intact Intimate Relationships*, 7 HOMICIDE STUD. 58 (2003).

[17] Helen Rhoades, *The 'No Contact Mother': Reconstructions of Motherhood in the Era of the 'New Father'*, 16 INT'L J. L. POL'Y & FAM. 71 (2002).

[18] LORRAINE RADFORD & MARIANNE HESTER, MOTHERING THROUGH DOMESTIC VIOLENCE (2006) Ch. 6; HELEN RHOADES, REGINA GRAYCAR, & MARGARET HARRISON, THE FAMILY LAW REFORM ACT 1995: THE FIRST THREE YEARS 23 (2000). *See also* The Hon. Justice Brenda Hale, *The View from Court*, 11 CHILD & FAM. L.Q. 377 (1999).

general community studies, the patterns of violent conflict in families often involve different dynamics. The majority of the violence revealed in such community studies is not coercive controlling violence, but what researchers have variously classified as "conflict instigated violence,"[19] "common couple violence,"[20] "situational couple violence,"[21] or, in the language of the U.S. Wingspread Conference, "violence driven by conflict."[22] The Wingspread Conference defined this as follows:[23]

> This type of violence takes place when an unresolved disagreement spirals into a violent incident, but the violence is not part of a larger pattern of coercive control. It may be initiated by either the male or female partner. However, female victims are more likely to suffer negative consequences, including injury, than are men.

Violence driven by conflict typically involves intimate partners losing control rather than using violence to assert it.[24] In their anger, either partner or both may use verbal abuse or emotional abuse. Arguments may escalate into hitting, punching, and throwing things,[25] but the incidence of injuries resulting from this is not nearly as great as would be seen in coercive controlling violence.[26] Nor are the relational dynamics the same. Women who report coercive controlling violence report a pattern of intimidation, isolation, and control, as well as assault. For this reason, Ellis and Stuckless have drawn the fundamental distinction between *conflict-initiated* and *control-initiated* violence.[27]

The language of "victim" and "perpetrator," "abused parent" and "violent parent" does not easily fit with the nature of violence driven by conflict and neither does an analysis that insists that only one gender

---

[19] Jaffe et al., *supra* note 9.
[20] Johnson, *supra* note 12, at 1126.
[21] Kelly & Johnson, *supra* note 10.
[22] Nancy Ver Steegh & Clare Dalton, *Report from the Wingspread Conference on Domestic Violence and Family Court*, 46 FAM. CT REV. 454 (2008).
[23] *Id.* at 458.
[24] MICHAEL JOHNSON, A TYPOLOGY OF DOMESTIC VIOLENCE: INTIMATE TERRORISM, VIOLENT RESISTANCE, AND SITUATIONAL COUPLE VIOLENCE (2008) Ch. 4.
[25] Michael Johnson & Kathleen Ferraro, *Research on Domestic Violence in the 1990s: Making Distinctions*, 62 J. MARRIAGE & FAM. 948, 949 (2000).
[26] Nicola Graham-Kevan & John Archer, *Physical Aggression and Control in Heterosexual Relationships: The Effect of Sampling Procedure*, 18 VIOLENCE AND VICTIMS 181 (2003); Kelly & Johnson *supra* note 10, at 481.
[27] DESMOND ELLIS & NOREEN STUCKLESS, MEDIATING AND NEGOTIATING MARITAL CONFLICTS (1996).

is responsible,[28] even if the patterns of female violence within intimate partnerships are different from male violence.[29]

Whereas violence driven by conflict predominates in general community studies, coercive controlling violence is much more common in cases that go to court and for women in domestic violence shelters. Michael Johnson, reviewing Frieze's U.S. data from the 1970s[30] derived from the general community, courts, and women's shelters, classified the patterns of violence within that study in accordance with four categorizations: mutual violent control, intimate terrorism, violent resistance, and situational couple violence. Focusing on wives' reports of violence by husbands, he reported that 89 percent of the violence in a general community sample was best characterized as situational couple violence, and 11 percent was intimate terrorism. In the court sample, only 29 percent of the violence was situational couple violence and 68 percent was intimate terrorism. In the sample of women who had been in shelters, 19 percent of the violence was situational couple violence and 79 percent was intimate terrorism.[31]

---

[28] The research evidence from general population studies make it clear that both women and men engage in physically aggressive altercations in intimate relationships. In a meta-analysis of eighty-two studies, it was found that women were slightly more aggressive than men. John Archer, *Sex Differences in Aggression between Heterosexual Partners: A Meta-analytic Review*, 126 PSYCHOLOGICAL BULLETIN 651 (2000). *See also* Williams & Frieze, *supra* note 10. Although many of these studies rely on use of the Conflict Tactics Scale (Murray Straus, *Measuring Intrafamily Conflict and Violence: The Conflict Tactics [CT] Scales*, 41 J. MARRIAGE & FAM 75 [1979]), the same patterns are discerned using other measures. *See e.g.* Fergusson et al., *supra* note 3. This research has proved highly controversial for those committed to a single causal factor theory of domestic violence centered in patriarchy and male control. For discussion, *see* Murray Straus, *Future Research on Gender Symmetry in Physical Assaults on Partners*, 12 VIOLENCE AGAINST WOMEN 1086 (2006). A single causal factor theory of domestic violence also does not take account of the perspectives of women from positions of difference, including indigenous women and lesbians. *See* Rosemary Hunter, *Narratives of Domestic Violence*, 28 SYD. L.R. 733, 744–49 (2006).

[29] *See e.g.* Russell Dobash & Rebecca Dobash, *Women's Violence to Men in Intimate Relationships: Working on a Puzzle*, 44 BRITISH J. CRIMINOLOGY 324 (2004); MARIANNE HESTER, WHO DOES WHAT TO WHOM? GENDER AND DOMESTIC VIOLENCE PERPETRATORS (2009), http://www.bristol.ac.uk/sps/research/projects/reports/2009/rj4843/whodoeswhat.pdf

[30] Irene Frieze, *Investigating the Causes and Consequences of Marital Rape*, 8 SIGNS 532 (1983); Irene Frieze & Angela Browne, *Violence in Marriage, in* LLOYD OHLIN & MICHAEL TONRY (EDS.), FAMILY VIOLENCE 163 (1989); Irene Frieze & Maureen McHugh, *Power and Influence Strategies in Violent and Nonviolent Marriage*, 16 PSYCHOLOGY OF WOMEN Q. 449 (1992).

[31] Michael Johnson, *Conflict and Control: Gender Symmetry and Asymmetry in Domestic Violence*, 12 VIOLENCE AGAINST WOMEN 1003, 1011 (2006).

Even taking account of mutual and female-perpetrated violence in general population studies, there is ample justification, from a public policy perspective, in treating violence as a gendered issue given the far greater risk of harm that arises from male-perpetrated violence.[32] As Elizabeth Reed and her colleagues put it:[33]

> Use of this "reciprocal violence" framework for understanding adolescent and adult IPV ignores the world beyond our databases. We should not frame and interpret research in the absence of well-accepted historical and political realities. That is not to say that both males and females cannot or do not enact unhealthy relationship behaviors, including aggression, or that such unhealthy relationship behaviors do not negatively impact both males and females. Such behaviors, however, likely have differing etiologies and are displayed differently based on the gender of the actors.

Other Patterns of Intimate Partner Violence

Coercive controlling violence and violence driven by conflict are not the only patterns of violence identified in research. Violent resistance and separation-instigated violence have also been identified.[34] Violent resistance is most commonly seen when women respond to coercive controlling violence by male partners. It is force used in self-defense.

Separation-instigated violence was identified by Johnston and Campbell, who observed, in their studies of ongoing and entrenched disputes over postseparation parenting, that there was a group of parents where uncharacteristic acts of violence were precipitated by the separation or were reactions to traumatic postdivorce events. In these cases, violence occurred only during or after the separation period and was not present during the marriage itself. They noted that physical violence was perpetrated by the partner who felt abandoned.[35]

---

[32] In another Australian study of incidents of domestic assault reported to the police in 2004, nearly 74 percent of women who reported assault by their partners or former partners had suffered injuries, compared with 36 percent of men who reported assault by their partners or former partners. Julie People, *Trends and Patterns in Domestic Violence Assaults*, CRIME AND JUSTICE BULLETIN, (no. 89), 9 (2005), available at http://www.lawlink.nsw.gov.au/lawlink/bocsar/ll_bocsar.nsf/vwFiles/CJB89.pdf/$file/CJB89.pdf. *See also* Richard Felson & Alison Cares, *Gender and the Seriousness of Assaults on Intimate Partners and Other Victims*, 67 J. MARRIAGE & FAM. 1182 (2005).

[33] Elizabeth Reed, Anita Raj, Elizabeth Miller, & Jay Silverman, *Losing the "Gender" in Gender-Based Violence: The Missteps of Research on Dating and Intimate Partner Violence*, 16 VIOLENCE AGAINST WOMEN 348, 350 (2010).

[34] *See* Kelly & Johnson, *supra* note 10.

[35] Johnston & Campbell, *supra* note 10, at 196–97.

THE RELEVANCE OF DOMESTIC VIOLENCE TO DECISION
MAKING ON PARENTING AFTER SEPARATION

The problem with treating domestic violence as homogenous is that it leads to one-size-fits-all responses in terms of legislation and public policy. As Ver Steegh and Dalton write, reporting on the consensus achieved at the Wingspread Conference in the United States in 2007:[36]

> In many jurisdictions domestic violence cases, identified principally by evidence of physical violence, are handled on a one-size-fits-all basis … once the label of "domestic violence" attaches, important differences among families are often ignored. Legal definitions of domestic violence encompass a broad range of behaviors and statutes provide little guidance with respect to distinguishing among them. It is commonly assumed that, in families that have experienced at least one seriously violent incident or in which there is a pattern of physical violence, the recipient of the violence should obtain a protective order, the perpetrator of the violence should be subject to legal presumptions regarding child custody, and both partners should be prevented from using (or alternatively should be required to use) services such as mediation. While such assumptions may be appropriate in many cases, their rigid application is based on the mistaken assumption that all families experiencing domestic violence are alike.

A history of violence is relevant to decision making about parenting after separation for a range of reasons. Courts need to be future-focused in determining the postseparation parenting arrangements, but they must be guided by the parents' past behavior as the clearest indication of how they might act in the future.

Prioritizing Safety

It is appropriate that an absolute priority be given to the safety of victims of violence and their children when there is a serious risk of harm resulting either from a pattern of violence and control in the past or a clear risk of murder-suicide.[37] In Australia, for example, this priority is expressed in terms of the test of "unacceptable risk."[38] The legislation provides that

---

[36] Ver Steegh & Dalton, *supra* note 22, at 456.

[37] CAROLYN JOHNSON, COME WITH DADDY: A STUDY OF CHILD MURDER-SUICIDE AFTER SEPARATION (2005).

[38] The test of unacceptable risk was first devised by the High Court of Australia in *M v. M* (1988) 166 C.L.R. 69, 78, in dealing with allegations of child sexual abuse. The Court held that "a court will not grant custody or access to a parent if that custody or access would expose the child to an unacceptable risk of sexual abuse." The test was included in

judges, in deciding what parenting orders to make, "must, to the extent that it is possible to do so consistently with the child's best interests being the paramount consideration ... ensure that the order does not expose a person to an unacceptable risk of family violence."[39] One of the two primary considerations for courts in determining what is in the best interests of the child is "the need to protect the child from physical or psychological harm from being subjected to, or exposed to, abuse, neglect or family violence."[40]

Even though the risk of intimate partner violence may be lessened when the parents are no longer living together and may indeed be living some considerable distance apart, the history of violence is nonetheless relevant to the logistics of any changeover arrangements. Where there is a risk of violence toward the primary caregiver, measures need to be put in place as far as possible to ensure that the parents do not meet, or meet only in a public place where the risk of violence is lessened. Contact centers to facilitate handovers offer one way in which this can occur.[41]

Violence and Children's Well-Being

A history of violence is also an important issue to explore in terms of the children's attitudes toward living with, or going on visits to, a violent parent. A child's fear of the violent parent, or concern about the parent's unpredictability, are relevant matters to explore in a custody evaluation or other expert report, as are the ways in which witnessing the violence has affected the children's love for, and trust in, the parent.[42] The sensitive discussion of children's fears concerning conflict between their parents may

---

legislation in 1995 to address the issue of family violence more generally. In *M v. M*, the High Court affirmed the decisions of the trial judge to deny access entirely even though he was not satisfied on the balance of probabilities that the father was guilty of sexual abuse of the child. He could not say that the father had *not* sexually abused the child, and expressed himself in terms of "lingering doubts" about the child's safety if access were to be allowed. The test of "unacceptable risk" therefore did not require affirmative findings either that the child had been abused or that, if she had, the father was responsible.

[39] Family Law Act, 1975, s.60CG. On problems in the courts' handling of cases involving domestic violence in Australia, *see* Miranda Kaye, Julie Stubbs & Julia Tolmie, *Domestic Violence and Child Contact Arrangements*, 17 AUSTRALIAN J. FAM. L. 93 (2003); KATHRYN RENDELL, ZOE RATHUS, & ANGELA LYNCH, AN UNACCEPTABLE RISK: A REPORT ON CHILD CONTACT ARRANGEMENTS WHEN THERE IS VIOLENCE IN THE FAMILY (2000).

[40] Family Law Act, 1975, s.60CC(2)(b).

[41] Contact centers exist in many jurisdictions, typically run as a voluntary service or a nonprofit organization. *See e.g.* in Britain, National Association of Child Contact Centres, http://www.naccc.org.uk

[42] Honore Hughes, *Psychological and Behavioral Correlates of Family Violence in Child Witnesses and Victims*, 58 AM. J. ORTHOPSYCHIATRY 77 (1988); PETER JAFFE, DAVID

bring out continuing fears about safety in visiting or living with one parent, which would not be revealed otherwise.

A tendency to violence also reflects adversely on the suitability of that parent to have the daily care of the children, or even to care for them on overnight visits. The overlap between violence and physical abuse is such that where a pattern of domestic violence has been demonstrated in the course of the parental relationship, there must be concerns about the possibility that the children will be physically abused as well.[43] A parent's tendency to be violent may well represent an unacceptable risk to the safety of the child.

Assessing Maternal Care and Attitudes to the Violent Parent

Understanding a history of coercive controlling violence may also be relevant to other kinds of assessment in determining parenting arrangements after separation, including the mother's capacity for parenting and her attitude toward contact between the child and the other parent. For many women who experience this kind of subjugation and control, the psychological effects may have a greater lasting impact than physical abuse. These effects include fear and anxiety, loss of self-esteem, depression, and posttraumatic stress.[44] They may impact significantly on a mother's capacity to parent,[45] particularly in the context of coping with the stresses of the relationship breakup and the litigation about the parenting arrangements. Mothers

WOLFE, & SUSAN WILSON, CHILDREN OF BATTERED WOMEN (1990); Zoe Hilton, *Battered Women's Concerns about Their Children Witnessing Wife Assault*, 7 J. INTERPERSONAL VIOLENCE 77 (1992); Patrick Parkinson, *Custody, Access and Domestic Violence*, 9 AUSTRALIAN J. FAM. L. 41 (1995); Patrick Parkinson & Cathy Humphreys, *Children Who Witness Domestic Violence – The Implications for Child Protection*, 10 CHILD & FAM. L. Q. 147 (1998); Jeffrey Edleson, *Children's Witnessing of Adult Domestic Violence*, 14 J. INTERPERSONAL VIOLENCE 839 (1999); ROBERT GEFFNER, PETER JAFFE, & MARLIES SUDERMANN (EDS.), CHILDREN EXPOSED TO DOMESTIC VIOLENCE: CURRENT ISSUES IN RESEARCH, INTERVENTION, PREVENTION AND POLICY DEVELOPMENT (2000); David Wolfe, Claire Crooks, Vivien Lee, Alexandra McIntyre-Smith, & Peter Jaffe, *The Effects of Children's Exposure to Domestic Violence: A Meta-Analysis and Critique*, 6 CLINICAL CHILD & FAM. PSYCH. REV. 171 (2003); Marian Brandon & Ann Lewis, *Significant Harm and Children's Experiences of Domestic Violence*, 1 CHILD & FAM. SOCIAL WORK 33 (2007); Stephanie Holt, Helen Buckley, & Sadhbh Whelan, *The Impact of Exposure to Domestic Violence on Children and Young People: A Review of the Literature*, 32 CHILD ABUSE & NEGLECT 797 (2008).

43 MARIANNE HESTER, CHRIS PEARSON, & NICOLA HARWIN, MAKING AN IMPACT: CHILDREN AND DOMESTIC VIOLENCE : A READER (2nd ed., 2007) Ch. 2.

44 Kelly & Johnson, *supra* note 10, at 483–84.

45 *See e.g.* Alytia Levendosky & Sandra Graham-Bermann, *Behavioral Observations of Parenting in Battered Women*, 14 J. FAM. PSYCH. 80 (2000).

may be misdiagnosed as suffering from various psychopathologies,[46] even though their deficiencies and problems are situational and reactive to the experience of abuse.[47]

The experience of coercive controlling violence may also explain a mother's resistance to regular contact between the children and the father even if it can be made safe through contact handovers, or her desire to relocate a long way from the other parent when there is not a convincing rationale for the move other than to get away.

It would be a mistake nonetheless to see any history of violence within intimate partnerships as being in some way a disqualification to parent. Van Krieken has observed that in the political debates on family law, there is a tendency in some quarters to advocate restrictions on contact between nonresident parents and their children as a punishment for past misbehavior, alongside a view that victims of domestic violence should be entitled to sever their associations with their former partners.[48] The clean break in the relationship between the parents is thus a remedy for the wrong of domestic assault. It punishes the offender and rewards the victim not only with sole custody but also with postseparation autonomy.

This may be appropriate in some cases. Indeed, there are certainly cases of serious violence when contact should be denied entirely, not just because of continuing physical risk, but because the mother's psychological well-being requires it. Yet violence is, regrettably, such a common feature of intimate partnerships that there has to be a realistic differentiation of cases along the spectrum of family violence. This is something that is not easily translated into legislation, where the tendency has been to treat family violence as homogenous and based on incidents of physical assault. This focus on domestic violence as involving incidents in which there is a perpetrator and a victim sits uncomfortably alongside the social science evidence on the nature and dynamics of intimate partner violence, and may lead to inappropriate approaches to legislation and policy.

---

[46] For an analysis, *see* Nancy Erikson, *Use of the MMPI-2 in Child Custody Evaluations Involving Battered Women: What Does Psychological Research Tell Us*, 39 FAM. L. Q. 87 (2005).

[47] *Id.*

[48] Robert van Krieken, *The "Best Interests of the Child" and Parental Separation: On the "Civilizing of Parents*," 68 MODERN L. REV. 25, 36 (2005).

INTIMATE PARTNER VIOLENCE AND LEGISLATION ON
POSTSEPARATION PARENTING

Legislatures around the western world have addressed the issue of violence and its relationship to decision making about children in a variety of different ways. At one end of the spectrum are legislatures that have given very little guidance to courts at all concerning how to determine the best interests of children, or if they have a list of factors to consider, do not mention domestic violence as an issue. One example of this is the Children Act 1989 in Britain. In determining the welfare of the child, courts are required to consider a range of factors, and whereas harm to the child is a consideration, the violence of one parent toward another is not listed as a specific matter to which the court should direct its attention.[49] Guidance has nonetheless been given by case law[50] and by a Practice Direction issued by the President of the Family Division of the High Court.[51]

Other jurisdictions have sought to identify violence as a specific consideration in legislation, with a focus on acts of violence that can be proven. In some states, there is just a general requirement to take acts of violence into account. The law in New York illustrates this:[52]

> Where either party to an action concerning custody of or a right to visitation with a child alleges ... that the other party has committed an act of domestic violence against the party making the allegation or a family or household

---

[49] The factors listed in the Children Act, s.1(3), are: the ascertainable wishes and feelings of the child concerned (considered in the light of his age and understanding); his physical, emotional, and educational needs; the likely effect on him of any change in his circumstances; his age, sex, background, and any characteristics of his that the court considers relevant; any harm that he or she has suffered or is at risk of suffering; how capable each of the parents, and any other person in relation to whom the court considers the question to be relevant, is of meeting his or her needs; and the range of powers available to the court under this Act in the proceedings in question.

[50] The English Court of Appeal reconsidered its approach in *Re* L (a child) (contact: domestic violence), [2001] FAM. 260 in response to a great deal of criticism that the courts were insensitive to the victims of domestic violence. For criticisms in Britain of the failure to recognize adequately the problem of domestic violence and other situations in which shared parental responsibility and regular contact is contraindicated, *see* John Eekelaar, *Rethinking Parental Responsibility*, 31 FAM. L. 426 (2001); John Eekelaar, *Contact – Over the Limit?*, 32 FAM. L. 271 (2002); JANE FORTIN, CHILDREN'S RIGHTS AND THE DEVELOPING LAW 401–13 (2nd ed. 2003).

[51] *Practice Direction: Residence and Contact Orders: Domestic Violence and Harm*, 9 May 2008, http://www.hmcourts-service.gov.uk/cms/files/pd-residence-contact-orders-domestic-violence-090508.pdf

[52] Domestic Relations Law § 240(1).

member of either party ... and such allegations are proven by a preponderance of the evidence, the court must consider the effect of such domestic
violence upon the best interests of the child, together with such other facts
and circumstances as the court deems relevant in making a direction pursuant to this section and state on the record how such findings, facts and
circumstances factored into the direction.

Three features of this legislation are noteworthy. First, the legislation does
not specify how the act of domestic violence is to be taken into account
other than that the court must consider what effect the violence has on
the well-being of the child. Secondly, it focuses attention on a history of
domestic violence rather than current safety concerns. Thirdly, it defines
domestic violence in terms of incidents of assault rather than in terms
of the impact of that assault on the victim and the relational context
within which that physical violence occurs. For female victims of coercive
controlling violence, physical abuse is just one dimension of an oppressive
relationship that subjugates, entraps, and disempowers. All three of these
are weaknesses of other legislation as well.

Domestic Violence as Incidents

Characterizing domestic violence in terms of incidents of assault places the
focus on provable incidents of assault, each as a discrete crime. Such an
approach does not give courts an appropriate understanding of the ongoing experience of coercive controlling violence. Evan Stark's observations
are apposite in relation to this pattern of violence:[53]

> With a few exceptions, our field has been dominated by a definition adapted
> from criminology that equates abuse with discrete episodes of force designed
> or likely to hurt or injure a partner. One result of the incident-specific vio-
> lence definition is that criminal justice intervention has failed to affect the
> problem. Because the vast majority of domestic violence involves "minor"
> assaults (e.g., pushes, shoves), when the law requires police and the courts to
> view abuse through the prism of discrete acts of violence, woman battering
> is downgraded to a second-class misdemeanor.... The emphasis on discrete
> acts of violence contrasts markedly with experience-based accounts where
> battered women report abuse is "ongoing"; includes a pattern of intimida-
> tion, isolation, and control as well as assault; and exacts high levels of fear
> and entrapment even when violence has stopped. Nor does the paradigm

---

[53] Evan Stark, *Commentary on Johnson's "Conflict and Control: Gender Symmetry and
Asymmetry in Domestic Violence,"* 12 VIOLENCE AGAINST WOMEN 1019, 1019–20
(2006).

account for the duration of abusive relationships. A related issue is that the harms victims identify are more often the cumulative result of ongoing "entrapment" than of discrete assaults, a fact that makes injury a poor way to assess risk.

The treatment of domestic violence in terms of provable events has a number of deficiencies. First, if the assaults were intermittent and not at the most serious end of the spectrum of violence in terms of physical injury, a court focused on discrete and provable incidents of criminal conduct might minimize the significance of the assaults in terms of the woman's overall experience of victimization.

A second problem with the focus on provable incidents of violence derives from the binary nature of fact-finding. Either an assault is proven or it is not. The abuse happened, or it did not. In law, a finding of "not guilty" is equated with innocence. Yet domestic violence occurs behind closed doors. Victims may not be able to recall many incidents of violence with the specificity concerning dates and circumstances needed to prove an incident to the satisfaction of a court. The police may only have been called on two or three occasions out of many. The laws of evidence may constrain what evidence is admissible.[54] It follows that where the focus is on provable events rather than the experience of oppression in its relational context, what is recorded as the history of violence may well understate the significance of that history in terms of decision making about parenting after separation.

While these considerations go to the risk that a history of power and control, backed up with the threat of or occurrence of violent assaults, will not be given sufficient weight by the courts, there is also a concern of a different kind about this focus on a provable event of violence: it might cast the net too wide. If the majority of both women and men who have been separated or divorced report physical assaults in the course of their previous relationship,[55] albeit in many cases assaults such as pushing and hitting that did not occasion physical injury, then a substantial proportion of the population, both men and women, may be covered by legislation that requires courts to respond in certain ways to any proven history of assault.

Like driftnets in ocean fishing, laws on family violence can capture a lot of fish within them that are not the targets of the operation.

---

[54] *See* generally, Jane Aiken & Jane Murphy, *Evidence Issues in Domestic Violence Civil Cases*, 34 FAM. L.Q. 43 (2000).

[55] In the context of Australia, *see* Sheehan & Smyth, *supra* note 4, and for Arizona, *see* Beck, Walsh, & Weston, *supra* note 5.

A pattern of coercive controlling violence is highly relevant to the question of postseparation parenting arrangements; so too are other threats to the ongoing safety of parents and children following separation. But laws designed to address these patterns of violence and ongoing safety concerns, if drafted in too wide a way, can catch up in the net any case where there has been a provable history of physical altercation within the relationship by either mothers, fathers, or both. That is, it catches in the net any incidents of violence driven by conflict, at any stage of the relationship.

PRESUMPTIONS AGAINST CUSTODY

In some U.S. states, there is a presumption against custody being awarded in favor of someone who has been proved to have committed an act of violence against the other parent or one of the children.[56] In these states, the failure to differentiate between different patterns of violence and the focus on individual incidents may well lead to overinclusive presumptions. The issue can be illustrated by the law in California, which has a presumption against any form of legal custody, including joint legal custody, if a parent has perpetrated a domestic assault in the previous five years. Section 3044 of the California Family Code provides:

(a) Upon a finding by the court that a party seeking custody of a child has perpetrated domestic violence against the other party seeking custody of the child or against the child or the child's siblings within the previous five years, there is a rebuttable presumption that an award of sole or joint physical or legal custody of a child to a person who has perpetrated domestic violence is detrimental to the best interest of the child, pursuant to Section 3011. This presumption may only be rebutted by a preponderance of the evidence.

(b) In determining whether the presumption set forth in subdivision (a) has been overcome, the court shall consider all of the following factors:

(1) Whether the perpetrator of domestic violence has demonstrated that giving sole or joint physical or legal custody of a child to the perpetrator is in the best interest of the child. In determining the best interest of the child, the preference for frequent and

---

[56] On the effectiveness of these provisions, *see* Allison Morrill, Jianyu Dai, Samantha Dunn, Iyue Sung, & Kevin Smith, *Child Custody and Visitation Decisions When the Father Has Perpetrated Violence against the Mother*, 11 VIOLENCE AGAINST WOMEN 1076 (2005).

continuing contact with both parents ... may not be used to rebut the presumption, in whole or in part.

(2) Whether the perpetrator has successfully completed a batterer's treatment program that meets the criteria outlined in subdivision (c) of Section 1203.097 of the Penal Code.

(3) Whether the perpetrator has successfully completed a program of alcohol or drug abuse counseling if the court determines that counseling is appropriate.

(4) Whether the perpetrator has successfully completed a parenting class if the court determines the class to be appropriate.

(5) Whether the perpetrator is on probation or parole, and whether he or she has complied with the terms and conditions of probation or parole.

(6) Whether the perpetrator is restrained by a protective order or restraining order, and whether he or she has complied with its terms and conditions.

(7) Whether the perpetrator of domestic violence has committed any further acts of domestic violence.

If both men and women have used violence in the course of the relationship (whatever the context), a presumption against having sole or joint custody may well apply to both parents, with the outcome of the case influenced by the extent to which either parent can prove particular incidents of assault to the satisfaction of the court.

If this approach were applied only to the more severe cases of coercive controlling violence, an outcome that was both just to the victim and likely to be in the best interests of the children would result. Coercive controlling violence against an intimate partner is a window on the soul. It reveals much about the character of a person. It is likely to be indicative of a tendency to dominate and control the children rather than to nurture and empower them. There is a strong likelihood of ongoing issues about the safety of the mother and of high levels of conflict between the parents. Laws that are really targeting men who engage in coercive controlling violence, where any form of joint parenting is likely to be contraindicated, can apply to very different patterns of conflict that do not give rise to ongoing safety concerns.

The legislation in California is particularly problematic because it appears that even one physical assault triggers the presumption, and it may be applied, of course, to both genders whenever a physical assault can be proven to occur, whatever the circumstances and whether or not any harm has resulted. Presumptions of this kind are blunt instruments for dealing with mutual aggression.

PRESUMPTION AGAINST UNSUPERVISED VISITATION

New Zealand goes further than other jurisdictions in having a presumption against unsupervised contact when a parent has committed an act of violence.[57] Sections 60 and 61 of the Care of Children Act 2004 provide that if the court is satisfied that a party to the proceedings has used violence against the child or a child of the family, or against the other party to the proceedings, then the court must not make an order giving the violent party the role of providing day-to-day care for the child or any order allowing the violent party contact (other than supervised contact) with that child, unless the court is satisfied that the child will be safe with the violent party. In considering whether a child will be safe, the court must have regard to:

- the nature and seriousness of the violence used;
- how recently the violence occurred;
- the frequency of the violence;
- the likelihood of further violence occurring;
- the physical or emotional harm caused to the child by the violence;
- whether the other party to the proceedings
    o considers that the child will be safe while the violent party provides day-to-day care for, or has contact with, the child; and
    o consents to the violent party providing day-to-day care for, or having contact (other than supervised contact) with, the child;
- any views the child expresses on the matter;
- any steps taken by the violent party to prevent further violence occurring;
- all other matters the court considers relevant.

The court also has a discretion to order supervised contact if the judge is not sure whether the child will be safe in a parent's care.[58] New Zealand takes a "safety first" approach to postseparation parenting.

A presumption against unsupervised contact where there is any history of violence certainly has the benefit of erring on the side of safety, but by catching all cases in which any violence or abuse is alleged to have

---

[57] For the origins of these provisions, and early experience, *see* Ruth Busch & Neville Robertson, *Innovative Approaches to Child Custody and Domestic Violence in New Zealand*, 3 J. AGGRESSION, MALTREATMENT & TRAUMA 269 (2000). For a critical view, *see* Ian Freckelton, *Custody and Access Disputation and the Prediction of Children's Safety: A Dangerous Initiative*, 2 PSYCHIATRY, PSYCHOLOGY AND LAW 139 (1995).
[58] Care of Children Act, 2004, s.60(4).

occurred at any time in the past, it casts the net very wide. Indeed there may be an inquiry about safety in relation to both parents in cases of mutual aggression. However, a proven act of violence is only a catalyst for further inquiry, not a disqualifying factor in itself. It leads to a focus on safety, requiring the court to examine specifically the question of whether the child will be safe in that parent's care, with a starting point being that unsupervised contact will not be permitted.

There are nonetheless significant resource implications in adopting this approach, and legislation without adequate resourcing will not be effective. One issue is the resourcing needed to make a proper risk assessment. An evaluation of these provisions a few years after their introduction found that frequently the courts had very little information on which to make a proper risk assessment, and in most cases did not make orders restricting contact. In 18 percent of the cases where violence or abuse was an issue, the court made orders for supervised access, and in another 12 percent there were orders for no access.[59]

A presumption against unsupervised contact where there is any history of violence also requires either that the government invests in an adequate network of supervised contact centers or that public policy countenances a significant number of parents being denied any face-to-face contact with their children. New Zealand has apparently struggled with having enough supervised contact places across the country to meet the need.[60]

How often are supervised contact orders made in New Zealand, and against whom? Of 4,068 final contact orders made in favor of parents in 2007, 252 supervised contact orders were made in relation to fathers and 94 in relation to mothers.[61] This represents 8.8 percent of all contact orders made in favor of fathers and 7.8 percent of all contact orders made in favor of mothers. Slightly more than 2 percent of orders made in relation to fathers were indirect contact orders only (that is, the orders

---

[59] Alison Chetwin, Trish Knaggs, & Patricia Te Wairere Ahiahi Young, The Domestic Violence Legislation and Child Access in New Zealand (1999).

[60] Judge Rosemary Riddell, *Protecting Children from Family Violence* (Paper presented at the International Conference on Child Labour and Child Exploitation, Cairns, 3–5 August 2008), http://www.justice.govt.nz/courts/family-court/publications/speeches-and-papers/protecting-children-from-family-violence. She wrote: As at 2007, "New Zealand had 31 centres, leaving many areas unserved. The lack of adequate resources can pose a challenge to Judges who are mandated to keep the welfare and best interests of the child as the paramount consideration in any proceedings. Enabling a child to maintain a safe relationship with his or her father can be stymied where sufficient formally supervised options do not exist."

[61] Ministry of Justice, Family Court Statistics in New Zealand in 2006 and 2007, at 32 (2009).

did not allow for face-to-face contact), and exactly the same percentage of contact orders in relation to mothers were also for indirect contact. It appears therefore that even in a jurisdiction with a presumption against unsupervised contact where there is any history of violence or abuse, in only a small minority of cases is such an order actually made. The New Zealand experience also demonstrates the extent to which such orders may be made against mothers as well as fathers.[62] Laws designed to protect women and children from violent men are necessarily gender-neutral in their application.

DIFFERENTIATING BETWEEN KINDS OF FAMILY VIOLENCE

Clare Dalton has observed how professionals with different theoretical orientations tend to "see" violence and abuse in different ways:[63]

> At the level of research and theory, there are at least three separate bodies of learning that describe problematic intimate relationships…. One set of literature deals with conflict, another with violence, and a third with abuse. A prime source of tension between specialists in partner abuse and the majority of mental health professionals who work within the family court system is that where the former see abuse, the latter tend to see conflict. A second difference that contributes to this tension is that before taking a relationship out of the conflictual category and putting it into the abusive category, the mental health professional looks for significant evidence of a one-sided pattern of physical violence. Those who specialize in abuse, on the other hand, understand abusive relationships as being first and foremost about power and control. They know that physical violence, while usually a potent residual source of power within the relationship, may play only a small part in the overall dynamic of control. A third related difference is that abuse specialists will always suspect that violence in a relationship indicates the presence of a power and control dynamic, whereas the mental health professional is quicker to associate violence with conflict between relatively evenly matched partners.

These conflicting paradigms lie at the heart of the problem in responding to violence and abuse in the context of parenting after separation. Whenever professionals in the family law system view violence

---

[62] Indeed, the legislation may have an adverse impact on victims of violence. *See e.g.* De Leeuw v Edgecumbe, [1996] N.Z.F.L.R. 801.

[63] Clare Dalton, *When Paradigms Collide: Protecting Battered Parents and Their Children in the Family Court System*, 37 FAM. & CONCIL. CTS REV. 273, 275 (1999). *See also* Janet Johnson's response to this article, *supra* note 13.

through one-size-fits-all theoretical lenses, the dynamics of interparental relationships within a particular family are prone to being misunderstood. This can have deleterious outcomes for those affected by the decisions reached.

Peter Jaffe and his colleagues have suggested that as a means of differentiating between types of violence for the purposes of making decisions in parenting disputes, it is important to consider three factors: the potency, pattern, and primary perpetrator of the violence. They refer to this as PPP screening and describe these three factors as follows:

> First, level of potency – the degree of severity, dangerousness, and potential risk of serious injury and lethality – is the foremost dimension that needs to be assessed and monitored so that protective orders can be issued and other immediate safety measures taken and maintained. Prior incidents of severe abuse and injuries inflicted on victims are an important indicator of the capacity of an individual to explode or escalate to dangerous levels. In some cases, explosive or deadly violence can erupt with little or no history of abuse, but other warning signs are often evident …
>
> Second, the extent to which the violence is part of a pattern of coercive control and domination (rather than a relatively isolated incident) is a crucial indicator of the extent of stress and trauma suffered by the child and family and the potential for future violence …
>
> Third, whether there is a primary perpetrator of the violence (rather than it being mutually instigated or initiated by one or the other party on different occasions) will indicate whose access needs to be restricted and which parent, if either, is more likely to provide a nonviolent home, other things being equal.

Certain of these factors can be found in the legislation of various jurisdictions. For example, in Massachusetts, where a pattern of abuse or serious incident of abuse has occurred, there is a rebuttable presumption that it is not in the best interests of the child to be placed in sole custody, shared legal custody, or shared physical custody with the abusive parent.[64] A "serious incident of abuse" is defined as the occurrence, between a parent and the other parent or between a parent and child, of (a) attempting to cause or causing serious bodily injury; (b) placing another in reasonable fear of imminent serious bodily injury; or (c) causing another to engage involuntarily in sexual relations by force, threat, or duress.

The requirement to identify a pattern of violence rather than sporadic incidents goes some way to addressing the problem of how to deal with

---

[64] MASSACHUSETTS GENERAL LAWS, Ch. 208, § 31A.

violent incidents in the context of separation. However, to properly differentiate between different patterns of violence, it is also important to focus on the context and severity of the violence, as well as the existence of a pattern. There may be a pattern of violence by both men and women where the violence erupts out of conflict.

Determining the Primary Aggressor

Wisconsin has tried to address the issue of mutual violence by requiring the court to try to identify the primary aggressor. There is a rebuttable presumption that it is detrimental to the child and contrary to the best interest of the child to award joint or sole legal custody to a party if the court finds by a preponderance of evidence that the party has engaged in a pattern or serious incident of interspousal battery or domestic abuse.[65] Where the court finds that both parties engaged in a pattern or serious incident of interspousal battery or domestic abuse, the presumption against joint or sole legal custody applies only to the party who was the "primary physical aggressor." If one, but not both, of the parties has been convicted of a crime of domestic abuse, he or she must be determined to be the primary aggressor. Otherwise, the court is required to consider:

- prior acts of domestic violence between the parties;
- the relative severity of the injuries, if any, inflicted upon a party by the other party in any of the prior acts of domestic violence;
- the likelihood of future injury to either of the parties resulting from acts of domestic violence;
- whether either of the parties acted in self-defense in any of the prior acts of domestic violence;
- whether there is or has been a pattern of coercive and abusive behavior between the parties;
- any other factor that the court considers relevant.

It is nonetheless open to the court to find that both parties engaged in a pattern or serious incident of violence or abuse and that neither party was the primary physical aggressor.

The Wisconsin legislation does seem to represent a sensible legislative model that requires courts to examine the three factors of potency, pattern, and whether or not there is a primary aggressor.

---

[65] Wis. Stat § 767.24(2)(d)1.

CURRENT SAFETY CONCERNS

Another approach is to focus attention on current safety concerns. This is the focus, for example, in Oregon. In that state, the court is required to give "primary consideration to the best interests and welfare of the child."[66] One of the factors to consider is "the abuse of one parent by the other."[67] Furthermore, although Oregon has a version of the friendly-parent rule[68] – namely that the court must consider the willingness and ability of each parent to facilitate and encourage a close and continuing relationship between the other parent and the child – this does not apply where the other parent has engaged in a pattern of abuse against the parent or a child and that a continuing relationship with the other parent will endanger the health or safety of either parent or the child.[69] The legislation defines abuse as:[70]

(a) Attempting to cause or intentionally, knowingly or recklessly causing bodily injury.
(b) Intentionally, knowingly or recklessly placing another in fear of imminent bodily injury.
(c) Causing another to engage in involuntary sexual relations by force or threat of force.

The law in Oregon further provides that when reviewing a proposed parenting plan, the court must ensure the safety of the parties but not deny parenting time to the noncustodial parent unless the court finds that parenting time would endanger the health or safety of the child. If the court awards parenting time to a noncustodial parent who has committed abuse, the court has to make "adequate provision for the safety of the child and the other parent."[71]

---

[66] O.R.S. § 107.137(1).   [67] O.R.S. § 107.137(1)(d).
[68] O.R.S. § 107.137(1)(f). For criticism of this rule, *see* Margaret Dore, *The Friendly Parent Concept: A Flawed Factor for Child Custody*, 6 LOY. J. PUB. INT. L. 41 (2004).
[69] O.R.S. § 107.137(1)(f).   [70] O.R.S. § 107.705.
[71] *Id.* § 107.105. Section 107.718(6) states that the order of the court may include:

(a) That exchange of a child between parents shall occur at a protected location.
(b) That parenting time be supervised by another person or agency.
(c) That the perpetrator of the abuse be required to attend and complete, to the satisfaction of the court, a program of intervention for perpetrators or any other counseling program designated by the court as a condition of the parenting time.
(d) That the perpetrator of the abuse not possess or consume alcohol or controlled substances during the parenting time and for 24 hours preceding the parenting time.
(e) That the perpetrator of the abuse pay all or a portion of the cost of supervised parenting time, and any program designated by the court as a condition of parenting time.
(f) That no overnight parenting time occur.

A focus on current safety concerns rather than a history of violence during the course of the relationship per se is important to allow a concentrated focus of resources on the parents and children who are at most risk as a result of postseparation parenting arrangements. A much smaller number of parents have concerns about either their own safety or the safety of their children a year or two after separation than report a history of violence or emotional abuse during the course of the relationship. The Australian Institute of Family Studies found that 26 percent of mothers and 17 percent of fathers reported being physically hurt by their partners. A further 39 percent of mothers and 36 percent of fathers reported emotional abuse[72] defined in terms of humiliation, belittling insults, property damage, and threats of harm during the course of the relationship. Yet in interviews conducted on average fifteen months after separation, a much smaller number of parents had current safety concerns either for themselves or their children than had reported a history of violence or emotional abuse. Four percent of fathers and 12 percent of mothers were concerned about their personal safety; 15 percent of fathers and 18 percent of mothers expressed concerns about the safety of their child – either alone or in addition to concerns about personal safety.

The researchers found that a history of family violence did not necessarily impede friendly or cooperative relationships between the parents. Sixteen percent of mothers who reported being physically hurt by their ex-partner during the course of the relationship reported friendly relationships at the time of the interview, and a further 23.5 percent reported having a cooperative relationship. Although others reported distant or conflictual relationships, only 18.5 percent reported a continuing fearful relationship. Fifty-five percent of mothers and 50 percent of fathers who reported emotional abuse by their ex-partner during the course of the relationship reported friendly or cooperative relationships by the time of the interview.[73]

By way of contrast, where a parent had current safety concerns either for themselves or for their child, it was much more likely that they would report difficult relationships with the other parent. Forty-nine percent of fathers and 54 percent of mothers with concerns about their own or their

---

[72] Rae Kaspiew, Matthew Gray, Ruth Weston, Lawrie Moloney, Kelly Hand, & Lixia Qu, Australian Institute of Family Studies, Evaluation of the 2006 Family Law Reforms 26 (2009).

[73] *Id.* at 31–32.

child's safety indicated that their current interparental relationship was marked by either conflict or fear.[74]

Parents who had concerns about the safety of their children reported that the children had a significantly lower level of well-being than those parents who did not have such concerns, while a history of family violence was no longer statistically significant in terms of child well-being once sociodemographic characteristics and family dynamics were controlled for.[75]

WHEN FAMILIAL RELATIONSHIPS CAN NO LONGER ENDURE

What are the limitations on the efforts that should be made to support the enduring family? Recognition of the notion that families endure beyond the separation of the parents does not necessarily involve an assumption that all families can or should endure. Nor does it mean that the goal of interventions in all cases ought to be to try to build a cooperative coparenting relationship.

There is nonetheless a reluctance to sever face-to-face contact between a parent and a child entirely, and one compromise position is to order handover between the parents to take place at a contact center. Where there are ongoing issues of violence, abuse, or serious dysfunctionality requiring professional interventions to sustain the parent-child relationship, questions need to be asked about the purpose of those interventions.[76]

This has been an issue, for example, in France. Some contact centers, developing out of the mediation movement, have seen their role in terms of assisting parents to develop a cooperative parenting relationship despite the demise of their relationship as a couple.[77] Others disagree entirely.

Jean Gréchez, a leading figure in the contact center movement in France, has written of how he envisages the work of staff in his Point Rencontre center in working with parents in conflict.[78] In his philosophy, the role of contact center personnel is not to mediate between the two parents, but to help them come to terms with the death of their relationship. He sees much

---

[74] *Id.*at 32–33.   [75] *Id.*at 269.

[76] For discussion in the American context, *see* Elizabeth Brandt, *Concerns at the Margins of Supervised Access to Children*, J. LAW & FAM. STUD. 201 (2007).

[77] Benoit Bastard, *Different Approaches to Post-Divorce Family Relationships: The Example of Contact Centers in France, in* FAMILY LAW: PROCESSES, PRACTICES AND PRESSURES 271 (John Dewar & Stephen Parker eds., 2003).

[78] Jean Gréchez, *Apprentissage de la Loi et Processus D'évolution Psychique au Point-Rencontre*, 132 DIALOGUE 79 (1996).

of the conflict between parents as occurring because one or both parents refuse to accept that their relationship is clinically dead and prefer to "keep it on a drip" of bitterness and conflict. The counselor's role, in his view, is to help the parents come to accept the ending of their relationship, not to continue it, and to promote the separate relationship of the child with each parent, independent of the other parent. Talk of maintaining a relationship between the parents in their role as parents, in his view, represents an ideological or unrealistic view of postdivorce parenting:[79]

> I ... understand what is meant by a parental couple which is at the same time a conjugal couple, however I am unable to understand what is meant by a parental couple once that union is dissolved.... To speak of a parental couple surviving a conjugal couple could well be a vague reminiscence of the indissolubility of the marital relationship in the Catholic religion, the transfer of religious elements or childish fantasy onto current social discourse.

The rejection of any concept of the indissolubility of parenthood, of course, goes too far and flies in the face of what seem like irreversible trends in much of the western world.[80] Gréchez's position does, nonetheless, seem more realistic when one considers the circumstances of many parents who need to use contact centers. Nonetheless, some therapeutic work with parents may be necessary and helpful where, by improving the level of cooperation and trust between the parents, the primary caregiver can build enough trust and confidence in the other parent that she feels safe to move beyond the security of using the contact handover service.[81]

Where the reason for the use of the center is because of ongoing concerns about safety, the notion that the parents can be assisted toward a healthy enough coparental relationship is, for the most part, likely to be unrealistic. In contact centers, there can be a conflict between an institutional imperative to help the parents to self-manage to the extent that they no longer need the services of the center, and the need for ongoing protection from violence or abuse. Services that have high levels of demand will want to move people off their books in order to place others on them.

Although some parents will move on to self-management, with the handover center providing an important halfway house in terms of building

<hr>

79   *Id.* at 85–86, Edwina Dunn trans.
80   *See* Chapter 4.
81   Grania Sheehan, John Dewar, and Rachel Carson, *Moving On: The Challenge for Children's Contact Services in Australia*, in Parenting after Partnering: Containing Conflict after Separation 147 (Mavis Maclean ed, 2007).

trust, in other cases, the threat of violence, controlling behavior, or abuse may be ongoing.[82] The question then remains for how long services should be a source of life support, and how far the family law system should go before taking the hard decisions by prioritizing safety and the well-being of the primary carer.

DOMESTIC VIOLENCE: THE NEED FOR A BIFURCATED RESPONSE

The issue of domestic violence is one of the central issues in the debates about the future of family law. For some women's groups and commentators, the need to protect women and children from domestic violence has been a primary factor in arguing against laws that encourage shared parenting or otherwise promote the greater involvement of nonresident fathers. The two policy directions are expressed as being in opposition to one another.[83] The argument essentially is that the more that legislation supports and encourages the involvement of nonresident parents, the more it exposes women to the risk of violence and abuse. The problem of domestic violence has thus taken center stage in campaigns against changes to the law that promote joint custody, shared parenting, and greater contact between nonresident parents and children. Typically, in the criticisms of a procontact culture that exposes women and children to a risk of violence, there is no differentiation between patterns of intimate partner violence, and only violence by men against women is addressed as a problem.

As a rhetorical device, there is no doubt as to the political influence of such arguments. No one wants to promote laws that make women and children less safe; however, the way in which views on this issue are polarized between two conflicting paradigms is unhelpful. There are not two sides – greater involvement of nonresident fathers on the one hand and protection from domestic violence on the other. As Dalton argues, what we need to do is to focus on "outcomes that will protect abused parents and their children from further violence and trauma, while continuing to

---

[82] Christine Harrison, *Implacably Hostile or Appropriately Protective? Women Managing Child Contact in the Context of Domestic Violence*, 14 VIOLENCE AGAINST WOMEN 381 (2008); Tracee Parker, Kellie Rogers, Meghan Collins, & Jeffrey Edleson, *Danger Zone: Battered Mothers and Their Families in Supervised Visitation* 14 VIOLENCE AGAINST WOMEN 1313 (2008).

[83] *See* e.g. Peter Jaffe & Claire Crooks, *Partner Violence and Child Custody Cases: A Cross-National Comparison of Legal Reforms and Issues*, 10 VIOLENCE AGAINST WOMEN 917 (2004); Michael Flood, *"Fathers' Rights" and the Defense of Paternal Authority in Australia*, 16 VIOLENCE AGAINST WOMEN 328 (2010).

foster strong relationships between children and those parents who can be counted on to treat their former partners and their children with respect, even if sources of conflict remain."[84]

Diminishing the emphasis on the meaningful involvement of both parents will do little to ensure the safety of women and children, because at the most, it will lead to many nonresident parents having less time with their children rather than no time at all. Conversely, strengthening the family law system's capacity for better risk assessment and evidence gathering in relation to family violence will do nothing at all to diminish the law's support for children to maintain meaningful relationships with both parents where there are no significant safety concerns.

There is no evidence of a linear relationship between the amount of time fathers spend with their children and the risk of violence to the mother. That is, a father who sees the children for four nights every two weeks is not more likely to engage in violence toward the other parent than a father who has the children for only three nights every two weeks. Certainly, the more frequent the handovers between the parents, the more opportunity there is for interaction, but increased duration of contact does not necessarily equate with increased frequency of handovers. Contact between parents during school term can in any event be avoided by structuring the arrangements to involve collection after school, with a return to school.

Issues about the mother's safety in the light of serious concerns about ongoing violence either have to be addressed by denying contact entirely, by organizing the handover of children through contact centers or other third parties, or by allowing a relocation of the mother to a distant location.

The position is different where there are safety concerns for the children, because the more time the father spends with the children, the more opportunity there is for harm to occur. The linear relationship between time and safety is therefore in terms of threats to the well-being of children rather than to the primary caregiver. Having said this, where there is a history of serious and ongoing violence in an intimate partnership, the risk of abuse to the children ought to be presumed.

What is needed, therefore, is a bifurcation in terms of policy. There are families in which contact between the nonresident parent and the children presents serious safety issues for mother, children, or both, and given the history of violence, ongoing contact could bring little conceivable benefit to the children. There are other families where at least for a period of time, contact needs to be supervised. There are many other families where the

---

[84] Dalton, *supra* note 63, at 287.

history of violence by one parent toward the other ought to have a decisive impact on choice of primary caregiver, and where the evidence of violence has implications for the assessment of the character of the nonresident parent and his capacity to meet the children's emotional and other needs, leading to consequential decisions about the amount of contact that is appropriate in the circumstances.

A bifurcation in terms of policy reflects the natural demographic of postseparation families, with some fathers dropping out of children's lives within a few months or years after separation, whereas others continue with regular contact for many years.[85] By no means all father-child relationships do – or should – survive parental separation, and family law systems need to come to terms with that. As the poet Arthur Clough once wrote: "Thou shalt not kill; but need'st not strive/officiously to keep alive."[86] Sometimes, perhaps, family law systems around the world try too hard to keep alive relationships that are not sufficiently healthy to survive without intensive care.

A bifurcation in terms of policy can be achieved without diminishing the importance given to the role of nonresident parents in children's lives, as long as there is a recognition in a procontact culture that an absolute priority must be given to the safety of women and children from a significant risk of serious harm, and clear messages are given to the community that a history of violence and abuse may lead courts to deny contact. The values of the family law system must be consistent with the kinds of decisions made in child protection cases in determining whether it is safe to leave a child in the care of his or her parents, and should not offer less protection than would be made in a child protection case. Making that decision is often an agonizing judgment call – and one that, without the benefit of prophetic foresight, is not always made correctly in either the child protection system or in the context of family law disputes. However, the issues are similar, and therefore a similar balance needs to be struck between the recognition of the importance of parent-child relationships to both parents and children, and the need to ensure as far as possible that children are protected from harm.

---

[85] Jacob Cheadle, Paul Amato, & Valarie King, *Patterns of Nonresident Father Contact*, 47 DEMOGRAPHY 205 (2010).

[86] Arthur Clough, "The Latest Decalogue" in THE POEMS OF ARTHUR HUGH CLOUGH, (2nd ed, 1974).

7

Relocation

Relocation cases are the San Andreas Fault of family law,[1] because they involve a fundamental clash between two competing ideas about postseparation family life, one in which the family is seen to be at an end, ushering in a freedom for people to begin a new life for themselves, and the other in which the family is seen to endure beyond separation.[2]

THE DILEMMA OF RELOCATION

Relocation cases, or "mobility" or "moving away" cases as they are sometimes known in North America, are among the most difficult cases that family courts have to deal with.[3] A New York court wrote in a leading case that relocation cases "present some of the knottiest and most disturbing problems that our courts are called upon to resolve."[4]

Relocation is a commonplace event in the aftermath of separation. Indeed for many parents, it is likely to be a necessity. As a result of the property settlement, the matrimonial home may have to be sold, and one or both parents will need to gravitate to areas of lower housing costs. In the big cities, these areas are often on the perimeter of the city or beyond, leading to the creation of some distance between the parents' homes. Separation has a centrifugal effect on many parents in terms of where each can afford to live after separation. Moves of residence may necessitate practical changes

---

[1] Richard Chisholm, *The Paramount Consideration: Children's Interests in Family Law*, 16 AUSTRALIAN J. FAM. L. 87, 107 (2002).

[2] *See e.g.* Bauers v Lewis, 770 A 2d 214, 217 (N.J. Sup. Ct, 2001).

[3] Dennis Duggan, *Rock-paper-scissors: Playing the Odds with the Law of Child Relocation*, 45 FAM. CT REV. 193 (2007); Tim Carmody, *Child Relocation: An Intractable International Family Law Problem*, 45 FAM. CT REV. 214 (2007).

[4] Tropea v. Tropea, 665 N.E.2d 145, 148 (1996).

to preexisting arrangements for contact between the nonresident parent and the child. Contact may be made more difficult or expensive, or less frequent. These changes are normal incidents of relationship breakdown. They are not major changes affecting the relationship between the nonresident parent and the child.

Where, however, the proposed relocation by one parent involves moving such a distance from the nonresident parent that frequent contact becomes impossible, then a major question arises. In what circumstances should a resident parent be prevented from relocating with a child where the relocation would disrupt continuing regular contact with the nonresident parent?

Relocation and the Problem of Prediction

While the best interests of the child is the paramount consideration, working out what is best for children in these cases can be very difficult because decision making often depends on making predictions about the outcomes of quite different alternative scenarios. If the child is allowed to move, then how will that affect his or her relationship with the nonresident parent? Is it possible for the nonresident parent to relocate as well? How will the child adjust to the new location with all the changes that this entails? If the court declines to permit the move, will the parent decide to move anyway without the child? If neither parent nor child move, will the mother adjust to the court's decision and make the best of her situation? If she continues to be unhappy about being unable to move to her preferred location, how will this affect the children?

Migration, Mobility, and the New Technologies

The problem of relocation is one that is attracting more and more attention and litigation.[5] One factor in this is the increase in international mobility. The proportion of Americans born in another country is estimated at 13.6 percent.[6] The percentage of all children living in the United States with at

---

[5] For evidence of the increase over time in the number of decided 'mobility' cases in Canada, *see* Elizabeth Jollimore & Ramona Sladic, *Mobility – Are We There Yet?*, 27 CAN. F.L.Q. 341 (2008).

[6] ORGANISATION FOR ECONOMIC COOPERATION AND DEVELOPMENT, INTERNATIONAL MIGRATION DATA 2009, STOCKS OF FOREIGN-BORN POPULATION IN SELECTED OECD COUNTRIES, http://www.oecd.org/document/52/0,3343,en_2649_33931_42274676_1_1_1_37415,00.html

least one foreign-born parent rose from 15 percent in 1994 to 22 percent in 2008.[7] In Australia, the level of migration is even higher. The proportion of the population who were born overseas increased from 10 percent in 1947 to 24 percent in 2000.[8] Currently, the Australian population has a net gain of one international migrant every two minutes.[9] In the context of such global mobility, relationships between people of different national origins are increasingly common, as well as migration by couples from one country to another. The breakup of such relationships may lead one to want to return to his or her country of origin.

International migration and the extent of international relationships are only part of the picture. Mobility within countries is also a major factor in the relocation problem. In the United States, for example, nearly 2.5 million people moved to a different region of the country in 2008–09.[10]

Another factor is changes in dating patterns. In the aftermath of separation and divorce, new relationships may form between people who live long distances from each other. Internet dating is a particular reason for this. Whereas a generation ago, separated parents' opportunities to find a new partner would mainly be limited to those they met through work or community involvement, and those opportunities were particularly limited for single parents whose care responsibilities made it difficult to go on dates, all that has now changed. Modern internet-based introduction services have radically increased the opportunities for separated parents to meet new people, and the connections thus formed are supported by very cheap modes of communication such as email, Internet chat programs, and Web-based telephone or video communication. Distance is little obstacle to the development of such relationships in the early stages. Although it may make personal contact more difficult, the opportunities for inexpensive plane travel both within countries and, to a lesser extent, between countries are such that those difficulties can readily be overcome by many. It is often only much further down the track – when the couple have formed strong emotional attachments – that the complexities of forming a new life partnership have to be confronted.

---

[7] Federal Interagency Forum on Child and Family Statistics, America's Children: Key National Indicators of Well-Being 8 (2009), http://www.nichd. nih.gov/publications/pubs/upload/Americas-Children-2009.pdf

[8] Australian Bureau of Statistics, International Migration, 2002, http://www. abs.gov.au

[9] As of July 2010. See Australian Population Clock, http://www.abs.gov.au

[10] U.S. Census Bureau, Geographical Mobility, 2008–09, Current Population Survey tbl. 1 (2009), http://www.census.gov/population/www/socdemo/migrate/ cps2009.html

THE CONFLICT IN LEGISLATURES AND COURTS

On the issue of relocation, it is safe to say that the jurisprudence of the common law world is far from uniform. The traditional position in the common law world[11] was that a choice of location was an aspect of the custody allocation. Civil law countries had a similar rule.[12] As a consequence, children went with the custodial parent wherever he or she chose to live. The common law principles date back to the nineteenth century.[13]

That changed over time, as awareness grew of the importance of both parents being involved in children's lives after separation. What emerged was not a new and coherent approach to relocation but a kaleidoscope of different approaches and positions around the western world.

When Is a Move a "Relocation"?

An area of fundamental disagreement concerns what constitutes a relocation. In England, for example, the law requires leave to remove a child from the jurisdiction,[14] with the consequence that a move beyond the borders of the United Kingdom is a relocation, but a move within the jurisdiction, however much it may disrupt existing patterns of contact, is not. Thus the definition of a relocation has nothing to do with the impact of a proposed move on the existing parenting arrangements; it is defined by whether a move involves crossing a geographical border. Some American jurisdictions impose a distance limitation, with notification required to the other parent if the primary caregiver intends to move more than a certain specified distance away, and with the nonresident

---

[11] On the traditional interpretation of the common law in Canada, see Douglas v. Douglas, [1948] 1 W.W.R. 473 (Sask. K.B.); Beck v. Beck, [1950] 1 D.L.R. 492 (BCCA); Wright v. Wright [1973] 40 D.L.R. (3d) 321 (Ont. CA).

[12] For the traditional position in France, see GABRIEL MARTY & PIERRE RAYNAUD, LES PERSONNES 288 (3rd ed. 1976).

[13] Wood v. Wood, 5 Paige Ch. 596 (Ch. NY) (parent or guardian has right to change residence of children from one state to another subject to the power of the court to restrain removal in extreme cases). The position was similar in the common law of England. Lord Justice Fry said in the English Court of Appeal in Hunt v. Hunt, (1884) 28 Ch. D. 606 that a noncustodial mother had no right to restrain the father from taking two of their children with him to Egypt, where he had been posted with the army. Commenting on the mother's right of access, he said that it meant nothing more than that the mother had a right to see the children where they happen to be. He wrote: "to hold that it obliges the husband to keep the children in such a place that she can conveniently have access to them, would create formidable difficulties." Id. at 613.

[14] Children Act, 1989, s.13.

parent having a right to object.[15] In Australia, there is no definition of what constitutes a relocation and no particular need for such a definition because there is not a specific set of statutory considerations that applies to proposed moves.[16]

Different Legal Approaches

Not only does the definition of a relocation vary from one jurisdiction to another, but the legal process by which the relocation issue is determined also varies. In some jurisdictions, the issue will be presented as one about whether leave should be granted or refused to move with the child; in others, the issues may be explored as a question about modification of the existing custody arrangements, with different statutory criteria applying to that question.

There are also considerable differences between jurisdictions on the substantive law. In the United States, for example, by the mid-1980s, one author commented that "a bewildering diversity of legal rules is brought to bear on the issue of relocation."[17] Positions ranged from a burden on the relocating parent to show compelling reasons for being allowed to move, through a neutral best-interests test, to a burden on the parent opposing the move to show that harm to the children would result from the relocation. No consensus of opinion was discernible.

In the 1990s, that diversity of approaches continued to be evident, but the trend at least in some of the most populous states was for liberalization of the freedom to move. In New York, the Court of Appeals abandoned its restrictive approach to relocation in its 1996 decision in *Tropea v. Tropea*,[18] in favor of a test of what is in the best interests of the child without recourse to presumptions.

In recent years, the trend has been to move toward an approach that uses an open-ended best interests of the child test.[19] This is a position similar to

---

[15] Linda Elrod, *A Move in the Right Direction?: Best Interests of the Child Emerging as Standard for Relocation Cases, in* RELOCATION ISSUES IN CHILD CUSTODY CASES 29, 33ff. (Phillip Stahl & Leslie Drozd eds., 2006). This volume was copublished simultaneously with volume 3, issues 3–4 of the JOURNAL OF CHILD CUSTODY (2006).

[16] Morgan & Miles (2007) F.L.C. ¶¶93–343.

[17] Anne Spitzer, *Moving and Storage of Postdivorce Children: Relocation, the Constitution and the Courts,* ARIZ. ST. L. J. 1, 4 (1985).

[18] Tropea v. Tropea, 665 N.E.2d 145 (1996).

[19] For reviews of the various approaches in the United States, *see* Theresa Glennon, *Divided Parents, Shared Children – Conflicting Approaches to Relocation Disputes in the USA,* 4 UTRECHT L. REV. 55, 57 (2008); Elrod, *supra* note 15.

that in other English-speaking jurisdictions.[20] There remains in the United States, nonetheless, a bewildering variety of approaches, with states adopting different approaches to the question of who has the burden of persuading the court of his or her case in relation to the proposed move, and whether a relocation constitutes a change of circumstances in itself justifying reopening the custody allocation. In some states, constitutional arguments about freedom of movement for the custodial parent have been brought into play.[21] Linda Elrod has described the current state of relocation law across America as a "hodge-podge of presumptions, burdens, factors and lists."[22]

Even within jurisdictions, the law has fluctuated over time, indicating ongoing battles over the issue. Nowhere is this clearer than in California. In 1996, the Supreme Court handed down its decision in *Burgess v. Burgess* that was favorable to parents who wanted to relocate with their children.[23] In 2003, the Supreme Court gave leave to reopen *Burgess*. The legislature then made a preemptive strike, passing a law in 2003 to affirm the position adopted in *Burgess v. Burgess*. Section 7501 of the Family Code was amended to read:

(a) A parent entitled to the custody of a child has a right to change the residence of the child, subject to the power of the court to restrain a removal that would prejudice the rights or welfare of the child.

(b) It is the intent of the Legislature to affirm the decision in In *re Marriage of Burgess* (1996) 13 Cal. 4th 25, and to declare that ruling to be the public policy and law of this state.

Cases normally interpret statutes, but here, the legislature aligned itself to a particular case. The Supreme Court was not deterred. Appearing to maintain conformity with precedent and deference to the statute while bringing about change, the Supreme Court chose to explain *Burgess*, offering an interpretation that was less sympathetic to parents who wanted to move.[24]

---

[20] In Canada, see Gordon v. Goertz: Women's Legal Education and Action Fund (LEAF), 134 D.L.R. (4th) 321 (1996). In Australia, see AMS v. AIF 199 C.L.R. 160 (1999) (relocation within Australia); U v. U 211 C.L.R. 238 (2002) (relocation overseas). *See also* A v. A: Relocation Approach F.L.C. ¶93–035 (2000); Taylor and Barker F.L.C. ¶93–345 (2007); McCall v. Clark 41 FAM. L.R. 483 (2009).

[21] *See e.g.* Watt v. Watt, 971 P.2d 608 (Wyo. Sup. Ct. 1999). On the constitutional issues, *see* Arthur LaFrance, *Child Custody and Relocation: A Constitutional Perspective*, 34 U. LOUISVILLE J. FAM. L. 1 (1995–96).

[22] Elrod, *supra* note 15, at 48.

[23] *In Re* Marriage of Burgess, 13 Cal. 4th 25 (1996).

[24] LaMusga v. LaMusga, 32 Cal. 4th 1072 (2004). The Court affirmed Burgess and explained aspects of its judgment in that case in the light of subsequent consideration by the Court

The battle over relocation has also seen appellate courts in conflict with trial court judges who are reluctant to follow the principles of appellate judgments that require relocation to be allowed.[25]

The conflict is not only in the courts. There are acrimonious policy debates about how the needs of the children to have a relationship with their parents can be reconciled with a primary caregiver's desire to live where she or he chooses.[26] So difficult are these issues that the Uniform Law Commission in the United States decided in 2009 to give up its attempt to develop a model law on the subject.[27]The President of the Uniform Law Commission explained in a letter that "given that the various interest groups are contentious and the states have adopted varying approaches on how to deal with the issue of relocation of children ... any act drafted by the ULC on this subject, no matter how much an advancement of the law, would not be enacted in a significant number of states."[28]

---

of Appeal. It concluded that "this area of law is not amenable to inflexible rules" (at 1101) and gave guidance to lower courts on how to exercise their discretion:

"Among the factors that the court ordinarily should consider when deciding whether to modify a custody order in light of the custodial parent's proposal to change the residence of the child are the following: the children's interest in stability and continuity in the custodial arrangement; the distance of the move; the age of the children; the children's relationship with both parents; the relationship between the parents including, but not limited to, their ability to communicate and cooperate effectively and their willingness to put the interests of the children above their individual interests; the wishes of the children if they are mature enough for such an inquiry to be appropriate; the reasons for the proposed move; and the extent to which the parents currently are sharing custody." (at 1101)

[25] Bruch and Bowermaster have noted the extent of conflict between lower courts and appellate courts: "State supreme courts ... have often operated against a tide of restrictive lower court rulings that prohibit a child's relocation in order to preserve or enhance existing visitation schedules. Indeed, supreme court opinions that support relocation opportunities have sometimes encountered so much resistance that the courts that rendered them have been moved to either issue further, more strongly worded opinions or, where they have had the option, to summarily reverse strings of decisions that have sought to avoid their logic." Carol Bruch & Janet Bowermaster, *The Relocation of Children and Custodial Parents: Public Policy, Past and Present*, 30 FAM. L. Q. 245, 247 (1996).

[26] For law reform proposals, see American Academy of Matrimonial Lawyers, *Proposed Model Relocation Act: An Act Relating to the Relocation of the Principal Residence of a Child*, 15 J. AM. ACAD. MATRIM. L. 1 (1998); AMERICAN LAW INSTITUTE, PRINCIPLES OF THE LAW OF FAMILY DISSOLUTION: ANALYSIS AND RECOMMENDATIONS §2.17 (2002). In Australia, see FAMILY LAW COUNCIL, RELOCATION (2006).

[27] Peter Messitte, *Relocation of Children: Law and Practice in the United States*, Paper given at the Judicial Conference for Common Law and Commonwealth Jurisdictions, Windsor, England, August 2009, at 6–7.

[28] Letter to the Chairperson of the Drafting Committee, February 2009, cited in Messitte, *supra* note 27.

The conflict over policy extends to the social science literature on relocation. Research that appears to support an opposing view is attacked with a ferocity rarely seen in response to empirical findings in other fields of study.[29] All research requires evaluation, critique, and testing (including the research studies that support one's favored position), but in the response to research findings on relocation, critique has been particularly vehement.

RELOCATION: BETWEEN TWO MEANINGS OF DIVORCE

The debates about relocation reflect the fundamental problem confronting modern family law today. What weight should be given to postseparation autonomy and how much weight should be given to the importance to a child of a meaningful relationship with both parents, and conversely, the nonresident parent's interest in maintaining that relationship?

The conflict between these two competing values – postseparation autonomy and continuing familial relationships in the postdivorce family – can be clearly seen in the different views expressed by judges of the Supreme Court of Canada in the leading case of *Gordon v. Goertz*,[30] which involved a request from a custodial mother to relocate from Canada to Australia.[31] In the outcome, the Court was unanimous in allowing the mother to relocate, but differed sharply in the reasons

[29] A particularly critical reception was given to a retrospective study on relocation. Sanford Braver, Ira Ellman & William Fabricius, *Relocation of Children after Divorce and Children's Best Interests: New Evidence and Legal Considerations*, 17 J. FAM. PSYCH. 206 (2003). *See e.g.* Carol Bruch, *Sound Research or Wishful Thinking in Child Custody Cases? Lessons from Relocation Law*, 40 FAM. L Q. 281 (2006). For a measured evaluation of their study, *see* Robert Pasahow, *A Critical Analysis of the First Empirical Research Study on Child Relocation*, 19 J. AM. ACADEMY MATRIMONIAL LAWYERS, 321 (2005). The research team provided further data subsequently in a response to critics. William Fabricius & Sanford Braver, *Relocation, Parent Conflict, and Domestic Violence: Independent Risk Factors for Children of Divorce*, in RELOCATION ISSUES IN CHILD CUSTODY CASES 7 (Phillip Stahl & Leslie Drozd eds., 2006).

[30] Gordon v. Goertz: Women's Legal Education and Action Fund (LEAF), 134 D.L.R. (4th) 321 (1996) (hereafter, *Gordon*). For commentary, *see* Perminder Basran, *Gordon v. Goertz: The Supreme Court Compounds Confusion over Custody and Access*, 61 SASKATCHEWAN. L. REV. 159 (1998). *See also* Susan Boyd, *Custody, Access and Relocation in a Mobile Society: (En)gendering the Best Interests Principle*, in LAW AS A GENDERING PRACTICE 158 (Dorothy E. Chunn & Dany Lacombe eds., 2000). For analysis of cases since *Gordon v. Goertz*, *see* Rollie Thompson, *Relocation and Relitigation: After Gordon v Goertz*, 16 CAN. FAM. L. Q. 461 (1999); Rollie Thompson, *Ten Years after Gordon: No Law, Nowhere*, (2007) 35 R.F.L. (6th) 307.

[31] The mother had custody and sought to vary the order so that the child could relocate with her from Saskatchewan to Australia. She also wanted the father to have access to the

given for coming to that conclusion.[32] Both the majority and minority judgments were delivered by women justices, Justice McLachlin and Justice L'Heureux-Dubé.

The majority of the court took the view that the interests of the child were the only relevant concern. Canadian law reinforced the importance of contact with the nonresident parent, but this gave way ultimately to the best interests of the child.[33] This required a balancing of the competing interests of the child; on the one hand, the importance of the child continuing in the custody of the same parent, but in a new location, and on the other hand, the significance to the child of continuing a significant level of contact with the noncustodial parent, the extended family, and the child's community.[34] In treating the question as merely a matter of balancing competing interests of the child, the majority opposed any notion of starting points, presumptions, or an onus of proof.[35] Justice McLachlin, for the majority, wrote: "A presumption in favour of the custodial parent has the potential to impair the inquiry into the best interests of the child. This inquiry should not be undertaken with a mind-set that defaults in favour of a pre-ordained outcome absent persuasion to the contrary."[36]

The contrasting position may be seen in the judgment of L'Heureux-Dubé who agreed in the result.[37] Justice L'Heureux-Dubé preferred a clear principle that the custodial parent has a right to determine place of residence. In her view, if a court has decided that one parent is to be preferred over the other as a primary caregiver, then that decision gives

child only in Australia, placing the onus of travel entirely on him. The trial judge and the Saskatchewan Court of Appeal were prepared to make orders to this effect. The Supreme Court of Canada unanimously upheld the mother's right to go with the child to Australia but allowed the father to exercise access in Canada.

[32] For an analysis of the arguments of the parties and interveners, *see* Susan Boyd, Child Custody, Law, and Women's Work 137–152 (2003).

[33] *Gordon*, at 333. The Divorce Act, s.16(8) (1985) (Can.), applied in this case provides: "In making an order under this section, the court shall take into consideration only the best interests of the child of the marriage as determined by reference to the condition, means, needs and other circumstances of the child." Section 16(10) provides a principle for the award of contact:

"In making an order under this section, the court shall give effect to the principle that a child of the marriage should have as much contact with each spouse as is consistent with the best interests of the child and, for that purpose, shall take into consideration the willingness of the person for whom custody is sought to facilitate such contact."

[34] *Gordon*, at 343.

[35] Justice McLachlin, for the majority, wrote: "The Act contemplates individual justice. The judge is obliged to consider the best interests of the particular child in the particular circumstances of the case. Had Parliament wished to impose general rules at the expense of individual justice, it could have done so." *Gordon*, at 337–38.

[36] *Id*. at 340.

[37] La Forest J concurred with the judgment of L'Heureux-Dubé.

that parent the right to relocate with the child wherever he or she may choose to go, and the fact that such a move may necessitate changes in the existing arrangements for contact between the nonresident parent and the child does not in itself justify reopening the decision as to who should have the custody of the child. The onus of proof must be on the noncustodial parent to show that the proposed change of residence will be detrimental to the child. She considered that such an approach provides clarity and certainty, and reduces the likelihood of acrimonious negotiations or traumatic and costly litigation.[38]

The contrast between the majority judgment and L'Heureux-Dubé's minority judgment reveals quite different visions of the postdivorce family. For the majority, the role of the court was to determine the best interests of the child in the new circumstances presented by the planned relocation, and in the context of continuing family relationships. The role of the court was not merely to select a custodial parent in the case of dispute. Rather, accepting that the new circumstances were not the same now as when the custodial decision was originally made, the court needed to look at all the circumstances in determining what now would be in the best interests of the child, taking into account a range of factors.[39] The relocation decision was to be made in the context of seeking to preserve as far as possible, the child's relationships with both parents, and other relationships significant to the child.[40]

Justice L'Heureux-Dubé's approach could not have presented a greater contrast, and reflected many of the assumptions underlying the substitution model of postdivorce parenting. She quoted from her judgment three years earlier in *Young v. Young*[41] on the traditional decision-making power of the custodial parent. In that judgment, she cited Goldstein, Freud, and Solnit's ideas in *Beyond the Best Interests of the Child* in support of the

[38] *Gordon*, especially at 349–61.

[39] Justice McLachlin, who delivered the judgment of the majority, set out a number of factors to consider in relocation cases:

> the existing custody arrangement and relationship between the child and the custodial parent;
> the existing arrangement and the relationship between the child and access parent;
> the desirability of maximizing contact between the child and both parents;
> the views of the child;
> the custodial parent's reason for moving, *only* in the exceptional case where it is relevant to the parent's ability to meet the needs of the child;
> disruption to the child of a change in custody;
> disruption to the child consequent on removal from family, schools, and the community he or she has come to know.

[40] In practice, the application of *Gordon* to relocation disputes has meant that the majority of relocations are allowed. *See* Jollimore & Sladic, *supra* note 5.

[41] [1993] S.C.R. 3.

propositions that the most important consideration was to preserve the relationship between the child and his or her "psychological parent," and that a custodial parent should have the autonomy to raise the child as he or she sees fit without interference with that authority by the state or the noncustodial parent.[42] In adopting this approach, L'Heureux-Dubé reaffirmed the traditional notion of custody as involving the sole right to exercise all aspects of parental authority to the exclusion of the other parent.[43] The difference between the two judges, and between the majority and minority positions in the court, was the difference between a belief in the substitution model of the family and the notion that the family endures after separation in two households.

A similar division of view about the meaning of divorce may be found also in the scholarly literature on relocation. Judith Wallerstein, for example, whose amicus brief strongly influenced the Supreme Court of California in *Burgess* and later relocation cases in other jurisdictions,[44] emphasized the importance of the bond between custodial parent and child as the primary concern. Her amicus brief was later revised for publication in an article coauthored with the lawyer in the case, Tony Tanke.[45] They explained their rationale for opposing restrictions on relocation in terms reminiscent of the substitution model of the postseparation family, arguing that on separation and divorce, the parents "effectively establish, with or without legal contest, a new kind of family unit in which the child resides."[46] They continued:[47]

> Court intervention designed to maintain the geographical proximity of divorced parents is fundamentally at odds with a divorce decision that necessarily determines that each parent will rebuild his or her life separate from the other. To require divorcing parents to spend their lives in the same geographic

---

[42] *Gordon*, at 365–66, quoting Young v. Young [1993] S.C.R. 3, 214–15, 233.

[43] In *Young v. Young* [1993] S.C.R. 3, L'Heureux-Dubé wrote (para 112):"The longstanding rule at common law is that an order of custody entails the right to exercise full parental authority. In the case of a sole custody order, that authority is vested in one parent to the exclusion of the other." Her judgment reflected the arguments of the interveners in the case. The Women's Legal Education and Action Fund (LEAF) wrote at para 37 of its factum: "The custodial parent and the child are a new family unit on separation. The court must consider the effect on the mother, and thus on the family unit, of restricting where she can live" (cited in BOYD, *supra* note 32, at 145).

[44] Janet Richards, *Children's Rights Versus Parents' Rights: A Proposed Solution to the Custodial Relocation Conundrum*, 29 NEW MEX. L. REV. 245, 258–261 (1999).

[45] Judith Wallerstein & Tony Tanke, *To Move or Not to Move: Psychological and Legal Considerations in the Relocation of Children Following Divorce*, 30 FAM. L.Q. 305 (1996).

[46] *Id.* at 314.   [47] *Id.* at 314–15.

vicinity is unrealistic. The state cannot legitimately confine individuals to a particular location in their quest for love or the good things in life.

Thus the rules about relocation ought to follow from the meaning of divorce. They went on to argue that restraining relocation would not be in the best interests of the children because it might lead to frustration and disappointment for the custodial parent.

Law professors Carol Bruch and Janet Bowermaster also put their argument supporting a general entitlement to relocate in terms strongly reminiscent of the old substitution model of the family. They wrote:[48]

> An initial custody decision between parents is, of course, handled with the best interests standard. But once made, whether consensually or by court order, a new family unit results that deserves protection for many of the same reasons that parents are protected from strangers in other contexts.

The analogy between a nonresident parent and the legal position of a stranger is telling. In their conceptualization of the effect of divorce, the nonresident parent becomes an outsider to the family unit that comprises the custodial parent and the children, together with any new partner of the custodial parent.[49]

While scholars such as Wallerstein, Bruch, and Bowermaster have sought to address the issue of relocation by restating the assumptions of the divorce revolution, others have sought to rethink those assumptions. Psychologist Richard Warshak, for example, is highly critical of Wallerstein's position and argues on the basis of the available research concerning children's need for a relationship with both parents, that the law should encourage both parents to remain in proximity to their children.[50] However, he recognizes that the impact of relocation on children is dependent on several factors, and argues that there needs to be an individualized determination in each case of whether relocation should be supported.[51]

---

[48] Bruch & Bowermaster, *supra* note 25, at 265.

[49] For a similar view that the family unit after divorce is the custodial parent and the child, *see* Tropea v. Tropea, 665 N.E.2d 145 (1996); Kenward v. Brown, 87 N.Y. (2d) 727, 740 (N.Y.C.A., 1996), per Titone J. By way of contrast, the Supreme Court of Canada described the custodial parent, access parent and children as a "post-divorce family unit" in Thibaudeau v. Canada, [1995] S.C.R. 627.

[50] Richard Warshak, *Social Science and Children's Best Interests in Relocation Cases: Burgess Revisited*, 34 FAM. L.Q. 83 (2000).

[51] *Id. See also* Joan Kelly & Michael Lamb, *Developmental Issues in Relocation Cases Involving Young Children: When, Whether and How?*, 17 J. FAM. PSYCH. 193, 196 (2003). Lamb and Kelly note that a range of factors need to be evaluated in determining a

BEYOND POLARIZATION

Developing a coherent policy on relocation in the age of the enduring family requires something other than just the restatement of entrenched positions for or against relocation in the abstract, focused on adult interests. The problem in this area lies in the competing policy positions represented by these very different understandings of what divorce ought to mean and the balance between freedom and responsibility that it entails. There is nonetheless value in clearer thinking about the issue of relocation, in a way that helps to move beyond the polarized positions of the gender war. Two issues in particular require more careful analysis. The first is the argument that prohibitions on relocation are discriminatory, and the second is that only women's freedom of movement is restrained as a consequence of the indissolubility of parenthood.

Gender and Relocation

When there are disputes about relocation, it is almost always women who want to move, and men, the nonresident parents, who oppose that move.[52] Restrictions on relocation may thus appear to be discriminatory, but arguing about children's issues using the rhetoric of gender equality and discrimination leads quickly into dangerous waters. Child support is, after all, predominantly a male obligation. Few would seek to argue that because child support laws disproportionately impose obligations on fathers, that therefore they are discriminatory. The reason why the child support obligation is in general terms morally incontestable (whatever contest there may be about the level of that obligation) is that there is a widely accepted moral value that parents should support their children financially.

Patterns of custody decisions could also be argued to be discriminatory because fathers are disproportionately the nonresident parents, but the issue is not whether outcomes disproportionately favor mothers or fathers. The issue is whether the policy settings in any given jurisdiction are set optimally to promote the well-being of children and to ensure that

relocation case. However, they consider that if a relocation is necessary, it should ideally be postponed until children are two or three years old in order to allow the relationship with the nonresident parent to be developed to the point that a long-distance relationship can be sustained.

[52]   For commentary, *see e.g.* Chris Ford, *Untying the Relocation Knot: Recent Developments and a Model for Change,* 7 COLUM. J. GENDER & L. 1 (1997). In Australia, *see* Kirby J in AMS v. AIF 199 C.L.R. 160, 206 (1999); Gaudron J in U v U 211 C.L.R. 238, 248 (2002). *See also* Juliet Behrens, *A Feminist Perspective on B and B (The Family Court and Mobility),* 2 SISTER IN LAW 65 (1997).

as far as possible, individual custody decisions are made in children's best interests.

The challenge, in relation to relocation policy, is to remain child-focused without being distracted by arguments about gendered impacts. Gendered impacts are everywhere in family law.

Nonetheless, restrictions on relocation may involve gender discrimination if the question is not asked whether the nonresident parent could move as well when there is a dispute about the mother's move. Justice Mary Gaudron, hearing an appeal in a relocation case in Australia's final court of appeal, commented on the fact that there had been little consideration in the lower courts of whether the father could move. In this case, both parents were Indian, and the mother wanted to return to India. Justice Gaudron wrote: [53]

> [I]t is noteworthy that in this case there was no consideration of the possibility that the father could return to India permanently to avail himself of frequent and regular contact with his daughter. The failure to explore that possibility, particularly given the father's origins, his professional qualifications and family contacts in India, seems to me to be explicable only on the basis of an assumption, inherently sexist, that a father's choice as to where he lives is beyond challenge in a way that a mother's is not.

Even though this was a dissenting judgment, the majority agreed with that proposition,[54] and since the decision in that case, Australian courts have been required to consider whether nonresident parents could move.[55]

Freedom of Movement

A primary caregiver does not have the same freedom to move as the nonresident parent if the relocation is opposed, at least if she or he wants to remain the primary caregiver of the children. In practical terms, there is

[53] U v U, 211 C.L.R. at 248 (High Court of Australia). On this issue, *see also* Merle Weiner, *Inertia and Inequality: Reconceptualizing Disputes Over Parental Relocation*, 40 U.C. DAVIS L.R. 1747 (2007).

[54] *See* Hayne J, U v U, 211 C.L.R. at 285 ("When one parent (for whatever reason) wishes a child who is, or is to be, resident with that parent to move to a place distant from the other parent, it should not be assumed that that other parent cannot, or should not, contemplate moving to be near the child.") Gleeson CJ (at 240) and McHugh J (at 249) agreed with Hayne J. For commentary on this case, *see* Juliet Behrens, *U v U: The High Court on Relocation*, 27 MELBOURNE U. L. REV. 572 (2003).

[55] The Court of Appeal of British Columbia has expressed a similar view. *See* S.S.L. v. J.W.W, [2010] B.C.J. No.180, 2010 BCCA 55.

little that can be done if nonresident parents choose to move away from their children, even if the effect in terms of disruption in the parent-child relationship is similar. Nonresident parents cannot readily be compelled to maintain a particular level of involvement with their child. They need to choose to do so. Restrictions on freedom of movement are effectively restraints on children moving, not parents moving. It follows that there is a gendered dimension to the issue of freedom of movement in that nonresident parents who want to move away from their children cannot readily be restrained.

However, the gendered nature of this issue is not so obvious as it may at first appear. Indeed, the proposition that only one parent's freedom of movement is limited must be questioned. Both parents are tied to one another by the indissolubility of parenthood. Certainly, only one parent's freedom of movement may be restrained as a matter of law. The equality of restraint may, however, be more evident when one considers the practical restraints on a nonresident parent who wants to remain closely involved with the children. To remain close to the children means staying within a reasonable distance of the children's primary caregiver, and that is a restraint that a great many nonresident parents accept. A study of data from the Netherlands found that when nonresident fathers moved, they moved the least distance of any of the groups in the study. This was hypothesized to be because of their desire to stay near to their children. The estimated moving distance of single mothers with children did not differ from women with children in a first intact family relationship.[56]

RELOCATION AND THE BEST INTERESTS OF THE CHILD TEST

Like the majority of the Supreme Court of Canada in *Gordon v. Goertz*, the solution that many jurisdictions have adopted has been just to leave it up to the courts, applying the best interests test. There are problems, nonetheless, in applying a best interests of the child test without presumptions or starting points, because it leaves unresolved the balance to be struck between postseparation autonomy and enduring close relationships with both parents.

This is well illustrated by the New Zealand litigation of *D v. S*, which was finally settled in 2002.[57] In this case, which involved the desire of a

---

[56] Peteke Feijten & Maarten Van Ham, *Residential Mobility and Migration of the Divorced and Separated*, 17 DEMOGRAPHIC RESEARCH 623 (2007).

[57] [2002] N.Z.F.L.R. 116.

mother to relocate to Ireland, nine judges eventually heard the matter, in five different hearings at first instance or on appeal. The case was heard in the New Zealand Family Court, with the outcome that the mother was not permitted to move out of New Zealand, appealed to the High Court, which held she should be allowed to move, appealed again to the highest court, the Court of Appeal, which held that the High Court was in error, remitted back to the Family Court for rehearing, which decided that the children should live in New Zealand, and taken on appeal again to the High Court which decided they could live in Ireland.[58] In this case, the best interests of the child test led to a quagmire for this family, with different decisions representing different value judgments about the importance of the father-child relationship in relation to the resident parent's entitlement to postseparation freedom.

Without the fundamental policy issues being resolved, the rhetoric of the child's best interests simply masks competing policy positions based often on the weight given to the different adult interests. Indeed, relocation cases have been the stimulus for judicial interpretations of the principle that children's interests are paramount, which give much more weight to considerations apart from the welfare of the child than is usually the case in disputes concerning postseparation parenting.[59]

Leaving it all up to individual judges to determine what they consider to be in the best interests of the child has all the attraction of deferral to an established standard; but indeterminacy is only a good political solution, not a sensible social policy. In Australia, where there is an open-ended best interests test for relocation, one of the consequences is that the likelihood of a relocation being allowed varies significantly from region to region, even though all judges are meant to be applying the same law. This may reflect different interpretations of the law and beliefs about the best interests of children among clusters of judges who work together in the same location.[60]

Indeterminacy has its costs, not least in terms of legal expenses. Relocation disputes are often pyrrhic victories, with the price for the

---

[58] Despite this "final" decision, as at 2010, the mother, the father and children are now all living in Christchurch, New Zealand.

[59] For an analysis, *see* Richard Chisholm, *The Paramount Consideration: Children's Interests in Family Law*, 16 AUSTRALIAN J. FAM. L. 87 (2002). *See also* Jonathan Crowe & Lisa Toohey, *From Good Intentions to Ethical Outcomes: The Paramountcy of Children's Interests in the Family Law Act*, 33 MELB. U. L. REV. 391 (2009).

[60] Patrick Parkinson, *The Realities of Relocation: Messages from Judicial Decisions*, 22 AUSTRALIAN J. FAM. L. 35 (2008).

"winner" of the dispute coming at enormous cost, at least in a system where each litigant normally pays his or her own legal fees.

Evidence of the hardship resulting from legal expenses has emerged from a prospective longitudinal study of relocation disputes in Australia, being conducted at the University of Sydney.[61] Eighty people involved in relocation disputes (forty women[62] and forty men) are being followed up for up to five years after the relocation dispute was resolved, one way or another. Although the criteria for admission to the study was that the person had sought legal advice about a relocation dispute, the majority of cases went through to a trial, indicating that these disputes are very difficult to settle.[63] Eleven participants out of eighty had to sell the family home in order to meet legal costs; others borrowed from family members.

While there are numerous reasons why relocation disputes are so difficult to settle, not least the difficulties of finding any compromise positions, the indeterminacy of the law is likely to be one factor. People cannot bargain in the shadow of the law if the law casts no shadow. There is a moral responsibility on legislatures and courts to give clearer guidance at least about the factors that will weigh heavily in the determination of the outcome.

What then is a way forward on relocation, given the conflicting claims of postseparation autonomy and connectedness?

REASONS FOR RELOCATION

A starting point in differentiation of cases must be to examine why it is that parents (almost always mothers) want to relocate with their children. Whereas in litigated cases, a parent might give one particular reason for relocation that could be expected to elicit a favorable response,[64] in the University of Sydney study, the majority of women interviewed who wanted to relocate had more than one reason for so doing.[65]

---

[61] The author, a family lawyer, and Judy Cashmore, a developmental psychologist, are leading the study, together with the Hon. Richard Chisholm, a former Family Court judge.

[62] There are thirty-nine mothers and one grandmother in the study. The grandmother sought primary care of her grandchildren and wanted to move them from one city in Australia to her home city in order to live with her.

[63] Patrick Parkinson, Judy Cashmore, & Judi Single, *The Need for Reality Testing in Relocation Cases*, 44 FAM. L.Q. 1 (2010).

[64] For reasons given in more than 600 U.S. cases on Westlaw, see Theresa Glennon, *Still Partners? Examining the Consequences of Post-Dissolution Parenting* 41 FAM. L.Q. 105, 125ff (2007).

[65] *Id.* This was also the finding from a smaller retrospective relocation study in Australia. Juliet Behrens & Bruce Smyth, *Australian Family Court Decisions about Relocation: Parents' Experiences and Some Implications for Law and Policy*, 38 FEDERAL L. REV. 1 (2010).

Support from the Family of Origin

Almost two-thirds of the women gave as at least one reason for relocating a desire to return home and/or to move to an area where they had support from family or friends. In countries with high levels of mobility for work and other such reasons, it is not uncommon for parents to have moved away from their family of origin. As long as the parents' relationship endures, they provide support to one another; however, it may be a different story if the relationship ends, and the mother finds herself managing most of the child care on her own, in circumstances where her financial circumstances are much more straitened than when the parents were living together. Being isolated from friends and family support, living in a community in which she has not yet put down many roots, and coping with significant financial difficulties may well represent a severe hardship for many women, leading to depression and other adversities.

Although this may in some circumstances provide a compelling reason to relocate, other options can also be explored to bridge the gulf of distance from a family of origin. One option, if a court considers it is in the best interests of the children not to allow a relocation in the circumstances of the case, is to require the father to provide airfares to allow the mother to visit her family of origin on a regular basis. In this way, the costs of not relocating can be more evenly distributed and recognition given to the importance of the mother maintaining these familial connections. In many cases, this is likely to reflect the situation before the parents separated, when the family budget was stretched to accommodate visits by the mother, or perhaps the whole family, to the mother's family of origin. Issues about relocation cannot be separated from financial issues in the enduring family.

Escaping Violence

In the University of Sydney study, four women said that escaping violence was a reason for relocating.[66] Others said that getting away was a motivation, and among them were those who had experienced serious violence in the course of the relationship. In total, seven mothers out of the thirty-nine who referred either to getting away or escaping violence had experienced abusive relationships.

---

[66] For an analysis of decided cases in the United States where escaping domestic violence was an issue, *see* Janet Bowermaster, *Relocation Custody Disputes Involving Domestic Violence*, 46 KANSAS L. REV. 433 (1998).

Lifestyle Factors

In other cases, the reason for relocation may be less compelling and other solutions might be found. More than a third of the women in the University of Sydney study gave a better "lifestyle" as a reason for relocation. It was quite a common primary reason for moving and the most common secondary reason. Lifestyle encompassed a range of different factors such as warmer weather, wanting a better job, a larger house, or having more opportunities for hobbies and out of school activities. Sometimes financial considerations were a factor, but not necessarily because the current location was unaffordable. Some interviewees explained that they could afford to buy a house outside of the city where they lived but could only afford to rent if they remained in the city. The unwillingness of fathers to recognize the financial difficulties that some mothers had in staying was a factor in driving the mother to want to move.

Another issue therefore to be considered in those cases where a woman's application to relocate is based on financial issues is the economic hardship that she may experience from being required to stay in a particular location if the relocation is refused. There seems no reason in principle why financial orders should not be made against the nonresident parent in these circumstances, subject to his capacity to pay.[67] That might be achieved by varying a discretionary child support award, or by an award of spousal maintenance where applicable. In some jurisdictions, such as Australia, legislative amendment might be needed to authorize this.

New Relationships

In the University of Sydney study, nine women (less than a quarter of the mothers) gave new relationships as a reason why they wanted to relocate. For seven out of nine, this was the primary reason for the move. Internet dating was the means by which some new partnerships were formed.

The issue of repartnering raises profound questions in the age of the enduring family, given what we now know about the importance to so many children of a close relationship with both of their parents. What responsibilities do separated parents, and indeed their new partners, have to act in a manner that protects as much as possible the relationships that are important to their children? It is not enough that the law should regulate the postseparation family. A new ethic is also needed, one that is

---

[67] Glennon, *supra* note 64.

internalized by parents and affirmed by courts. The internet in particular has opened up a universe of possibilities. People we have never met face to face and who live on the other side of the globe can become friends and share much that is most intimate about themselves while writing on a computer.

Yet personal morality has always involved restraint in the face of possibility, and this restraint, in the context of repartnering, derives from responsible parenthood, which affects both genders.[68] The mother or father who is seeking a new partner may need to consider what limitations ought to be placed on her or his search because of the children's needs – including for parents with primary care, the children's relationship with the other parent. This may mean being realistic about distances when pursuing relationships over the internet or other electronic forms of communication. For new partners of mothers with primary care, there may also need to be some realism about the extent to which the mother is free to move, and what other constraints will be placed on their relationship by the children's continuing relationship with the father. Fathers' new partners also need to do some reality testing around the constraints that the enduring connection with the father's children may impose on the new relationship both in terms of child support payments and constraints on the father's freedom of movement if he wants to remain in reasonably close proximity to his children.

SHOULD NONRESIDENT PARENTS MOVE?

In the University of Sydney study, which is following families over a period of five years, six fathers out of twenty-four have so far moved to the same location as the mother. This is approximately three-to-four years since the relocation dispute was resolved.[69]

Many nonresident parents will have legitimate reasons not to move, including the difficulty of finding comparable work in the new location,

---

[68] As two members of the High Court of Australia have written in the context of a relocation case: "The reality is that maternity and paternity always have an impact upon the wishes and mobility of parents: obligations both legal and moral, the latter sometimes lasting a lifetime, restrictive of personal choice and movement have been incurred." U v. U 211 C.L.R. 238, 263 (2002).

[69] Parkinson et al., *supra* note 63, at 17. Similarly, in a New Zealand study involving interviews with 114 parents, 3 fathers out of 41 had moved to be near their children following the mother's relocation. NICOLA TAYLOR, MEGAN GOLLOP, & MARK HENAGHAN, RELOCATION FOLLOWING PARENTAL SEPARATION: THE WELFARE AND BEST INTERESTS OF THE CHILDREN 89 (2010).

commitments to a new partner or to the care of elderly parents, or other such factors limiting him or her to the current location. In relation to overseas relocations, immigration constraints may also provide a barrier to the nonresident parent's relocation.

The discussion of the issue of the nonresident parent's mobility often assumes that the primary caregiver would want the other parent to move. This is not necessarily the case. In one U.S. study, researchers found that 40 percent of both male and female movers stated that they left the community in which they had lived while married in order to create physical distance between themselves and their former spouse.[70] If a motivation for relocation is to put distance between mother and father, for whatever reason, then the last thing that a relocating parent will want is for the other parent to move as well. This is particularly the case where the motivation for the move is to get away from a violent or abusive relationship. Where the issue for the parent is the need to get away from the other parent, the issues that have led the parent to that desire to move need to be addressed on their merits, without being diverted by asking a question that neither parents wants to be asked.

A further issue is that it will be unreasonable to expect a nonresident parent to move if the evidence indicates that the relocating parent may not settle for long in the new location.[71] This is an issue in particular for parents or partners of parents in the military, for whom postings are a regular part of life.

If a case is to be resolved on the basis that it is reasonably practicable for the nonresident parent to move, is this sufficient, or must the court be satisfied also that on the balance of probabilities, the nonresident parent *will* move if the primary caregiver's relocation is allowed? It may be argued that the latter is necessary for the court to ensure that children have the benefit of a meaningful relationship with both of their parents. However, courts cannot, by order, ensure that parents have meaningful relationships with their children; they can only create or maintain the circumstances that make meaningful relationships possible. Giving a parent the opportunity to continue to spend substantial time with a child by moving location,

---

[70] Shirley Asher & Bernard Bloom, *Geographic Mobility as a Factor in Adjustment to Divorce*, 6 J. OF DIVORCE 69, 73 (1983).

[71] In Western Australia, for example, Thackray J took account of the fact that if he were to decide the case concerning a young child on the basis that the father could follow the mother, it might be the first of a number of moves he would have to make because the mother's previous lifestyle indicated that she was unlikely to settle for a long time in the next location. G and A [2007] F.C.W.A. 11, para. 61.

when there are very good reasons to allow a primary caregiver to relocate, may be as much as a court can do. Determining the reasonableness of a move by the relocating parent, rather than the reasonable prospects of such a move actually occurring, is all that judges, who are not blessed with omniscience or prophetic foresight, can realistically do.

SHOULD NEW PARTNERS MOVE?

In the University of Sydney study,[72] in none of the cases was the relocation dispute resolved by the mother's new partner deciding to move to be with the mother. Mothers routinely sought to relocate to join new partners.

There seems to be no reason in principle why courts should not have to consider whether the new partner could move to be with the mother, as well as considering whether the father could relocate. Indeed, the moral case for doing so is overwhelming. The new partner makes a choice to form a relationship with someone who has ties through the children to another location. The mother needs to accept some measure of responsibility for the consequences of her choice of a new partner. Even in cases where the mother and her new partner met locally and the relocation dispute arose from a better employment opportunity for the new partner, choices are being made. The father who is the respondent to a relocation application may have had no choice in the matter at all. A new partner's choice as to where he lives should not be beyond challenge in a way that a father's is not.

MAINTAINING A MEANINGFUL RELATIONSHIP
WITH THE NONRESIDENT PARENT

A key factor in relocation cases will be the quality of the father-child relationship and the impact of the mother's move on the closeness of the relationship between the father and the child. It is not per se the distance involved in the proposed relocation that matters as much as the impact of that relocation on the relationship between the nonresident parent and the child. This in turn will be affected by factors such as the financial circumstances of the parties in terms of being able to afford the cost of travel.[73]

In cases where that relationship is not marked by great closeness, a relocation may make little difference to the child's well-being, even though

---

[72] Parkinson et al., *supra* note 63.
[73] Morgan & Miles (2007) F.L.C. 93–343.

it may not be a change welcomed by the father. In other cases, where there is a close relationship characterized by warmth and parental engagement with the daily life of the child, distance may mean significant loss for the child of a relationship that is vitally important to him or to her.

The capacity to cope with that loss, for the child, may depend on age. There is some evidence that adolescents can sustain close relationships with a nonresident parent if they stay with a nonresident parent for an extensive period during the summer holidays, even if they do not see that parent during the school year.[74]

Electronic forms of communication, such as videoconferencing programs, certainly help bridge the distance, but the extent to which they substitute for face-to-face interaction and caring for children can be exaggerated. In the University of Sydney research,[75] and a similar study in New Zealand,[76] fathers whose children had been allowed to relocate did not report significant use of Skype or other forms of video communication, nor that it made much difference to their experience of loss.

THE DIFFICULTIES OF CONTACT

Another issue that has emerged from the University of Sydney study is that contact often does not proceed in the way that the court orders allowing relocation require.[77] When judges allow relocations, they do so on certain conditions, in particular in relation to the arrangements for the other parent to spend time with the children. Whether or not a child will be able to maintain a meaningful relationship with a parent following a relocation depends, critically, on whether those orders are complied with. Yet in numerous cases, contact did not proceed in accordance with the court orders.[78]

Why were there problems with contact following the relocation? In some cases, contact seems to have been lost due to estrangement, and

---

[74] Eleanor Maccoby, Christy Buchanan, Robert Mnookin, & Sanford Dornbusch, *Postdivorce Roles of Mothers and Fathers in the Lives of Their Children*, 7 J. FAM. PSYCH. 33, 33 (1993). CHRISTY BUCHANAN, SANFORD DORNBUSCH, & ELEANOR MACCOBY, ADOLESCENTS AFTER DIVORCE, 85 (1996).

[75] Parkinson et al., *supra* note 63.   [76] TAYLOR ET AL., *supra* note 69, at 96.

[77] Problems with contact arrangements were also found in Marilyn Freeman's British study of international relocations. MARILYN FREEMAN, RELOCATION: THE REUNITE RESEARCH (2009), http://www.reunite.org/edit/files/Library%20-%20reunite%20Publications/Relocation%20Report.pdf

[78] Parkinson et al., *supra* note 63.

this was particularly the case in overseas relocations. The relationship between the parent and the children had largely broken down, for whatever reason, before the relocation and did not survive the move because the children were unwilling to see the nonresident parent. In a few situations, contact appears to have been lost, or become very intermittent, owing to the disengagement of the nonresident parent. In other cases, however, the loss of contact, or the difficulties about contact, appear to have been the consequence of deliberate actions by the mother to make contact difficult for the father – for example, by not providing a new address or contact details.

Apart from deliberate obstruction of contact, problems have also arisen because the arrangements appear to have been unrealistic given the travel costs involved once the parents live a long way apart. Particularly where there have been orders for regular contact, including weekends during school term, the cost to one or other parent of exercising contact has proved considerable. In the Australian study, there were cases where the annual costs of travel for one parent alone was between a quarter and a third of full-time earnings for men and women in Australia.[79] Distant relocations may impose financial burdens on parents, which can make the planned levels of contact unsustainable in the long term.

The costs are not only in the children's airfares. Young children are likely to have to be accompanied by a parent, at least until the age when they are permitted to travel as unaccompanied minors – and ready to do so. Prior to that stage, if the visit is for a significant period, then two adult return airfares and one child's return airfare are likely to be involved in order to facilitate each visit for one child. In a situation, for example, where the child's primary caregiver is responsible for the travel, she may have to travel to the other parent's home and then return to her own because of her work commitments, and then, at the end of the visit, fly back again to collect the child. The cost of this on a regular basis could be prohibitive and lead either to a breakdown in the arrangements for the child to spend time with the other parent or significant financial stress for a parent. This in turn could have deleterious effects on the well-being of the child.

The alternative of staying in the other parent's town for the duration of the visit may also impose a financial stress if there is no free accommodation,

[79] Average weekly ordinary full-time earnings in February 2007, about the time that these interviews were conducted, was $1,070.40 per week or $55,661 per year. The statistics on average weekly earnings are available at the Australian Bureau of Statistics. http://www.abs.gov.au

or if it would not be possible to hold down a regular full-time job because the frequency and extent of the visits are such as to exceed the amount of annual leave the relocating parent has.

This problem – that relocation may in practice deprive the nonresident parent of face-to-face contact with the children because of the costs of travel – raises issues about how far the freedom to terminate a relationship in an age of no-fault divorce should be deemed to extend. It is clear that it means that one spouse can bring an end to the adult relationship, but should it also mean the end to the other parent's relationship with his or her child other than through email, internet video conferencing, letters, or telephone contact? One may choose this consequence for oneself, but should it be able to be visited on the other parent? In the absence of fault or serious inadequacy as a parent, it is at least arguable that the preservation of a parent's opportunities to spend time with his or her children and to have a meaningful relationship with them should not be unilaterally terminated, and should only be permitted after careful examination of all the circumstances by a court, including the option for the nonresidential parent to relocate as well. Courts in other circumstances will not deprive a parent of contact with a child, or the child with a parent, except for very good reasons such as a history of violence and child abuse, or where a mature child does not want contact.

In a worst-case scenario, the relocation of a parent with the children to the other side of the country, or to another country, may effectively deny the nonresident parent the chance to spend time with his or her children. For parents who operate on subsistence budgets, and struggle to meet basic needs in the aftermath of separation, such cross-continental or international travel is beyond contemplation.[80]

THE BURDEN OF TRAVEL

Another issue to consider is the burden of travel on the child. New Zealand research indicates that children who have experienced living a long distance apart from one parent vary considerably in their reactions to the traveling, with some enjoying the travel and others finding it difficult or tiresome.[81] Although it is difficult to generalize about how children will

---

[80] For an example of a relocation case litigated to trial in which both parents were impecunious, *see* O'Donnell v. Chambers, [2000] N.B.J. No 202 (Q.B., F.D.) cited in BOYD, *supra* note 32, at 155 (custodial mother on social assistance denied permission to relocate from New Brunswick to Alberta because of impact on eleven-year-old son's contact with father, who was on disability benefits.)

[81] TAYLOR ET AL., *supra* note 69, at 121–24.

react to traveling long distances, and doing so multiple times, it is an issue that needs careful consideration in the evaluation of a proposed move.

In the University of Sydney research,[82] there have been examples of children flying vast distances on a regular basis to see the nonresident parent. Such arrangements are particularly troubling with young children for two reasons. The first is the evident stress on some children of such frequent dislocation from his or her normal home and routine, for long periods. The other concern is the effect on young children of such long separations from their primary caregiver in the cases where the primary caregiver delivers the child to the other parent and then returns home before coming back to collect the child again. Seven- or eight-day absences from a primary caregiver represent a very long time in the life of young children. Thus, sharing the parenting across a continent may appear to solve the problem of reconciling a parent's freedom of movement with the need to involve both parents in the child's life, but perhaps at great cost to the well-being of the child.

Why then are such troubling orders being made? It is a common pattern in the Australian cases that generous arrangements are proposed by the parent who wants to relocate for the other parent to spend time with the child. The onerous travel requirements to maintain the relationship with the other parent are the initiative of the relocating parent, rather than being imposed by the court. In other cases, they have been the outcome of settlement negotiations. Of course, the fact that a parent proposes to fly children there and back on a regular basis does not mean that this amount of travel is in the best interests of the child. Attention has to be given to the question of how the children will cope with such travel.

DIVORCE, COHABITATION, AND THE ENDURING FAMILY

Another issue that needs to be confronted in terms of relocation is whether the marital status of the parents matters. Australian law, for example, states, as general principles, that "children have the right to know and be cared for by both their parents, regardless of whether their parents are married, separated, have never married or have never lived together" and that they "have a right to spend time on a regular basis with both their parents." These principles apply except when it would be contrary to the child's best interests.[83] Yet are all parental relationships really equivalent? Are women to be tied to the fathers of their children through inhibitions on their freedom of movement, or fathers with primary care tied to mothers,

---

[82] Parkinson, *supra* note 63.   [83] Family Law Act, 1975, s.60B(2) (Austl.).

irrespective of whether they ever made a commitment to that other person to form an enduring family?

The question is a vital one. In the United States, for example, the number of births to unmarried women increased 26 percent between 2002 and 2007. The 2007 total was 2.5 times the number reported in 1980.[84] Of the 4.2 million women fifteen to fifty years old in the 2006 American Community Survey who had a birth in the past twelve months, 36 percent were not married at the time of the survey.[85] From other studies, it has been estimated that only about 40 percent of unmarried mothers are living with the father at the time of the child's birth.[86] The rate of births outside of any cohabiting relationship is thus a significant feature of patterns of fertility in America.

Contact between fathers and children born outside of marriage is typically more tenuous after separation than for couples who have been married.[87] An analysis of data from the Fragile Families and Child Wellbeing Study found that about five years after the birth of an ex-nuptial child, only 43 percent of fathers had seen the child in the last month and 37 percent had lost contact.[88]

When children are born outside of marriage, and particularly where the parents were either not living together at the time of the birth or separated relatively soon after birth, the prognosis for the development of a long-term coparenting relationship that is meaningful and important to the child is not good. To what extent then should the maintenance of that relationship with the father take precedence over the reasonable desire of a mother to relocate in the event of a dispute?

[84] Stephanie Ventura, Changing Patterns of Nonmarital Childbearing in the United States, National Center for Health Statistics, (Data Brief, no. 18, May 2009), http://www.cdc.gov/nchs/data/databriefs/db18.htm

[85] U.S. Census, Fertility of American Women: 2006 (2008), http://www.census.gov/prod/2008pubs/p20-558.pdf

[86] Paul Amato, *The Impact of Family Formation Change on the Cognitive, Social and Emotional Wellbeing of Children*, 15 Future of Children 75, 78 (2005).

[87] Paul Amato, Catherine Meyers, & Robert Emery, *Changes in Nonresident Father-Child Contact From 1976 to 2002*, 58 Fam. Rel. 41 (2009). *See also* Jacob Cheadle, Paul Amato, & Valarie King, *Patterns of Nonresident Father Contact*, 47 Demography 205 (2010).

[88] Marcia Carlson, Sara McLanahan, & Jeanne Brooks-Gunn, *Coparenting and Nonresident Fathers' Involvement with Young Children after a Nonmarital Birth*, 45 Demography 461 (2008). *See also* Laura Tach, Ronald Mincy, & Kathryn Edin, *Parenting as a "Package Deal": Relationships, Fertility, and Nonresident Father Involvement among Unmarried Parents*, 47 Demography 181 (2010).

The incidence of relocation disputes among parents whose relationship to one another was short term or tenuous can be seen in another Australian study of relocation, in which thirty-eight participants were recruited whose relocation cases had all gone to trial. Ten of these thirty-eight parents had had short and unhappy relationships with the other parent, with separation occurring either during pregnancy or shortly after the birth of an only child.[89] In all of these cases, there was significant conflict both prior to and after the relocation. It should not be assumed that all relocation disputes occur in the context of well-established parental relationships with a substantial history of mutual care and good communication between the parents about child-rearing.[90]

When parents have not made a commitment to each other, or where the commitment was tenuous, as with some couples who cohabit for a limited period of time, it must be asked how justified it is to place constraints on the freedoms of one parent because of the biological connection that their child has with the other. There have to be limits on the extent to which those who have never formed families that include both biological parents should be treated as if they had done so. Maintaining contact between biological parents and children can be achieved in other ways than by restraining the relocation of the mother.

This is particularly the case where the relationship has been characterized by conflict from the beginning, or near the beginning, of the child's life. Furthermore, the overwhelming evidence from the social science research is that ongoing high conflict between parents who are not living together is deleterious to children's well-being.[91] Where the relationship is characterized by serious and ongoing conflict, and in a context where the connection between the parents was from the beginning short term or tenuous, the case for restraining the primary caregiver's relocation seems weak.

---

[89] Juliet Behrens, Bruce Smyth, & Rae Kaspiew, *Australian Family Law Court Decisions on Relocation: Dynamics in Parents' Relationships Across Time*, 23 AUSTRALIAN J. FAM. L. 222 (2009).

[90] Behrens & Smyth, *supra* note 65.

[91] *See* e.g. Catherine Ayoub, Robin Deutch, & Andronicki Maraganore, *Emotional Distress in Children of High-Conflict Divorce: The Impact of Marital Conflict and Violence*, 37 FAM. & CONCIL. CTS. REV. 297 (1999); Jennifer McIntosh, *Enduring Conflict in Parental Separation: Pathways of Impact on Child Development*, 9 J. FAMILY STUDIES 63 (2003); Joan Kelly & Robert Emery, *Children's Adjustment Following Divorce: Risk and Resilience Perspectives*, 52 FAM. REL. 352 (2003).

THE RISKS OF RELOCATION

While in many cases it is not difficult to see that the children's interests will be best served by a move that improves the situation for the custodial parent, there will be other cases where children have interests that diverge from those of the custodial parent. Relocation for a parent is dislocation for the child. For a mother, it may mean returning to the locality where she spent her earliest years and where she can find support from her parents. For the child, it may mean moving away from the locality where he or she lived in the earliest years, and away from the nurture of one parent.

The arguments against relocation will often be arguments about the importance to the child of the status quo, providing continuity in the child's schooling, friendships, and continuing, frequent, and meaningful contact with the other parent. Conversely, the change of environment can also be a significant stressor for children. Although many children manage change well, moves of home, school, and neighborhood are sometimes stressful for children in intact families.[92] Why would they not be also in the context of relationship breakdown?[93] The disruption to a child of relocating is not to be compared, of course, with the disruption that would occur if there were to be a change in the child's primary caregiver, but it is not insignificant.

Parental separation and divorce is a significant risk factor for some children in terms of long-term emotional well-being.[94] So also is residential mobility, for some children. School-age children who have moved three or more times have twice as high a risk of emotional and behavioral problems, and difficulties at school, as children who have never moved, after controlling for relevant sociodemographic factors, including mother's marital status and income.[95] In combination, the risks are multiplied.[96] Sara McLanahan and colleagues found that residential mobility explained

---

[92] For a review of the literature on how children adjust to relocations in intact families, and what insights it may provide for relocation disputes, *see* Briony Horsfall & Rae Kaspiew, *Relocation in Separated and Non-Separated Families: Equivocal Evidence from the Social Science Literature*, 24 AUSTRALIAN J. FAM. L. 34 (2010).

[93] For a review, *see* Paula Raines, *Joint Custody and the Right to Travel: Legal and Psychological Implications*, 24 J. FAM. L. 625, 648–56 (1986).

[94] JAN PRYOR & BRYAN RODGERS, CHILDREN IN CHANGING FAMILIES: LIFE AFTER PARENTAL SEPARATION (2001).

[95] Gloria Simpson & Mary Glenn Fowler, *Geographic Mobility and Children's Emotional/Behavioral Adjustment and School Functioning*, 93 PEDIATRICS 303 (1994).

[96] William Austin, *Relocation, Research and Forensic Evaluation, Part I: Effects of Residential Mobility on Children of Divorce*, 46 FAM. CT REV. 137 (2008).

two-thirds of the difference between children in single-parent families and two-parent families in terms of dropping out of high school. The rest of the difference was due to family income.[97] Residential mobility explained all of the difference between step-families and two-parent families in high school dropout rates. The researchers also found that residential mobility accounts for 30 percent of the increase in the risk of a teen birth, compared with two-parent families.[98]

There are also particular risks concerning secure attachments if a relocation is proposed when children are very young.[99] These risk factors associated with residential mobility need to be balanced by considerations about the risk to the child's well-being if the child's primary caregiver has severe depression arising from her circumstances in a particular location, which could be ameliorated if a relocation were permitted.

DETERMINING PUBLIC POLICY ON RELOCATION

Being honest about the relocation issue means facing the fact that relocation cases raise fundamental issues about the importance of the best interests of children in the postseparation family. There was a time when the question of divorce was debated in terms of whether or not it may be better to stay in an unhappy relationship for the sake of the children. Now the question raised by the relocation problem is whether divorce means staying in close proximity to one another for the sake of the children, at least in circumstances where both parents are devoted to the children, take their parental responsibilities seriously, and where there are no significant issues of safety for a parent or for the children in the care of either parent.

Ultimately, the problem of relocation can only be resolved by developing a prima facie policy position on where the balance is to be found between postdivorce autonomy and the importance to both the child and to the non-resident parent of their parent-child relationship. Thus far, the empirical research on relocation would not appear to support a general presumption in favor of parental relocation as being in the best interests of children.

---

[97] Sara McLanahan & Garry Sandefur, Growing Up with a Single Parent: What Hurts, What Helps 129 (1994).

[98] *Id.* at 131. The authors concluded that: "Since many parents are in a position to reduce the number of times they move, and since judges are often in a position to limit or minimize residential mobility, these findings may be especially useful to parents and policymakers in improving the lives of children." *Id.* at 133. *See also* Nan Marie Astone & Sara McLanahan, *Family Structure, Residential Mobility and School Dropout: A Research Note*, 31 Demography 575 (1994).

[99] Kelly & Lamb, *supra* note 51.

Nor does it support a general presumption against relocation. There are many different reasons for relocation – some stronger than others. Some nonresident parents are also much more involved in their children's lives than others. The role of legislatures in this area is at least to express the values to which the courts need to have most regard and to identify the most important issues on which evidence ought to be led, concerning children's well-being in the alternative scenarios put forward by the parents.

PART FOUR

The Family Law System and the Enduring Family

8

Dispute Resolution for the Enduring Family

In the new conceptualization of postdivorce parenting, the family does not go through a death so much as a metamorphosis from a nuclear household to become a family in two locations, with new relationships extending the range of adults and children associated with that family. If the family is understood to be enduring in spite of the breakdown of the parents' relationship, then the improvement of the relationship between parents so that they will be more likely to cooperate into the future emerges as an important goal of services to support families following separation.

What does that mean for dispute resolution? Around the western world, there has been a shift in thinking about the role of dispute resolution in promoting enduring family relationships, but dispute resolution still tends to occur, in many countries, within a context of case management of disputes by courts.

MEDIATION AS AN ALTERNATIVE TO LITIGATION

Alternative dispute resolution processes, notably mediation, have long played a role as an alternative to litigation in family law disputes.[1] In many jurisdictions, it is a requirement before a case can proceed to trial. These dispute resolution strategies emerged as alternatives to lawyer-led negotiation and adjudication in the event that settlement negotiations failed.

The development of alternative dispute resolution as part of the process of resolving cases through the courts was the beginning of a recognition that disputes about parenting after separation should not be regarded as

---

[1] On the development of family mediation in North America, *see* Connie Beck & Bruce Sales, *A Critical Reappraisal of Divorce Mediation Research and Policy*, 6 PSYCHOL. PUB. POL'Y & L. 989 (2000).

merely a legal problem requiring the interventions of lawyers and courts for its resolution. However, mediation was still seen as an option within a legal framework, and as part of a process of dispute resolution managed by the courts.

This form of mediation did not change the orientation of the family law system away from its focus on what was presumptively once-for-all decision making about the children in the aftermath of relationship breakdown. The major focus of services to support families going through separation remained on helping the parties reach agreement on their disputes concerning the parenting arrangements. Mediation and conciliation strategies were typically directed toward this goal and, where ordered by courts, sought to bring an end to the legal conflict between the parties.

Because mediation was court-ordered and often court-annexed, the model still placed lawyers and the courts at the center of the process of dispute resolution about postseparation parenting, with pathways to settlement being created to divert people off the litigation pathway. Forty years on from the beginnings of the divorce revolution, this still remains the dominant paradigm for dispute resolution in family law in many parts of the western world. However, this is changing in many jurisdictions, and a new paradigm is emerging.

THE PARADIGM SHIFT IN FAMILY DISPUTE RESOLUTION

As a consequence of the recognition that the parental relationship needs to survive the ending of the intimate partnership, there is now a much greater focus on therapeutic interventions that will assist parents to separate their conflicts as former spouses from their continuing role as parents, and which encourage better communication and cooperation in the parenting role over time.[2] For example, Edward Kruk has written:[3]

> The main purpose of intervention with a family during and after divorce should be the redefinition of family roles, relationships, and boundaries

---

[2] *See e.g.* Hugh McIsaac & Charlotte Finn, *Parents Beyond Conflict: A Cognitive Restructuring Model for High-Conflict Families in Divorce*, 37 FAM. & CONCIL. CTS REV. 74 (1999) (parent education program in Portland, Oregon); Alicia Homrich, Michelle Muenzenmayer Glover, & Alice Blackwell White, *The Court Care Center for Divorcing Families*, 42 FAM. CT. REV. 141 (2004) (court-annexed program in Orlando, Florida).

[3] Edward Kruk, *The Disengaged Noncustodial Father: Implications for Social Work Practice with the Divorced Family*, 39 SOC. WORK 15, 22 (1994). *See also* Constance Ahrons, *Divorce: Before, During and After, in* STRESS AND THE FAMILY, VOL 1, COPING WITH NORMATIVE TRANSITIONS 102, 114 (Hamilton McCubbin & Charles Figley eds., 1983); ELIZABETH SEDDON, CREATIVE PARENTING AFTER SEPARATION 150–91 (2003).

to allow the family to continue as a divorced family system. Intervention should focus primarily on the clarification of boundaries so that the spousal role does not contaminate the parental role, that is, on helping parents to separate their previous marital conflicts from their ongoing parental responsibilities.

Jana Singer has noted five features of the paradigm shift in dispute resolution in the last two decades.[4] The first is the development of nonadversary dispute resolution mechanisms designed to avoid adjudication of family cases. This includes not only the ubiquitous development of court-connected mediation but also other problem-solving approaches such as collaborative law. The second has been the recognition that most family disputes are not discrete legal events, but ongoing social and emotional processes. This necessitates interventions that are collaborative, holistic, and interdisciplinary, with the goal of addressing the underlying dysfunction and emotional needs of families. The third feature has been a reformulation of the goal of legal intervention in the family, moving away from a backward-looking process of assigning blame and allocating rights to a forward-looking task of supervising a process of family reorganization. The fourth feature is a therapeutic goal for dispute resolution, away from third-party dispute resolution and toward capacity-building processes that seek to empower families to resolve their own conflicts. Mandatory divorce-related parenting education programs have been one aspect of this. Finally, there has been an increased emphasis on predispute planning and preventive law, for example by encouraging prenuptial agreements, domestic partnership contracts, and dispute resolution clauses in parenting plans so that there is a planned mechanism for resolving future disagreements.

The focus on mediation and conciliation is not, of course, without its dangers. Not only is there the issue of screening out cases that are not suitable because of violence or other imbalances of power,[5] but there is a danger too in mediation that the forward-looking focus, and the desire to reach agreement, will minimize the significance of histories of violence or abuse and risk factors associated with ongoing parent-child contact.[6] Liz Trinder and her colleagues, in an analysis of recorded conversations

---

4   Jana Singer, *Dispute Resolution and the Postdivorce Family: Implications of a Paradigm Shift*, 47 FAM. CT. REV. 363, 363–65 (2009).

5   *See e.g.* Nancy Johnson, Dennis Saccuzzo, & Wendy Koen, *Child Custody Mediation in Cases of Domestic Violence: Empirical Evidence of a Failure to Protect*, 11 VIOLENCE AGAINST WOMEN 1022 (2005).

6   Zoe Rathus, *Shifting the Gaze: Will Past Violence Be Silenced by a Further Shift of the Gaze to the Future under the New Family Law System?*, 21 AUSTRALIAN J. FAM. L. 87 (2007).

between conciliators and the parties in the context of court-based dispute resolution in Britain, has shown that the way conciliators structure the dialogue in such sessions is often aimed at keeping a lid on conflict and focusing on settlement at the expense of risk management.[7] Because mediators are not fact finders and do not have an investigatory or adjudicatory role, concerns about safety are all too easily overlooked.

A focus on settlement may be a particular pressure for court-annexed conciliation and mediation services, for in the context of time-poor courts and long waiting lists for trial dates, the strong temptation is to see any settlement as a good settlement. Separated out from the structures and institutional imperatives of courts, mediators may be more free to pursue their distinctive role in those cases where mediation is likely to be helpful and appropriate.

This is the journey on which Australia has now embarked. In that country, there is now a coordinated approach, led and funded by government, which has brought about a revolution in service provision to support families after separation. There has been a concerted effort to try to recognize and support different pathways to the resolution of postseparation parenting arrangements, with litigation being just one of those pathways.[8] The creation of alternatives to the pathway of lawyers and courts in resolving disputes about children is not an easy one, however. It requires the development of a service system to support families in making parenting arrangements after separation without needing to operate within court-managed processes.

At the heart of that service system in Australia is a network of highly visible and accessible centers, known as Family Relationship Centers, located, for the most part, in the main business districts of urban and regional communities. Whereas the move in the United States has been in the direction of more in-court therapeutic services, with the court at the center of a problem-solving team,[9] in Australia, the move has been away from the courts into community-based services that are nonetheless systemically integrated with the family law system in a cohesive framework of services to families after separation.

---

7   Liz Trinder, Alan Firth, & Christopher Jenks, *"So Presumably Things Have Moved on Since Then?" The Management of Risk Allegations in Child Contact Dispute Resolution*, 24 INT. J L. POLICY & FAM. 29 (2010).

8   In Australia, *see* FAMILY LAW PATHWAYS ADVISORY GROUP, OUT OF THE MAZE: PATHWAYS TO THE FUTURE FOR FAMILIES EXPERIENCING SEPARATION (2001). This group, established by the federal government, recognized three major pathways to dispute resolution: a self-help pathway that depended mainly on getting information, a supported pathway for people who could resolve their disputes with the assistance of professionals (e.g., mediation), and a litigation pathway.

9   On American developments in court-annexed services, *see* Jessica Pearson, *A Forum for Every Fuss: The Growth of Court Services and ADR Treatments for Family Law*

THE AUSTRALIAN FAMILY RELATIONSHIP CENTERS

The Family Relationship Centers (FRCs) emerged as a strategy for reform of the family law system in Australia in the mid-2000s following major debates about the future of that system.[10] There are now sixty-five centers all over the country, with approximately one servicing every 300,000 of the population, in all the major population centers and regions. The first of them opened in July 2006.

The FRCs are funded by the government and operate in accordance with guidelines set by the government. However, they are actually run by nongovernment organizations with experience in counseling and mediation, selected on a tender basis and staffed by professional counselors and mediators. Although actually run by different service providers in different localities, the FRCs have a common identity and logo for the public.

FRCs are an early-intervention initiative to help parents work out postseparation parenting arrangements, managing the transition from parenting together to parenting apart. They are there to help resolve disputes not only in the aftermath of separation, but also in relation to ongoing conflicts and difficulties as circumstances change.

The FRCs do not only have a role in helping parents after separation. They are not "divorce shops." They are meant also to play a role in strengthening intact relationships by offering an accessible source for information and referral on relationship and parenting issues, and providing a gateway to other government and nongovernment services to support families. One such source of assistance is relationship counseling, but the FRCs are also meant to offer a more holistic assessment of need. The breakthrough for one family might be to get the father to attend an anger management program. For another, it might be for the mother to seek help with an addiction such as gambling or alcohol. Another parent's need may best be met through

---

Cases in the United States, in CROSS CURRENTS: FAMILY LAW AND POLICY IN THE US AND ENGLAND 513 (Sanford Katz, John Eekelaar, & Mavis Maclean eds., 2000); James Bozzomo & Gregory Scolieri, *A Survey of Unified Family Courts: An Assessment of Different Jurisdictional Models,* 42 FAM. CT. REV. 12 (2004); Richard Boldt & Jana Singer, *Juristocracy in the Trenches: Problem-Solving Judges and Therapeutic Jurisprudence in Drug Treatment Courts and Unified Family Courts,* 65 MARYLAND L. REV. 82 (2006).

[10] For the history of this and the emergence of the FRCs following the acceptance by the Prime Minister of a proposal by this author, *see* Patrick Parkinson, *Keeping in Contact: The Role of Family Relationship Centers in Australia,* 18 CHILD & FAM. L. Q. 157 (2006). *See also* Patrick Parkinson, *Changing Policies Regarding Separated Fathers in Australia, in* THE ROLE OF THE FATHER IN CHILD DEVELOPMENT 518 (5th ed., Michael Lamb ed., 2010).

parent-adolescent mediation services, or services to assist in troubled step-family relationships. The FRC cannot possibly provide all the services that people need, but it is designed as a gateway to those services.

The potential for a supportive and preventive role in strengthening family life and in helping people whose relationships are beginning to experience significant difficulties was a key rationale for the development of the FRCs.[11] The extent to which a Center does so, nonetheless, depends on the organization running it and the level of demand for postseparation services in each community.

The FRCs also provide an educational, support, and counseling role to parents going through separation with the goal of helping parents understand and focus on children's needs, and by giving initial information to them about such matters as child support and welfare benefits. They act as a gateway to a range of postseparation services, such as support programs for separated fathers. The FRCs are thus about organizing postseparation parenting, but they are much more than this. They may be the gateway also to services that help people cope with the emotional sequelae of relationship breakdown.

The FRCs serve not only parents, but grandparents as well. To ensure that there were sufficient services for the FRCs to be able to refer clients to, the government also expanded the range of other services for families, particularly postseparation services to support parents.

The centers are intended to be highly visible. The government launched the Centers with a major advertising campaign. The Centers were required to find a location that is central for the community being served, being in the places that people go to for their shopping and other business needs. Leaflets about the Centers can be found in such places as doctors' surgeries, out-of-school care services, and community health centers. Referrals also come, of course, from family lawyers. The Centers achieved a high level of public awareness very quickly indeed.

The Role of FRCs in Postseparation Parenting

One of the aims of the FRCs is to achieve a long-term cultural change in the pathways people take to resolve disputes about parenting arrangements

---

[11] Commonwealth of Australia, *Operational Framework for Family Relationship Centres*, 2 (2007), http://www.ag.gov.au/www/agd/agd.nsf/Page/Families_FamilyRelationship-ServicesOverviewofPrograms_ForFamilyRelationshipServicesPractitioners_Family-RelationshipCentreResources

after separation. The concept behind the FRCs is that when parents are having difficulty agreeing on the postseparation parenting arrangements, they have a relationship problem, not necessarily a legal one. If no other solution can be found, the dispute may need to go to an adjudication by someone who can make a binding decision; but it should not be seen as a legal issue from the beginning.

Although there are some variations in the model around the country, parents inquiring at the FRC are usually offered an individual session with an adviser to receive initial, basic advice about options and sources of help for dealing with whatever problems might have led them to call into the Center. If the parent needs help with working out postseparation parenting arrangements, then the adviser will explain about mediation. Many people who come into the Centers have recently separated, although some may have separated years before but are coming because of ongoing difficulties with the parenting arrangements. The kinds of issues that might be covered with a person who has recently separated would be information about how to apply for welfare support payments if needed; applying for child support; and referral to sources of support for people with personal safety concerns. Of course, the relevant agencies would remain the most appropriate source of detailed advice on such matters as child support or welfare benefits.

Mediation in the FRCs

The primary service offered by the FRCs is mediation. The use of mediation as a central strategy in the resolution of family disputes is, of course, not new in Australia. Mediation and related forms of dispute resolution such as conciliation have long been a central feature of the Family Court system. A court-based Counselling Service was established from the inception of the Family Court of Australia in 1976. Although the staff were meant to have a role in relationship counseling, mainly counselors engaged in conciliation to try to resolve disputes without the need for a judicial determination, and this normally had to be attempted before a case could be set down for trial. The Counselling Service, which later became known as the Mediation Service, was part of the structure of the court. Sessions took place on court premises. For a while, before the late 1990s, the Counselling Service was sufficiently well resourced that it could conduct conciliation sessions without parents even filing proceedings in court. This early intervention approach proved particularly successful. However, with a decline in funding, conciliation was confined to cases in which proceedings had been commenced.

Part of the package of reforms introduced in 2006[12] was to make prefiling mediation compulsory in most cases. "Family dispute resolution" as it is called in the legislation, is now a requirement before a person can file an application for parenting orders in court, unless a person is exempted on application to the Court or screened out as unsuited to mediation.[13] The grounds of exemption include a history of family violence or the risk of it.[14] Parents may be screened out as unsuitable for mediation on that ground or if the mediator decides for other reasons that a parent is unable to negotiate freely in the dispute.[15] A new assessment program has been developed for this purpose.[16] While it is not possible to compel a person to attend mediation, if one person seeks it and the other refuses to attend, a certificate will be issued noting the failure of the parent to participate. That notice will form part of the court file.

People can go to any mediation service they choose, but the advantage of the FRC is that it is free (for the most part) and readily available. FRCs are not in a position to offer legal advice, and those who access the service without lawyers may not have had any such advice prior to mediation. However, the government is examining the option of linkages between legal advice services and FRCs. Premediation screening is an important part of the mediation process in the FRCs, as it is for all mediation services. Another requirement prior to engaging in mediation at an FRC is likely to be attendance at a parenting-after-separation seminar. The information sessions may cover such issues as the way people deal with separation emotionally; the need to separate the parents' conflicts from issues about the children; the value of a parenting plan; what helps children get through the divorce process; what harms them; how parenting arrangements need to take account of the needs of children at different developmental stages; options for structuring postseparation parenting arrangements; shared parenting, and when shared parenting is contraindicated; the issue of children's participation in decision making about arrangements; sources of help to deal with domestic

---

[12] Family Law Amendment (Shared Parental Responsibility) Act, 2006, amending the Family Law Act, 1975.
[13] Family Law Act 1975, s.60I. For a review of the impact of mandatory mediation in a county in North Carolina, *see* Suzanne Reynolds, Catherine Harris, & Ralph Peeples, *Back to the Future: An Empirical Study of Child Custody Outcomes*, 85 N.C. L. Rev. 1629 (2007).
[14] Family Law Act, 1975, s.60I(9).
[15] Family Law (Family Dispute Resolution Practitioners) Regulations 2008.
[16] Gail Winkworth & Morag McArthur, Framework for Screening, Assessment and Referrals in Family Relationship Centers and the Family Relationship Advice Line (2008).

violence and child protection issues; and comparing mediation and litigation as options for dealing with disputes about the children.

The main focus for mediation in the FRC must be on parenting issues. However, financial matters may also be discussed in mediation as long as the primary focus is on resolving the parenting arrangements. This is because it is often impossible to separate the division of property from the discussion of where the children will live. The initial model was that the mediation was free for up to three hours (excluding the premediation session with each participant). Thereafter, it was means-tested. The parents could return for a further three hours of free mediation on two further occasions in a two-year period, as long as the mediation was dealing with new issues.

Funding cuts announced by the government in 2010 now threaten the concept of free mediation, and it is possible that a modest charge per hour may be applied in some circumstances. However, even with these funding cuts, the mediation services will be at a very low cost to those participants who are required to make a contribution.

The provision for ongoing family mediation is part of the philosophy of the FRCs. The goal of the mediation is not to reach a final resolution of all the issues for the long term. There is really no such thing as final arrangements with children. There are too many things that can and do change, both for the parents and in terms of children's needs. Rather, the goal of mediation in FRCs is to help parents work out parenting arrangements for the time being. In an initial mediation, within a few weeks or months of separation, it is hoped that at the very least, short-term parenting arrangements can be put in place that allow both parents to remain involved in caring for the children, and that these will then form the basis of more enduring arrangements.

Another reason for allowing more than one free or heavily subsidized mediation in any two-year period is to allow for experimentation and reality testing. Mediators can suggest an arrangement that works for other parents in similar circumstances, and the parents can just try it for a few weeks or months. The opportunity to come back for further free or subsidized mediation encourages this kind of experimentation.

The FRCs have a particular role to play in the resolution of disputes about alleged contraventions of court orders. Experience in the courts has shown that at least some contravention disputes concern problems that arise from court orders, frequently made by consent, that are either unworkable or have become unworkable as circumstances have changed.[17] The FRCs offer an option to help resolve these cases.

---

[17] FAMILY LAW COUNCIL, IMPROVING POST-PARENTING ORDER PROCESSES (2007).

At the conclusion of a mediation, a certificate may be given if the parents have been unable to agree and one parent wants to take the matter to court. A certificate is required when filing an application in court unless a ground for exemption is claimed. A certificate may also be given if the mediation did not proceed because the other person was unwilling to participate, or if the family dispute resolution practitioner decided that mediation would not be appropriate under the circumstances.

Success of the Family Relationship Centers and Other Support Services for Families

The FRCs achieved success very quickly. An evaluation of the family law reforms by the Australian Institute of Family Studies found that the overall number of applications for final orders in children's matters (including cases where there were also property issues being litigated) declined by 22 percent, from 18,752 in 2005–06 to 14,549 in 2008–09.[18] This needs to be read in the context that there has been a steady and persistent increase in applications for such orders over the last twenty years,[19] and that the FRCs were opened in stages. Fifteen centers were established in the first twelve months from July 2006. Another twenty-five were opened in July 2007. Almost all the remaining ones opened in July 2008.

In the three years following the introduction of the reforms to the family law system in 2006, the use of counseling and mediation services by parents during and after separation increased from 67 percent to 73 percent, and recourse to lawyers diminished to a corresponding degree. Contact with courts dropped from 40 percent before the reforms to 29 percent afterward.[20] Use of specialist domestic violence services almost doubled, indicating that there was greater awareness of the availability of these services.[21]

The evaluation also indicated that FRCs deal with parents with complex problems and significant needs – they do not just "cream off" the cases most likely to settle, leaving the hard cases for the courts. Those using family relationship services, including the FRCs, were much more likely than those not using services to have reported the experience of some form of family violence, mental health problems, or drug and alcohol issues, as

---

[18] Rae Kaspiew, Matthew Gray, Ruth Weston, Lawrie Moloney, Kelly Hand, & Lixia Qu, Evaluation of the 2006 Family Law Reforms 304–05 (2009).
[19] *See* Chapter 1.   [20] Kaspiew et al., *supra* note 18 at 50.
[21] *Id.* at 39.

well as distant, conflicted, and fearful relationships. They also reported much less cooperative relationships.[22]

Seventy-three percent of people who went to FRCs reported that they treated everyone fairly, and 55 percent said they got the help they needed. Overall, 70 percent of clients gave the FRCs a favorable rating.[23] The research team commented:[24]

> Taken as a whole, these client satisfaction ratings are quite positive, particularly when it is considered that a substantial proportion of clients have mental health issues, substance misuse issues, and/or a highly conflictual relationship with the other parent, or there are violence issues or safety concerns ... all of which tend to make it more challenging for services to meet the needs of a client.

In the long term, one of the most important measures of their success in relation to parenting after separation will be in the extent to which nonresident parents (mostly fathers) are able to maintain involvement with their children, and the extent to which conflict between parents after separation is reduced.

NEW APPROACHES TO IN-COURT COUNSELING SERVICES

Australia has also trialed a new approach to the use of specialist counselors and mediators within the court structure. This followed from the development of the FRCs. The requirement that family dispute resolution be attempted prior to filing an application for parenting orders, and through services available in the community, raised issues about the future role of the Family Court mediators. They had always had two functions. In addition to seeking to resolve disputes, they also acted as writers of family reports, conducting what in other jurisdictions are called "custody evaluations." This role was distinct from the dispute resolution role, and the mediator who conducted the dispute resolution session did not go on to write a family report since the dispute resolution phase was confidential.

With the move to community-based mediation, the Family Court's professional staff, known from 2006 as Family Consultants, took on a new role. If a family consultant is involved in a case, typically he or she is assigned early on in the process and continues to be involved for

[22] *Id.* at 49.   [23] *Id.* at 60.
[24] *Id.* at 61.

the duration of the case. The basic elements of what is known as "the child-responsive model" have been described by those involved in its development as follows:[25]

> "The program aims to educate and better focus parents from the point of entry to court on the views and needs of their children, to facilitate out-of-court settlement where possible and, where agreement cannot be reached, to assist judicial decision making when the matter proceeds to trial. Following evidence elsewhere of the potential impacts of child-inclusive divorce mediation, specialist child and family practitioners, known as family consultants, are involved in interviewing and observing children, carefully formulating their needs, and discussing with parents and their lawyers the children's experience of separation and their views about future arrangements. Each family is assisted by a nominated Family Consultant, who remains a constant presence for that family, assisting to enhance each parent's capacity to reflect on their children's needs and to plan a co-parenting approach and living plan to better meet these needs.

The dispute resolution processes conducted by Family Consultants are not confidential. The rationale for this is that normally, confidential mediation has either already been attempted prior to filing the proceedings or the case has been deemed inappropriate for mediation. The Family Consultant's involvement with the family is thus on a nonconfidential basis, and if the case cannot be resolved without adjudication then the Family Consultant is likely to be the person who prepares a family report for the judge and gives evidence about his or her observations of the family.

Resource constraints nonetheless limit the applicability of this model for all cases filed in the courts, because in some cases it is not possible to appoint a Family Consultant to the family, or another kind of expert report is needed in the circumstances of the case, such as a report from a psychiatrist.

COMPETITION OR PARTNERSHIP? MEDIATORS, LAWYERS, AND THE COURT SYSTEM

These changes in the system of dispute resolution have not been achieved without difficulty. The provision of substantial government expenditure

---

[25] Jennifer Mcintosh, Hon. Diana Bryant, & Kristen Murray, *Evidence of a Different Nature: The Child Responsive and Less Adversarial Initiatives of the Family Court of Australia*, 46 FAM. CT. REV. 125, 127 (2008).

on the resolution of family disputes without lawyers was bound to be treated with suspicion by some family lawyers – and it was.[26] There were certainly numerous complaints from lawyers that the money would have been better spent on appointing more judges or providing more legal aid for indigent litigants. The development of the FRCs occurred at a time when the waiting lists for trial dates in many parts of Australia were long and the family court system was overstretched. This indeed remains the case.

The significant decline in the number of court applications over the three-year period since the introduction of the FRCs shows how a well-organized and funded system of mediation and other family support, away from the court system, can have collateral benefits for the courts. However, it would be a mistake to measure the success of the FRCs only in these terms. It is apparent that they are meeting the needs of many people who would not have gone on to court at all, who would have given up or joined the ranks of the disaffected. They have the potential to offer a service to that large body of people who cannot realistically afford private lawyers but who also do not qualify for state-funded legal assistance. The FRCs are part of a long-term strategy to promote more consensual arrangements for parenting after separation and to encourage nonresident parents to remain involved in their children's lives.

Lawyers can and do play an important role in fulfilling that strategy. Lawyers work in partnership with mediators by giving initial advice prior to mediation, in reality-testing agreements reached in mediation, and in writing up agreements in such a way as to give them legal effect. Lawyers in particular play a vital role in hosing down the unrealistic expectations of their clients. Litigation also continues to be an important strategy in many cases, not least in bringing a reluctant parent to the negotiating table.

There are also cases that cannot or should not be mediated and cases that should not be settled without safety concerns being adequately addressed. Some cases will only settle after a custody evaluation or other expert report; others need adjudication. Lawyers and other professionals who work in resolving parenting disputes do not need to be in competition. What was needed in Australia, and is no doubt needed elsewhere, is to illuminate

---

[26] For an empirical study, *see* Georgina Dimopoulos, *Gateways, Gatekeepers or Guiding Hands? The Relationship Between Family Relationship Centres and Legal Practitioners in Case Management and the Court Process*, 24 Australian J. Fam. L. 176 (2010).

9

Adjudication for the Enduring Family

The transformation of the meaning of divorce from the old idea that the family is at an end to the acceptance of ongoing linkages between parents has profound implications not only for the substance of the law but also for legal processes. Just as hospitals have quite different functions depending on whether their role is to preserve life or to assist the family following the death of a loved one, so the family law system has also had to change profoundly – or needs to do so still.

NEW APPROACHES TO ADJUDICATION

Parenting disputes range enormously in their intensity and in what is at stake. Traditional models of adjudication in family courts were built around the typical custody dispute in which both parents were seeking the primary care of the children, relegating the other parent to the role of the visitor. This reflected the assumptions of the substitution model of the family. American scholar Andrew Schepard describes well the nature of the court's role in the substitution model. He writes that:[1]

> courts conceived of a custody dispute much like a will contest. The parents' marriage, like the decedent, was dead. Parents, like the heirs, were in dispute about the distribution of one of the assets of the estate – their children ... The goal of the proceeding was a one time determination of custody "rights" which created "stability" for the future management of the asset.

If this was the role of the court, then traditional adversarial processes, applying strict rules of evidence, were not necessarily an inappropriate way

---

[1] Andrew Schepard, *The Evolving Judicial Role in Child Custody Disputes: From Fault Finder to Conflict Manager to Differential Case Management*, 22 U. Ark. Little Rock L. Rev. 395, 395 (2000).

to adjudicate between warring parents. It remains so in cases where fact finding about such issues as child sexual abuse or other serious allegations are at the heart of the dispute between the parents.

However, three changes have occurred in the nature of family law disputes in the aftermath of the divorce revolution. Firstly, it is no longer the case that family law disputes are binary, either/or propositions. Although most relocation cases and cases that turn on an allegation that a parent is unfit to care for the child tend to be binary in nature, most family court cases do not present the court with a stark choice between two alternatives. As long as the parents live within a reasonable proximity to one another, there is a range of options for structuring parent-child contact, from limited involvement by the nonresident parent through to shared care. Depending on the law in the jurisdiction, parental responsibility may be able to be allocated and divided in different ways. The smorgasbord of options that courts have to resolve parenting disputes are limited by the circumstances of the parties and the needs of the children, but do not necessarily involve a clear choice between the position of one party and the position of the other.

The second change that has occurred in family law disputes arises from the enduring nature of the postseparation family. As long as the decision that courts faced was essentially only about which parent should have custody, it could be a once-off decision subject to modification where there was a significant change of circumstances. The application of the best interests of the child test meant working out which of the alternative households would be better for the children, together with deciding whether any constraints should be placed on visitation if that was an issue. There was no thought given to the impact of the litigation on the coparental relationship, because divorce meant the end of the family.

That has all changed now, with a recognition that it is in the best interests of children to try to reduce their exposure to conflict between their parents. This requires a focus on how the best interests of children could be served by the processes of adjudication, as well as using the best interests test to determine the appropriate outcome of the dispute. Unified family courts, influenced in some cases by the insights of therapeutic jurisprudence, have been a growing feature of the landscape in the United States for this reason.[2]

---

[2]   Barbara Babb, *Reevaluating Where We Stand: A Comprehensive Survey of America's Family Justice Systems*, 46 Fam. Ct. Rev. 230 (2008). For a critical view of the family court as a problem-solving court, *see* Jane Spinak, *Romancing the Court*, 46 Fam. Ct Rev. 258 (2008).

Thirdly, there has been a recognition that the notion of a "final" order in children's cases, subject to an application for "custody modification" is problematic. While there are good reasons to ensure that decisions on primary residence are not lightly reopened, the idea that once-for-all adjudications can be made in children's cases is unrealistic given the dynamic, rather than static, nature of family life. Adjudications on parenting matters involve making decisions at a moment in time, based on the circumstances of that time. Those circumstances change constantly as children grow older. The needs of a child at the age of three may be quite different from his or her needs at age eight, and in the intervening years, many changes are likely to have occurred in the circumstances of the parents such as moving house, repartnering, and changing jobs.

Of particular significance may be changes in the level of acrimony in the relationship with the other parent as time begins to heal the wounds of the separation and the initial grief, anger, and resentment associated with relationship breakdown has subsided. Maclean and Eekelaar in Britain found that relationships between parents improved markedly in the years after separation where contact was maintained.[3] Similar findings have been made in an older longitudinal study in Australia.[4] What may be the best available option for a child when parents are in very high conflict may not be the best at a later time when the parents are capable of a more civil and cooperative relationship.

The level of change that in fact occurs in parenting arrangements after separation is borne out by longitudinal research with parents.[5] Maccoby and Mnookin in California found that over the three and a half years of their study of custody and visitation arrangements following separation and divorce, 28 percent of the children had switched residence and in 45 percent of the families in which children were in the primary care of their mothers, there were significant changes in the amount of contact with their fathers. In about two-thirds of the cases where there were changes in contact patterns, there was a decline in father-child contact, but in the remainder, the change was in the direction of increased father-child contact or shifts

---

3 Mavis Maclean & John Eekelaar, The Parental Obligation: A Study of Parenthood across Households 123–126 (1997). This was the case even where personal protection had been discussed with a lawyer in the aftermath of separation.

4 Kate Funder, *Exploring the Access-Maintenance Nexus, in* Settling Down: Pathways of Parents after Divorce 177–78 (Kate Funder, Margaret Harrison, & Ruth Weston eds., 1993).

5 For an international review, *see* Bruce Smyth & Lawrie Moloney, *Changes in Patterns of Post-Separation Parenting Over Time: A Brief Review,* 14 J. Fam. Studies 7 (2008).

from daytime contact to overnight stays.[6] These changes can be in more than one direction, with some families establishing coparenting arrangements after beginning with a residence/contact arrangement, whereas in other cases the father's involvement decreased over time.

Similarly, Smart and Neale in Britain found that 53 percent of the parents they interviewed had experienced significant changes in parenting arrangements between the time of separation and the time of the second interview (which took place between three and seven years after separation).[7]

At least some of the heat might be taken out of disputes about parenting after separation if lawyers, mediators, and courts make it clear that the process of decision making is not a process of allocation that is final, but rather is a decision for the time being, based on the circumstances at that time, and that the parenting arrangements need not remain the same throughout the children's minority. Of course, there are some parents who also need to be advised that the court will not look kindly on attempts to begin a new cycle of litigation as a means of reversing the initial custody decision soon after it has been made. Courts also need to act robustly toward vexatious litigants whose use of further applications to the court destabilizes the child's primary care.

There is a particular reason to treat the detail of contact and visitation orders as relatively short-term in duration, with further negotiation being encouraged over time, taking into account the views of children themselves. An order for "reasonable visitation" is flexible, but the tendency now is to define much more precisely how much parenting time the nonresident parent will have. Particularly in high-conflict families, this may be specified with a great deal of precision. Such detailed orders may quickly become unworkable as circumstances change, even in such day-to-day matters as the commitments children have to sports and other extracurricular activities. Making only short-term contact orders, perhaps for two to three years in the first instance, is more realistic than trying to craft orders covering the long term, and would send a message to the parties that future contact arrangements need to be a matter for continuing negotiation.

The Family Relationship Centers in Australia offer one accessible means to renegotiate contact arrangements over time as circumstances change without requiring necessarily a fresh engagement with the family law system. Where mediation is suitable, this offers a means to renegotiate arrangements, but it is not for all and there are those who in any event will not reach a consensual agreement.

---

6   ELEANOR MACCOBY & ROBERT MNOOKIN, DIVIDING THE CHILD: SOCIAL AND LEGAL DILEMMAS OF CUSTODY 198–99 (1992).
7   CAROL SMART & BREN NEALE, FAMILY FRAGMENTS? (1999).

Where the dispute is essentially about levels of contact and details of the arrangement rather than the issue of who should be the primary caregiver, the dispute ought to be able to be resolved without another full-blown trial in court. A model for quick and inexpensive resolution of contact disputes is the Danish system.

DENMARK: THE ROLE OF COUNTY GOVERNORS' OFFICES

The system for resolving contact (visitation) disputes in Denmark illustrates the possibilities for developing new forms of adjudication, other than the traditional adversarial trial, that are quick and inexpensive. Contact disputes are an example of where the remedy will only be reasonably effective if it is speedy and affordable. Yet typically, courts in common law jurisdictions adopt the same adversarial processes and legal structures to the resolution of contact disputes as they do for the major allocation decision of custody or primary residence.

In Denmark and Norway, certain functions have traditionally been exercised by the County Governors' Offices.[8] These are administrative authorities. Their role in relation to family law is a historical one, which dates back hundreds of years to a time when the monarch was able to grant divorces as a matter of executive decision. This continued in Denmark and Norway into the modern age of divorce, so that the courts and the administrative authorities have a parallel jurisdiction in relation to divorce, and certain ancillary matters, such as child support.[9]

In Denmark, the County Governors' Offices are given a lot of responsibility for resolving disputes and making orders.[10] Consensual divorces are almost always handled by the County Governors' Offices. They also deal with how much should be paid as spousal maintenance, if the court

[8] In Danish, *statsforvaltning*; in Norwegian, *fylkesmann*.
[9] Svend Danielsen, *The Scandinavian Approach: Administrative and Judicial Resolutions of Family Conflicts, in* FAMILLES ET JUSTICE 139 (Marie Thérèse Meulders-Klein ed., 1997).
[10] The description of the Danish system for resolving contact disputes is derived from the author's research in Denmark in 2002, and interviews with Svend Danielsen, a former senior family law judge in Denmark, senior members of the Ministry of Justice, and with a judge of the Sheriff's Court. Prof. Danielsen provided an update in 2010. *See also* MARIANNE HESTER & LORRAINE RADFORD, DOMESTIC VIOLENCE AND CHILD CONTACT ARRANGEMENTS IN ENGLAND AND DENMARK (1996); Marianne Hester, *One Step Forward and Three Steps Back? Children, Abuse and Parental Contact in Denmark*, 14 CHILD & FAM. L. Q. 267 (2002); Christina Jeppesen de Boer, *A Comparative Analysis of Contact Arrangements in the Netherlands and Denmark, in* PERSPECTIVES FOR THE UNIFICATION AND HARMONISATION OF FAMILY LAW IN EUROPE 378 (Katharina Boele-Woelki ed., 2003).

decides there should be a duty to pay, child support, contact arrangements, and adoption. The courts resolve the major issue of who should have custodial responsibility, but can only make contact orders in connection with disputes on custody or the child's residence. Other disputes about contact are left to the County Governors' Offices to deal with.[11]

The procedure for initiating the involvement of the County Governor's Office in a contact problem is simple. If a father is having problems seeing his children, or is otherwise unhappy with the arrangements, he can write to the County Governor's Office asking for it to get involved. There are no forms to fill in or applications to file, and there is no fee payable.

The matter will be dealt with initially by a lawyer in the County Governor's Office. He or she will contact the mother and seek her response. There will often be a meeting. The couple can be referred to counseling, paid for by the County Governor's office, or to mediation. It used to be the case that counseling was only offered if both parties were willing to participate. Counseling may now be offered to one party even if the other is not willing to join in.

If the problems cannot be resolved by counseling or informally, then the lawyer in the County Governor's office will proceed to make a determination. This takes effect as an order, enforceable in the courts.[12] Usually matters are resolved within six weeks. There is a right of appeal to a directorate under the Ministry of Justice (*Familiestyrelsen*) in Copenhagen. Generally these are dealt with on the papers, but a parent will never be denied a personal meeting if that is requested.[13]

These different ways of adjudicating disputes concerning children that cannot be resolved by mediation or negotiation demonstrate what might be possible in common law countries with the support of legislatures.

REFORMING THE ADVERSARIAL SYSTEM

Another area where change needs to occur in an age of the enduring family is in relation to legal processes in those cases that need to go to trial.

---

[11] For further detail on the role of the County Governor's Office in resolving contact disputes, *see* the leaflet put out by the Ministry of Justice, *Med Barnet I Centrum* (2006), http://www.familiestyrelsen.dk/samvaer/publikationer/1/

[12] The decisions of County Governors' Offices are enforceable, and this enforcement occurs through the court system. The Danish have a special enforcement court for all kinds of court orders, including contact orders. It can be translated as either the Bailiff's Court or the Sheriff's Court (Danish: *Byret*).

[13] Between 1997 and 2000, appeals were lodged in about 17 percent of cases. CivilRetsDirektoratet, Samvær Børnesagkyndig Rådgivning Konfliktmægling, Statistik 2001 (2002).

It has long been recognized that a trial system based on adversarial processes is not well suited to family cases in which the desirable outcome for most families will be an ongoing relationship between both parents and the children.[14] Much research on family law practice demonstrates that family lawyers tend to be oriented towards settlement rather than litigation, particularly in children's cases.[15]

Nonetheless, in the cases that do not settle, the adversarial system remains a norm in many common law jurisdictions, even if the trial itself takes place in a specialist family court setting.[16] There are grounds for concern about the impact that litigation has on the coparental relationship. A study in the United States involving a twelve-year follow-up of families who had been randomly assigned to mediate or litigate their child custody disputes indicated that nonresidential parents who mediated were more involved in multiple areas of their children's lives, maintained more contact with their children, and had a greater influence in coparenting twelve years later than families who litigated custody.[17]

In the light of these concerns, another feature of the Australian reforms has been changes to the adversarial nature of the trial in parenting disputes[18] to try to reduce conflict between parents in those few cases that go to trial.[19]

14 Gregory Firestone & Janet Weinstein, *In the Best Interests of Children: A Proposal to Transform the Adversarial System*, 42 FAM. CT REV. 203 (2004).
15 GWYNN DAVIS, PARTISANS AND MEDIATORS (1988); RICHARD INGLEBY, SOLICITORS AND DIVORCE (1992); GWYNN DAVIS, STEPHEN CRETNEY, & JEAN COLLINS, SIMPLY QUARRELS (1994); AUSTIN SARAT & WILLIAM FELSTINER, DIVORCE LAWYERS AND THEIR CLIENTS (1995); JOHN EEKELAAR, MAVIS MACLEAN, & SARAH BEINART, FAMILY LAWYERS (2000). *See also* Craig McEwen, Lynn Mather, & Richard Maiman, *Lawyers, Mediation, and the Management of Divorce*, 28 L. & SOC. REV. 149 (1994); Janet Walker, *Is There a Future for Lawyers in Divorce?*, 10 INT'L J.L. & FAM. 51 (1996), Bren Neale & Carol Smart, *"Good" and "Bad" Lawyers? Struggling in the Shadow of the New Law*, 19 J. SOC. WELFARE L. 377 (1997); Michael King, *"Being Sensible": Images and Practices of the New Family Lawyers*, 28 J. SOC. POL'Y 249 (1999).
16 For discussion of the position in the United States, *see* ANDREW SCHEPARD, CHILDREN, COURTS AND CUSTODY: INTERDISCIPLINARY MODELS FOR DIVORCING FAMILIES 40–42, 50–51 (2004).
17 Robert Emery, Lisa Laumann-Billings, Mary Waldron, David Sbarra, & Peter Dillon, *Child Custody Mediation and Litigation: Custody, Contact, and Coparenting 12 Years after Initial Dispute Resolution*, 69 J. CONSULTING & CLINICAL PSYCHOL. 323 (2001).
18 *See generally,* Peter Rose, *The Road to Less Adversarial Trials and Beyond*, 21 AUSTRALIAN J. FAM. L. 232 (2007).
19 As in other jurisdictions, most cases are resolved without a trial. In family law disputes in Australia, generally only 13 percent of cases reach the stage of commencement of a trial, with 6 percent of cases being resolved by a formal judgment. FAMILY AND COMMUNITY AFFAIRS COMMITTEE OF THE HOUSE OF REPRESENTATIVES, PARLIAMENT

Alastair Nicholson, the former Chief Justice of the Family Court of Australia, initiated the changes to procedure, arguing that major reform of the adversarial process is necessary to address "the weaknesses of the traditional processes that allow the parties via their legal representatives (where they have them) to determine the issues in the case, the evidence that is to be adduced and the manner of its use."[20] Looking back over sixteen years as Chief Justice, he wrote that:[21]

> These weaknesses have been exacerbated in recent years as the proportion of litigants who represent themselves has increased. Judges find themselves being presented with reams of unnecessary material, usually dwelling on events long past, adult rather than child focused, and replete with allegations about what each party is alleged to have done to the other. Witnesses are called who can provide little or no relevant information, and trials become lengthier and more expensive. The relationship between the parties – if it is not already in tatters – deteriorates to the extent that they are unable to effectively co-parent their children in the future to any extent without hostility.

As a consequence of the rethinking of the place of adversarial processes for children's cases, the Family Court of Australia developed the Less Adversarial Trial. This followed on from a pilot program known as the Children's Cases Program conducted from 2003 onward.[22] In developing this new style of adjudication, the Family Court of Australia was particularly influenced by its examination of the German approach to the management of trials as it stood in the early part of the decade.[23]

The Less Adversarial Trial represents a significant reform of the traditional adversarial trial in the common law tradition. It is mainly used in children's cases and contains many features that differentiate the process from a traditional trial.[24] The Court uses introductory questionnaires to

---

OF AUSTRALIA, EVERY PICTURE TELLS A STORY: REPORT OF THE INQUIRY INTO CHILD CUSTODY ARRANGEMENTS IN THE EVENT OF FAMILY SEPARATION 6–7 (2003).

[20] The Hon. Alastair Nicholson, *Sixteen Years of Family Law: A Retrospective*, 18 AUSTRALIAN J. FAM. L. 131, 144 (2004).

[21] *Id.* at 144–45.

[22] Rosemary Hunter, *Child-Related Proceedings Under Pt VII Div 12A of the Family Law Act: What the Children's Cases Pilot Program Can and Can't Tell Us*, 20 AUSTRALIAN J. FAM. L. 227–48 (2006).

[23] MARGARET HARRISON, FINDING A BETTER WAY: A BOLD DEPARTURE FROM THE TRADITIONAL COMMON LAW APPROACH TO THE CONDUCT OF LEGAL PROCEEDINGS 38–42 (2007).

[24] Division 12A of Pt VII of the Family Law Act, 1975, provides the statutory basis for the less adversarial trial. This form of trial is mainly used in children's proceedings, but if there are children's and property issues combined in the one proceeding, then the same

gain a lot of the basic information about the case. The trial itself proceeds in stages, usually some weeks apart. On the first day of the hearing, the parties are sworn in, so that anything said thereafter constitutes evidence. The parties are each given an opportunity to explain at the beginning of the hearing what the dispute is about. The parties may, of course, speak through their lawyers, but the normal practice – one encouraged by the court – is for each party to speak directly to the judge. The judge then usually identifies areas of agreement and disagreement. Some issues in dispute may be clarified and resolved at this stage.

The issues that cannot be resolved will be determined at a subsequent stage. The judge will give directions for the next phase of the trial, including what evidence will need to be adduced. The judge has considerable discretion in determining how the case should be conducted. The rules of evidence are applied very flexibly. Most evidence is conditionally admitted unless the judge determines otherwise.[25]

An evaluation of the pilot program, the Children's Cases Program, indicated that four months after the conclusion of court proceedings, parents who went through the Children's Cases Program were significantly more likely to report better management of conflict, less damage to the coparental relationship, and greater satisfaction with the parenting arrangements. There were also significantly lower levels of overall conflict.[26]

ADJUDICATION IN FAMILIES WITH
CONTINUING HIGH CONFLICT

A minority of families continue to be in high conflict for a long time after separation. An innovation in various parts of the United States offers a means of ongoing dispute resolution in these high-conflict families. In some jurisdictions, courts appoint someone to mediate and, if necessary, to adjudicate on disputes arising in high-conflict families if the parents cannot agree.[27] These appointees are variously described as special

process can be used for both aspects of the case if the parties agree. The principles for the less adversarial trial are contained in s.69ZN of the Family Law Act.

[25] FAMILY COURT OF AUSTRALIA, LESS ADVERSARIAL TRIAL HANDBOOK, 34–35 (2009).

[26] JENNIFER McINTOSH, THE CHILDREN'S CASES PILOT PROJECT: AN EXPLORATORY STUDY ON IMPACTS ON PARENTING CAPACITY AND CHILD WELL-BEING, FINAL REPORT TO THE FAMILY COURT OF AUSTRALIA (2006).

[27] Joan Kelly, *Psychological and Legal Interventions for Parents and Children in Custody and Access Disputes: Current Research and Practice*, 10 VA. J. SOC. POL'Y & L. 129, 142–44 (2002); AFCC Taskforce on Parenting Coordination, *Parenting Coordination: Implementation Issues*, 41 FAM. CT REV. 533 (2003); Christine Coates,

masters,[28] parenting coordinators,[29] or arbitrators, depending on the jurisdiction and the manner of their appointment.[30] Such an appointee is most often a psychiatrist or psychologist,[31] but may be a lawyer. Joan Kelly explains the most common features of such programs:

> In Special Master or Parent Coordinator programs, experienced custody evaluators, mediators, and family law attorneys are given limited and court-ordered authority to settle parenting disputes outside of the court setting. This non-confidential intervention is intended to provide a non-adversarial forum for quick resolution of parental disputes involving their children. While Special Masters function outside of the adversarial system, in a non-adversarial manner, they are responsible to the court, write and file decisions, adhere to rules for appeal and judicial review, and can be subpoenaed to testify. Focusing on children's developmental, social and psychological needs, instead of the parents' power struggles and grievances, these arbitration programs have the goal of reducing the amount of parental conflict experienced by children ... Most often, these professionals meet with parents and children separately to gather information about disputed issues as they arise, assist parents when possible to mediate differences, and make timely decisions if parents cannot agree.

Models vary in the role given to the professional. In some jurisdictions, they may have significant decision-making powers, whereas in others, their role may be more one of counseling, mediating, and making recommendations to the court. Their role involves dealing with ongoing disputes about parenting arrangements and scheduling, as well as sorting out the myriad other problems that can arise when parents are so conflicted that all trust has broken down.

Even though parenting coordinators and other professionals appointed to play a similar role may offer a useful addition to the range of options open to courts in dealing with high-conflict cases, their use is limited in the United States by the problem of cost. Unless states provide a free or

---

Robin Deutsch, Hugh Starnes, Matthew Sullivan, & Bea Lisa Sydlik, *Parenting Coordination for High-conflict Families*, 42 FAM. CT REV. 246 (2004).

[28] Matthew Sullivan, *Have a Problem? Hire a Special Master as Decision-Maker*, 21 FAM. ADVOCATE 41 (1998).

[29] Doris Truhlar, *Use of a Parenting Coordinator in Domestic Cases*, 27 COLORADO LAWYER 53 (1998). For a critical view of the idea of parenting coordinators, *see* Jane Ellis, *Caught in the Middle: Protecting the Children of High Conflict Divorce*, 22 N.Y.U. REV. L. & SOC. CHANGE 253 (1996).

[30] Kelly, *supra* note 27, at 142–44.

[31] Robert Zibbell, *The Mental Health Professional as Arbitrator in Post-Divorce Child Oriented Conflict*, 33 FAM. & CONCIL. CTS REV. 462 (1995).

subsidized program, the services of a parenting coordinator typically must be paid for in full by the parents themselves, usually at mental health professionals' hourly rates. Where a parenting coordinator needs to make a significant time commitment to resolving the ongoing disputes occurring in a high-conflict family, the costs may be out of reach for all but the most wealthy.

Even if such a service is affordable, there remains the question of whether it is desirable. As a short-term intervention to try to build a more positive and cooperative relationship between the parents, the strategy may be very useful. If, however, the parents need the ongoing services of a neutral arbitrator to resolve conflicts in the long term, it is questionable whether the notion of joint parental responsibility is worth sustaining. The involvement of both parents in the life of a child cannot be purchased at any price, and beyond the financial cost of such interventions there is the issue of exposing the child to ongoing conflict and uncertainty. In some cases, the old custody/visitation model, with visitation fixed by court orders, may provide the least detrimental environment for the child.

PART FIVE

Financial Transfers in the Enduring Family

10

Child Support and the Obligations
of Parenthood

MAINTAINING AND CREATING TIES BETWEEN PARENTS

One significant factor that has shaped government policies toward parenting after separation around the world has been the issue of financial support for children. Child support has become enormously significant in tying together the fortunes of mothers and fathers in the enduring family, and in this dimension, more than any other, government is deeply involved in maintaining the indissolubility of parenthood.[1] For this reason, child support has been called the "new coparenting".[2] Whereas once, governments were persuaded, under the tutelage of the Church,[3] to keep marriages together through laws prohibiting or restricting divorce, now the focus is on the need to keep families together after separation, at least in a financial sense. This indissolubility of parenthood arises whether or not they were ever married or even lived together, and whether or not a parent sees the children. Huge efforts are now made to ensure, to the greatest extent possible, that nonresident parents meet their obligations, at least if the parent can be traced and has an income or savings against which a child support liability can be enforced. Around the western world, considerable government expenditure is incurred in that effort.

This change has been a response to the massive growth in the number of one-parent families. This growth has occurred not only as a consequence of the rise in divorce rates following the no-fault divorce revolution, but also because of the huge increase in the numbers of children born outside marriage in western countries.

---

[1] For a review of policies in the United States and other countries, see CHILD SUPPORT: THE NEXT FRONTIER (Thomas Oldham & Marygold Melli eds., 2000).
[2] ALISON DIDUCK, LAW'S FAMILIES, 167 (2003).
[3] For a history, see MARY ANN GLENDON, STATE, LAW & FAMILY (1977).

This can be illustrated, for example, by Britain. In the early 1970s, less than 10 percent of all births were outside marriage. In 1995, 34 percent of live births were outside marriage[4] and in 2009 the percentage was 46 percent.[5] The majority of these children would have been born to parents who were cohabiting,[6] but the dissolution rates of cohabitation are much higher than for marriages.[7]

There are significant variations between western countries in the proportion of single-parent families. In the United Kingdom, and the United States around the year 2000, nearly a quarter of families with children were headed by a lone parent. By way of contrast, the proportion in certain continental European countries was much lower.[8]

Reform was also driven by concern for the effects of poverty on the future life chances of children. The payment of child support when parents are living apart is an important strategy in the reduction of child poverty[9] and more generally in improving child well-being.[10] American studies indicate that awareness of the likelihood of child support enforcement also reduces the likelihood of births out of wedlock and influences the choice of partner with whom to have children.[11]

---

[4] NATIONAL STATISTICS, POPULATION TRENDS no 126, at 45 tbl. 3.2 (2006), http://www.statistics.gov.uk/downloads/theme_population/PopTrends126.pdf

[5] NATIONAL STATISTICS LIVE BIRTHS IN ENGLAND AND WALES BY CHARACTERISTICS OF MOTHER 2009 (2010), http://www.statistics.gov.uk/statbase/Product.asp?vlnk=14408. *See also* Louise O'Leary, Eva Natamba, Julie Jefferies, & Ben Wilson, *Fertility and Partnership Status in the Last Two Decades*, POPULATION TRENDS no 140, at 5 (2010).

[6] Of the births registered outside marriage in 2005, 63 percent were registered jointly by parents living at the same address. NATIONAL STATISTICS, *supra* note 4. *See also* O'Leary et al., *supra* note 5, at 27.

[7] Kathleen Kiernan, *Cohabitation in Western Europe*, POPULATION TRENDS no 96, at 25 (1999), http://www.statistics.gov.uk/downloads/theme_population/PT96book.pdf. In a study of eleven European countries, Kiernan found that cohabiting relationships that did not result in marriage were much more fragile than marriages either preceded by a period of cohabitation or without a prior period of cohabitation. In Britain, only 18 percent of such relationships survived for ten years.

[8] *See* Christine Skinner & Jacqueline Davidson, *Recent Trends in Child Maintenance Schemes in 14 Countries*, 23 INT. J. L. POLICY & FAM. 25, 30 (2009).

[9] Judi Bartfeld, *Child Support and the Postdivorce Economic Well-being of Mothers, Fathers, and Children*, 37 DEMOGRAPHY 203 (2000); Daniel Meyer & Mei-Chen Hu, *A Note on the Antipoverty Effectiveness of Child Support Among Mother-only Families*, 34 J. HUMAN RESOURCES 225 (1999).

[10] Laura Argys, Elizabeth Peters, Jeanne Brooks-Gunn, & Judith Smith, *The Impact of Child Support on Cognitive Outcomes of Young Children*, 35 DEMOGRAPHY 159 (1998).

[11] Anna Aizer & Sara McLanahan, *The Impact of Child Support Enforcement on Fertility, Parental Investments, and Child Well-being*, 41 J. HUMAN RESOURCES 28 (2006). *See also* Robert Plotnick, Irwin Garfinkel, Sara McLanahan, & Inhoe Ku, *Better Child*

This need to ensure child support is paid does not have to be connected with laws encouraging greater nonresident parent involvement, but the evidence from many studies internationally is that there is a strong association between regularity of contact and child support compliance, giving governments a motivation for encouraging continued father-child involvement.[12] Furthermore, it is difficult for governments on the one hand to regularize the payment of child support while on the other hand turning a deaf ear to nonresident parents' complaints about the little time they are able to spend with their children. Child support is, in theory, separate from the issue of contact with children, but in the minds of citizens it is often linked, and dissatisfaction with the lack of enforceability of court-ordered contact arrangements can be displaced into anger about the rigorous enforcement of child support obligations.[13] This practical nexus in the minds of citizens, if not in the law itself, has become a driver for law reform.

CHILD SUPPORT AND THE DIVORCE REVOLUTION

This governmental interest in enforcing child support has transformed child support from being a private matter between parents to being a matter of considerable public interest and concern.

As seen in Chapter 2, for the majority of divorced men in many countries, the divorce revolution meant walking away from the marriage, or being shown the door, without attribution of blame, but also without continuing responsibilities. In theory, spousal support could be awarded, and all noncustodial parents who were in employment were expected to pay child support. However, the reality differed greatly from the ideal. Less than a third of single mothers in America received child support in the 1960s and 1970s, and spousal support was much rarer still. Freedom from the bonds of matrimony came at a terrible price for many women in

---

Support Enforcement: Can It Reduce Teenage Premarital Childbearing?, 25 J. FAM ISSUES 634 (2004).

[12] Judith Seltzer, Nora Schaeffer, & Hong-Wen Charng, *Family Ties after Divorce: The Relationship between Visiting and Paying Child Support*, 51 J. MARRIAGE & FAM. 1013 (1989). Kate Funder, *Exploring the Access-Maintenance Nexus*, in SETTLING DOWN: PATHWAYS OF PARENTS AFTER DIVORCE (Kate Funder, Margaret Harrison, & Ruth Weston eds., 1993); Bruce Smyth & Belinda Fehlberg, *Child Support and Parent-Child Contact*, 57 FAM. MATTERS 20 (2000).

[13] Stacey Bloomer, Theresa Sipe, & Danielle Ruedt, *Child Support Payment and Child Visitation: Perspectives from Nonresident Fathers and Resident Mothers*, 29 J. SOCIOLOGY AND SOCIAL WELFARE 77 (2002).

terms of adverse financial consequences; it exacted a different kind of toll for divorced fathers.

There has long been court-based enforcement of child support,[14] sometimes involving jail terms for fathers who would not pay, but the systematic efforts to improve child support compliance, involving the active role of government, can be traced to the mid-1970s onward in the United States, and somewhat later elsewhere, in response to rapidly rising welfare expenditures. In the United States, for example, the growth in one-parent families over the period from the mid-1950s to the mid-1970s had been considerable. Welfare expenditure rose threefold in real terms, with little actual increase in the rates of payment to each family.[15] There were similar issues in other countries. If nonresident parents are not contributing to their children's support, the State is left as the default provider for low-income female-headed households with children, placing a considerable strain on welfare budgets.

Governments needed to find ways to privatize the obligation to support children, or at least to reduce the extent of taxpayers' responsibility for ensuring that children did not live in poverty. Governments could provide a social safety net, and they did, but fiscal realities ensured that it would become a governmental priority to recoup at least some of that expenditure, where possible, from the noncustodial parent. Although there were those who called for recognition of the mother-child dyad as the family unit deserving privacy and protection without the need to locate a father,[16] and for treating single parenthood as an event like sickness or disability that should be covered by social security,[17] the prevailing consensus was that fathers should be made accountable for procreation, and that this should be a private and noninsured obligation.

What emerged was a close nexus between welfare systems and child support enforcement, with the private obligations of support between parents becoming a matter of public interest and concern.

---

[14] DAVID CHAMBERS, MAKING FATHERS PAY: THE ENFORCEMENT OF CHILD SUPPORT (1979).

[15] Irwin Garfinkel, Daniel Meyer, & Sara McLanahan, *A Brief History of Child Support Policies in the United States, in* FATHERS UNDER FIRE: THE REVOLUTION IN CHILD SUPPORT ENFORCEMENT 14, 18 (Irwin Garfinkel, Sara McLanahan, Daniel Meyer, & Judith Seltzer eds., 1998).

[16] MARTHA FINEMAN, THE NEUTERED MOTHER, THE SEXUAL FAMILY AND OTHER TWENTIETH CENTURY TRAGEDIES 212, 230–33 (1995).

[17] Stephen Sugarman, *Financial Support of Children and the End of Welfare As We Know It*, 81 VIRGINIA L. REV. 2523 (1995).

NONMARITAL FAMILIES AND THE
INDISSOLUBILITY OF PARENTHOOD

One of the consequences of the crisis of burgeoning welfare expenditures was that new families were sometimes formed. Fatherhood was first biological, then economic. In some cases, economic fatherhood created artificial families where none had previously existed before. These families were not born out of mutual intention and consent, other than the consent to sexual intercourse, but were formed at the behest of the State to ensure that children had adequate means of support and that the burden on governments of supporting single mothers would be reduced. Precisely because men were tied by the obligations of child support into an ongoing and long-term commitment to their children, it legitimized their role in having an ongoing parental involvement as well.

In jurisdictions that conferred parental responsibility on nonmarital fathers by reason of biological parenthood, or acknowledgment on the birth certificate, fathers were given the same legal status whether the child was the result of a one-night stand or had been cared for by both mother and father from the cradle through the years of infancy, preschool, and primary school until the time that the parents separated. All such men had child support obligations flowing from their biological connection, and with that came the other aspects of parenthood, often involving a continuing relationship with the child's mother.

THE PUBLIC ROLE IN CHILD SUPPORT
ASSESSMENT AND COLLECTION

The public interest in child support compliance had three major strands to it. The first was to identify fathers of ex-nuptial children to pay child support. This involved efforts to obtain information from mothers about the identity of fathers and to ensure that a child support claim was made. The second dimension was enforcement, with the state taking a role in collecting child support that was similar in some respects to the enforcement of the obligation to pay taxes. The third dimension was ensuring adequate levels of child support, replacing the individualized assessment of courts with general formulas that had at least the status of a presumptive guideline, and in some jurisdictions, binding statutory force.

The growth of this public role in child support collection and assessment and its underlying rationale can be seen in the way in which law and practice developed both in the United States and elsewhere.

The United States

In 1975, Congress established a federal Office of Child Support Enforcement and required all states to establish similar offices. It operated both with sticks and carrots. The stick was loss of some of their federal funding under a combined federal state welfare program, the Aid to Families with Dependent Children (AFDC).[18] The carrot was substantial federal funding of state enforcement programs, as long as they complied with federal standards.[19] One drive was to increase the identification of fathers who would be liable to pay child support. For example, legislation made it a requirement for mothers to cooperate with child support enforcement officials to identify absent fathers as a condition for eligibility for welfare payments.[20] States were also required to extend their statutes of limitations on paternity suits.[21] A national parent-locator system was also established, assisted by access to a wide range of government records.

There was also a focus on collection. Although the primary focus in the early years was on obtaining child support for mothers on welfare, there was a limited level of support given also to collection efforts on behalf of other mothers, and by 1984, these efforts at child support enforcement had become a universal service.[22]

In the drive to improve collection, automatic withholding of child support from wages became the front-line strategy. Federal legislation passed in 1984 obliged states to withhold child support from wages if the child support payer was more than a month behind in payments.[23] Legislation in 1988 extended the obligation of automatic withholding to all cases where mothers were on welfare, with a further extension in 1994 to all new or modified child support cases.[24] Tax refunds could also be intercepted, liens could be imposed on property, and a range of more punitive measures such as cancellation of driving licenses were made available to support enforcement efforts.[25] Between 1975 and 1999,

---

[18] This is now known as Temporary Assistance for Needy Families (TANF).
[19] Harry Krause, *Child Support Reassessed: Limits of Private Responsibility and the Public Interest*, 1989 U. ILL. L. REV. 367, 372.
[20] 42 U.S.C. § 602(a)(26)(B) (1988).
[21] 42 U.S.C. § 666(a)(5)(A); § 652(g).
[22] Garfinkel et al., *supra* note 15, at 19.
[23] Child Support Enforcement Amendments of 1984, Pub. L. No. 98–378, 98 Stat. 1305.
[24] Garfinkel et al., *supra* note 15, at 23–24.
[25] For examples, *see* Solangel Maldonado, *Beyond Economic Fatherhood: Encouraging Divorced Fathers to Parent*, 153 U. PA. L. REV. 921, 936–37 (2005).

$30 billion was spent implementing this child support enforcement program.[26]

This effort at child support enforcement was backed by a level of rhetoric that climbed to the heights of moral judgment. Senator Moynihan urged government to "hunt, hound and harass" the absent parent.[27] President Clinton said in his 1994 State of the Union address:[28]

> We'll ... say to absent parents who aren't paying child support, if you're not providing for your children, we will garnish your wages, we will suspend your license, we will track you across state lines, and, if necessary, make some of you work off what you owe. People who bring children into this world cannot and must not just walk away from them.

It was a soaring rhetoric that made no reference to the other side of the moral coin – that in an age of no-fault divorce, many of these fathers were not the leavers, but the left, not those who abandoned their children but those who, sometimes for good reasons, sometimes not, were abandoned by their former partners. Such fathers, forced by circumstances into being absent, may have felt less than committed to reimbursing the government for its welfare expenditure in support of their former partners, however much they cared about their children. Many also were too poor themselves to be able to provide for their children – a continuing dilemma in the enforcement of child support obligations.[29]

Despite all the efforts made from the mid-1980s onward to improve child support collection, the overall effect of these efforts has been comparatively modest. Between 1976 and 1997, the numbers of single mothers receiving child support increased by less than 1 percent.[30] However, research has shown that this overall lack of progress disguises the dramatic changes in the demographics of the family in America that have led to problems in improving child support compliance. In 1976, 83 percent of mothers who were not living with the father of their child or children were or had been married. By 1997, that percentage had dropped to 54 percent.[31] In that period, the number of never-married mothers increased fivefold, while the number of divorced and separated mothers increased at a much slower

---

[26] ELAINE SORENSEN & ARIEL HALPERN, CHILD SUPPORT ENFORCEMENT: HOW WELL IS IT DOING? (Urban Institute, Discussion Paper) 1 (1999).

[27] DANIEL MOYNIHAN, FAMILY AND NATION 180 (1986), cited in Krause, *supra* note 19, at 379.

[28] Available at http://www.let.rug.nl/usa/P/bc42/speeches/sud94wjc.htm

[29] *See* David Chambers, *Fathers, the Welfare System, and the Virtues and Perils of Child Support Enforcement*, 81 VIRGINIA L. REV. 2575 (1995).

[30] SORENSEN & HALPERN, *supra* note 26, at 1.   [31] *Id.*

rate, rising from 3.6 million to 4.6 million.[32] Single, never-married mothers have much lower rates for receipt of child support. This is in part due to the characteristics of those who father their children.

There are also issues about establishing the child support liability. For a proportion of single mothers, paternity would need to be established before a child support claim could be made. In 1993, the father was identified for only about a third of the children born to unmarried women.[33] Where single mothers are on welfare, most of the father's child support payments might well go to reimbursing the government, and so the incentive for fathers to pay is limited.

The introduction of unilateral no-fault divorce also played a part in reducing the prevalence of child support awards. Anne Case and her colleagues, working from data from the Panel Study of Income Dynamics, showed that while in 1968, 39 percent of single mothers had an alimony or child support award, by 1984, that had dropped to 28 percent.[34] In 1968, only 2 percent of single mothers lived in states with unilateral divorce laws, and less than 1 percent of these mothers had never been married. By 1984, 50 percent of single mothers lived in states with unilateral divorce laws.[35] Case and colleagues commented that:[36]

> States' adoption of unilateral divorce legislation has a large, negative and statistically significant effect on the receipt of child support among ever-married mothers.

It was only after all the efforts made to increase child support compliance that this proportion rose again, reaching 46 percent of single mothers in 1997. This study did not indicate whether these amounts were actually paid.

Compliance among those with formal child support orders is also not particularly high. Data from 2007 published by the U.S. Census Bureau indicates that 46.8 percent of those who had formal child support orders received the full amount and 29.5 percent received a portion of the total due. The other quarter did not receive child support in that year.[37]

Another important strategy in the promotion of adequate levels of child support was the development of guidelines for the calculation of

---

[32] *Id.* at 3.   [33] Chambers, *supra* note 14, at 2589.
[34] Anne Case, I-Fen Lin, & Sara McLanahan, *Explaining Trends in Child Support: Economic, Demographic and Policy Effects*, 40 DEMOGRAPHY 171, 177 (2003).
[35] *Id.* at 180.   [36] *Id.* at 184.
[37] TIMOTHY GRALL, CUSTODIAL MOTHERS AND FATHERS AND THEIR CHILD SUPPORT: 2007 (2009), http://www.census.gov/prod/2009pubs/p60–237.pdf

child support. These were first developed in a few individual states such as Wisconsin and Washington State,[38] before the federal government further encouraged their development. They began as advisory only. They were aimed at increasing the levels of child support payments ordered by courts by specifying a percentage of income that a child support payer could reasonably be expected to pay, rather than starting, as courts traditionally had done, with an assessment of the "costs" of the child.

U.S. legislation in 1984 required states to establish numeric guidelines, although they did not need to be binding. The Family Support Act of 1988[39] mandated that states develop mathematical formulas for setting child support that had the status of a presumption, and also that the guidelines be reviewed every four years to ensure that they result in appropriate levels of child support.[40]

Australia

Australia developed a comprehensive child support scheme in the late 1980s, establishing an assessment and collection regime that all but ousted the jurisdiction of the courts in relation to child support. Like the schemes in other countries, it was largely driven by the need to ensure as far as possible that private transfers of money from fathers to mothers reduced the burden of the state in terms of welfare expenditure.[41] Between 1974 and 1985, the proportion of sole-parent households rose from 9.2 percent to 14.4 percent of all families with dependent children – an increase of 57 percent in the proportion of one-parent households,[42] with high levels of

---

[38] Robert Williams, *An Overview of Child Support Guidelines in the United States, in* CHILD SUPPORT GUIDELINES: THE NEXT GENERATION 1, 1 (Margaret Campbell Haynes ed., 1994).

[39] 102 STAT. 2343 (1988).

[40] For federal regulations on these reviews *see* 45 C.F.R. § 302.56. *See also* Jane Venohr & Robert Williams, *The Implementation and Periodic Review of State Child Support Guidelines,* 33 FAM. L.Q. 7 (1999).

[41] Stephen Parker & Margaret Harrison, *Child Support in Australia: Children's Rights or Public Interest?,* 5 INT'L J. L. & FAM. 24 (1991). In Australia, according to the 2001 census, 18 percent of children under fifteen years of age (over 660,000 children) lived in a household with no employed parent, with more than half (61 percent) of these living in one-parent families. In 83.5 percent of one-parent families where the parent was not in the workforce, that parent was not looking for work. Australian Bureau of Statistics, *Families with No Employed Parent, in* AUSTRALIAN SOCIAL TRENDS (2004), http://www.abs.gov.au

[42] MINISTERIAL TASKFORCE ON CHILD SUPPORT, IN THE BEST INTERESTS OF CHILDREN: REFORMING THE CHILD SUPPORT SCHEME 43 (2005).

dependence on welfare support. Only 26 percent of sole parents who were receiving income support payments were also receiving maintenance.[43] Another major concern was to reduce the incidence of children living in poverty. Between 1972 and 1986, the proportion of children living in poverty had increased from 7.2 percent to 17.5 percent.[44]

The Child Support Agency was established by legislation in 1988. Legislation passed in 1989 imposed a mandatory formula for all parents who separated after October 1 of that year, or in relation to children born after that date or children who had siblings born after that date.

The amount of child support payable is worked out by the Child Support Agency based on the parties' tax records and other information (such as tax withholding information from employers), which provide a reasonably reliable indication of income. When the scheme was first introduced, parents had access to the Family Court to seek to vary the statutory formula on one or more of a strictly defined set of grounds, but by 1992, the legislation was amended to set up an administrative process for such a "change of assessment," leaving the courts to an appellate role.

The use of tax records or other information on incomes available to the taxation authorities allows for updating of the child support assessment every twelve-to-fifteen months. This means that the child support payable keeps pace with increases – or decreases, for that matter – in the earnings of the liable parent. This use of income tax records as the basis for calculating child support payments has been a key aspect of the success of the Australian scheme, but it is not a magic bullet. A review of the scheme that reported in 2005 discovered that 25 percent of all liable parents had not filed a tax return in the last four years.[45] This was despite a legal obligation to do so. Furthermore, the capacity to pay of those who are self-employed is a vexed issue for any child support collection system, particularly as a consequence of the opportunities to conceal income or structure one's tax affairs in an advantageous manner that is not open to pay-as-you-earn employees.

In current practice, collection takes a variety of forms. The majority of all cases handled by the Agency involve private transfers by parents; that is, the Agency is involved in assessment but not collection. Where the payee feels the need for Agency collection, and certainly if there is a history of default in private transfers, the Agency will get involved in

[43] *Id.*
[44] *Id.*
[45] *Id.* at 97.

collection. It encourages voluntary payments to the Agency, but failing that, the main options are automatic withholding, tax refund intercepts, raiding bank accounts held by the liable parent, and court-based enforcement measures such as seizing property. A particularly effective measure has been Departure Prohibition Orders. An order of this kind can be made administratively by the Agency preventing a person going overseas until they have reached a satisfactory arrangement with the Agency concerning their child support debts.

Other Countries

The arrangements concerning the assessment and collection of child support vary significantly between countries. Britain and New Zealand have child support agencies that are similar in function to that in Australia. The Agency has the power to issue assessments based on a statutory formula. Norway[46] and Denmark[47] have similar administrative agencies. In other jurisdictions, there are hybrid systems in which both courts and governmental agencies are involved.[48] In others still, courts have the main role in establishing liability but do so in accordance with guidelines. This is the position in North America and also in Germany[49] and Sweden. France

---

[46] In Norway, parents are encouraged to make their own agreements. If they cannot agree, they may apply to the Norwegian Work and Welfare Agency for a determination. *See* Skinner & Davidson, *supra* note 8.

[47] The position in Denmark is similar to Norway. Private agreements can be registered, and the agency has the same enforcement powers in respect of both registered and agency determined child support decisions. *See* Skinner & Davidson, *supra* note 8.

[48] *See* Skinner & Davidson, *supra* note 8, at 33–37.

[49] In Germany, the judges of the Provincial High Courts and Courts of Appeal (*Oberlandesgerichte*) have developed tables and guidelines for the standardization of their decisions. Even though these tables do not have the quality of legal norms or legislation, they are treated as such by the courts. The most well-known table is the *Düsseldorfer Tabelle*. For the tables, *see* e.g. the MONATSSCHRIFT FÜR DEUTSCHES RECHT, http://www.mdr.ovs.de/13593.htm. The Federal Constitutional Court has held that the means by which the government calculated the basic needs of adults and children in determining the level of welfare benefits was seriously inadequate, because it was based on a flawed methodology: BVerfG, 9.2.2010–1 BvL 1/09 u.a., NEUE JURISTISCHE WOCHENSCHRIFT 505 (2010). It was unconstitutional, because Art 20 of the German Constitution (the right to a "menschenwürdiges Existenzminimum") was held to be violated. The German legislature must now amend the social welfare legislation, and this will have implications for the way that minimal child support (§ 1612a BGB), the "Selbstbehalt" of the liable parent (that is, the amount of money that the person who has to pay support can use for himself) (§§ 1603, 1581 BGB) and the minimal needs of recipients (§§ 1610, 1615l, 1361, 1578 BGB) will be assessed.

and Belgium are examples of countries that retain court-based discretion, with no guidelines to determine the level of child support.[50]

REVENUE RECOVERY, SUPPORTING CHILDREN, AND PARENT-CHILD CONTACT

One of the major tensions in child support schemes around the western world has been between revenue recovery and reducing child poverty. Where child support policy has been driven by revenue recovery as the dominant motivation, its success in achieving substantial compliance with child support obligations across the population has been limited.

In the early years especially, enforcement efforts in the United States were substantially driven by the need to reduce welfare expenditures by casting the burden of support for children, to the greatest extent possible, on nonresident fathers. Even though there is evidence of success in that endeavor,[51] it also came at a significant cost. Harry Krause, reviewing the state of affairs in 1989, observed that "at the bottom of the social pyramid, the fact is that … we currently spend as much on collection as we collect – and in many states more. Child support collection actually has been turned into an income transfer program from poor fathers to lawyers and welfare bureaucrats."[52]

There are numerous issues in this, not least the low incomes of so many fathers whose former partners are in receipt of welfare support payments, but a significant issue is whether the strategy of "hunting, hounding and harassing" nonresident parents[53] with the goal of revenue recovery could ever be effective in achieving high rates of compliance. Early child support enforcement policies had altogether too few incentives for voluntary compliance and failed to take account of the importance of child support within an overall approach to parenting after separation that did not treat

---

[50] *See* Skinner & Davidson, *supra* note 8. Empirical research has indicated substantial variations between judges in terms of the levels of child support they would award in a given factual scenario: Cécile Bourreau-Dubois et al, *Les Obligations Alimentaires vis-à-vis des Enfants de Parents Divorcés : une Analyse Économique au Service du Droit*, (rapport pour le compte du GIP 'Mission-recherche Droit et Justice' et la Missionrecherche CREDES-ADEPS, Université Nancy 2 et CNRS) (2003). *See also* Cécile Bourreau-Dubois, Bruno Jeandidier & Bruno Deffains, *Un Barème de Pension Alimentaire pour L'entretien des Enfants en Cas de Divorce*, Revue Française des Affaires Sociales, n° 4, 101 (2005); Bruno Jeandidier & Jean-Claude Ray, *Pensions Alimentaires pour Enfants lors du Divorce: les Juges Appliquent-ils Implicitement un Calcul Fondé sur le Coût de L'enfant?* 84 Enfance: Recherches et Prévisions 5 (2006).
[51] *See* Sorensen & Halpern, *supra* note 26.
[52] *See* Skinner & Davidson, *supra* note 8.
[53] Moynihan, *supra* note 27.

nonresident fathers only as recalcitrants from whom money should be extracted to reimburse governments.

Indeed, the research evidence is that fathers who do not pay child support through the formal child support system may not be as recalcitrant as the rhetoric of "deadbeat dads" might suggest. U.S. studies that have gathered information on informal transfers directly from father to mother, and in-kind payments, have indicated quite significant levels of informal child support that bypass the revenue recovery systems put in place by governments. For example, in the Fragile Families and Child Wellbeing Study, data was collected between 1998 and 2000, almost entirely from unwed parents across twenty U.S. cities. Only 16.6 percent received child support through the formal system, but 58.9 percent received informal payments. It diminished as children got older, which is consistent with declines in parent-child contact.[54]

In demonstrating the importance of retaining incentives for parents to cooperate with the child support system, the contrast between the experiences of Australia and Britain is instructive. The Australian scheme, like others that emerged in the late 1980s and early 1990s, was certainly motivated by concerns about growing welfare expenditure; however, as the scheme developed, governments concentrated on ensuring that both payers and payees had a strong incentive for voluntary compliance. To maintain an incentive for both payers to comply and payees to chase compliance, payees who are in receipt of government benefits are entitled to keep a substantial proportion of the child support paid by the nonresident parent. The payment of child support has no effect at all on the basic income support payment for single mothers. It is linked to another government benefit paid to support children on a per-child basis, and also to the level of rent assistance to assist low-income families in meeting housing costs. Parents are entitled to keep all of the child support paid up to a certain amount (which depends on how many children they have). Child support (or spousal maintenance) income above the free area reduces the parent's entitlement to the child benefit and rent assistance by 50 cents in the dollar. The advantage of this approach is that the payee retains an incentive to maximize the amount of child support payable because she or he gets to keep 50 cents in every dollar above the disregarded amount.

[54] Steven Garasky, Elizabeth Peters, Laura Argys, Steven Cook, Lenna Nepomnyaschy, & Elaine Sorensen, *Measuring Support to Children by Nonresident Fathers, in* HANDBOOK OF MEASUREMENT ISSUES IN FAMILY RESEARCH 399, 410 (Sandra Hofferth & Lynne Casper eds., 2007).

By way of contrast, in Britain, revenue recovery was by far the dominant motivation for child support reform. Britain followed the Australian model to some extent in setting up its own Child Support Agency, utilizing a statutory formula for the calculation of child support.[55] However, unlike the Australian scheme, there was initially no incentive for voluntary compliance. Social security acted as a guaranteed form of income support for parents with care of children, and money was then recouped to the greatest extent possible from the paying parent. Only if there was more child support payable than the money that the government could reclaim would the parent with care receive any of the child support for use in providing for the children. This meant there was no incentive either for the payee on benefits or for the payer to cooperate with the Child Support Agency.

When the Child Support Scheme was redesigned as a result of the Child Support, Pensions and Social Security Act 2000 (implemented in 2003), the government introduced a £10 disregard. That is, the payee parent could keep the first £10 of each scheduled child support payment. However, the disregard only applied to those on the new scheme. In December 2006, the government announced further reforms to the Scheme, raising the disregard level and extending its scope.[56] In December 2008, the government announced further changes, saying that a full child maintenance disregard would be introduced in all income-related benefits from April 2010.[57] This meant that having been motivated initially by fiscal considerations, the government had finally abandoned any revenue recovery function for the child support scheme. The new rationale is the reduction in child poverty.[58]

---

[55] The British child support scheme has struggled since its inception in multiple respects. *See* Nicholas Wikeley, Child Support – Law and Policy (2006) Ch 5. The British government has now established a new Child Maintenance and Enforcement Commission to take over the work of the Child Support Agency. *See Child Maintenance and Other Payments Act,* 2008.

[56] Department of Work and Pensions, A New System of Child Maintenance (2006). This was built on the recommendations of an independent inquiry. Sir David Henshaw, Recovering Child Support: Routes to Responsibility (July 2006). For commentary, *see* Patrick Parkinson, *Reengineering the Child Support Scheme: An Australian Perspective on the British Government's Proposals,* 70 Modern L. Rev. 812 (2007).

[57] Department of Work and Pensions, Raising Expectations and Increasing Support: Reforming Welfare for the Future (2008). This was implemented on April 12, 2010. *See* Ministerial Statement, the Parliamentary Under-Secretary of State for Work and Pensions, *Child Maintenance Disregard,* 23rd March 2010, http://services.parliament. uk/hansard/commons/ByDate/20100323/writtenministerialstatements/part007.html

[58] On the effectiveness of the British scheme in this respect, *see* Jonathan Bradshaw, *Child Support and Child Poverty,* 14 Benefits 199 (2006); Christine Skinner & Daniel Meyer, *After All the Policy Reform, Is Child Support Actually Helping Low-Income Mothers?,* 14 Benefits 209 (2006).

DEVISING FORMULAS – THE SEARCH FOR PRINCIPLE

Calculating appropriate levels of child support transfers in the postseparation family is not an exact science. There is plenty of room for argument about both the objectives for child support transfers[59] and the methods of calculation on which child support guidelines should be based.[60]

Maintaining Preseparation Standards?

Policy makers might want to shelter children – and therefore their primary caregivers – from a loss of living standards stemming from a parental separation, but such a goal is unachievable given the harsh realities of separation. For families who use up most or all of their household income on providing one house together with its furnishings – as most do – to move to having two households inevitably means a diminution of living standards in one home, or possibly both. Separation means an irretrievable loss of the financial efficiencies of the unitary family.[61]

Furthermore, the child support system is dealing with many children born outside of any cohabiting relationship, and so child support formulas based on maintaining preseparation standards of living as far as possible would not be of universal application.

Equalizing Living Standards?

Another approach that might have some theoretical attraction would be the equalization of living standards across the mother's and father's households. Such an approach would require all available income to be divided between the two households according to the equivalent number of people to support in each household, using a formula to allocate proportionate

---

[59] For a review and assessment of the major theoretical approaches and objectives, *see* David Betson, Eirik Evenhouse, Siobhan Reilly, & Eugene Smolensky, *Trade-offs Implicit in Child-Support Guidelines*, 11 J POLICY ANALYSIS & MANAGEMENT 1 (1992). *See also* Marsha Garrison, *Child Support Policy: Guidelines and Goals*, 33 FAM. L.Q. 157 (1999); Tim Graves, *Comparing Child Support Guidelines*, 34 FAM. L.Q. 149 (2000). On philosophical approaches to child support obligations, *see* Marsha Garrison, *Autonomy or Community? An Evaluation of Two Models of Parental Obligation*, 86 CAL. L. REV. 41 (1998); Scott Altman, *A Theory of Child Support*, 17 INT'L. J. L. POL'Y & FAM. 173 (2003).

[60] Ira Ellman, *Fudging Failure: The Economic Analysis Used to Construct Child Support Guidelines*, 2004 U. CHICAGO LEGAL FORUM 167.

[61] *See* Chapter 11.

costs between children and adults. For example, the Organisation for Economic Co-operation and Development's (OECD) modified equivalence scale, which is widely used, gives a value of 1 to the first adult in the family, 0.5 to another adult, and 0.3 to each child.[62]

Such a system of equalizing living standards between households might operate fairly when there is only the mother's income and the father's income, but new partners, and indeed new children from those partnerships, complicate matters immeasurably. A policy of equalizing living standards would need to take account of the administrative realities of trying to calculate child support based on up to four incomes if both parents have repartnered. Arguments would open up about whether a shared housing arrangement, or "living together-apart" relationship, is an intimate relationship that should be taken into account in the formula. Complaints would be generated from new partners of primary caregivers who argue that their incomes should not be used to relieve the liable parent of his or her responsibility, and from new partners of liable parents that their incomes should not be included in calculations in such a way as to increase the liable parent's obligations to provide for the household of his former partner.

The child support system needs to operate at a reasonable cost to taxpayers and in a way that reduces, as much as possible, the grounds for complaint on the basis of fairness. For these reasons, a policy of equalizing living standards is really not feasible.

The Continuity of Expenditure Principle

Perhaps because of the complexities involved in other approaches, the dominant rationale that legislatures have adopted for calculating child support in the United States, Britain and Australia is the continuity of expenditure principle.[63] This principle is based on the notion that the non-resident parent should contribute a similar level of support to the children as he or she would contribute if the parents were living together.[64]

---

[62] Organisation for Economic Co-operation and Development – What are Equivalence Scales?, http://www.oecd.org/dataoecd/61/52/35411111.pdf

[63] In Britain, for example, *see* Department of Social Security, A New Contract for Welfare: Children's Rights and Parents' Responsibilities 9–10 (1999). In the United States, *see* Venohr & Williams, *supra* note 40.

[64] For example, the Committee that proposed the formula for Australia in 1988 explained the rationale as follows: "As a starting point in considering what proportion of income should be shared, the Consultative Group accepted the proposition that wherever possible, children should enjoy the benefit of a similar proportion of parental income to

The continuity of expenditure principle does not mean that children will necessarily be able to maintain the same living standards after their parents' separation as they enjoyed before, because children's living standards depend on the overall income of the households in which they spend their time. For that reason, the continuity of expenditure principle does not, and cannot, protect children from a loss of living standards after separation.

Even though the continuity of expenditure principle does not protect children from a fall in living standards in each parent's home, it has been accepted around the western world as offering the fairest basis for calculating the extent of the contribution that nonresident parents should be expected to pay, given the extra burdens in terms of housing costs and other expenses now to be distributed in some way across the two households. It is also seen as operating most fairly over the duration of childhood. The standard of living of many resident parents falls after separation, but this loss in living standards tends to be ameliorated if they repartner.[65] The child support formula needs to apply generally until the children reach adulthood, and the circumstances of parents can change considerably over this time. Although a child support requirement that is substantially in excess of the amount justified by the continuity of expenditure principle may seem reasonable in the first year or two after separation, it may look grossly inequitable if the payee repartners and has the benefit of another income in the household, while the payer only has his own income to support him.

The idea that a parent ought to contribute approximately what he or she would have been paying if the parents had not separated is a reasonable moral position to take. It justifies the requirement that liable parents on higher incomes pay more than those on lower incomes. It allows the children to continue to share to some extent in the living standard of the liable parent. It is a morally defensible basis for calculating child support even where for the liable parent with new housing costs and other additional costs after separation, finances are much tighter than they were before.

---

that which they would have enjoyed if their parents lived together. This proposition is based on the view that children should not be the economic losers from the separation of the parents or where the parents never lived together." CHILD SUPPORT CONSULTATIVE GROUP, CHILD SUPPORT: FORMULA FOR AUSTRALIA 67 (1988).

[65] *See* SETTLING UP: PROPERTY AND INCOME DISTRIBUTION ON DIVORCE IN AUSTRALIA (Peter McDonald ed., 1986); KATE FUNDER, MARGARET HARRISON & RUTH WESTON, SETTLING DOWN: PATHWAYS OF PARENTS AFTER DIVORCE (1993); Stephen Jenkins, *Marital Splits and Income Changes Over the Longer-Term*, in CHANGING RELATIONSHIPS (Malcolm Brynin & John Ermisch, eds) 217 (2009).

THE "COSTS" OF CHILDREN

Working out what children "cost" in intact families is not straightforward. Children do not have a fixed cost. The "cost" of children depends on a range of factors including their ages, their needs, the expenses of the household of which they are a part, and the choices that parents make concerning their discretionary expenditure. Once basic needs are met, the "costs" of children depend on the resources available to their caregivers and how much they choose to spend on them.

There is an extensive body of research now on the costs of children, and the methodologies that are used to provide estimates of those costs, based on responses to survey data, are well established.[66] The costs of children include infrastructure costs. That is, they are calculated as a proportion of the costs of all goods shared by members of the household, such as housing, running a car, and fuel bills. Depending on which methodology is used, account may also be taken of depreciation costs.

No single method of calculating expenditures involved in raising children is unproblematic, however. There are two basic ways in which expenditures on children are calculated. The first is to look at survey data on actual household expenditure. The second is to look at what a family needs to achieve a certain standard of living, for example one experienced by 50 percent of families, or 75 percent of families. This is known as the "budget standards" approach.

In order to work out the additional cost of children, the question is asked how much more income a family with one, two, or more children requires in order to be as well off as a family with no children. This requires finding bases for comparing standards of living between childless couples and couples with children, which allow for meaningful assessments about the additional costs of having children to be made. There are value judgments to be made at various levels in such calculations.

Furthermore, even if the measures of comparison and methods of calculation were widely accepted, research on the costs of children would still only provide a broad estimate. For example, because it includes a proportion of the housing costs incurred by the family, the costs of children will vary depending on the location of the family. For the purposes of working out a generalizable child support formula, housing costs in different

---

[66] For a discussion of the methodological issues involved in calculating expenditures on children for the purposes of an Australian review of the child support formula, *see* Matthew Gray, *Costs of Children and Equivalence Scales: A Review of Methodological Issues and Australian Estimates* (May 2005), http://www.fahcsia.gov.au/sa/childsupport/pubs/ChildCostEquivilantScales/Pages/default.aspx

locations have to be averaged out. Averages across a population also take no account of the gender mix of children. There are likely to be greater economies of scale in a family with two children of the same gender than if the family has a boy and a girl.

Two approaches have been adopted to the calculation of child support based on the continuity of expenditure principle. The first is the percentage of obligor income approach. The second is the income shares approach.[67] Whatever the basis for the formula, special account needs to be taken of families where liable parents may have obligations to more than one mother, and other more complex situations.[68]

THE PERCENTAGE OF OBLIGOR INCOME APPROACH

The first guidelines typically adopted a simple approach in which a percentage of the liable parent's gross or net income was payable depending on how many children he (or she) had to support. The leader in this regard was Wisconsin, which retains this simple approach.[69] The formula is based on the parent's annual gross income, divided by 12 to yield a monthly income. Parents are required to pay 17 percent of income for one child, 25 percent for two children, 29 percent for three children, 31 percent for four children, and 34 percent for five or more children. For low-income earners, there is a table of payments that gradually increases with increases in income until the normal statutory percentages become applicable.[70] For shared-care families, where each parent has the care of the child for at least 25 percent of the year, each parent is ordered by the court to assume the child's basic support costs in proportion to the time that the parent has with the child, applying a modified formula.[71]

---

[67] In the United States, there is a third formula, called the Melson formula, which has been adopted in three states. It is really a variant on the income shares model. *See* Jo Beld & Len Biernat, *Federal Intent for State Child Support Guidelines: Income Shares, Cost Shares and the Realities of Shared Parenting*, 37 FAM. L.Q. 165, 167, 175–77 (2003).

[68] Adrienne Jennings Lockie, *Multiple Families, Multiple Goals, Multiple Failures: The Need for "Limited Equalization" as a Theory of Child Support*, 32 HARV. J. L. & GENDER 109 (2009).

[69] *See now* DCF 150.03, available at http://www.legis.state.wi.us/rsb/code/dcf/dcf150.pdf. The origins and rationale for the Wisconsin formula are explained in Irwin Garfinkel & Marygold Melli, *The Use of Normative Standards in Family Law Decisions: Developing Mathematical Standards for Child Support*, 24 FAM LQ 157 (1990).

[70] *See* table in Department of Children and Families, Child Support Obligation of Low–Income Payers at 75% to 150% of the 2009 Federal Poverty Guidelines app. C at 47 (2009), http://www.legis.state.wi.us/rsb/code/dcf/dcf150_app_c.pdf

[71] *See now* DCF 150.04, available at http://www.legis.state.wi.us/rsb/code/dcf/dcf150.pdf

A similar approach was adopted in Australia from 1989 to 2008, influenced by the work in Wisconsin. It modified that approach by setting a self-support amount for the liable parent before the formula percentage was applied.[72] The percentages adopted were 18 percent for one child, 27 percent for two children, 32 percent for three children, 34 percent for four children, and 36 percent for five children, with a maximum level to which those percentages could be applied. Unlike in the Wisconsin scheme, the payee parent's income was factored in above the threshold of average weekly earnings for all employees. However, this was a factor in only 12 percent of cases in 2004.[73]

THE INCOME SHARES APPROACH

About three-quarters of U.S. jurisdictions have now adopted an income shares approach, taking account of the income of both parents.[74] This formula was devised by the Child Support Guidelines Project of the National Center for State Courts, following the enactment of the Family Support Act of 1988, and completed in 1990. The income shares approach begins with a dollar figure for the costs of the child based on combined parental income, and then distributes that cost between the parents in accordance with their respective capacities to pay. The primary caregiver is assumed to meet her or his share of that cost in kind. The nonresident parent's share becomes the child support obligation. An income shares approach can also be adjusted to take account of parents' proportionate share of the child's care.

If parents spend approximately the same proportion of their income on child-related expenditure across the income range, then it makes no difference whether a percentage of the liable parent's income is used or an income shares approach. The outcome is exactly the same.[75] However, the income shares approach is much fairer and more transparent if, as the

---

[72] The Committee wrote: "However, in designing an appropriate formula it was necessary to temper the application of this proposition in order to ensure a workable scheme and one which took into account the realities of capacity to pay and maintained appropriate incentives to work for both parents ... The recommended formula therefore guarantees the non-custodial parent a protected component of income, the self-support component, on which no child support is levied." CHILD SUPPORT CONSULTATIVE GROUP, *supra* note 63, at 67.

[73] MINISTERIAL TASKFORCE ON CHILD SUPPORT, *supra* note 42, at 89.

[74] *See* generally LAURA MORGAN, CHILD SUPPORT GUIDELINES: INTERPRETATION AND APPLICATION (1996 with annual supplements).

[75] This is explained by Ira Ellman as follows, comparing the Percentage of Obligor Income Approach (POOI) and the income shares approach:

Assume Dad is support obligor. Let
D = Dad's Income
M = Mom's Income,

preponderance of the international research evidence shows, child-related expenditure falls as a percentage of income as that income increases. Although there is some debate in the literature about this,[76] the prevailing interpretation of the empirical research now seems to indicate that the lower the income, the greater the proportion of that income that is spent on children.[77] However, much depends on how one classifies shared family consumption goods such as housing and transportation. On any view of this, at the point that income exceeds consumption and therefore generates savings and investments – including substantial equity in the home in advance of a typical twenty- to twenty-five-year mortgage – the proportion of income devoted to the costs of raising children necessarily must decline. As child support guidelines expert Robert Williams has written:[78]

> As income increases, *total* family current consumption declines as a proportion of net (after-tax) income because non-current consumption spending increases with the level of household income. Non-current consumption spending includes savings (broadly defined), gifts, contributions, and

---

D% = Dad's percent of combined income = D/(D+M).
CE% be the constant percent of aggregate parental income (D+M) that parents spend on their children, throughout the entire income range. Then
a) In POOI: Dad pays CE% of D, i.e., (CE%)(D)
b) In Income Shares:
(1) Total Child Support Obligation is (CE%)(D+M)
(2) Dad's Share is D%.
(3) Dad pays (D%)(CE%)(D+M)
But since D% = D/(D+M), we can substitute in (3)
(4) (D/(D+M))(CE%)(D+M)=(D)(CE%), the identical value as in POOI.
Ellman, *supra* note 59, at 181 n.29.

[76] For example Ellman, supports the view that expenditure on children remains constant across a substantial income range. He wrote (*supra* note 59, at 182 n.31):
"The 1990 Betson study commissioned by H.H.S., widely relied upon in nearly all later child support expenditure studies done for support guidelines, concluded that "the cost of children expressed as a percentage of total expenditures is almost constant across all levels of total expenditures." David Betson, *Alternative Estimates of the Cost of Children from the 1980–86 Consumer Expenditure Survey*, Final Report to the U.S. Department of Health and Human Services, Office of the Assistant Secretary for Planning and Evaluation 50 (1990). Betson looked only at families with total expenditures up to $75,000, which is approximately $112,000 in current dollars. Whether child expenditures are a constant percentage of *income* depends largely on whether expenditures are a constant percentage of income. There is clearly some level of family income above which consumption declines as a percentage of income. The question, in writing guidelines that set support awards by income, is the point at which that decline begins—only at the upper reaches of the income distribution, or throughout a large part of the income distribution range?"

[77] Jo Beld, *Improving Child Support Guidelines in Minnesota: The "Shared Responsibility" Model for the Determination of Child Support*, 28 WILLIAM MITCHELL L.R. 791, 797 (2001).

[78] Williams, *supra* note 38.

personal insurance. Moreover, family current consumption declines even more as a proportion of gross (before tax) income because of the progressive federal and state income tax structure.

For this reason, in American jurisdictions that utilize the income shares approach, the percentage of income required for the calculation declines as combined parental income increases.[79]

Australia adopted an income shares approach in 2008, following a comprehensive review of the child support formula and other aspects of the scheme.[80] The Child Support Taskforce utilized three different methodologies to make its estimates of the costs of children in Australian families.[81] The Household Expenditure Survey was used to examine actual patterns of expenditure on children.[82] The budget standards approach was utilized to assess how much parents would need to spend to give children a specific standard of living, taking account of differences in housing costs all over Australia.[83] A review was also done of all previous Australian research,[84] so that the outcomes of these two studies could be compared with previous research findings.

The research evidence was that the percentage of obligor income approach (after deducting a self-support component) could not be justified as representing a reasonable assessment of what was required by the continuity of expenditure principle, taking account not only of private income but also the impact of government benefits paid to all families with children.[85]

COMMUNITY VIEWS ON CALCULATING
THE CHILD SUPPORT OBLIGATION

Research both in the United States and Australia indicates support for the basic concepts of the income shares approach. A survey of community

---

[79] *See* Ira Ellman, Sanford Braver & Robert MacCoun, *Intuitive Lawmaking: The Example of Child Support*, 6 J. EMPIRICAL STUD. 69, 73–75 (2009).

[80] *See* MINISTERIAL TASKFORCE ON CHILD SUPPORT, *supra* note 42.

[81] For an overview, *see* Patrick Parkinson, *The Future of Child Support*, 33 U. WESTERN AUSTRALIA L. REV. 179 (2007).

[82] RICHARD PERCIVAL & ANN HARDING, THE ESTIMATED COSTS OF CHILDREN IN AUSTRALIAN FAMILIES IN 2005–06: COMMISSIONED RESEARCH REPORT FOR THE MINISTERIAL TASKFORCE ON CHILD SUPPORT (May 2005), http://www.fahcsia.gov.au/sa/childsupport/pubs/EstimatedCostsofChildren/Pages/default.aspx

[83] PAUL HENMAN, UPDATED COSTS OF CHILDREN USING AUSTRALIAN BUDGET STANDARDS (May 2005), http://www.fahcsia.gov.au/sa/childsupport/pubs/CostsofChildrenUsingAusStandards/Pages/default.aspx

[84] Gray, *supra* note 65.

[85] For findings from France about the need to take account of government benefits in the assessment of child support, *see* Alain Jacquot, *Divorce, Pension Alimentaire et Niveau de*

attitudes in Australia as part of the review of the Child Support Scheme found strong support for the idea that both parents' income should be taken into account in working out child support liabilities.[86] Even though there may be no difference between the percentage of obligor income approach and the income shares approach if a flat-rate percentage of combined income is used across the income range, perceptions of fairness are important. When both parents' incomes are included in the calculation, then it is much more transparent that the formula is taking account of the resources available to both parents and not only to the nonresident parent.

A study in Arizona also indicates that there is community support for both incomes to be taken into account. Members of the public were asked to give their views on what would be an appropriate level of child support under different scenarios that included changes in the income level of both resident and nonresident parent. The researchers found that as the resident parent's income increased in the scenarios (and when the nonresident parent's income was kept constant), respondents considered that the nonresident parent's child support obligation should diminish.[87] This is what happens in income shares jurisdictions.

CHILD SUPPORT AND SHARED PARENTING

The need to enforce child support transfers has undoubtedly strengthened the importance to governments of the involvement of both parents, but at the same time, the greater involvement of nonresident parents in caring for children after separation brings challenges and difficulties in terms of child support policy.

If the liable parent spends time regularly with the children, then the total family expenditure related to the children is necessarily much higher than it would be if the relationship had not broken down, or if the children were cared for after separation entirely by one parent. In particular, there are duplicated infrastructure costs from having two households suitable for children to stay in, and there are transportation costs involved in the other parent seeing the children. Children need a suitable place to sleep in each home, and if not a separate bedroom then age- and gender-appropriate arrangements for sharing a room. There are other costs that are duplicated also, apart from the cost of bedrooms

---

Vie des Parents et des Enfants: une Etude à Partir de Cas Types 67 ENFANCE: RECHERCHES ET PRÉVISIONS 37, 57–58 (2002).

[86] BRUCE SMYTH & RUTH WESTON, A SNAPSHOT OF CONTEMPORARY ATTITUDES TO CHILD SUPPORT, (2005).

[87] Ellman et al., *supra* note 78.

and their furnishings. Children will need some toys and clothes in both homes. Consequently, the cost of caring for the children across two households is very much greater than if the children spent all their time with one parent.[88]

If nonresident parents routinely had much more disposable income than primary caregivers, and that disposable income was sufficient to meet all the costs of accommodating and looking after the children without diminishing the level of support for primary caregivers, shared care would be less problematic. However, the reality is that many liable parents are also at the bottom of the socioeconomic pyramid.[89] Unless some allowance is made for the costs associated with having children staying regularly overnight in the child support equation, as well as some allowance for direct expenditures on the children while they are in the liable parent's care, there are some nonresident fathers and mothers who might not be able to have their children staying overnight at all. There is evidence in a number of countries for an association between low socioeconomic status and not seeing children regularly.[90]

The difficulty, in terms of child support policy, is that because these infrastructure costs are duplicated rather than shared, expenditure in the liable parent's household does little to reduce the primary caregiver's costs associated with looking after the children. Certainly there are some savings, for example, in reduced food and utility costs when the children are staying with the other parent, and there might be some savings in child care costs for working parents. Nonetheless, such savings do not greatly diminish the problem that when nonresident parents see their children regularly, costs are duplicated more than they are shared.

---

[88] Marygold Melli & Patricia Brown, *The Economics of Shared Custody: Developing an Equitable Formula for Dual Residence*, 31 HOUSTON L. REV. 543 (1994).

[89] For Australian analysis, *see* Jerry Silvey & Bob Birrell, *Financial Outcomes for Parents after Separation*, 12 PEOPLE & PLACE 45 (2004). In June 2009, the median taxable income of liable parents on the Child Support Agency database who had lodged tax returns (and were therefore likely to be in employment) was $40,677. The average income was $47,044. *See* CHILD SUPPORT AGENCY, FACTS AND FIGURES 08–09, at 32 (2009). The average full-time weekly earnings in Australia in May 2009, seasonally adjusted, was $1,242.70 per week or an annual average income of $64,620.

[90] In the Scandinavian context, *see* e.g. Anne Skevik, "Absent Fathers" or "Reorganized Families? Variations in Father-Child Contact after Parental Break-up in Norway*, 54 SOCIOLOGICAL REV. 114 (2006). In Australia, *see* Bruce Smyth, & Patrick Parkinson, *When the Difference is Night & Day: Some Empirical Insights into Patterns of Parent–child Contact after Separation*. Paper presented at the 8th Australian Institute of Family Studies Conference, Melbourne, 2003, available at http://www.aifs.gov.au/institute/afrc8/papers.html#p

This problem is resolved in different ways in different jurisdictions. In the United States, an approach used in some states is to increase each parent's income notionally by 50 percent in order to take account of the increased costs of raising the children across the two households, before making an allowance for the amount of time the children spend in each household.[91]

In Australia, a different approach was adopted. If a liable parent has the children for between 14 percent and 34 percent of the nights per year (that is, fewer than five nights every two weeks), then he or she gets a credit of 24 percent in the level of child support. However, as a trade-off, the primary caregiver gets all the child benefit paid by the government unless the parents share care.[92] This benefit represents a significant part of the total household income for lower-income families. When the children stay overnight for 35 percent of nights per year, he or she is given a credit of 25 percent for the costs of the children in his or her own household. This percentage rises gradually between 35 percent and 48 percent of nights, reaching a 50 percent allowance when the children are in an equal time arrangement. This recognizes that the primary caregiver is likely to bear the major costs for such items as clothing and school uniforms, and extra-curricular activities, where the cost is incurred only from time to time or at the beginning of a school term.

Another problem with dealing with shared care is when modified or different formulas should apply. If a modified formula is applicable when certain thresholds are met, for example, 25 percent, 30 percent, and 40 percent of nights per year,[93] then small variations in the parenting arrangements may make a substantial difference to the amount of child support when that threshold is crossed. This is known as a "cliff effect." It creates perverse incentives for liable parents to seek extra nights with the children in order to reduce their child support obligation, and also for primary caregivers to resist children spending more time with the other parent to avoid a reduction in the child support obligation. The Australian scheme was devised to try to minimize these cliff effects by making the level of care irrelevant when the children are staying at least one night per week with the nonresident parent, but less than five nights per fortnight. If there are negotiations between parents for extra nights of care beyond this, then

---

[91] *See* Beld & Biernat, *supra* note 66, at 195.

[92] Shared care is defined as at least 35 percent of nights for each parent. The child benefit is termed Family Tax Benefit.

[93] *See* Marygold Melli, *Guideline Review: Child Support and Time Sharing by Parents*, 33 FAM. L.Q. 219 (1999).

the effects on child support from each extra night of care is so small that it should not be a major issue between parents.

The nexus between levels of care and child support payments makes it imperative that legislative policy on child support is coordinated with legislative policy on parenting after separation. As far as possible, cliff effects and perverse incentives need to be avoided, and legislative policies in these areas should be in harmony rather than conflict. This is not as straightforward as it sounds, because policies are often developed in different eras, by different government departments, with different objectives, and responding to different political imperatives.

A further issue is whether there should be child support transfers when parents are sharing the care approximately equally. In a study of child maintenance in fourteen countries, national reporters indicated that in ten of those countries, the child maintenance obligation could in principle be annulled completely.[94] This is the case, for example, in Sweden.[95] If the parents have an approximately equal earning capacity, this seems like a sensible approach – indeed it would be the outcome of applying an income shares formula or a percentage of obligor income approach in which respective liabilities are offset against one another. However, it is often the case that one parent – almost invariably the mother – has sacrificed her earning capacity to care for children in the earliest years of their lives, interrupting workforce participation or going to work part time to prioritize the needs of the children, with long-term impacts on income levels. If there is no contribution from the higher-income earner to the lower-income earner through child support, then the sacrifice of earning capacity falls entirely on one parent, to the detriment of the children.

CHILD SUPPORT AND THE INTERDEPENDENCE OF PARENTS

In modern child support systems, and in particular where both incomes are taken into account, the fortunes of separated parents are tied together in a way that could not have been contemplated in the heady days of the divorce revolution. This is particularly so when child support obligations are calculated administratively, and in accordance with annual changes in parental income.

This can be illustrated by the Australian scheme, which is an income shares scheme that relies on annual assessments by the Child Support

---

[94] *See* Skinner & Davidson, *supra* note 8, at 38.
[95] Anna Singer, *Time is Money? – Child Support for Children with Alternating Residence in Sweden*, in FAMILY FINANCES 591 (Bea Verschraegen ed., 2009).

Agency, based on the latest information about taxable income for each parent. Just as the financial well-being of the intact family would be affected by changes in the father's income, such as a loss of a job or a decline in the fortunes of the family business, so the income of the other parent and children is affected by the same fluctuations.

In an income shares scheme, changes in the circumstances of either parent may affect the well-being of the other. For example, where the mother is earning $50,000 per year in paid employment and has repartnered, her income may well drop to zero if she falls pregnant to her new partner and decides to stay at home after giving birth. If this happens, then the next time a child support assessment is conducted, based on the mother's new financial circumstances, the father's child support obligation will be increased. In effect, this is to pay for a child who is not his own. Such consequences are unavoidable in income-based schemes. Voluntary reductions in income can be dealt with by deeming a liable parent to have the income that he would have had but for his decision to reduce his workforce participation, but the consequences of involuntary losses of income, or changes for socially acceptable purposes such as child-rearing, are necessarily shared by both parents.

When it comes to child support, divorce does not end the marriage – it changes it. Not only does the nonresident parent have a continuing duty of support (that was always the case), but the parents' economic fortunes are tied to one another for as long as child support transfers are made between the parents. The ties that bind parents together do not depend only on having been married.

Even parents who have never lived together are now tied to one another by the indissolubility of parenthood. It is an interconnectedness that could hardly have been contemplated in the early days of the divorce revolution, when it seemed so simple for people who were in unhappy marriages just to separate, allocate, and walk away.

Spousal Support and the Feminization of Poverty

One of the major consequences of the divorce revolution and the rapid growth of unmarried parenthood has been the increased feminization of poverty,[1] particularly for women, with children, who do not repartner. The focus of attention around the world has been on child support, but there has also been a revival of attention given to spousal support, in some jurisdictions at least. This is seen as another means of addressing the problem of women's economic vulnerability following relationship breakdown.

THE DIVORCE REVOLUTION AND THE CLEAN BREAK

As noted in Chapter 2, an important feature of the divorce revolution was the idea that, as far as possible, a clean break should be achieved financially between the parents through a once-for-all property division, with child support being the only obligation that continued, where awarded. Each party to the failed marriage was to be encouraged to put the past behind them and offered the opportunity to begin a new life - one not overshadowed by the relationship that had broken down.[2]

The practical outworking of this, in many jurisdictions at least, was that spousal support – otherwise known as alimony – was not to be a normal and commonplace incident of postseparation relationships. As much as possible, each party was to be encouraged to stand on his or her own feet, free of ongoing financial commitments to each other. Child

---

[1]   Diane Pearce, *The Feminization of Poverty: Women, Work, and Welfare*, 11 URBAN & SOCIAL CHANGE REV. 28 (1978); Janice Peterson, *The Feminization of Poverty*, 21 J. ECONOMIC ISSUES 329 (1987).

[2]   *See* e.g. Minton v. Minton, [1979] AC 593, 608 (per Lord Scarman).

support was left outside the clean-break concept, for that was about a father's obligations toward his child, not about his obligations to his former wife. Even still, child support was far from a universal obligation in practice in the 1960s and 1970s, and many fathers paid nothing at all.

Different Approaches to Spousal Support

Jurisdictions varied quite significantly in their approach to spousal support in the years after the divorce revolution.[3] Spousal support has continued to play a role in England and Wales, where the law of "financial provision" does not make the sharp distinction between property division and spousal support that is made in other jurisdictions. Assets and income are dealt with together by reference to the same set of principles.[4] In France, the concept of the compensatory payment was introduced for divorce by consent (although this could be paid in installments), whereas traditional spousal support was retained for fault-based divorce.[5] Variations may be seen in the laws of other European countries.[6]

Some jurisdictions seek to ameliorate the economic disadvantage of primary caregivers through weighting property division in their favor, whereas others provide for an equal division of the community property while remedying disadvantage through spousal support. Jurisdictions vary also in the levels of child support required of nonresident parents, with implications for capacity to pay spousal support in addition. Tax issues also influence the practice in jurisdictions; the attractiveness of income transfers as opposed to property transfers will be influenced by whether such income payments are tax-deductible to the transferor.

For these reasons, the role of spousal support in remedying women's disadvantage varies around the world. The clean-break principle was emphasized much more in some jurisdictions than others.

---

[3]　*See* Chapter 2.　　　　　　　　　　[4]　Matrimonial Causes Act, 1973.

[5]　*See* Chapter 2.

[6]　For a survey of the position in the early part of the decade, *see* 2 European Family Law in Action, Maintenance between Former Spouses (Katharina Boele-Woelki, Bente Braat, & Ian Sumner eds., 2003). For policy proposals, *see* Katharina Boele-Woelki, Frédérique Ferrand, Cristina González-Beilfuss, Maarit Jänterä-Jareborg, Nigel Lowe, Dieter Martiny & Walter Pintens, Principles of European Family Law Regarding Divorce and Maintenance Between Former Spouses, European Family Law Series No 7 (2004).

The U.S. Experience

Even in the United States, where the concept of the clean break certainly gained some traction, the impact of changes to the law of spousal support on the frequency of awards may not have been all that great. Although the Uniform Marriage and Divorce Act (UMDA) offered a very clear approach, eliminating fault as an issue in relation to property division or spousal support, this was one aspect of the UMDA approach that did not achieve widespread adoption. A no-fault approach to spousal support has only been taken in about half the U.S. states.[7]

Furthermore, Census data reveals that courts made awards of permanent alimony in only 9.3 percent of the divorces between 1887 and 1906, only 15.4 percent of divorces in 1916, and only 14.6 percent of those in 1922.[8] This was about the same percentage (14.3 percent) as was awarded in 1978, toward the beginning of the no-fault divorce revolution.[9] As Twila Perry has commented:[10]

> [T]o a large degree, the institution of alimony is a myth ... the reality is that the vast majority of divorced women have never been awarded alimony. Those who did receive it have not gotten much and often received awards of limited duration. It also seems increasingly likely that none of the theories that have been advanced to justify alimony is likely to adequately protect the economic interests of most women who subordinate their careers to those of their husbands. Alimony may present fascinating intellectual problems for scholars of family law, but, as an institution, it has never been widespread.

However, changes to the law in various U.S. jurisdictions did make a difference to the proportion of cases in which alimony was ordered for the long term. Although the levels of spousal support hovered around 14–15 percent in the first half of the 1980s,[11] the evidence from at least some

---

7   AMERICAN LAW INSTITUTE, PRINCIPLES OF THE LAW OF FAMILY DISSOLUTION: ANALYSIS AND RECOMMENDATIONS sec. 1, Topic 2, at 43 (2002).

8   PAUL JACOBSEN, AMERICAN MARRIAGE AND DIVORCE 126 (1959), *cited in* LENORE WEITZMAN, THE DIVORCE REVOLUTION: THE UNEXPECTED SOCIAL AND ECONOMIC CONSEQUENCES FOR WOMEN AND CHILDREN IN AMERICA 180 (1985).

9   Margo Melli, *Alimony Trends*, 19 FAM. ADVOC. 21 (1996–1997).

10 Twila Perry, *Alimony: Race, Privilege, and Dependency in the Search for Theory*, 82 GEO. L.J. 2481, 2503–04 (1994). *See also* Constance Shehan, Felix Berardo, Erica Owens, & Donna Berardo, *Alimony: An Anomaly in Family Social Science*, 51 FAM. REL. 308 (2002).

11 Robert Kelly & Greer Fox, *Determinants of Alimony Awards: An Empirical Test of Current Theories and a Reflection on Public Policy*, 44 SYRACUSE L. REV. 641, 643 (1993).

jurisdictions is that levels of permanent awards fell sharply, with a focus on rehabilitative maintenance. In New York, for example, 81 percent of spousal support awards in one study were permanent in 1978; this had dropped to 41 percent, by 1984.[12] There was also a decline of 43 percent in the number of cases in which spousal support was awarded at all. In other jurisdictions also, there was a significant decline in the proportion of women receiving spousal support.[13]

Conversely, in some jurisdictions, changes went in the opposite direction. Jana Singer, reviewing Weitzman's much-publicized data from California,[14] noted that the likelihood of spousal support was reduced only for women married less than five years. There was a substantial increase in the proportion of homemakers in long marriages who received spousal support compared to the time prior to the divorce revolution. Even though spousal support awards were more likely to be limited in duration under the new laws of divorce, Singer pointed out that in practice, so-called permanent awards of alimony under the old fault-based divorce could be modified or terminated for a range of reasons, which included the payer's voluntary assumption of new support obligations through remarriage.[15]

Thus even in the United States, the extent to which the changes brought about by the divorce revolution actually affected spousal support rates may have been overstated. Nonetheless, the debates about spousal support continue, and need to continue, as part of the range of options available to legislatures and courts in remedying women's economic disadvantage.

The German Experience

That spousal support has a limited role to play in practice is also evident from the German experience. Spousal support remained an entitlement in a range of circumstances following separation after the introduction of no-fault divorce in 1976. In Germany, the concept of postmarital "solidarity"

---

[12] Marsha Garrison, *Good Intentions Gone Awry: The Impact of New York's Equitable Distribution Law on Divorce Outcomes*, 57 BROOKLYN L. REV. 621, 698 (1991).

[13] *See e.g.* Robert McGraw, Gloria Sterin, & Joseph Davis, *A Case Study in Divorce Law Reform and its Aftermath*, 20 J. FAM. L. 443, 473 (1981–82) (Cleveland, Ohio); James McClindon, *Separate But Unequal: The Economic Disaster of Divorce for Women and Children*, 21 FAM. L. Q. 351 (1987). *See further*, Marsha Garrison, *The Economics of Divorce: Changing Rules, Changing Results*, *in* DIVORCE REFORM AT THE CROSSROADS 75 (Stephen Sugarman & Herma Hill Kay eds., 1990).

[14] WEITZMAN, *supra* note 8.

[15] Jana Singer, *Divorce Reform and Gender Justice*, 67 N.C. L. REV. 1103, 1107–09 (1989).

is used to justify spousal support. Although readily available in theory, the practice has been rather different, and actual receipt of spousal support has for a long time been quite uncommon.

This was so even a decade after the divorce revolution in West Germany. A study published in 1985 found that in 61 percent of cases, women renounced their right to spousal maintenance, and only 21 percent of men were obliged to pay maintenance by court order.[16] This proportion did not change much in the ensuing years, even after further reforms in 1986. A large-scale study conducted between 1999 and 2001 found that ten months after divorce, only 21 percent of women who shared parental responsibility with their former partners and only 12 percent of women with sole parental responsibility received spousal support.[17] By 2001, some two years after the divorce, the levels of spousal support had fallen. Only 18 percent of women with shared parental responsibility and 9.5 percent of those with sole parental responsibility received spousal support.[18] The main reasons given for the decline in the incidence of spousal support over the interval between the two surveys was remarriage and the former partner's inability to pay.[19] Women did not, of course, receive spousal support if they were not entitled to it under the legislation; but even when they were eligible, pursuing it might have been pointless.

This can be illustrated by another study of 1,500 divorced couples, published in 2003, that examined receipt of spousal maintenance during the period of separation but before they obtained a divorce. Seventy-six percent of women were eligible, but only 28 percent of these received spousal maintenance in full whereas another 9 percent received some but not all that had been agreed, or received it irregularly.[20] Further reform to the law of spousal maintenance occurred in Germany in 2007, placing greater emphasis on self-sufficiency, which may further reduce the incidence of spousal support in that country.[21]

---

[16] Beatrice Caesar-Wolf, Dorothee Eidmann, & Barbara Willenbacher, *Gleichberechtigungsmodelle im neuen Scheidungsfolgerecht und deren Umsetzung in die familiengerichtliche Praxis*, 6 ZEITSCHRIFT FÜR RECHTSSOZIOLOGIE 16 (1985).

[17] ROLAND PROKSCH, RECHTSTATSÄCHLICHE UNTERSUCHUNG ZUR REFORM DES KINDSCHAFTSRECHTS 172, (2002).

[18] *Id.* at 18.   [19] *Id.*

[20] HANS-JÜRGEN ANDREß, BARBARA BORGLOH, MIRIAM GÜLLNER, & KATJA WILKING, WENN AUS LIEBE ROTE ZAHLEN WERDEN. DIE WIRTSCHAFTLICHEN FOLGEN VON TRENNUNG UND SCHEIDUNG, 15 (2003).

[21] Gesetz zur Änderung des Unterhaltsrechts (UÄndG 2007) vom 21.12.2007, BGBl I 3189. The law entered into force on 1.1.2008.

ROLE DIFFERENTIATION IN THE MODERN FAMILY

It was very common at the time of the divorce revolution for women and men to have quite discrete roles, one doing most of the homemaking and parenting whereas the other brought in the income for the household. Such specialization was an optimal arrangement if the marriage lasted; but if the relationship broke down, women who had withdrawn from workforce participation entirely, in order to devote themselves to the care of the family, and remained single thereafter, were particularly vulnerable to adverse economic effects on separation.

This was because of the impact of withdrawal from the workforce on their earning capacity, and it had long-term consequences. Where retirement incomes depend on building up pension entitlements through years of workforce participation, the adverse impact of disengagement with the workforce, or limiting that engagement due to child-rearing responsibilities, affects the level of pension entitlement that can be built up. In countries where the courts are able to split pensions, and do so routinely, mothers are able to gain some benefit, in terms of retirement income, from the socioeconomic partnership they had with their husbands, but this does not help in terms of the ongoing effect of impaired earning capacity after separation.

Much has changed in recent years.[22] Although pure role-divided marriages still exist, the patterns of life for the majority of mothers in western countries now is one in which the care of home and children is combined with workforce participation, with women moving in and out of part-time or full-time work at different stages of their lives.[23]

Workforce Participation of Mothers in the United States

In the United States, workforce participation of married women jumped from 28 percent in 1960 to 68 percent in 1987.[24] The largest fall in the proportion of marriages with stay-at-home mothers occurred in the 1980s, levelling off by about 1991.[25] Women who remain connected with the

---

[22] For a review of these changes in the American context, *see* Thomas Oldham, *Changes in the Economic Consequences of Divorces, 1958–2008*, 42 Fam. L. Q. 419 (2008).

[23] Catherine Hakim, Work-lifestyle Choices in the 21st Century : Preference Theory (2000).

[24] Oldham, *supra* note 22, at 424.

[25] Ira Ellman, *Marital Roles and Declining Marriage Rates*, 41 Fam. L. Q. 455, 465 (2007). Since the late 1990s, there has been a modest increase in the proportion of stay-at-home mothers in marriages, but this must be read in the context of a decline in marriage rates and corresponding rise in cohabitation.

workforce through their years of raising young children are more likely to maintain an earning capacity similar to childless women.[26]

The improvement in the earning capacity of American mothers over the last thirty years is evident from McKeever and Wolfinger's study comparing married and divorced women (excluding women who had repartnered) in 1980 and 2001 respectively. The data came from the large-scale, longitudinal Current Population Survey. They found that by 2001, only those women with three children or more earned significantly less than women without children.[27] Women with children under the age of six were still earning substantially less than their childless counterparts, because only a minority of women with children under that age were in paid work; but the differential had at least declined since 1980.[28]

Over that period, divorced women's educational levels had also increased significantly. Per capita income had increased 48 percent whereas married women's per capita income had increased 34 percent. The increase in the lowest income quartile was only a little lower than the average, indicating divorced women across the spectrum had gained increases in living standards.

This has meant that child support and spousal support are less significant than they once were as a proportion of household income. McKeever and Wolfinger found that although the amount of money that women received in spousal support or child support increased substantially between 1980 and 2001,[29] these income transfers, for those who received them, represented only 14 percent of total family income in 2001, compared with 31 percent in 1980.[30]

Other Countries in the OECD

The evidence from the Organization for Economic Co-operation and Development (OECD) is that there remain significant variations in women's rates of workforce participation between countries. In Sweden, 82.5 percent of women with a child under the age of sixteen were in the workforce in 2007. In Hungary, this figure was 45.7 percent. The Scandinavian and

---

[26] Heather Joshi, Pierella Paci, & Jane Waldfogel, *The Wages of Motherhood: Better or Worse?*, 23 CAMBRIDGE J. ECON. 543 (1999).

[27] Matthew McKeever & Nicholas Wolfinger, *Shifting Fortunes in a Changing Economy: Trends in the Economic Wellbeing of Divorced Women*, in FRAGILE FAMILIES AND THE MARRIAGE AGENDA 127, 143–45 (Lori Kowaleski-Jones & Nicholas Wolfinger eds., 2006).

[28] *Id.*

[29] Expressed in 2001 dollars, the average payment in 1980 was $5,224 and in 2001 it was $6,944. *Id.* at 144.

[30] *Id.* at 149.

English-speaking countries generally have much higher rates of workforce participation by mothers than the countries of Southern and Eastern Europe.[31]

Variations may even be seen in the workforce participation patterns of mothers with very young children. Nearly 53 percent of British mothers with a child aged two years or younger were connected to the workforce (either working or on maternity leave) in 2007. The figure was 54 percent for American women and nearly 59 percent for Canadian women.[32] In the old Soviet bloc countries, the Czech Republic, and Hungary, less than 20 percent of women with children under the age of three maintained a connection with the workforce. These differences between countries in patterns of maternal employment explain the differences observed in terms of the "wage penalty" for child rearing between countries.[33]

There are also significant differences between countries in the extent to which mothers work full time. A typical pattern of part-time employment of mothers may be seen in Australia, the Netherlands, Switzerland, and the United Kingdom, with mothers in the Netherlands and Switzerland likely to continue in part-time employment after the children start school.[34] The common pattern in these countries therefore remains for mothers and fathers to make differential life-course investments, with fathers' primary investment being in the marketplace of career or self-employed business, whereas women's life investments are more diversified and include a major orientation toward the care of children.[35]

This is not so everywhere. For example, in Denmark, Canada, Finland, Portugal and Sweden, mothers typically continue to work full time following the birth of children.[36]

---

[31] Organisation for Economic Co-operation and Development, Babies and Bosses – Reconciling Work and Family Life: A Synthesis of Findings for OECD Countries (2007). Table 3.2 is available at http://www.oecd.org/document/45/0,3343,en_2649_34819_39651501_1_1_1_1,00.html

[32] *Id.* For more explanation of detail on the proportions actually at work or on paid maternity leave respectively in different countries, *see id.* at 48–49.

[33] Wendy Sigle-Rushton & Jane Waldfogel, *Motherhood and Women's Earnings in Anglo-American, Continental European, and Nordic Countries* (Luxembourg Income Study Working Paper Series, No. 454, 2006).

[34] OECD, *supra* note 31, at 47.

[35] *See* e.g. in Australia, Janeen Baxter, Belinda Hewett, & Michele Haynes, *Life Course Transitions and Housework: Marriage, Parenthood, and Time on Housework*, 70 J Marriage & Fam. 259 (2008); Michael Bittman, Juggling Time: How Australian Families Use Their Time (1991).

[36] OECD, *supra* note 31, at 47. There is evidence that partnered mothers who work full time in Britain tend to be the primary earner in the relationship or an equal earner. *See* Shireen Kanji, *What Keeps Mothers in Full-time Employment?*, European Sociological Rev. (forthcoming).

The Continuing Economic Disadvantage of
Mothers without Partners

Because of changes in maternal workforce participation and improved child support systems, the level of disadvantage suffered by mothers on separation is likely to be less across the western world than it was thirty years ago.[37] However, it still exists, particularly in those countries with lower levels of maternal workforce participation and where the majority of such work is part time. The evidence from many countries around the western world is that the continuing role specialization of women in caring for children – and the elderly – continues to have economic repercussions.[38] There is also evidence from the United States that the economic consequences of the breakdown of cohabiting relationships are very similar to those of marriage breakdown.[39] This is not surprising, to the extent that patterns of role differentiation are similar, where the couple has children.

THE ECONOMIC CONSEQUENCES OF
SEPARATION AND DIVORCE FOR MEN

The impact of separation and divorce on the economic well-being of men is much less well understood than for women. It was widely reported in studies conducted in the 1980s[40] that men's standard of living increased

---

[37] In the United States, *see* e.g. Matthew McKeever & Nicholas Wolfinger, *Reexamining the Economic Costs of Marital Disruption for Women*, 82 *Social Science Quarterly* 202 (2001). In this study of data from the National Survey of Families and Households (NSFH), the researchers found that women who were married or cohabiting in 1987–88 and who had separated by the time of the second interview in 1992–94 experienced a decline of 14 percent in median per capita income if they remained single and 3 percent if they had repartnered. This was lower than in previous studies. Multivariate analysis indicated that women's higher postdivorce incomes could be attributed primarily to labor force participation and human capital.

[38] For international evidence, *see* Hans-Jürgen Andreß, Barbara Borgloh, Miriam Bröckel, Marco Giesselmann, & Dina Hummelsheim, *The Economic Consequences of Partnership Dissolution – A Comparative Analysis of Panel Studies from Belgium, Germany, Great Britain, Italy, and Sweden*, 22 EUROPEAN SOCIOLOGICAL REVIEW 533 (2006). For recent Australian research, *see* Bruce Smyth & Ruth Weston, Australian Institute of Family Studies, *Financial Living Standards after Divorce: A Recent Snapshot* (2000); Jerry Silvey & Bob Birrell, *Financial Outcomes for Parents after Separation*, 12 PEOPLE AND PLACE 45 (2004); Simon Kelly & Ann Harding, *Love Can Hurt, Divorce Will Cost*, (AMP/NATSEM Income and Wealth Report Issue 10, AMP, April 2005).

[39] *See* Sarah Avellar & Pamela Smock, *The Economic Consequences of the Dissolution of Cohabiting Unions*, 67 J. MARRIAGE & FAM. 315 (2005).

[40] *See* Chapter 2.

after separation, raising the prospect that even after paying decent levels of child support, nonresident fathers could afford to make further transfers to their former partners by way of spousal support. Although that may well be true in some cases, the reality may be somewhat different across the population of separated parents.

Studies that have reported an increase in the standard of living of men following divorce have based this on a comparison of incomes and needs. Here, the assessment of need plays a critical part. Does a nonresident father need more than a one-bedroom apartment? The answer to that question depends critically on whether he is seeing his children regularly for overnight stays. Early studies, using equivalence scales to work out income needs per person in the household, typically treated nonresident parents as single people without others living in the home. That may have been true in the 1970s and 1980s for a substantial number of separated and divorced fathers who did not have their children to stay regularly overnight, and who therefore needed only a much more modest level of accommodation than the mother.[41] With the changing demographics of postseparation parenting, and the greater level of involvement that nonresident parents have with their children, including regular overnight stays, that assumption is no longer sustainable.

Even those nonresident fathers who do not have to accommodate the children for regular visits may find that their housing costs do not vary significantly from the former family home. Major cities may well have a plentiful supply of small apartments, but the housing stock of many towns and rural communities may be based almost entirely on family-size homes. No doubt there are differences between countries in this respect. The assumptions of economists do not always sit easily with real-world experience.

Whatever the situation may have been in the 1970s and 1980s, the situation now is that many men as well as women suffer from the loss of the other partner's income when relationships break down. The changing patterns of workforce participation of women over the last thirty years, and diminishing male earnings relative to women's as a consequence of deindustrialization,[42] has meant that more intact families are dependent

[41] For an analysis of the impact of different equivalence scales on the assessment of separated men's living standards, *see* Sarah Jarvis & Stephen Jenkins, *Marital Splits and Income Changes: Evidence from the British Household Panel Survey*, 53 POPULATION STUDIES 237 (1999).

[42] Annette Bernhardt, Martina Morris, & Mark Handcock, *Women's Gains or Men's Losses? A Closer Look at the Shrinking Gender Gap in Earnings*, 101 AM. J. SOCIOLOGY 302 (1995).

on the earnings of both parents to sustain their standard of living. In families where men work full time and women work part time, the loss of the male income will impact disproportionately on women, but both parents will suffer a loss of standard of living from the loss of the other's income.

Taking all these factors into account, studies of the impact of separation on men's income indicate that the outcomes for men are as heterogeneous as for women. The impact of separation financially depends on the extent to which a man relied on his partner's income in the preseparation household, on household composition before and after separation, and on what income transfers are required to be made in the aftermath of separation.[43]

Even though the economic effects of separation and divorce on women and men depends greatly on both their preseparation circumstances and their postseparation household composition, it is evident that in most cases, both parents will suffer a loss in standard of living as long as both are having to meet the housing needs of the children in their separate households. People cannot go from one household to two households, with a duplication of housing costs, furnishings and appliances, and other such expenses, without suffering a significant loss of living standards. Where the children are visiting regularly, transport costs also add to the total impact of separation on the finances of the parents. The greatly increased costs of having two households instead of just one being supported by the same private earnings can be ameliorated to some extent by the provision of welfare benefits to primary caregivers, but even with such taxpayer support, the economics of separation inevitably dictate loss. The one budget that the family had together while intact has to stretch across two households with whatever support the taxpayer may provide.

In situations where the children are not spending a significant amount of time with both parents, and the father has not taken on a commitment to a new family, the position may well be different, provided that he is able to find housing that is no more than needed for a single person.

JUSTIFYING SPOUSAL SUPPORT IN AN AGE OF NO-FAULT DIVORCE

Even though there are often adverse economic effects of separation and divorce for both parents, concern has quite properly been focused on the

---

[43] Patricia McManus & Thomas DiPrete, *Losers and Winners: The Financial Consequences of Separation and Divorce for Men*, 66 Am. Sociological Rev. 246 (2001).

position of women, and particularly homemaker spouses, for whom the losses stemming from separation and divorce can be catastrophic. In the last twenty years, this has led to a rethinking of the role of spousal support in addressing the financial aspects of relationship breakdown.

There are significant difficulties in justifying spousal support in an age of no-fault divorce, especially where divorce can be unilateral and does not require the agreement of the other partner to the marriage. It is much easier to justify ongoing spousal maintenance for the fifty-year-old "displaced homemaker" who is abandoned for a younger woman, or for the woman who leaves her husband because of his violence, than it is to justify maintenance for the woman who makes the decision to leave, for other reasons, such as boredom with the relationship or because she forms a new relationship that does not result in remarriage.

The problems of justification are particularly great in those jurisdictions that insisted on removing the fault-based aspects of entitlement to spousal support. In common law countries, at least, the no-fault approach took away the moral basis for spousal support, its conceptual justification, and its method of quantification, leaving nothing left but the idea that one spouse might have to pay money periodically to the other for some period and for some reason. The traditional law of spousal support rested, mainly if not only, on the premise that a wife who was not legally at fault for the breakdown of the marriage was entitled to a form of expectation damages for the loss of that consortium, at least for as long as she remained unmarried.[44] The principle of quantification, at least in theory, was that she should be allowed to retain the standard of living she enjoyed in the course of the marriage for the rest of her life if need be – or at least until her former husband passed away. The duty of support relied on the nature of the marriage contract, which for the husband involved a continuing obligation of support for the wife. That obligation survived the divorce if he deserted her or was otherwise at fault. The continuing financial obligation was part of marriage's indissolubility even after a divorce ended the consortium vitae.

What basis could there be for spousal support after no-fault divorce? In many jurisdictions following the divorce revolution, "need" replaced "fault" as the moral basis for awarding spousal maintenance. It represented

---

[44] Historically, there were also other rationales for spousal support, including the concept of the dower. *See* June Carbone, *The Futility of Coherence: The ALI's Principles of the Law of Family Dissolution, Compensatory Spousal Payments*, 4 J.L. & FAM. STUD. 43 (2002). Carbone traces the history of awards of spousal support and demonstrates that it has always had multiple justifications and served multiple purposes.

not the continuing obligation of support but rather a residual obligation of support. A man who had once taken on the obligation of supporting a woman (or was at least deemed to have done so by entering into matrimony) still had some kind of moral and legal obligation to look after her welfare if she was in need and unable to support herself. "Need" both represented the justification for a residual obligation of support and offered a principle of quantification. To the extent that he had the capacity to pay, the former husband should be required to meet the need. Need also offered a principle to determine duration. The spousal support payments should continue only for as long as the former wife needed them. She had a duty to endeavor to become self-sufficient.

The obligation of support, residual as it may have been on the "needs" approach, did not extend to cohabiting couples because it was still founded, as the traditional law of spousal support was, on the obligation of support contained in the marriage contract. Men who cohabited with women did not have any legal obligation to support them after the relationship was over.

RECONCEPTUALIZING AND REVIVING SPOUSAL SUPPORT

The research findings on the adverse financial circumstances and loss in living standards of so many single mothers has led to a search for new justifications for spousal support that go beyond merely meeting the needs of those who were unable to support themselves.[45] Two new approaches have emerged to respond to the need to justify spousal support in an age of no-fault divorce. These are the compensatory rationale, and spousal support as income sharing arising from the nature of marriage as a socioeconomic partnership.

Spousal Support as Compensation

The most significant new approach that has emerged from this search for justifications has been a compensatory role for spousal support. This is a particularly important theme of the law in Canada. In that country, the law of property division varies from province to province, whereas the

---

[45] *See* e.g. Margaret Brinig & June Carbone, *The Reliance Interest in Marriage and Divorce*, 62 TUL. L. REV. 855 (1988); Ira Ellman, *The Theory of Alimony*, 77 CAL. L. REV. 1 (1989); June Carbone, *Economics, Feminism and the Reinvention of Alimony: A Reply to Ellman*, 43 VAND. L. REV. 1463 (1990); Carl Schneider, *Rethinking Alimony: Marital Decisions and Moral Discourse*, [1991] BYU L. REV. 197.

law of spousal maintenance, being contained in the Divorce Act, is federal. Although decisions of the Supreme Court of Canada in the late 1980s were seen as promoting the idea of financial self-sufficiency and a clean break,[46] the Divorce Act 1985, then as now,[47] offered several bases for awarding spousal support. These are:

- To recognize any economic advantages or disadvantages to the spouses arising from the marriage or its breakdown;
- To apportion between the spouses any financial consequences arising from the care of any child of the marriage over and above the obligation apportioned between the spouses through child support;
- To relieve any economic hardship of the spouses arising from the breakdown of the marriage;
- Insofar as practicable, to promote the economic self-sufficiency of each spouse within a reasonable period of time.

In its 1992 decision in *Moge v. Moge*,[48] the Supreme Court of Canada rejected earlier decisions to the extent that they promoted the importance of the clean break at the expense of the other factors given. It emphasized that there were a number of different bases for spousal support payments. In particular, and given the research evidence on the economic disadvantage of divorced women, the Court focused on the compensatory role of spousal support as a means of distributing fairly between the former spouses the economic advantages and disadvantages of marriage. Most commonly, the Court recognized, disadvantage flows from situations where a spouse withdraws from workforce participation to care for children. In this case, the husband had been paying spousal support to the wife for sixteen years, but after the children had grown up, he sought to terminate his obligation. Both had quite low incomes, but Mrs. Moge's income was much lower than her former husband's. The Supreme Court held that the obligation to pay should continue. It was quite a modest level of spousal support that had not been adjusted for inflation.

This compensatory theory of spousal support, based on the notion that the law should provide compensation to a primary caregiver for

---

[46] Pelech v. Pelech, [1987] 1 S.C.R. 801; Richardson v. Richardson, [1987] 1 S.C.R. 857; Caron v. Caron, [1987] 1 S.C.R. 892. *See supra* Chapter 2.

[47] Divorce Act, 1985, s.15(7)(d) (as originally enacted). *See now* Divorce Act, 1985, s.15.2(6)(d). *See also* subsection (4) that lists factors to be taken into account.

[48] Moge v. Moge, [1992] 3 S.C.R. 813. *See* Nick Bala, *Spousal Support Law Transformed—Fairer Treatment for Women*, 11 Can. Fam. L.Q. 13 (1994); Carol Rogerson, *Spousal Support After Moge*, 14 Can. Fam. L.Q. 281 (1996).

lost earning capacity, has been very influential in thinking about spousal support in other jurisdictions as well. In England, the House of Lords took this approach in *Miller v. Miller* and *McFarlane v. McFarlane*, two cases decided together that reshaped the law of financial provision on divorce in England and Wales.[49] One basis for financial provision, the House of Lords held, was compensation for relationship-generated disadvantage aimed at redressing any significant prospective economic disparity between the parties arising from the way they conducted their marriage. In *McFarlane*, the parties were both in their forties and had divorced after being married for sixteen years. They had three children who were aged fifteen, thirteen, and eight, respectively. The husband was an accountant earning about £750,000 per year. The wife was a qualified solicitor who had stopped work after the birth of their second child. The trial judge awarded her one-third of his before-tax income, £250,000 per annum. This was upheld by the House of Lords for an indefinite period. One of the rationales was that the wife had given up a career potentially as lucrative as the husband's in order to make a home for both of them and the children.

In the United States, the American Law Institute has developed the concept of compensatory spousal payments as the justification for income sharing between former partners (including cohabitees) following relationship breakdown.[50] One of the bases for that compensation is loss of earning capacity due to child-rearing responsibilities. Of course, a compensatory approach need not be limited to couples with children. Childless women may also make career sacrifices for their partners, for example, by moving to another country where they are not eligible to continue in their profession without requalifying.

One problem with the compensatory model, however, is how to quantify the loss. Potentially at least, the compensation approach offers both a principled justification for spousal support awards and also a principle of quantification.[51] Yet in practice, there are enormous difficulties in evaluating the adverse impact of interrupted workforce participation in any given case. Such a calculation involves an attempt to construct what might have been. We cannot know whether a woman who had low educational qualifications at the time of the marriage and a limited earning capacity might have upgraded her educational qualifications or in other ways enhanced

---

[49]   [2006] 2 AC 618.
[50]   AMERICAN LAW INSTITUTE, *supra* note 7, at Chapter 5.
[51]   On the distinction between principles of justification and principles of quantification in family property law, *see* Patrick Parkinson, *Quantifying the Homemaker Contribution in Family Property Law*, 31 FEDERAL L. REV. 1 (2003).

her modest earning capacity if she had remained single. We cannot know, in any individual case, whether a teacher who last taught before the birth of her first child ten years ago would have risen to be a school principal or otherwise hold a senior position within a school. In few occupations is age and experience alone a criterion for promotion. Furthermore, many people go through a series of different occupations and careers in the course of their lifetime, and sometimes make sacrifices in terms of pay and seniority to do so. In any individual case, the calculation of the losses associated with child rearing can be little more than guesswork.

For this reason, perhaps, Canadian courts, ostensibly applying the compensatory approach laid out by the Supreme Court in *Moge v. Moge*, have eschewed the use of expert evidence to calculate the extent of lost earning capacity due to child rearing. Instead, they have in practice reverted to need (assessed in the light of the marital standard of living) and capacity to pay as proxies for the calculation of losses associated with role division in the course of the marriage.[52] The means of justification may have changed, but the practice has reverted to the familiar and quantifiable.[53]

Similarly, the American Law Institute used compensation as the justification for spousal payments, but this rationale was not translated into principles of quantification. The ALI Principles relied instead on the difference in income between the former partners, together with the duration of the relationship, to guide quantification.[54] When principles

---

[52] Carol Rogerson, *The Canadian Law of Spousal Support*, 38 Fam. L. Q. 69, 71–72 (2004).

[53] Canadian scholars Carol Rogerson and Rollie Thompson, in work commissioned by the Department of Justice, have developed guidelines for the quantification of spousal support payments and duration of awards that are used to guide judges in making appropriate orders for spousal support once the justification for an award has been established. Carol Rogerson & Rollie Thompson, *Spousal Support Advisory Guidelines* (2008), http://www.law.utoronto.ca/faculty/rogerson/ssag.html. These guidelines distinguish between cases where the spousal support is in addition to child support (with child support payments being the first priority) and those where the recipient is not also in receipt of child support. They address all the bases for making awards, including noncompensatory spousal support, based on what judges do in practice, rather than as an outworking of a theoretical principle of quantification.

[54] Although much discussed in the academic literature, the ALI proposals have not been translated into significant legislative or case law developments in the United States. In a review of the impact of the ALI proposals eight years on, researchers found no adoptions by legislatures and only eight references to the chapter on compensatory spousal payments in case law. Three references were positive. *See* Michael Clisham & Robin Wilson, *American Law Institute's Principles of the Law of Family Dissolution, Eight Years after Adoption: Guiding Principle or Obligatory Footnote?*, 42 Fam. L.Q. 573, 600, 604 (2008).

of justification are not consistent with principles of quantification, the consequence is both undercompensation and overcompensation. Some losses are not compensated because the principles of quantification do not address the degree of loss, whereas in other cases, the level of compensation may exceed any measurable loss.

Spousal Support and the Marriage Partnership

The other major justification for spousal support has been an extension of the idea of marriage as a partnership. This justifies not only the sharing of the assets acquired in the course of the marriage, but also a degree of income sharing after its separation. The rationale for the long-established concept of community property arising out of the status of marriage becomes, on this view, a justification also for community of income.[55] The entitlement to spousal support flowing therefrom might be continued for a set period calculated by reference to the length of the marriage and terminating abruptly after the set period, or a dwindling right that tapers off gradually over time until it is finally extinguished.[56]

This justification for spousal support has also made its way into the ALI's Principles.[57] Under those principles, a partner even in a childless marriage would be obliged to make "compensatory spousal payments" to a partner who was earning less, if their relationship lasted a sufficient length of time. Even though categorized as a form of compensatory spousal payment for loss of the marital standard of living, this is a different rationale from role differentiation within the marriage.

The Practical Convergence of the New Justifications

Although conceptually distinct and offering quite distinct bases for quantification, the two approaches may well merge in practice. If the measure of what the homemaker might have earned if she had not devoted her attention to the home and family is what her former partner actually

---

[55] *See* e.g. Jana Singer, *Alimony and Efficiency: The Gendered Costs and Benefits of the Economic Justifications for Alimony*, 82 GEORGETOWN L. J. 2423, 2454ff. (1994); Stephen Sugarman, *Dividing Financial Interests on Divorce, in* DIVORCE REFORM AT THE CROSSROADS 130 (Stephen Sugarman & Herma Hill Kay eds., 1990).

[56] Jane Ellis, *New Rules for Divorce: Transition Payments*, 32 U. LOUISVILLE J. FAM. L. 601 (1993–94) (proposes an initial period of income sharing followed by a period of gradually decreasing economic interdependency).

[57] AMERICAN LAW INSTITUTE, *supra* note 7.

earns, as it was, for example, in the English case of *McFarlane*, then the differences between the compensation approach and the income sharing approach largely disappear at the stage of quantification.

COMPENSATION, INCOME SHARING, AND THE DECISION TO END THE MARRIAGE

A major question about both these approaches concerns the extent to which people should be expected to take responsibility for their own decisions to end marriages.

The income sharing approach, giving the claimant spouse a right to share equally in the other's income, is akin to expectation damages, mitigated, in the case of time-limited awards, by a duty to become self-sufficient over that period.[58] The compensation approach, remedying the losses arising from the role division in the relationship, is akin to reliance damages. Both expectation damages and reliance damages are predicated on the breach of contract being the fault of the person against whom the remedy is sought.

Much of the criticism levelled at the ALI's approach to spousal support in its Principles of the Law of Family Dissolution has been about its no-fault approach. Certainly, any mention of the notion of "fault" tends to make family lawyers unsettled. The accepted wisdom is that it is not possible to attribute responsibility for marriage breakdown. Yet in the United States at least, the issue of fault in relation to spousal support has been raised by numerous leading family law scholars.[59]

Acknowledging all the complexity of marital relationships, the variety of reasons why marriages break down, and the difficulties of judicial

---

[58] The concept of earning capacity as an asset of the marriage partnership is problematic as an explanation of the income-sharing approach because if it were treated as property to which both parties have an equal entitlement, its division could not reasonably be time-limited.

[59] *See* e.g. the contributions to a volume on the ALI Principles. RECONCEIVING THE FAMILY, CRITIQUE ON THE AMERICAN LAW INSTITUTE'S PRINCIPLES OF THE LAW OF FAMILY DISSOLUTION (Robin Wilson ed., 2006). Critiques of no-fault in relation to spousal support include Lynn Wardle, *Beyond Fault and No-Fault in the Reform of Marital Dissolution Law*, at 9; June Carbone, *Back to the Future: The Perils and Promise of a Backward-Looking Jurisprudence*, at 209; Katharine Silbaugh, *Money as Emotion in the Distribution of Wealth at Divorce*, at 234; Katherine Spaht, *Postmodern Marriage as Seen through the Lens of the ALI's 'Compensatory Payments'*, at 249. *See also* David Westfall, *Unprincipled Family Dissolution: The American Law Institute's Recommendations for Spousal Support and Division of Property*, 27 HARV. J.L. & PUB. POL'Y 917, 931ff. (2004).

enquiry, it is a legitimate question to ask what place notions of responsibility ought to play before we require anyone to pay damages to another. It is not obvious that one partner should have to pay for the other's choice if, though it is made only after long soul searching and consideration, it is nonetheless a choice ultimately to pursue her fulfillment rather than theirs, or to fulfill her search for meaning rather than being content with a shared meaning, or even the humdrum of daily meaninglessness.

The no-fault approach to spousal support does not offer convincing answers to this conundrum. June Carbone, for example, posits the hypothetical case of a sixteen-year childless marriage that ended after the husband indicated to the wife that he had had an affair and was leaving her. At the commencement of the marriage, she earned about one-third more than he did. The gap between their respective earnings increased substantially during the course of the marriage. Under the ALI Principles, based on income sharing, or compensation for the loss of the marital standard of living, she might have to pay thousands of dollars per month in compensation to him, at least for some years. This would be in recognition of the fact that the ending of the marriage meant a loss in his living standards. Yet he was the one who decided to leave, and in Carbone's hypothetical, she is devastated by his decision.[60] What justice is there in requiring her to compensate him for the choices he has made?

Such an example is particularly poignant in a situation where it is the woman who is required to make income support payments to the man, as would be the case, for example, in more than a quarter of American marriages.[61] As in other areas of family law, a good way to test the intuitive fairness of a gender-neutral rule is to reverse the usual gender patterns of its application and then to examine how fair the rule seems. The example is also poignant because, in the hypothetical, the husband acknowledged that he had had an affair. There is a widespread acceptance of the immorality of adultery in U.S. society,[62] and community surveys indicate that

---

[60] Carbone, *supra* note 59, at 229.

[61] In 2004, 25.5 percent of women in marriages earned more than their husbands, and in about 5 percent of cases, the wife was earning and the husband was not. The latter may include a number of men who had retired while their younger wives were still working. *See* Ellman, *supra* note 25, 464–66.

[62] A national survey conducted in the United States in 1993 found that 77 percent of respondents considered that extramarital sex is always wrong. NATIONAL OPINION RESEARCH CENTER, GENERAL SOCIAL SURVEYS 1972–1993 (1994), *cited in* STEVEN NOCK, MARRIAGE IN MEN'S LIVES 22 (1998). *See also* the surveys reported by Wardle, *supra* note 59, at 17, n.41.

this is a major cause of marriage breakdown both in the United States and elsewhere.[63]

Yet the example would raise issues of justice even if he had not committed adultery. What if he just tired of living with her and wanted to embark on a new direction? And what if, reversing the gender positions to the more common scenario, where the wife earns less, she tired of living with him, ended the relationship, and then sought compensation from him for the loss of her marital standard of living? What price must one spouse pay for the other's midlife crisis?

Although the notion of compensation has its problems, the financial losses cannot be left to fall where they occur, because those losses usually fall on women. This is why need (broadly defined to include also the housing costs of primary caregivers), in most cases, still represents a more satisfying rationale for spousal support than compensation. It is not that the concept of compensation for lost earning capacity is flawed; it may be a compelling rationale in many cases. The difficulty is that if a no-fault approach is taken to compensation, the problems of justice are too glaring. Legislators and judges alike will resist the idea that one person should have to compensate another when the circumstances that give rise to the demand for compensation arise from their own wrongdoing, or at least their own free choices. This is less of an issue with divorce by consent than unilateral no-fault divorce. In a situation where divorce can be entirely unilateral, and based solely on a separation period, the opportunity to negotiate about these issues as a condition for giving consent to a divorce is not there.

For these reasons, in the new rationales for spousal support, there has to be some recognition of responsibility for the breakdown of the relationship, if only at the margins. As Carl Schneider has observed, "the people the law seeks to affect themselves think in moral terms. A law which tries to eliminate those terms from its language will both misunderstand the people it is regulating and be misunderstood by them."[64]

One compromise position is that it could at least be a defense to a claim for spousal support or a consideration in relation to quantum, that

---

[63] Paul Amato & Denise Previti, *People's Reasons for Divorcing: Gender, Social Class, the Life Course, and Adjustment*, 24 J. FAM. ISSUES 602 (2003) (infidelity the most commonly cited cause of marital breakdown in survey of more than 200 respondents). *See also* ILENE WOLCOTT & JODY HUGHES, AUSTRALIAN INSTITUTE OF FAMILY STUDIES, TOWARDS AN UNDERSTANDING OF THE REASONS FOR DIVORCE, (Working Paper No. 20, at 14–18, 1999) (infidelity perceived as the main reason for divorce by 20 percent of both men and women in Australia).

[64] Schneider, *supra* note 45, at 243.

it would be contrary to the justice of the case to order one party to pay compensation to the other for the consequences flowing from marriage breakdown because the party seeking compensation was in some way responsible for it. Of course, this has the necessary, and perhaps disquieting, consequence that it will be most frequently women's responsibility for marriage breakdown that is likely to be an issue in family law proceedings. At the same time, it will be mostly women who are likely to receive the benefits of compensatory awards. An alternative would be to make it a precondition to the award of compensation over and above the asset sharing of the fruits of the marriage, that the man's responsibility for the marriage breakdown can be demonstrated. This would focus attention on men's responsibility but it would make it harder to obtain a compensation award. On the other hand, it would certainly provide grounds for substantial awards of spousal support based on the principles of expectation damages – for example, in circumstances where a woman has been driven out of the marriage by the man's violence toward her.

SPOUSAL SUPPORT AS INSURANCE

A further problem area in terms of the revival of spousal maintenance is the issue of spousal support as insurance. In a happy marriage, spouses insure each other against life's adversities; but the question is whether parties to failed marriages can be expected to act as insurers to their former spouses, especially in a system that refuses to examine any questions about responsibility for the marriage breakdown. It is, after all, only when marriages break down that the financial need for one person to live independently of the other arises.

Marriage, at least in jurisdictions that have unilateral no-fault divorce based on a period of separation, can no longer be seen as a covenant in which people commit to support one another for richer or for poorer, for better or for worse, in sickness and in health, till death parts them.[65] Of course, people may still make these promises – and mean them. Yet in no sense is there now an enforceable contract when the relationship is terminable by one party at will.

This has implications for the insurance role of marriage. The issue arose, for example, in another decision of the Supreme Court of Canada

[65] In three states in the United States, Arizona, Arkansas and Louisiana, there is now the option of covenant marriage, which is a form of marriage that cannot be as readily terminated as the default regime for marriage.

seven years after its landmark decision concerning compensatory spousal support in *Moge v. Moge*. In *Bracklow v. Bracklow*,[66] the Court held that in addition to a compensatory rationale for spousal support, the legislation also supported noncompensatory awards of spousal support. In that case, the parties had both been married previously. Their relationship lasted seven years and there were no children from it. The Supreme Court held that the former husband was under a duty to pay ongoing support to his ex-wife as a result of illness that had no connection with the circumstances of the marriage. In so doing, the Court indicated that as a matter of statutory interpretation, men were still required to act as social insurers for women against life's adversities, despite the removal of the conceptual rationale for such a support obligation in an age of no-fault divorce. The promise to the other spouse to support them in sickness as well as health remained enforceable even if all other promises contained in the marriage vows were not. To this extent, the indissoluble nature of marriage, as well as parenthood, has survived the no-fault divorce revolution.

Yet even with the changes in the law of spousal support in Canada after *Moge* and *Bracklow*, spousal support remains uncommon in Canada. Carol Rogerson wrote in 2002 that: "Reliable data on the actual incidence of spousal support does not exist, but the scant available suggests that spousal support is present in only a small percentage of divorce cases – ranging from the low twenties at best, to the low tens at worst."[67] Whatever the legal grounds on which spousal support is payable, Canada does not necessarily have a higher incidence of spousal support than the United States. The issues may be less about eligibility than that women who feel able to support themselves do not apply, or that pursuing spousal support from someone who does not have the capacity to pay is pointless.

SPOUSAL SUPPORT AND PROPERTY DIVISION

The relationship between spousal support and the rules for property division also need to be considered. If the rules for property division in a jurisdiction provide for the equal division of the acquests of the marriage or community property, as the case may be, then the argument for some additional compensatory payment to redress the consequences of role

---

[66] [1999] 1 S.C.R. 420. For commentary, *see* Carol Rogerson, *Spousal Support Post-Bracklow: The Pendulum Swings Again?*, 19 CAN. FAM. L.Q. 185 (2001).

[67] CAROL ROGERSON, DEVELOPING SPOUSAL SUPPORT GUIDELINES IN CANADA: BEGINNING THE DISCUSSION: BACKGROUND PAPER (Paper prepared for the Department of Justice, Canada) 59 (2002).

differentiation within the relationship becomes compelling. This was, for example, the position taken in France with its *prestation compensatoire*, a payment that, while normally a one-off payment, can be paid wholly or partially in installments, to compensate a party to a marriage for the consequences of its disruption.[68] Such a payment might, in other jurisdictions, be characterized as lump-sum spousal support, or periodic spousal support if paid in installments.

However, if compensatory considerations are built into the grounds for equitable distribution of property, the position may be different. If one of the rationales for property division is to meet future needs, with the consequence that typically women with the primary care of children get a substantial majority of the property on separation, then (unless tax consequences in the jurisdiction make a difference) the same result is achieved by characterizing the amount that in some jurisdictions might be called lump-sum maintenance as part of the property allocation instead.

An unequal division of the property in favor of the women who have, or have had, the primary care of children will in many cases be a form of income support.[69] A mother who receives the outright ownership of the matrimonial home free of a mortgage, or with a modest mortgage, receives an asset that provides the same benefit as ongoing income transfers. A mother who receives a transfer of the home subject to a mortgage as part of the property settlement, and who receives $300 per week in spousal support from the ex-husband, which covers the mortgage payments, is in much the same position as the mother who receives an outright transfer of the property and who therefore does not have to repay a mortgage. Indeed, from a woman's perspective, a clean break in terms of the property settlement is better for two reasons. First, typically periodic payments characterized as spousal support will end on remarriage (unless in the law of a particular jurisdiction, the traditional rule has been modified). Secondly, an outright transfer of property represents the equivalent of cash in hand, whereas the ex-partner may prove less than reliable in making payments of spousal support.

---

68   As a consequence of amendments to the Civil Code made by *Act no 2000–596* (30 June 2000), Article 274 now provides that the *prestation compensatoire* shall take the form of a capital amount. Article 275-1 provides that if the debtor is not able to pay a capital sum, the judge should set amounts to be paid in installments for up to eight years. Article 276 provides that in exceptional circumstances, where a former spouse cannot meet her or his needs, an indexed life annuity may be awarded. *See* further, ADELINE DASTE AND AUDE MORGEN-GUILLEMIN, DIVORCE: SÉPARATIONS DE CORPS ET DE FAIT, (19th ed., 2006).

69   Margaret Brinig, *Property Distribution Physics: The Talisman of Time and Middle Class Law*, 31 FAM. L. Q. 93, 95 (1997).

From this perspective, the clean break favors women, if the alternative is a lower level of property award together with periodic transfers characterized as spousal support. Conversely, men may be more advantaged by a system in which the matrimonial assets are evenly divided, but where they have an obligation to pay spousal support for a limited period or until the woman repartners, if that comes before the expiration of the period assigned to pay spousal support. If, as in the United States, the payment of spousal support is tax-deductible for the transferor, and taxable in the hands of the recipient,[70] the practical benefits deriving from the taxation of spousal support transfers may make it more advantageous than supporting the other parent through an unequal division of the property.

Any revival of spousal support must take into account the extent to which the property division, together with any pension splitting, if available, has already sought to address the issue of economic disadvantage stemming from the role differentiation within the marriage. There are legal limitations and practical limitations on this. The legal limitations are in terms of whether the law allows for equitable distribution that weights the share of the property in favor of a parent who has sacrificed his or her earning capacity because of caring roles or for other reasons. The practical limitations arise from the economic circumstances of the parties. For a great many parents who separate, there is very little property to divide. Spousal support is particularly important where there is not enough property to allocate between the parties in order to effect a fair and reasonable division of the losses associated with relationship breakdown. As Marsha Garrison notes, "[b]ecause of the relative infrequency of valuable assets among the divorce population, alimony and child support entitlements are far more important to the typical divorcing couple than is property distribution law."[71]

THE RELATIONSHIP BETWEEN CHILD SUPPORT AND SPOUSAL SUPPORT

Child support and spousal support also need to be considered together. Money is money, whether it is labeled as child support or spousal support. Financial transfers between parents with children, however

---

[70] *See* Stephen Comeau, *An Overview of the Federal Income Tax Provisions Related to Alimony Payments*, 38 Fam. L. Q. 111 (2004).

[71] Marsha Garrison, *The Economic Consequences of Divorce: Would Adoption of the ALI Principles Improve Current Outcomes?*, 8 Duke J. Gender L. & Pol'y 119, 128 (2001).

they are labelled, just go toward general household expenditure in an undifferentiated manner.

There is only so much money that is reasonably available for transfer between parents. If governments prioritize child support, and formulas or guidelines set expected payments at quite high levels, there may be little if any additional capacity for a parent also to pay spousal support. Conversely, if child support percentages are modest, there is more room for a person to pay spousal support as well.

This may be illustrated by the differences between two neighboring jurisdictions, Ontario and Wisconsin. In Canada, federal child support guidelines were introduced in 1997 and updated in 2006, although there are variations between provinces in terms of their detailed application. Wisconsin was a pioneer in developing child support guidelines and uses a simple percentage of obligor income approach comparable to that in Canada.[72] The following table compares the child support obligation of a child support payer in Ontario and in Wisconsin as a percentage of the payer's gross salary, where the payee has no income that affects the calculation, there are no special payments (for example for private school fees), and there is one child who is staying overnight on average for 2 nights per week, or 104 nights per year.[73] These conditions facilitate ready comparison between the guidelines, although typically the Canadian dollar trades at a little below parity with the American dollar, so that $50,000 Canadian represents a slightly lower income than $50,000 U.S.

Annual income	Ontario Per month child support	% of gross income	Wisconsin Per month child support	% of gross income
50,000	462	11.1%	708	17%
75,000	680	10.9%	1062	17%
100,000	877	10.5%	1377	16.5%

It is obvious that the differences in the percentages of gross income paid in child support are considerable, even in two adjoining jurisdictions.

There are sound pragmatic justifications for policy makers to elect to impose higher child support payments based on a standard percentage

---

[72] *See* Chapter 10.

[73] The figures for Ontario are taken from the website of the federal Ministry of Justice, http://www.justice.gc.ca/eng/pi/fcy-fea/lib-bib/legis/fcsg-lfpae/index.html#on. The figures from Wisconsin are derived from a calculator available at http://www.dwd4ocalculator.com/

of gross income at the expense of capacity to pay spousal support, rather than having lower child support payments supplemented by additional spousal support payments. Payments identified as being for the children carry less negative associations for payers than those ordered for the support of an ex-spouse in circumstances where there may be considerable bitterness about the breakup. Child support is also seen as a universal obligation in theory – if not in practice – for nonresident fathers, whereas spousal support is not. Furthermore, child support payments apply to all parents, whereas traditionally at least, spousal support has been an incident of postmarital relationships, not postcohabitation relationships or relationships that led to the birth of a child in which the parents never lived together.

However, in order to command community acceptance, levels of child support payments must bear some relationship to the measured expenditure patterns on children in intact families (including a proportionate share of housing and other infrastructure costs).[74] This is particularly a problem in formulas that take no account of the primary caregiver's income, as is the position in Wisconsin.[75]

Child support that contains a substantial element of spousal support may be justified in circumstances where the primary caregiver has not repartnered, and particularly where her earning capacity has been affected, and continues to be affected, by child-rearing responsibilities. The position is different if she has repartnered, as the preponderance of empirical research on the economic effects of relationship breakdown indicates that women who repartner tend to recover much the same standard of living as they had previously lost. Child support is typically calculated, around the world, on the incomes of one or both parents, ignoring the income of new partners. To do otherwise undermines the insistence of governments that the obligation to support children financially is an incident of biological parenthood. Furthermore, the difficulties in getting reliable information about incomes for one or both parents is great enough without going into the incomes of new partners or other members of the household in which a parent is living.[76] In jurisdictions, such as Wisconsin, that take account of the income of only one parent, an element of spousal support will over-compensate a parent who has maintained her earning capacity and has a substantial income from paid employment.

[74] These issues are discussed in Chapter 10.
[75] *See now* DCF 150.03, available at http://www.legis.state.wi.us/rsb/code/dcf/dcf150.pdf
[76] A new partner's income may nonetheless contribute indirectly to meeting a parent's child support obligation to the extent that they form a single economic household unit.

SHOULD SPOUSAL SUPPORT BE LIMITED
TO THOSE WHO WERE MARRIED?

The new frontier of maintenance is orders made for the support of former partners where there had been no marriage. Historically, cohabitation gave rise to no obligation of support. Yet in Australia[77] and New Zealand,[78] cohabitation has been assimilated with marriage, so that once a court establishes that a cohabiting relationship of sufficient duration existed, the legal rights and obligations that flow therefrom in terms of property division and maintenance are the same as for marriages. This includes maintenance.

New Zealand even has a provision allowing maintenance to be ordered against a natural parent where the parents have not lived together. Section 79 of the Family Proceedings Act 1980 provides:

Where

(a) The natural parents of a child are not married to, or in a civil union with, each other; and

(b) The natural father of the child is a person who is a parent from whom the payment of child support may be sought in respect of the child under section 6 of the Child Support Act 1991; and

(c) Either natural parent has or has had the role of providing day-to-day care for the child, the natural parent who has or has had the role of providing day-to-day care of the child may apply for a mainte-nance order in favour of that natural parent against the other natural parent.

There is a certain logic in this, if the basis for spousal maintenance is to compensate for the financial sacrifices involved in a caregiving role rather than as an outworking of the contractual duty of support arising from marriage. The indissolubility of parenthood extends to those who did not marry, and even did not live together.

DIVERGING APPROACHES AND THE MEANING OF DIVORCE

Because of the difficulties in rationalizing spousal support in an age of no-fault divorce, there is no longer much consensus about its role and justi-fication. The differences between jurisdictions in rules regarding property

---

[77] Family Law Act, 1975, Part VIIIAB.
[78] Family Proceedings Act, 1980, part 6.

division and levels of child support awards are part of the explanation. Some jurisdictions, such as Australia, seek to ameliorate women's disadvantage mainly through weighting property division in their favor (and dividing all the property, howsoever acquired), together with reasonable levels of child support; other jurisdictions – Canada falls into this category – divide only the marital property and rely much more on income transfers by way of spousal support. Jurisdictions vary also in the extent to which public support, not only through welfare payments but also through child benefits and other population-wide government payments, cushions the losses of income stemming from relationship breakdown.

There are also substantial variations between countries in patterns of maternal workforce participation. The need for spousal maintenance to compensate for lost earning capacity through child rearing is much greater in some countries than others.

All these differences matter, and matter very much; fundamentally, however, there is no international consensus about spousal support because there is no international consensus about what divorce is all about.

PART SIX

The Future of Family Law

12

Between Two Conflicting Views of Separation and Divorce

ABANDONING THE JUDEO-CHRISTIAN VIEW OF MARRIAGE

Thousands of years ago – so the story is told in the first book of Kings – Elijah stood on Mount Carmel and challenged his people as to which beliefs they would maintain, which deity they would follow. "How long will you waver between two opinions?" he asked. "If the Lord is God, follow him; but if Baal is God, follow him."[1]

Western societies have rather decisively cast off their Christian heritage when it comes to family life. The no-fault divorce revolution was just one of many social changes concerning marriage, family, and sexuality that occurred from the 1960s onward. The notion that marriage was, at least in principle, a lifelong commitment has given way to a practice of free terminability in many, but not all, western countries.[2] Marriage is also just one choice of partnering now; many people choose to live together without marrying either as a life-stage on the way to marriage (perhaps with that partner, perhaps with another) or as an alternative to marriage.[3] Same-sex relationships are recognized in various ways in many jurisdictions, some granting the right to marry, others giving legal effect to same-sex relationships through registered partnerships or civil unions. A plurality of forms of legal recognition has emerged for domestic relationships. In the Netherlands, for example, both heterosexual couples and homosexual

---

[1] 1 *Kings* 18 (New International Version).

[2] A marriage may be freely terminable in practice even where the ostensible ground for divorce is fault-based, if the grounds for divorce are sufficiently open-ended and the practice of the jurisdiction makes it not worth anyone's while to contest a divorce sought by the other. *See* in relation to the British experience, GWYNN DAVIS & MERVYN MURCH, GROUNDS FOR DIVORCE (1988).

[3] For Australian evidence, *see* Sandra Buchler, Janeen Baxter, Michele Haynes, & Mark Western, *The Social and Demographic Characteristics of Cohabiters in Australia: Towards a Typology of Cohabiting Couples*, FAMILY MATTERS No. 82, at 22 (2009).

couples may enter into either marriages or registered partnerships with almost identical consequences, or live together without formal recognition.[4] There is a smorgasbord of choice.

There is also a lot of choice about parenthood. Gone is the stigma of unmarried parenthood in many countries, and in cultural subgroups within countries. In some European countries, more than half of all births are ex-nuptial.[5] The figure is close to 40 percent in the United States,[6] with significant variations according to race.[7]

The notion that heterosexual marriage is the only acceptable form of partnering and the only appropriate context for parenting has well and truly been overthrown. In the choice between God and the modern Baals, there has been a clear societal decision. In some societies, and perhaps more so in the United States than any other western country, there is a disconnect between private adherence to faith and the practice of family life. Many of us worship God in the temple, but in our homes we worship Baal.

The road on which we are traveling is not entirely new. Modern western societies are now revisiting the experiments that took place nearly a century ago in the aftermath of the Russian revolution.

BOLSHEVIK RUSSIA REVISITED

After the October Revolution of 1917, Bolshevik legislation, first under Lenin and later under Stalin, was marked by three major features. The first was complete freedom to divorce. The right of unilateral no-fault divorce was introduced by legislation in 1918. The right to seek a divorce was reinforced in legislation passed in 1926, which provided for divorces to

---

4   Wendy Schrama, *Reforms in Dutch Family Law During the Course of 2001: Increased Pluriformity and Complexity*, IN INTERNATIONAL SURVEY OF FAMILY LAW 2002, 277 (Andrew Baiham ed., 2002); FAMILY LAW LEGISLATION OF THE NETHERLANDS (Ian Sumner & Hans Warendorf eds., 2003).

5   According to Organisation for Economic Co-operation and Development statistics (mostly from 2007), the highest level of ex-nuptial births, well over 60 percent, is in Iceland. Other countries with more than half the births occurring outside marriage are France, Norway, Sweden, and Estonia. *See* SOCIAL POLICY DIVISION, ORGANISATION FOR ECONOMIC CO-OPERATION & DEVELOPMENT, SHARE OF BIRTHS OUTSIDE MARRIAGE AND TEENAGE BIRTHS, http://www.oecd.org/dataoecd/38/6/40278615.pdf

6   In 2007, 39.7 percent of all births in the United States were nonmarital births. STEPHANIE VENTURA, CHANGING PATTERNS OF NONMARITAL CHILDBEARING IN THE UNITED STATES, NATIONAL CENTER FOR HEALTH STATISTICS, (Data Brief, no. 18, May 2009), http://www.cdc.gov/nchs/data/databriefs/db18.htm

7   The highest number of nonmarital births per 1,000 unmarried women was among Hispanic women in 2006, with the next highest being among black women. *Id.*

be granted without notice to the other party.[8] This major change to traditional Russian values concerning family life reflected the beliefs of Marx
and Engels. Engels thought that although romantic love was in its nature
exclusive, marriage should only continue for as long as love continued,[9]
and that meant that marriage should be freely dissoluble. Lenin asserted
that one "cannot be a democrat and a socialist without demanding full
freedom of divorce."[10]

The second feature of the Bolshevik concept of family life was the recognition of de facto marriages. Whereas some jurisdictions such as Australia
and New Zealand have now created two concepts of marriage, one de
jure and one de facto, with identical consequences other than the need
to divorce,[11] the Russians (more logically) maintained just one concept
of marriage. In Bolshevik law from 1926 onward,[12] registration merely
represented a means of evidencing a marriage. It was not necessary for a
marriage to exist. If there was no formal ceremony, no registration, then
the marriage could be demonstrated by evidence that the parties cohabited,
had the appearance of spouses as against third parties, mutually supported
each other economically, and jointly educated their children (if they had
any).[13] This is not dissimilar to the evidence that may be adduced to prove
a de facto marriage in Australia,[14] except that Australia, unlike Bolshevik
Russia,[15] recognizes de facto polygamy.[16] The Bolsheviks also had no
minimum time period for cohabitation to count as a marriage.[17]

The third feature of the Bolshevik idea of the family was that women
should be in the workforce and that therefore there was only a very limited

---

[8] Jacob Sundberg, *Recent Changes in Swedish Family Law: Experiment Repeated*, 23 Am. J.
Comp. Law 34, 44 (1975). *See also* Lynn Wardle, *The 'Withering Away' of Marriage: Some
Lessons from the Bolshevik Family Law Reforms in Russia, 1917–1926*, 2 Georgetown
J. L. & Public Policy 469 (2004).

[9] Kent Geiger, The Family in Soviet Russia, 22 (1968) (Engels noted that individual sex-
love varies in duration between people, especially among men). *See generally,* Freidrich
Engels, The Origin of the Family, Private Property, and the State (1884).

[10] *Cited in* Inga Markovits, *Family Traits*, 88 Mich. L. Rev. 1734, 1744 n.39 (1990) (book
review).

[11] This is also advocated by the American Law Institute. American Law Institute,
Principles of the Law of Family Dissolution: Analysis and Recommendations
ch. 6 (2002).

[12] Russian Socialist Federative Soviet Republic Code of 1926.

[13] Sundberg, *supra* note 8, at 45.   [14] Family Law Act, 1975, s.4AA(2).

[15] Sundberg, *supra* note 8, at 48.

[16] Family Law Act, 1975, s.4AA(5)(b): "a de facto relationship can exist even if one of the
persons is legally married to someone else or in another de facto relationship."

[17] In Leningrad, one-quarter of all marriages lasted between ten and forty-five days in 1927.
Sundberg, *supra* note 8, at 46.

role for spousal support. The duty of spousal support was attached to both registered and unregistered marriages, but it was limited in duration to twelve months from the termination of the marriage, and confined to those unable to work.[18]

In the postrevolutionary Russian society, women had the primary responsibility for child rearing after separation because custody was typically allocated to them[19] and because the dystopian vision of the Bolsheviks for the socialized rearing of children did not eventuate.[20]

The Bolshevik concept of marriage and family life was a massive departure from the prevailing cultural norms both in Russia and throughout the rest of the developed world at that time. Yet it represented a logical and coherent view of how a family law system allowing for free terminability of relationships could be structured, and what effect should be given to cohabiting relationships that are not formally registered. The Bolsheviks adopted the idea of the clean break and the allocation of custody to one parent, mostly the mother, after divorce. They focused on substance rather than form, not worrying whether the marriage was formally celebrated or merely a de facto union. The postseparation family was essentially a mother-child dyad, as others have recommended should be the norm in western societies.[21]

However, the Russian experiment with free terminability and de facto marriage was abandoned by 1944. A law passed in that year imposed major restrictions on divorce and abolished the recognition of de facto unions. The new laws required a judicial process for the grant of a divorce and it was a judicial function to encourage reconciliation. Divorce also became very expensive.[22] Stalin's regime suddenly embraced traditional family values.

There are multiple explanations for Stalin's about-face on family policy,[23] but the social dislocation caused by these family policies was certainly a major contributing factor.[24] The social cost of free terminability had proved to be enormous, with women and children as its primary victims.[25]

WAVERING BETWEEN TWO OPINIONS

In contrast to the Bolsheviks' intentional – if disastrous – social policy, western societies have stumbled from one family policy to another in

---

[18] John Hazard, *Law and the Soviet Family*, 1939 WIS. L. REV. 224, 246 (1939).
[19] GEIGER, *supra* note 9, at 97–98.   [20] *Id.* 47–48.
[21] MARTHA FINEMAN, THE NEUTERED MOTHER, THE SEXUAL FAMILY AND OTHER TWENTIETH CENTURY TRAGEDIES (1995).
[22] GEIGER, *supra* note 9, at 95.   [23] *Id.* at 97ff.
[24] *Id.*   [25] Wardle, *supra* note 8, at 490–96.

consecutively abandoning the regulation of the exit from marriage and then reinforcing the indissolubility of parenthood.

Most Western societies still waver between two opinions, two competing ideas of family relationships and of the consequences of separation. We have traveled far along the road to a radical reconceptualization of family life. Yet we have not been able to live with the consequences of the free dissolubility of marriage and the dissolution of the family that it was said to entail.

Economic Constraints on Free Terminability

Just as the Bolsheviks promoted complete freedom of divorce long before they had the employment conditions and communal provision for child rearing that could support free terminability of relationships, so a similar mistake has been made in many western countries. Perhaps the Scandinavian countries, with their tradition of high levels of maternal employment, socialized pension entitlements, and a strong welfare safety net, offered conditions for free terminability that avoided the worst economic consequences of divorce for women, but other societies lacked those conditions.[26]

Many countries stumbled into divorce reform without really thinking the issues through. Twenty-five years ago, British scholar Pamela Symes identified with great clarity the nub of the problem concerning financial issues following separation in her country. In all the debates about divorce law reform in England, she observed, the one question that was not answered was how it was going to be paid for. A large number of new households would be created, so where would the extra resources come from to finance this? The financial implications for taxpayers were enormous if divorce was to mean the termination of the support obligation. Yet there was no explicit recognition of the extent to which preventing women and children falling into poverty would fall to the public purse, and hence an unwillingness to accept the logic of divorce as ending spousal obligations. She wrote:[27]

> Unable to accept the full logic of the position that divorce should constitute a complete and final termination of the parties' legal and financial relationship with the parties reverting to being "legal strangers," we have been forced to accept that it must therefore be a readjustment of their former marital relationship.... A law was introduced which was effectively available only

[26] MARY ANN GLENDON, THE TRANSFORMATION OF FAMILY LAW: STATE, LAW AND FAMILY IN THE UNITED STATES AND WESTERN EUROPE 234ff. (1989).
[27] Pamela Symes, *Indissolubility and the Clean Break*, 48 MOD. L. REV. 44, 52–53 (1985).

to those who could afford it. For the unwitting who availed themselves of it, but could not afford it, poverty and misery has ensued.... For what does this "liberal divorce" amount to? If it is a readjustment rather than a termination (and this is the inescapable logic of the failure to provide the extra resources to finance a termination), then divorce brings about a curious change in the status of the parties. They do not revert, as one would have expected, to the status of non-spouse which was their old status when entering marriage for the first time. A new status of "former-spouse" has been created; one which carries many of the continuing obligations and responsibilities of the former marriage. We have coupled this with a licence to remarry and inevitably (and perhaps largely unwittingly) created thereby a kind of institutionalised successive polygamy.

The costs to the public purse from the divorce revolution in most western countries have certainly been immense. It is not that fault-based divorce had ever done much to prevent the economic calamity of divorce for homemaker mothers. The U.S. experience, at least, is that spousal support has always been something awarded to only a small minority of divorced women.[28] What it did do was to increase exponentially the numbers of such women – a problem continued in this century not so much in the breakdown of marriages as in the rupture of cohabiting relationships.

The immediate costs of relationship breakdown have been felt in the increase in welfare budgets primarily to support women with children; but there have been more hidden costs too. No-fault divorce not only disrupted the system by which the husband, as primary earner, supported his wife. In many families, the financial stresses resulting from divorce also affected the ability of people in midlife to provide for their elderly parents.

It is only in the last few years that the full impact of the divorce revolution on the aged population of western societies has begun to be felt. The cohort of those who divorced in their mid-thirties and forties in the late 1970s and 1980s have in recent years started to reach retirement age. Those women who did not gain a share of their former partner's retirement savings, and did not repartner, have been particularly vulnerable to economic hardship in their twilight years, with consequent dependence on public support.[29] The long-term economic effects of the divorce revolution have started to become apparent, beyond the immediate crises requiring welfare support for so many single mothers.

---

[28] Margo Melli, *Alimony Trends*, 19 FAM. ADVOC. 21 (1996–1997). *See* Chapter 11.
[29] For Australian Research, *see* DAVID DE VAUS, MATTHEW GRAY, LIXIA QU, & DAVID STANTON, AUSTRALIAN INSTITUTE OF FAMILY STUDIES, THE CONSEQUENCES OF DIVORCE FOR FINANCIAL LIVING STANDARDS IN LATER LIFE (2007).

Even though over time, increased workforce participation by mothers in many western countries has ameliorated the adverse economic repercussions of relationship breakdown, this has not occurred before a wholesale rethinking, in jurisdictions like Canada, of the role of spousal support. As a consequence of the waves of poverty that have resulted from the divorce revolution, and the costs to the taxpayer, there has been a reluctance on the part of legislators or courts in a number of jurisdictions to accept that there is no longer a justification for marriage to provide a form of insurance against postseparation adversities. The result has been the continuance of support obligations that are unrelated to the circumstances of the marriage, and an incoherence in terms of social policy.[30]

The law in western countries has hovered uncertainly between two different concepts of divorce. In the first, divorce terminates the support obligation, subject to the need for income transfers by way of transition. In the second, there is a readjustment of a continuing, lifelong support obligation that arises independently of the reasons for marriage breakdown and without reference to whether the ending of the relationship was the unilateral choice of one party. Like the people that Elijah addressed on Mount Carmel, we waver between two opinions.

The new frontier is to extend the obligations of marriage to those who have not chosen to commit themselves for better or for worse, for richer and for poorer, in sickness and in health, for as long as they both shall live. The imposition of maintenance obligations on nonmarried people, as occurs in Australia and New Zealand, is the ultimate triumph for the Judeo-Christian idea of marriage.

Parenting after Separation

Legislatures and courts in many western societies have also struggled to develop a coherent approach to the law of parenting after separation. Following the logic of free terminability of relationships, the no-fault divorce revolution promised a substantial measure of autonomy to each of the parties after the property was divided and the children were allocated. Mothers with sole custody had very limited legal obligations to the other parent of their children. That the other parent would visit the children, or

---

[30] That lack of coherence in social policy may be seen particularly in Canada following the Supreme Court's decision in Bracklow v. Bracklow, [1999] 1 S.C.R. 420. *See* Chapter 11. No clear rationale has emerged for the award of noncompensatory spousal support in an age of no-fault divorce. Carol Rogerson, *The Canadian Law of Spousal Support*, 38 FAM. L. Q. 69 (2004).

the children visit them, was perhaps an expectation, but there was not much of an obligation imposed on the primary custodian. The extent to which the custodial parent had a continuing relationship with the other parent beyond organizing the logistics of visits was largely a matter of choice. Men had more obligations than women after separation, but the ties that bound them to their former partners financially were only restraints for a minority of fathers who it was financially worthwhile to pursue.

As the law has had to come to terms with the importance of the relationship between nonresident parents and their children, so the concept of the enduring family has replaced the old substitution model of relationship breakdown. Here also, the law has wavered between two opinions. The emergence of the idea of the enduring family should not be seen necessarily as displacing the old substitution model of the postdivorce family. In some respects, it is in continuing conflict with it, for in the substitution model of the postdivorce family rests much of the hope and the promise of divorce itself. People in unhappy marriages do not look to divorce as a way to restructure the relationship with their partners. They look to divorce to end that relationship, to set them free to start a new life, perhaps to move to a new location and to form new relationships. This is true also for people who separate from cohabiting relationships. Yet in the enduring family, the promise of postseparation autonomy is much more qualified.

Nowhere is the conflict between the two competing conceptualizations of divorce greater than in the law of relocation, where the claims of personal autonomy and ongoing connectedness through the children are in almost irreconcilable conflict. A desire of a primary caregiver to relocate to another area or country has profound implications for the other parent – and for the children.

Not all families endure – or should – beyond separation. A history of coercive controlling violence by a father will often present a compelling case for the attenuation of the ties between the parents.[31] In other cases, the ties that bind are only as strong as the bond between each parent and the children. Where one parent is prepared to let go of a close connection with his or her child, or is resigned to that outcome, autonomy is possible for the primary caregiver.

THE CHALLENGE OF EXPERIENCE

Although western societies have all but abandoned the Judeo-Christian idea of marriage – and indeed marriage as practiced in other faiths – the

---

[31] *See* Chapter 6.

idea lives on in our experience if not in our allegiance. Marriage is now both optional and freely dissoluble; it need not be chosen, and even if it is, it need not be maintained in most western societies.

However, there is actually less choice than we think. Whether we choose marriage or not, whether we maintain it or not, our societal experience has been that parents' lives become intertwined when children are born. Marriages may be dissolved, but the freedom that this dissolution brings is limited by the connection of parenthood. Indeed, people who were never married to one another are entwined by the ties that parenthood brings. This is so in terms of the need to maintain parental relationships with children. Neither parent who wants to remain closely involved with the lives of his or her children, and to see them on a regular basis, is autonomous from the other. The circumstances of parents may also be tied to one another financially. Career success or career reversals for the primary earner may affect his or her liability for child support or spousal maintenance. The financial circumstances of one former partner is thus often affected by the success or otherwise of the other.

Marriage may be dissoluble, but parenthood is not. Human beings have never worked out a satisfactory way to combine the free terminability of relationships with parenthood in a way that does not lead to disaster or discontent. Stalin's Russia did not achieve it, nor has the western world in the last forty years. Eventually, there may come a time when policy makers in even the most liberal western countries survey the instability of family forms, and the effect of that instability on children, and seek to find ways again to promote order, stability, and cohesion in family life. Indeed, governments may be forced to do so by recognizing that an entirely libertarian view of family life and governmental neutrality between family forms is simply not affordable given the other demands that will be placed on the public purse in an ageing society. The enormous public costs of relationship breakdown from welfare payments and expenditure on the family law and child support systems, together with ancillary services such as publicly funded mediation, may eventually require a rethink of social policy.

THE IRRETRIEVABLE BREAKDOWN OF DIVORCE POLICY

Many of the battles that have consumed legislatures and other policy makers for a generation or more have been presented as battles between the genders. Lobby groups line up on each side of a contested issue of policy in family law, and they typically purport to represent women's interests and men's interests respectively. Who has the right to speak for the children's interests is heavily contested terrain. The battle lines are sometimes confused by the advocacy of new partners. Second wives or female partners of separated and divorced men sometimes align with their menfolk against the claims of former female partners. Yet largely, the conflicts are between women and men, whether or not men enlist female allies.

This destructive gender conflict, which is ongoing and irresoluble, masks a deeper reason for the battles over policy in family law. The model on which the divorce revolution was premised – the notion that once there was a division of the property and an allocation of the children, and perhaps a transitional period of rehabilitative spousal support, each person could walk away with limited obligations to the other – has irretrievably broken down. The promise of personal autonomy and a new beginning that the divorce revolution offered has proved largely to be an illusion. Yes, people can make fresh starts and form new partnerships, but most cannot shed the connections with former relationships when there are children involved. We do not practice serial monogamy, but rather experience multiple partner relationships simultaneously, living with one partner while maintaining a relationship with another (in a different household), because of the shared obligations of parenthood.

TOWARD NEW POLICIES FOR THE POSTSEPARATION FAMILY

The history of the last forty years has been the history of the piecemeal recognition that parenthood creates enduring connections. Legal systems throughout the western world have not created the indissolubility of parenthood. Slowly, painfully, and through much conflict in the legislatures and the courts, legal systems have had to come to terms with the reality of parenthood's indissolubility. Positive law has had to become realigned with natural law.[32] Having sought freedom from the pain of broken relationships, people have had to come to terms with the limitations on that freedom. Autonomy is limited by the connectedness of parenthood for as long as each parent desires that close connection with his or her children, and insofar as the law will refuse to sever or attenuate that connection.

The challenge for the future of family law is coming to terms with the implications of this in a more systematic and principled way than has so far occurred. Legal systems in many jurisdictions continue to oscillate

---

[32]   On the relationship of legal positivism to the idea of natural law, *see* HERBERT HART, THE CONCEPT OF LAW (1961).

between two irreconcilable conceptualizations of the postseparation family. Facing the challenge for the future of family law begins with the recognition that the old concept of "sole custody" is no longer viable as an organizing principle for postseparation parenting. It retains its utility in situations where domestic violence, abuse, or entrenched conflict makes it necessary to limit the contact between one parent and his or her children. However, as a default rule and pattern for postseparation parenting, it has long since disappeared in some jurisdictions and is likely to disappear everywhere that legislatures are in touch with community attitudes, values, and aspirations.

Facing the challenge presented by the indissolubility of parenthood also requires the redesign of court structures and service systems that support families through the transition from one household to two. No longer is it possible to gear laws and service systems just to the initial process of structuring postseparation parenting in the aftermath of separation and divorce. Court processes and service systems, still showing their origins in the substitution model of the postseparation family, have to be reengineered to meet the needs of a family that endures beyond the initial decisions about parenting after separation.

Facing up to the indissolubility of parenthood is one of the great challenges of our time.

Index

United States (*cont.*)
 spousal support, 240–41, 252, 254–56
 in child support, 27–28
 Uniform Marriage and Divorce Act, 20,
  27–28, 240
 violence in relationships, 122, 136–37,
  141–44
University of Sydney relocation study,
 166–75

violence in relationships
 adjudication as abuse, 125, 200
 autonomy, post-separation, 15, 132
 capacity to parent, 131–32
 children's wellbeing, 129–31
 contact center, 145–47

Family Relationship Centers, 192–93,
 195–96
gender, 125–28, 139–40
heterogeneity, 123, 129, 136–42, 147,
 See also types
mediation, family law, 185–86
parenting, 124–25, 132, 141, 148–49,
 276
rates, 121–22
safety, ensuring, 129–30, 147–49
types, 123–24, *See also* heterogeneity
 coercive controlling violence, 124–25,
  127, 132, 134–36, 137, 276
 intimate partner violence, 125–28
 separation instigated violence, 128
 violent resistance violence, 128